OXFORD CONSTITUTI

Series Editor.

Martin Loughlin, John P. McCorm , and Neil Walker

The Cultural Defense of Nations

OXFORD CONSTITUTIONAL THEORY

Series Editors:

Martin Loughlin, John P. McCormick, and Neil Walker

Oxford Constitutional Theory has rapidly established itself as the primary point of reference for theoretical reflections on the growing interest in constitutions and constitutional law in domestic, regional, and global contexts. The majority of the works published in the series are monographs that advance new understandings of their subject. But the series aims to provide a forum for further innovation in the field by also including well-conceived edited collections that bring a variety of perspectives and disciplinary approaches to bear on specific themes in constitutional thought, and by publishing English translations of leading monographs in constitutional theory that have originally been written in languages other than English.

ALSO AVAILABLE IN THE SERIES

The Cosmopolitan Constitution
Alexander Somek

The Structure of Pluralism
Victor M. Muniz-Fraticelli

Constitutional Courts and Deliberative Democracy
Conrado Hübner Mendes

Fault Lines of Globalization Legal Order and the Politics of A-Legality
Hans Lindahl

The Cosmopolitan State
H Patrick Glenn

After Public Law
Edited by
Cormac Mac Amhlaigh, Claudio Michelon, and Neil Walker

The Three Branches A Comparative Model of Separation of Powers
Christoph Möllers

The Global Model of Constitutional Rights
Kai Möller

The Twilight of Constitutionalism?
Edited by
Petra Dobner and Martin Loughlin

Beyond Constitutionalism The Pluralist Structure of Postnational Law
Nico Krisch

Constituting Economic and Social Rights
Katharine G. Young

Constitutional Referendums The Theory and Practice of Republican Deliberation
Stephen Tierney

Constitutional Fragments Societal Constitutionalism and Globalization
Gunther Teubner

Further praise for

The Cultural Defense of Nations: A Liberal Theory of Majority Rights

"Minority rights have commonly been promoted by liberals and leftists, majority rights by people on the political right. Liav Orgad challenges this too-simple polarity. He has written a resolutely liberal account, carefully and elegantly argued, of what majorities can and cannot do to defend their culture and way of life."

—**Michael Walzer**, Institute for Advanced Study, Princeton

"After innumerous theories of minority rights, we finally have a theory of majority rights. The notion may appear paradoxical, but Liav Orgad makes a compelling case that the old assumption that the majority 'can take care of itself' is no longer valid. A young star in the legal profession, Orgad navigates perilous waters with the ease of a sage. This is a book to read for all concerned about the future of liberalism."

—**Christian Joppke**, Chair in General Sociology, University of Bern

"Liav Orgad is perhaps the leading young scholar today analyzing the clash between the cultural claims of immigrants and the cultural defensiveness of the receiving societies. In a highly nuanced, empirically informed, and normatively scrupulous analysis, Orgad not only highlights one of the major crises facing liberal societies today (and tomorrow), but offers specific and persuasive solutions that, paradoxically, can protect liberal nation-states from some of their increasingly illiberal cultural defenses. This book is destined to be a classic in its field."

—**Peter Schuck**, Simeon E. Baldwin Professor Emeritus of Law,
Yale Law School

"This is a remarkable book. It makes a significant contribution to work on the management of immigration and diversity, along with the broader discipline of constitutional and liberal theory. It is an instant classic, establishing a clear, yet nuanced, position in the debate about how states are responding—and should respond—to the age of migration."

—**Robert Schertzer**, *The Modern Law Review*

"The Cultural Defense of Nations is an exceptional work that sounds a timely, provocative and very perceptive alarm about the looming challenges facing liberal democracies across the West ... given the importance of those questions and the thoughtfulness of Orgad's answers to them, policy makers of all sorts should make reading this book a top priority."

—**Daniel Falkiner**, *LSE Review of Books*

The Cultural Defense of Nations

A Liberal Theory of Majority Rights

Liav Orgad

OXFORD
UNIVERSITY PRESS

OXFORD
UNIVERSITY PRESS

Great Clarendon Street, Oxford, OX2 6DP,
United Kingdom

Oxford University Press is a department of the University of Oxford.
It furthers the University's objective of excellence in research, scholarship,
and education by publishing worldwide. Oxford is a registered trade mark of
Oxford University Press in the UK and in certain other countries

First published 2015
First published in paperback 2017

Published in the United States of America by Oxford University Press
198 Madison Avenue, New York, NY 10016, United States of America

British Library Cataloguing in Publication Data
Data available

Library of Congress Cataloging in Publication Data
Data available

ISBN 978–0–19–966868–7 (Hbk.)
ISBN 978–0–19–880691–2 (Pbk.)

For my father
Eliyahu (Eli) Orgad
1953–2005

Abstract

The changing patterns of global immigration have initiated a new form of majority nationalism. In recent years, liberal democracies have introduced an increasing number of immigration and naturalization policies that are designed to defend the majority culture. This trend is fed by fears of immigration—some justified, some paranoid—which explain the rise of extreme right-wing parties in the West. Liberal theory and human rights law seem to be out of sync with these developments. While they recognize the rights of minority groups to maintain their cultural identity, it is typically assumed that majority groups have neither a need for similar rights nor a moral basis for defending them. The majority culture, so the argument goes, "can take care of itself." This book shifts the focus from the prevailing discussion of minority rights and, for the first time, directly addresses the cultural rights of majorities. The findings reveal a troubling trend in liberal democracies, which, ironically, in order to protect liberal values, violate the very same values. The book criticizes this state of affairs and presents a liberal theory of "cultural defense" that distinguishes between justifiable and unjustifiable attempts by majorities to protect their cultural essentials. It formulates liberal standards by which liberal states can welcome immigrants without fundamentally changing their cultural heritage, forsaking their liberal traditions, or slipping into extreme nationalism.

Acknowledgments

I have always looked forward to writing the acknowledgements part of the book yet now, as I begin work on it, I am at a loss for words realizing how many individuals and institutions assisted me in this endeavor. During the years in which this book took shape, I was privileged to obtain the help of many friends and colleagues who inspired my thinking on issues pertinent to this topic. Ideas grow and develop over time and it is almost impossible to pinpoint all the people whose sage advice and guidance have made the book possible. Acknowledgements, however detailed, are a poor medium by which to express my heartfelt thanks for the support I have received.

Writing this book would have never been possible without the immense help that I have been fortunate enough to receive from friends, colleagues, and students, whose thoughtful discussions and excellent suggestions benefited me at different stages of the research. I owe a great intellectual debt to David Abraham, Shlomo Avineri, Keith Banting, Aharon Barak, Daphne Barak-Erez, Jürgen Bast, Linda Bosniak, Joseph Chamie, Mishael Cheshin, David Coleman, Noah Feldman, Monique Foudraine, Ruth Gavison, Anne Gladitz, Dieter Grimm, Malachi Hacohen, Kay Hailbronner, Dora Kostakopoulou, Shay Lavie, Natan Lerner, Stephen Macedo, Avishai Margalit, Michele Manspeizer, Martha Minow, Noah Pickus, Yoram Rabin, Guy Raveh, Daphné Richemond-Barak, Rahel Rimon, Adam Shinar, Jennifer Shkabatur, Avi Soifer, Daniel Thym, Kyriaki Topidi, Mark Tushnet, Patrick Weil, Alexander Yakobson, and Yaffa Zilbershatz. Offering a mere list does injustice to the hours, and often days, which so many of these people spent listening to my arguments, reviewing drafts, and challenging ideas.

Writing in an inspiring academic environment and a lively intellectual community is a valuable gift for an author. A number of universities have hosted me in the course of writing the book. At Columbia Law School, I learned a great deal about loyalty and the concept of "nation" from George Fletcher, and became familiar with U.S. immigration law in a seminar taught by Theodore Ruthizer. Their unwavering support and friendship is the biggest asset that I secured at Columbia. They have followed this project from its inception and forced me to rethink my positions and reflect on the arguments. At Harvard Law School, I was honored to be supervised by Sanford Levinson, Frank Michelman, and Gerald Neuman—all of whom have profoundly influenced my thinking, writing, and views on citizenship and constitutionalism; they generously shared their time and knowledge with me, welcomed me into their seminars, and commented on my articles. In such ideal conditions, it is no wonder that my year at Harvard was incredibly stimulating and productive. At NYU's Tikvah Center for Law & Jewish Civilization I began to reflect on the philosophical foundations related to majority rights. The academic seminars, led by Joseph Weiler and Moshe Halbertal, galvanized me into considering new ways of understanding citizenship and the depth of the parallel between religious affiliation and political membership, religious rituals and citizenship ceremonies. After spending a few years in the United States, I could not land in a better place to continue pursuing this project than the European University Institute in Florence. I am grateful to Rainer Bauböck for granting me the opportunity to benefit from this unique academic environment. The scholarly insights I received from members, fellows, and students during my time in Florence were truly thought-provoking. At Freie Universität Berlin, my gratitude goes to Philip Kunig, who opened a window into German constitutional law and the German academic world; his encouragement was central to the completion of this work.

A few individuals deserve separate mention in view of their profound influence of this book. Christian Joppke has been my mentor since my student days and has contributed tremendously to my intellectual development; I am grateful for his sharp criticism, inspiration, and indispensable guidance. It was a great pleasure to have an exchange with someone who seemed to understand my work better than I did myself. This book owes a great deal to his methodological suggestions and invaluable advice. Stephen Legomsky served as a reviewer of my doctoral dissertation at the Hebrew University of Jerusalem, providing me with the self-confidence—the most valuable asset a young scholar can acquire—needed to develop some of the ideas discussed in this book. He always found the time to assist me even when serving as Chief Counsel of the U.S. Citizenship and Immigration Services at the Department of Homeland Security. Barak Medina was my doctoral supervisor at the Hebrew University of Jerusalem and has instructed me on everything I have written thus far; his perceptive comments and remarkable insights have always been challenging and kept me busy for weeks. I could not wish for a better supervisor and owe him an enormous debt of gratitude. Shelly Simana has been my assistant throughout the writing process and became a partner for the journey; she has made the writing of this manuscript a joy. This book would not have been completed without her encouragement and enthusiasm, accompanied by exceptional research skills, uncanny ability to analyze legal issues, and original thinking. Peter Schuck gave me a precious opportunity of an intellectual exchange with him and his constructive criticism on citizenship tests and loyalty oaths substantially improved the manuscript. Much of what I know about citizenship theory is thanks to him. Peter believed in the project long before it deserved his trust.

I had various opportunities to present the ideas appearing in this book at conferences. In particular, I benefited from feedback offered at the Annual Meeting of the American Society for Legal History, European University Institute, FGV Direito Rio, Freie Universität Berlin, Harvard University, Interdisciplinary Center (IDC) Herzliya, Justus-Liebig-Universität Gießen, LSE, Texas A&M University at Qatar, the Institute for Advanced Study in the Humanities in Germany, the

Swiss Institute of Comparative Law, Universität Konstanz, Universität Luzern, and Wissenschaftszentrum Berlin für Sozialforschung. While a conference provides an opening for keen criticism, it is often a workshop—with a commentator—that proves priceless in improving a work-in-progress. I profited from the opportunity to participate in the Fourth Comparative Law Works-in-Progress Workshop at Princeton University, the Seventh International Workshop for Young Scholars at Humboldt University, the "Loyalty, Identity, and Migration" workshop in Kenan Institute for Ethics at Duke University, and the W.G. Hart Legal Workshop on Comparative Perspectives of Constitutions at the Institute of Advanced Legal Studies in London. I thank participants and commentators for their useful comments.

The project could not have been realized without financial support. Several fellowships have made this book a reality: an ISEF Fellowship at Columbia Law School and Harvard Law School; a Fulbright Fellowship, a Rothschild Fellowship, and a Tikvah Scholarship at NYU's Tikvah Center for Law & Jewish Civilization; a Jean Monnet Fellowship at the European University Institute; a research Fellowship at the Center for Comparative Constitutional Law and Religion, Universität Luzern; and DRS and Marie Curie Intra-European Fellowships at Freie Universität Berlin. During the years of research, a number of grants enabled me to employ research assistants and present my ideas at conferences: a Russell Sage Presidential Authority Award (RSF Project No. 88-13-04), a Minerva Grant by the Minerva Center for Human Rights at the Hebrew University, an Israel Institute Research Grant, and a grant of the Israel Science Foundation (Grant No. 434/13). I wish to convey my thanks to these foundations for their generous support. In particular, I am indebted to Nina Weiner, the President of ISEF, for years of assistance—she supported me during all my studies in Israel and abroad—but mainly for her friendship. The many hours we spent discussing issues relating to this book in New York are valuable and appreciated.

For the past fifteen years, IDC Herzliya has been my home. I have been blessed by an extraordinarily supportive President, Uriel Reichman, who has been dedicated to my success more than I could ever dream of. Uriel took me under his wing when I was a first-year student and believed in me from the beginning. Over the years, he has provided me with ideal conditions to flourish academically and his door has always been open to me and my never-ending requests. IDC has helped me grow as a scholar and a person, tolerating my mistakes and celebrating my triumphs. I also wish to express my appreciation to my former dean, Yishai Beer, my current dean, Sharon Rabin-Margalioth, and my vice dean, Ronen Kritenshtein, who allowed me to take a few years off to conduct this research. No doubt my greatest long-running, intellectual and personal debt is owed to Amnon Rubinstein, who befriended a research assistant ten years ago and convinced him to pursue an academic career. Amnon is hard to classify because he could easily fit all categories. He is an advisor, a colleague, a friend, and a role model. Amnon has not merely "influenced" my academic career; he has made and shaped it. I feel lucky to be able to work with him and owe him more than I could ever repay.

Writing a book is one thing; publishing it is another. I wish to thank Natasha Flemming and Elinor Shields at OUP for their professional approach that has exceeded my most extravagant hopes. They kindly tolerated my repeated delays in submitting the manuscript, as well as all my requests about the book cover, editing process, and numerous other issues characterized as "first book syndrome." Thanks are also due to Geetha Parakkat and Alison Floyd for excellent editing of the manuscript.

The book incorporates, in modified forms, ideas that were previously published elsewhere: "Illiberal Liberalism: Cultural Restrictions on Migration and Access to Citizenship in Europe," *American Journal of Comparative Law* 58, no. 1 (2010): 53–105; "Creating New Americans: The Essence of Americanism under the Citizenship Test," *Houston Law Review* 47, no. 5 (2011): 1227–1297; "Race, Religion and Nationality in Immigration Selection: 120 Years after the Chinese Exclusion Case," *Constitutional Commentary* 26, no. 1 (2010): 237–296 (with Theodore Ruthizer); *A Strategy for Immigration Policy in Israel*, Ruth Gavison, ed. (Jerusalem: The Metzilah Center, 2010) (with Shlomo Avineri and Amnon Rubinstein). Permission to use these materials is gratefully acknowledged.

Writing a book can be a burden on family members. My mother and two brothers, Shachar and Dan, have tolerated my lack of time and innumerable visits abroad. While I cannot compensate them for my absence, I can thank them for their unconditional love and support.

This book is dedicated to my father (and best friend), Eli Orgad, who did not live to see its publication.

Liav Orgad
Herzliya and Berlin
FEBRUARY 2015

Contents

List of Tables

Table of Cases

INTERNATIONAL LAW

ISRAEL

THE NETHERLAND

UNITED KINGDOM

UNITED STATES

OTHER

EUROPEAN LAW

FRANCE

INTERNATIONAL LAW

ISRAEL

UNITED STATES

Table of Legislation

FRANCE

GERMANY

ISRAEL

List of Abbreviations

CDU	Christian Democratic Union Party (Germany)
CSU	Christian Social Union (Germany)
EEA	European Economic Area
HCJ	High Court of Justice (Israel)
ICCPR	International Covenant on Civil and Political Rights
INA	Immigration and Nationality Act (1952) (United States)
OECD	Organisation for Economic Co-operation and Development
StAG	Staatsangehörigkeitsgesetz (1913) (Germany)
StAR-VwV	Allgemeine Verwaltungsvorschrift zum Staatsangehörigkeitsrecht (2000) (Germany)
SVP	Swiss People's Party
TFR	Total Fertility Rate
UNESCO	United Nations Educational Scientific and Cultural Organization
USCIS	U.S. Citizenship and Immigration Services

A Note on the Cover

The cover illustrates a world-famous painting, *The Threatened Swan* by Jan Asselijn (*c.* 1650), exhibited in the Rijksmuseum Amsterdam. The swan, conceived as an elegant, non-aggressive bird, feels threatened by a curious dog which, barely seen in the lower left side, seems intent on attacking the swan's nest. The swan is transformed into a raging beast, ferociously attacking the dog. Unlike its peaceful image, the swan is on the warpath.

While it is unknown what Jan Asselijn meant by this awe-inspiring painting, later owners added three inscriptions on the painting. One of the eggs is engraved *"Holland"*; above the dog's head appears the caption *"De Vijand van de Staat"* (enemy of the state); and underneath the swan it is stated *"De Raadspensionaris"* (Grand Pensionary)—the political title given to Johan de Witt (1625–1672), the most important political figure of his time in the Republic of the United Provinces. These three inscriptions have transformed the painting into a political allegory. The painting has become synonymous with Holland defending itself and the swan has become a symbol of a Dutch hero, de Witt, who led the wars against England and France and, as a republican, struggled against the return of the House of Orange to the throne. Thus, the swan can be regarded as defending the Dutch Republic against both external and domestic enemies.

The painting represents a conundrum. We do not know whether the dog is indeed threatening the swan—it may be that the swan is overestimating the threat—or whether the swan's reaction is overprotective. The painting, however, may be given a contemporary interpretation that is relevant to the subject of this book. The prosperous and usually docile West feels threatened by the influx of immigration. Is the threat, symbolized by the dog, real or perceived? Is the frightened reaction to it by the West, symbolized by the swan, just or unjust, proportional or disproportional? And is there a way of coping with the real or perceived threat other than through an aggressive defense? This book attempts to answer these questions.

Introduction: Citizen Makers

> To understand what a constitution (*politeia*) is, we must inquire into the nature of the city (*polis*); and to understand that—since the city is a body of citizens (*politai*)—we must examine the nature of citizenship.
>
> —Aristotle[1]

Liberal democracies are citizen makers. They have a long tradition of attempts to "Protestantize" Catholic immigrants and "Westernize" non-Western immigrants. In contemporary liberal democracies, the ultimate goal of the naturalization process is to "liberate" the illiberal and channel immigrants into the dominant customs, beliefs, and values of the dominant majority—by, for example, Anglifying or Germanizing the immigrants. This process is tricky—how to be citizen makers without being law breakers? More importantly, in order to make "good" citizens out of immigrants, liberal states must define not only the qualities that make one a good citizen, but also the specific qualities that make one a good *national* citizen (American, German, etc.). To answer this challenging question, states must explore who they are and which elements define their national character. The process which a non-citizen undergoes to become a citizen is one of the most fascinating disciplines through which to explore constitutional identity.

Immigration has become the topic of the day. Never in human history has so much attention been paid to human movement. Numbers matter. By 2013, the number of international immigrants soared to 232 million—10.8 percent of the total population in the developed regions. Numbers, however, are merely one factor. Other factors are the pace of immigration and its character. In some countries, the annual growth rate of immigration is rapidly increasing and the ethno-cultural composition

[1] Aristotle, *Politics*, Ernest Barker, trans. (Oxford: OUP, 1995): p. 84 (Book III, I).

of immigrants is relatively homogeneous. Contemporary immigration yields demographic shifts of historical significance between dominant majorities and immigrant communities. The changing patterns of immigration are linked to the changing nature of Western societies. The West faces an unprecedented population decline and has become more dependent on immigration due to demographic and economic needs. Alongside these transitions, the usual cultural changes brought about by immigration are strengthened by global forces—free markets, satellite television, and the Internet. Trans-cultural diffusion is greater today than in any other period in human history. The "other" is present in the national boundaries not just physically, but also spiritually.

The long-term cultural impact of immigration is uncertain at this point. It is too early to predict the consequences of immigration on sovereignty, self-determination, and the nation-state. Three consequences, however, are evident even at this early stage: the effect of massive population movements on the cultural composition and self-image of Western democracies—their national identities; the backlash against multiculturalism in immigration policy; and the rise of majority nationalism, or "cultural defense policies."

WHO WE ARE

Surveys show that a high percentage of British citizens "feel British." But what exactly does it mean to feel "British"? What do people have in mind when they state that they feel "British"? People may think differently about this question, and perhaps it is also British to give various meanings to British identity. Nevertheless, what does feeling "British" really mean: can you choose the top three characteristics without which one cannot feel or become British? If this is too difficult, can you define what is un-British or non-British, be it a pattern of behavior, a belief, or a way of doing things? Does feeling British entail devotion, identification, or faith?

In 2002, the British government established a committee to investigate the concept of Britishness. After long deliberation, the Home Office published a report on the essence of being British: "To be British seems to us to mean that we respect the laws, the elected parliamentary and democratic political structures, traditional values of mutual tolerance, respect for equal rights and mutual concern; and that we give our allegiance to the state.... To be British is to respect those over-arching specific institutions, values, beliefs and traditions that bind us all."[2] About a decade

[2] Home Office, "The New and the Old: The Report of the 'Life in the United Kingdom' Advisory Group," 2003: p. 11. See also Commission for Racial Equality, "Citizenship and Belonging: What is Britishness?," 2005.

later, following the "Trojan Horse affair" in Birmingham, in which Islamic leaders attempted to introduce Islamic ethos in schools, the *Daily Telegraph* published an editorial on what it means to be British, which included the top ten items that constitute the core of "Britishness":[3]

> We have never been especially good at defining what constitutes British values.... There was a time when this would not have been necessary, since they would have been inculcated into everyone in the land through their schools and shared cultural experiences. In an era of mass immigration and the segregation of some communities from mainstream society, as exposed by the so-called Trojan Horse affair in Birmingham, this is no longer so straightforward.

Britain is not the only nation in search of an identity. From Australia to the United States, France to the Netherlands, Germany to Israel, Japan to the Republic of Korea, nation-states seek to construct a unique national character to be shared and celebrated, and find distinguishing identities: what is uniquely Dutch or German National identity debates have become routine. In all cases, the debate has been related to the "other"—Muslims (Europe), Latinos (the United States), non-Jewish immigrants (Israel), the West (Japan), and the American and Chinese influence (Korea).

Immigration, more than anything else, has brought to the fore the question of national identity. Immigrants encourage nation-states to define themselves. As George Orwell rightly observed, "It is only when you meet someone of a different culture from yourself that you begin to realise what your own beliefs really are."[4] To a large extent, the substance of the requirements "we" demand of "them" is about "us." Immigration policy echoes national identity by mirroring not only the qualities that "we" value in others, but also by reflecting the essentials that define "us" as a nation. In a sense, drafting immigration requirements is a form of nation-building.[5]

Until not so long ago, Western countries had no immediate or foreseeable need to set boundaries to their collective identity; it was a given,

[3] Telegraph View, "The Core British Values that Define Our Nation," *Daily Telegraph*, June 11, 2014. See also GOV.UK, "British Values: Article by David Cameron," June 15, 2014.

[4] George Orwell, *The Road to Wigan Pier* (New York: Harcourt, Brace and Company, 1958): p. 197; Samuel P. Huntington, *Who Are We? The Challenges to America's National Identity* (New York: Simon & Schuster, 2004): p. 24 ("'you' and 'I' become 'we' when a 'they' appears.").

[5] Rogers M. Smith, "Foreword," in *Immigration & Citizenship in the 21st Century*, Noah M.J. Pickus, ed. (Oxford: Rowman & Littlefield Publishers, 1998): pp. xi–xv at xiii; Rogers Brubaker, "Immigration, Citizenship, and the Nation-State in France and Germany," in *The Citizenship Debates: A Reader*, Gershon Shafir, ed. (Minneapolis: University of Minnesota Press, 1998): pp. 131–164 at 132.

not something that had to be defined. In the post-World War II international system, Western countries did not struggle with the question "Who we are?" or search for a bond to bind them together; they had a solid sense of what was American, British, French, or German. But times have changed. The influx of immigrants, together with globalization processes and the rise of multiculturalism, has led to a new reality where it becomes more difficult to know what it means to have an American, British, French, or German identity. David Miller rightly observes that "People are both less sure of what it means to be French or Swedish, and less sure about how far it is morally acceptable to acknowledge and act upon such identities."[6] This process is particularly apparent in European Member States, whose national identities have been challenged by EU institutions.

National identities have traditionally not been legal concepts. Perhaps for the first time in human history, states currently offer, or attempt to offer, a *legal* definition of their national identity. Immigration law is the field (or rather the battlefield) in which this fascinating phenomenon is taking place.

THE CULTURAL DEFENSE

The six months between September 2010 and February 2011 witnessed a fierce attack on multiculturalism in political rhetoric. Angela Merkel, the German Chancellor, David Cameron, the British Prime Minister, and Nicolas Sarkozy, the French President—all denounced multiculturalism and declared that it had "utterly failed." Multiculturalism puts the emphasis not on what people have in common, but on their differences. Arguably, this has contributed to the reality in which, after years of encouraging people to acknowledge and celebrate ethno-cultural diversity, nation-states have difficulty in finding commonalities. Academically, the retreat from multiculturalism was recognized years earlier. Back in 2001, Brian Barry warned that "multiculturalism was bound sooner or later to sink."[7] The scope of the retreat from multiculturalism is disputed, but even the greatest supporters of multiculturalism agree that it is receding. According to Will Kymlicka, the backlash against multiculturalism does not apply to national minorities and indigenous peoples.

[6] David Miller, *On Nationality* (Oxford: Clarendon Press, 1995): p. 165.

[7] Brian Barry, *Culture and Equality: An Egalitarian Critique of Multiculturalism* (Cambridge: Harvard University Press, 2001): p. 6. See also Nathan Glazer, *We Are All Multiculturalists Now* (Cambridge: Harvard University Press, 1997): pp. 11, 19–20.

Rather, it is primarily restricted to *immigrant* groups and is limited geographically (for example, U.S. immigration law is generally more multicultural compared to European immigration law) and substantially (there are opposite trends even in European Member States).[8]

The most visible expression of the backlash against multiculturalism in the immigration context is the rise of what I term "cultural defense policies." Generally speaking, these are immigration and naturalization policies that are aimed at defending/preserving/protecting different forms and expressions of the national culture/identity/character. In Europe in particular, this has resulted in attempts to enforce, rather than encourage, cultural assimilation—integration is mandatory, sanctioned, and test-based. It is expressed in the extension of culture-based immigration selection to the requirements for entry—as pre-arrival integration. It applies to all types of immigrants, including family members, and it is more invasive than the classic requirements of familiarity with a country's history and civics. By and large, cultural defense policies are implemented through five principal measures: (a) citizenship tests; (b) integration contracts; (c) loyalty oaths; (d) attachment requirements; and (e) language requirements. Alongside these principal measures, some level of incompatibility between the immigrant's way of life and the host society's cultural identity has become a ground for exclusion.

In 2008, the Conseil d'Etat sustained the denial of French citizenship to a Muslim woman—who had been legally admitted into France, had married a French citizen, and had given birth to three French children—due to "insufficient assimilation into the French *communauté*." It ruled that the woman, who wore a *niqab* (face-covering), adopted a "radical religious practice," incompatible with the "values essential to the French *communauté*, notably the principle of gender equality." As of 2007, in order to receive a permanent residence permit, every immigrant must sign an "integration contract" in which he or she undertakes to take French language lessons and respect the fundamental values of the Republic. Noncompliance with the contract's terms can lead to a refusal to issue a residence permit, non-renewal of a permit, and a fine. Recently, France adopted a policy of "integration from abroad." According to this policy, even before they enter France, newcomers have to participate in language classes and orientation courses covering fundamental values of the Republic. As of 2012, immigrants are required to answer questions

[8] Will Kymlicka, *Multicultural Odysseys: Navigating the New International Politics of Diversity* (Oxford: OUP, 2007): pp. 66–77, 124.

about French history, culture, and society during an immigration interview. Topics include French history, the Constitution of France, and Republican values, but also the Eiffel Tower, Brigitte Bardot, Edith Piaf, and Molière.

France is not alone; similar policies are mushrooming worldwide. To become German, immigrants must "conform to the German living conditions" and answer questions such as: "What should parents of a 22-year-old girl do if they do not like her boyfriend?" To become British, immigrants must be familiar with rugby, cricket, and the Grand National, and answer questions such as: "Suppose you spill someone's pint in the pub. What usually happens next?" To become Dutch, immigrants must complete an integration course in the Dutch embassy in their country of origin and pass a citizenship test. The content of the test is secret because the new Dutch philosophy provides that "one cannot study to be Dutch, one has to feel Dutch." To become American, immigrants have long been required to be "attached to the principles of the constitution of the United States," take an oath of allegiance to "support and defend the Constitution," and pass a citizenship test on American history and civics.

Liberal democracies have implemented a variety of coerced cultural-defense measures, thereby directing immigrants to embrace the values and customs of the dominant group. They increasingly rely on the cultural character of the host society, and the cultural background of the immigrant, in setting up immigration rules. Although the law is phrased in terms such as "community," "society," and "state," and in spite of the fact that politicians try to show that cultural defense policies defend "shared," "common," and "prevailing" values, the defended culture essentially represents the tastes and preferences of the dominant majority. The underlying message is that liberal states have a fixed national identity, and that there is a correlation between the "state culture" and the "majority culture." By adopting cultural defense measures, states create an image of one culturally homogenous group, speaking the same language, sharing the same values, and celebrating the same holidays, as if all people are the same.

The cultural defense of the majority goes far beyond immigration and naturalization requirements, as demonstrated by a recent case in which the European Court of Human Rights upheld the ban on wearing a full-face veil in any public space in France. The case was brought to the Court by a devout female Muslim, who argued that the absolute ban—which applied to public highways, public transport, post offices, hospitals, shops, walkways, cinemas, banks, airports, etc.—unlawfully infringed her right to private life and her freedom of conscience and religion. France defended the ban on grounds of public safety and the values of the Republic—gender equality, human dignity, and a respect for minimum requirements of life in society. However, the European Court of Human Rights held that the only legitimate aim of an absolute ban on a full-face veil was to guarantee the minimum requirements of "living together" in society. It admitted that in a democracy, "the views of a majority must [not] always prevail," yet referred to the principle of living together as requiring minimum social interaction and community life. In spite of the neutral language of "living together," the Court did not protect a universal mode of life—it actually concluded that the French position was very much a minority in Europe—but rather safeguarded the values and traditions of the dominant majority. The French government indeed asserted that the wearing of a "full-face veil by certain women shocked the majority of the French population." The dissenting opinion, however, replied that "there is no right not to be shocked or provoked by different models of cultural or religious identity, even those that are very distant from the traditional French and European life-style."[9]

To be clear: cultural defense policies reflect a retreat from multiculturalism, but do not mark a return to policies of forced cultural assimilation. It actually reveals how difficult it is for a liberal state to return to those policies. Yet it also indicates that it is too early to talk about the end of nationalism; the nation-state is witnessing a rise of majority nationalism which is aimed at defending the culture of the majority. It is often difficult to capture exactly what this "culture" is, but in most cases it includes some national particularity—the national language(s), symbols, and institutions; religious icons; traditions and ways of life. Talk about cultural majority rights, from a non-jingoistic perspective, is something we are likely to hear more often going forward.

MAJORITY RIGHTS

Liberal thinking and human rights law recognize the right of minority groups to maintain their unique cultural identity. Thus far, majority groups have not been granted a similar right because it is assumed that their culture is not threatened within the state. The majority, so the

[9] *S.A.S.* v. *France* Application 43835/11 (E.Ct.H.R., July 1, 2014): paras. 128, 119 (majority) and para. 7 (dissenting), respectively.

argument goes, "can take care of itself"; it can use its numerical advantage to perpetuate its culture. Political liberalism and human rights law have thus been silent on the topic of cultural rights of majority groups. As it stands, international law does not suggest a theoretical framework for understanding the challenge which global immigration poses to the culture of the majority. International law focuses on the right of "peoples" to self-determination, as well as on cultural rights of "minorities," yet does not recognize a legal entity of a "majority." Since the "majority" is not explicitly recognized as synonymous with "people," it is assumed that it has no self-determination rights and, in fact, no particular legal rights at all.

Thus far, the cultural defense of the majority has been indirect. Four techniques can be identified. The first technique equates the majority with the state. The majority defends the "state culture," which simply mirrors the majority culture. This technique is used, or exists on an unconscious level, when protecting national languages, holidays, symbols, institutions, and values, thereby declaring them part of the state culture. A second technique is the "culturalization of religion." This technique is commonly used when protecting religious icons of the majority, which, due to human rights considerations, are better protected by reference to their cultural aspect. Thus, for instance, the display of crucifixes on the walls of public classrooms in Italy may be considered as part of Italy's cultural heritage, and a school visit in a Spanish Cathedral may be seen as a history lesson. A third technique is "universalizing the particular." This technique is used when the majority seeks to disguise the defense of a particular culture by using a universal argument. For example, the Italian government defends the display of the crucifix in public schools by claiming, among other things, that it transmits a humanist message that may be independent of its religious connotation. In this view, the crucifix is a "symbol of the principles and values which formed the basis of democracy and western civilisation."[10] Similarly, the French government defends its mode of life and particular version of secularism, *laïcité*, by invoking the universal principles of gender equality, human dignity, and "living together." A fourth technique is "legal white lies." This technique uses relatively neutral criteria, such as an income requirement or a minimum age of 24 for admission of a foreign spouse (a rule that exists in Denmark), which, although used to protect the welfare system and against forced marriages, are also designed to deal wisely with undesirable

[10] *Lautsi v. Italy* Application 30814/06 (E.Ct.H.R., March 18, 2011), para. 36.

immigrants. The law does not tell the truth because it is legally impermissible and thus offers a different story. For example, the law can seek to reduce the scale of certain immigrant groups by setting an income requirement based upon the assumption that immigrants from some countries have a low income level.

Liberal democracies, I believe, should stop beating about the bush and directly tackle the question of majority rights. Under which circumstances (if any), and based on what justifications, can majorities legitimately defend their cultural essentials by using immigration law? This question is one of the most pressing issues of our time. The book presents four patterns of cases in which majority groups claim that they are in need of protection in the immigration context: (a) *diminishing majorities*—this relates to a situation in which a fundamental component of the majority culture faces a significant challenge due to immigration; (b) *regional-minority majorities*—this relates to a situation in which there is a substantial gap between the cultural characteristics of the majority within the state and the regional characteristics outside the state so that the majority constitutes a cultural "regional minority"; (c) *victimized majorities*—this relates to a situation in which the majority has a rich history of being victimized and persecuted, and when threats are still persistent; and (d) *minoritized majorities*—this relates to a situation in which, for historical reasons, a national majority displays the state of mind of a national minority, and further immigration is perceived by the majority as a threat to its territorial integrity and sovereignty. Once it has recognized a principle, the book explores the extent of the protection: *when* is cultural defense justified; *what* does it justify; and *which* culture and *whose*?

THREE CASES OF DEFENSE

Culture is a notoriously difficult concept to capture. I use the concept of "culture" for two meanings: anthropological and normative. In the anthropological sense, culture is everyday experience, the way "of doing, seeing and organizing things that focuses on actual practices."[11] This aspect relates to what people actually do—their way of doing things in work, education, family life, social interaction, leisure, arts, politics, and almost all fields of life. Culture, in this sense, includes folkways, habits, manners, traditions,

[11] Veit Bader, "Associational Governance of Ethno-Religious Diversity in Europe: The Dutch Case," in *Citizenship, Borders, and Human Needs*, Rogers M. Smith, ed. (Philadelphia: University of Pennsylvania Press, 2011): pp. 273–300 at 274.

and mores. In the normative sense, culture centers on a concrete and bounded set of beliefs and norms that form a community's identity and shape its sense of right and wrong. It relates to those ideas, values, creeds, and philosophies that influence the moral commitment of a people and define who they are—be it a religion, reason, or rationality.[12] This aspect is supposed to be canonical and of sacred import. These two meanings are interrelated and influence one another.

The book presents three cases of "defense": (a) civic-political; (b) ethno-religious; and (c) ethno-cultural. Although the distinction between civic, cultural, and ethnic nationalism is blurred, traditional models are still useful in helping to understand similarities and differences. On the whole, in spite of wide variations, all countries attempt to defend a "culture"—as an umbrella-category. However, this typology is far from being an accurate description of a rich and complex story; reality is more contextualized. In the realm of culture, the dividing boundaries are not as clear-cut as the distinction between men and women, young and old, or black and white.

In adopting the typology of civic, cultural, and ethnic cultures, I follow a typology offered by Shmuel Eisenstadt and Bernhard Giesen. According to Eisenstadt and Giesen, there are three ideal types of collective identity: primordial, civic, and cultural. Primordial identity focuses on "kinship, ethnicity and race." Primordial characteristics are a given in the sense of being inborn; they are largely unchangeable "by voluntary action." One is born a member, granted membership via a relationship with a member, or achieves membership through a change of the primordial characteristics as in the case of religious conversion. There are no citizenship tests because, in principle, the test is birthright. In contrast, civic identity is constructed on familiarity with the community's rules of conduct, constitutional arrangements, and social mores. One can learn to become a member by knowing the history and civics, participating in the political life, following the laws, and adopting the local mores. These requirements may not be easy, but they are learnable. They focus on a minimal mandatory core of knowledge and familiarity with the community, and the rest is assumed to be acquired through social interaction. In between primordial and civic identities, cultural identity relates to confirmation of a community's cultural taboos. Becoming a member is a process of "communication, education, and conversion."

[12] Roger Scruton, *Culture Counts: Faith and Feeling in a World Besieged* (New York: Encounter Books, 2007): pp. 2–4.

Membership is open to anyone who is willing to subscribe to the tenets of the community. It is a form of cultural conversion—anyone can become a member "by converting to the right faith." The community has a "divine mission," "eternal values," and "moral zeal." Those who do not share in the project are "mistaken and erring; they have to be converted" by "cultural formation." The community, hence, implements a direct mechanism to verify the cultural conformity of new candidates.[13]

Although no political community entirely fits these types of collective identity, they help in distinguishing between different cases of defense. In primordial communities, one cannot become a member by just learning the language and history. In Israel, for example, unless one is a spouse of an Israeli citizen (Jewish or non-Jewish), one can become a naturalized Israeli in the usual manner only if one is born with essential primordial characteristics (being Jewish) or via a close family relationship with a Jew, or through changing one's primordial characteristics (Jewish conversion); naturalization of non-Jewish applicants, an option that officially exists, is rarely granted in reality. In civic communities, one can learn to become a member; membership is a function of civic knowledge, political participation, and legal obedience. In the United States, for instance, anyone can theoretically become a U.S. citizen by demonstrating, among other things, basic English language proficiency, knowledge and understanding of the fundamentals of U.S. history and principles and form of government, and attachment to the principles of the U.S. Constitution. In cultural communities, one can become a member by showing moral commitment to, and identification with, cultural taboos of the community. The Dutch philosophy according to which "one cannot study to be Dutch, one has to feel Dutch" can fit this model. In practice, however, all communities present a combination of the primordial, civic, and cultural types and the question is one of weight—which specific type of identity is more prominent in the overall assessment?

STRUCTURE AND METHODOLOGY

Outline of the book

The book is divided into six chapters organized in two parts. Part I is descriptive. It depicts a deviation from multiculturalism in the immigration context and its outcome—moral panic and "cultural defense."

[13] Shmuel Noah Eisenstadt and Bernhard Giesen, "The Construction of Collective Identity," *European Journal of Sociology* 36, no. 1 (1995): pp. 72–102 at 77, 82–84, 87.

Chapter 1, "New Challenge," argues that the challenge brought about by global migration is historically unprecedented. Identifying nine changes, Chapter 1 traces a transformation in the relationship between majority groups and minority groups. The nine changes occur in immigration patterns (scale, character, intensity), in Western society (population decline, changing lifestyles, new human rights regime), and in the world (geopolitics, technology, globalization). Chapter 1 documents the fast-changing reality in the West and shows that it is not adequately addressed by international law and political theory.

Chapter 2, "Demographic Anxiety," describes how the changing patterns of immigration produce public hysteria, what I term "demographobia." Conspiracy theories that immigrant groups plan a "take-over," attached to concerns over the erosion of national identities and traditional ways of life, contribute to the rise of right-wing parties in the West. Focusing on three cases—Hispanics in America, Muslims in Europe, and Palestinians in Israel—Chapter 2 demonstrates how immigration debates are often grounded on incorrect facts and false conclusions and prompt an extreme and disproportionate response.

Chapter 3, "Cultural Defense," addresses the legal response to global immigration—proactive immigration policies designed to defend the culture of majority groups. Chapter 3 presents three models of defense—ethno-religious, ethno-cultural, and civic-political—and explains how they represent different concepts of peoplehood. It further identifies five means of defense: citizenship tests, integration contracts, naturalization oaths, attachment requirements, and language requirements. On the whole, Chapter 3 finds that nationalism is undergoing a process of "cultural convergence" under which liberal states define the essence of their citizenship, and thus the rules of joining the community, in cultural terms.

After describing the new challenge of immigration (Chapter 1) and its political and legal responses (Chapters 2 to 3), Part II of the book presents a normative analysis that seeks to distinguish between the justifiable and unjustifiable efforts of liberal states to protect their culture. Chapter 4, "Illiberal Liberalism", reveals a troubling trend in liberal states, which, ironically, in order to protect liberalism, violate the very same values they seek to protect. This creates a paradox of liberalism. Liberal states, in order to defend what they perceive as a liberal regime, resort to illiberal means. Here lies the paradox: either the liberal must tolerate illiberal practices, or turn to illiberal means to "liberate" the illiberal. Chapter 4 criticizes the excessive reliance on culture as a criterion in immigration selection—not necessarily its use, but rather its abuse—as being illiberal, for three reasons: state neutrality, liberal tolerance, and policy motivation.

Chapter 5, "Majority Rights," advocates the recognition of a new concept, "majority groups"; presents three concepts of majorities—ethno-cultural majorities, sociological majorities, and idea-based majorities; identifies four cases in which majorities may be culturally "needy" in the immigration context—diminishing majorities, regional-minority majorities, victimized majorities, and minoritized majorities; and provides two justifications for cultural majority rights in immigration law. Generally, it asserts that the justifications for cultural majority rights are based upon similar rationales to those which justify cultural minority rights—the right of persons belonging to these groups to identity and personal autonomy.

Chapter 6, "National Constitutionalism," examines whether it is morally defensible for a liberal state either to set the continuity of the majority culture as a goal, or to adopt explicit cultural criteria for immigrant selection. It constructs a two-stage immigration regulation. First, for admission, immigrants would have to accept liberal-democratic principles as a prerequisite for admission; these principles are not culturally-oriented but rather constitute a system of rules governing human behavior in liberal states. Second, for naturalization, immigrants would have to accept fundamental constitutional principles essential for obtaining citizenship in a specific state—as long as these principles are just, given the state's circumstances. This concept, national constitutionalism, has five principal elements. It refers to: (a) *constitutional* principles; (b) which are *fundamental*; (c) *essential* for obtaining citizenship; (d) *just, given the circumstances* of a specific country; and (e) which should be *legally accepted* by the immigrant.

The book conducts a systematic analysis of immigration requirements in liberal states. But don't be mistaken: the book is more about "us" than about immigrants. We are those who define the type and number of people we permit to join our community, and what rules apply to the naturalization process. Immigration law, hence, is a unique platform to examine *our* choices. It shapes who we are as a people and, at the same time, functions as a mirror reflecting those qualities that we value in others. By putting immigrants to test, we put our own values to test. The final chapter, "Conclusion: Immigration Policy and Constitutional Identity," traces what immigration policy can teach us about constitutional identity. In an attempt to define what the process of becoming a citizen means—how to become British, French, and German—states are exploring their own ethos—what Britishness, Frenchness, and Germanness means. Regulating immigration is a journey into ourselves.

Methodology and limitation

The book focuses on three cases—the United States, Europe, and Israel. The cases present a different challenge, experience a different type of anxiety, have a different concept of nationhood, and are in a different chronological stage of development in terms of absorbing immigrants.[14] In Europe, the main countries analyzed are France, Germany, the Netherlands, and the United Kingdom. This is because they have been the largest receiving countries of immigrants in recent decades, have the highest percentage of Muslim population in the European Union (together with Austria, Belgium, and Sweden), have a strong sense of national identity, and face ongoing cultural tensions over the topic of immigration. Although these are limited examples, they provide a fairly good picture of current trends in Europe.

Five caveats should be considered. First, the starting point of the book is the premise that a state has "a qualified right to limit immigration"[15] and thereby set some criteria for exclusion and inclusion. It is possible to challenge this premise, as some scholars have done, but the still widely accepted proposition in international human rights law is that states can generally decide some qualifications for entry and citizenship. Second, the book tells a provincial story. The story is geographically limited to certain Western societies in North America and Europe with the addition of Israel. The lessons that can be inferred from this story are limited to the analyzed countries. Third, the book focuses on nation-states; it does not cover cases of multinational or bi-national states, a topic that raises different dilemmas. Fourth, the book addresses cultural changes brought about by voluntary migration—labor migration and family migration and, when relevant, humanitarian migration. It discusses neither forced population movements—population transfer, state succession, invasion, or occupation—nor interregional movements of

[14] The book uses the terms "migrants" and "immigrants" interchangeably. The terms "migrant" and "immigrant" have no commonly-accepted definition. This is a source of inconsistency and methodological problems. The definition used by the United Nations considers a long-term international migrant/immigrant as a person who has resided in a foreign country for more than one year, regardless of his or her motivation and status.

[15] John Rawls, *The Law of Peoples, with "The Idea of Public Reason Revisited"* (Cambridge: Harvard University Press, 2001): p. 39 (n 48).

people within federations, states, or unions. Most of these cases bring about cultural changes, but they deserve a separate discussion that goes beyond the scope of this book. And finally, cultural defense in the liberal state is a broad topic. Majorities employ ordinary means to protect their culture—public education, national feasts and ceremonies, limitations on cultural free trade, and constitutional safeguards—are all familiar examples of cultural protectionism. This book focuses only on cultural defense in one field—immigration and citizenship requirements.

Contribution

The book seeks to make four contributions: (a) to expose a new emerging trend—the rising power of culture in immigration selection—which partly refutes the generally-accepted view of liberalization in access to citizenship; (b) to set out a theory of cultural defense of nations based upon principles of international law and moral philosophy, and thus identify legal and moral constraints that should be imposed upon states' power to limit immigration based on culture and for the purpose of majorities' cultural continuity; (c) to provide liberal justifications for cultural rights of majority groups based upon rights of persons belonging to these groups to identity and autonomy; and (d) to develop a liberal concept of cultural defense, "national constitutionalism," as an instrument by which liberal democracies can pursue legitimate cultural goals without recourse to the more draconian measures recently adopted by, or proposed in, several states.

The question whether the majority has a right to defend its culture has not been the subject of much discussion in law and political liberalism. Theories of the rights of minorities to preserve their culture have been put forward, but it has been generally assumed by most thinkers either that the majority culture is not threatened, or that liberal states should not attempt to promote a particular culture but, instead, should remain neutral in the public sphere. Reality, however, has changed. The changing patterns of immigration and the changing face of the West have generated a form of majority nationalism and given rise to a series of new questions. The book addresses one of the most divisive questions—is it justified for a liberal state to restrict immigration in order to protect the culture of majority groups? It seeks to offer a form of cultural defense that is morally defensible and politically wise. This issue is one of the greatest challenges facing liberalism today.

PART I

BEFORE THE MAJORITY BECOMES THE MINORITY

1

New Challenge

As our case is new, so we must think anew, and act anew.

—Abraham Lincoln[1]

This chapter argues that international migration presents a new challenge. It challenges a fundamental premise in liberal thought under which majority groups can perpetuate their culture by controlling entry into the state. Grouping together nine macro and micro-level changes, the chapter traces a transformation in the relationship between majority groups and minority groups. The nine changes occur in migration patterns (scale, character, intensity), in Western society (population decline, changing lifestyles, new human rights regime), and in the world (geopolitics, technology, globalization). Each of these changes, individually, may not be entirely new, yet the combination of them all-together at one time has no historical precedent. This reality brings about political and legal responses (Chapters 2 to 3) and raises normative questions (Chapters 4 to 6). The aim of this chapter is to document the changing reality and show that it is not adequately addressed by political theory and international law.

LIBERALISM AND MAJORITY GROUPS

One of the most fundamental premises underlying contemporary immigration law is that immigration is about individuals, not collectives. Stephen Legomsky eloquently coined it by noting, "Countries don't immigrate. People do."[2] This premise is related to another well-established proposition in liberal theory under which majority groups can

[1] Ronald C. White, Jr., *A. Lincoln: A Biography* (New York: Random House, 2009): p. 522.

[2] Stephen H. Legomsky, "Immigration, Equality and Diversity," *Columbia Journal of Transnational Law* 31, no. 2 (1993): pp. 319–336 at 334.

perpetuate their power through immigration laws. Liberal thought and international human rights law recognize the right of minority groups to preserve their cultural identity. So far, majority groups have not been granted a similar right under the assumption that their culture is not threatened within the public sphere. The majority culture, so the argument goes, "can take care of itself."[3] It can dominate the public sphere by controlling entry into the community and by utilizing the forces of democratic decision-making.

The idea that the majority "can take care of itself" is shared by liberal theorists. In *Liberalism and the Right to Culture*, Avishai Margalit and Moshe Halbertal articulate this point by observing that while every human being has a right to culture, culture requires a group.[4] Not all groups are entitled to the right to culture—only those that have passed some numerical threshold and are "needy": "The right to culture demands that the state abandon its neutral position and actively assist needy cultures."[5] The "needy cultures" are minority cultures, not majority cultures. "The majority culture," Margalit and Halbertal hold, "is able to maintain a more or less homogeneous environment even without privileges by virtue of its being the culture of the majority."[6] This is because the majority group can perpetuate its power "through laws of entry to the state.... For if the matter were left to the forces of the market, the majority culture would soon take over the entire public space."[7] This reality creates an unequal situation that should be rectified by granting special privileges to minority groups.

Will Kymlicka proclaims a similar idea. Among the justifications for minorities' right to culture, Kymlicka refers to the disadvantage caused to minority cultures by the erosive effect of a majority-controlled laissez-faire democracy. A liberal state is not neutral because the common good reflects the preference of the majority group—vis-à-vis its language, values, holidays, and political institutions. The so-called "state culture" mirrors the culture of the majority. Consequently, "minorities must either play by the rules of the majority culture...or get out entirely."[8] Kymlicka describes the illusive concept of liberal neutrality, which "may appear to be 'neutral' between the various national groups,"

[3] Avishai Margalit and Moshe Halbertal, "Liberalism and the Right to Culture," *Social Research* 71, no. 3 (2004): pp. 529–548 at 530.

[4] Margalit and Halbertal, p. 537 (n 3) ("The last of the Mohicans does not seem to be someone with the right to a Mohican way of life since...the Mohican way of life requires a group.").

[5] Margalit and Halbertal, p. 530 (n 3).

[6] Margalit and Halbertal, p. 546 (n 3).

[7] Margalit and Halbertal, p. 547 (n 3).

[8] Will Kymlicka, *Liberalism, Community and Culture* (Oxford: Clarendon Press, 1989): p. 228.

yet "systematically privilege[s] the majority."[9] As a result, he shows, "Some groups are unfairly disadvantaged in the cultural market-place."[10] This inequality creates injustice that needs to be balanced by giving privileges to minority groups.

Guided by this philosophy, international law is silent on the issue of majority cultures. International law offers the notion of self-determination of "peoples," which does not overlap with the concept of "majorities," and apparently holds that the existing right of peoples to self-determination is sufficient to maintain the culture of the majorities. Since "peoples" have a right to self-determination, and this right includes a right to pursue their "cultural development," no further protection seems to be required. The forces of democracy would supposedly protect their culture. To compensate ethnic and religious minority groups, who do not enjoy a similar right of state-based cultural self-determination, international law provides them with a right to sub-state cultural self-determination. It declares that "In those States in which ethnic, religious or linguistic minorities exist, persons belonging to such minorities shall not be denied the right... to enjoy their own culture."[11]

Although the premise that the majority culture can take care of itself generally still stands, it has been questioned due to a few factual and normative developments. I shall briefly mention nine developments and group them into three categories: shifts in migration patterns, changes occurring in Western society, and transformations in the world. Taken together, these nine developments undermine one of the most fundamental premises of contemporary liberal thought and international human rights law.

THE CHANGING FACE OF MIGRATION

It's the immigrants—migration patterns are different

The first transformation is related to the scale, character, and intensity of contemporary migration. Let us focus on each of these factors, starting with the *scale* of migration. On the global level, the number of migrants has almost tripled in the past five decades. In the 1960s, the world had 75 million international migrants; in 2010, the number was 214 million. True, the proportional growth of international migrants remains constant

[9] Will Kymlicka, *Multicultural Citizenship: A Liberal Theory of Minority Rights* (Oxford: Clarendon Press, 2000): p. 51.

[10] Kymlicka, *Multicultural Citizenship*, p. 109 (n 9).

[11] International Covenant on Civil and Political Rights (New York, December 16, 1966, 999 U.N.T.S. 171): Arts. 1, 27.

TABLE 1.1 INTERNATIONAL MIGRANT STOCK AS A PERCENTAGE OF THE TOTAL POPULATION BY MAJOR REGIONS, 1960–2010

Area	*Percentage*		
	1960	*1990*	*2010*
World	2.6	2.9	3.1
More developed regions	3.6	7.2	10.1
Less developed regions	2.1	1.8	1.4
Africa	3.2	2.5	1.9
Asia	1.7	1.6	1.4
Europe	3.4	6.9	9.5
Latin America and the Caribbean	2.8	1.6	1.3
Northern America	6.7	9.8	14.2
Oceania	13.5	16.2	16.8

Source: U.N., Department of Economic and Social Affairs, Population Division, "Trends in International Migrant Stock: The 2008 Revision," U.N. Doc. POP/DB/MIG/Stock/Rev.2008, 2009.

Notes: (a) A "migrant" is a person who changes his or her country of usual residence; (b) The "more developed regions" comprise Australia, Europe, New Zealand, Japan, and Northern America; (c) The "less developed regions" comprise Africa, Asia (excluding Japan), Latin America and the Caribbean plus Melanesia, Micronesia, and Polynesia; (d) The distribution in Europe is as follows: Northern Europe—3.0% (1960) versus 10.9% (2010); Southern Europe—0.8% (1960) versus 9.5% (2010); Western Europe—5.7% (1960) versus 12.4% (2010); and Eastern Europe (including Russia)—3.8% (1960) versus 2.2% (2010).

in relation to the total population growth—international migrants were 2.6 percent of the world population in 1960 and 3.1 percent of the world population in 2010—yet it is much higher in the more developed regions (10.1 percent) than in the less developed regions (1.4 percent) (see Table 1.1). On the regional level, although there is a movement of people within the developing regions and within the developed regions, most interregional migration moves from the developing regions to the developed regions. In 2010, the developed regions hosted about 60 percent of the total migrant stock.[12] Net migration has grown steadily in absolute and relative numbers in developed regions.[13] In Europe, international migrant stock as a percentage of the total population climbed from 3.4 percent in 1960 to 9.5 percent in 2010. In North America, the figure more than doubled—from 6.7 percent in 1960 to 14.2 percent in 2010 (see Table 1.1).

[12] U.N., Department of Economic and Social Affairs, Population Division, "International Migration Report 2009: A Global Assessment," U.N. Doc. ST/ESA/SER.A/316, 2011: p. 1.

[13] U.N., Department of Economic and Social Affairs, Population Division, "World Population Prospects: The 2006 Revision, Highlights," U.N. Doc. ESA/P/WP.202, 2007: pp. 24–25.

TABLE 1.2 INTERNATIONAL MIGRANT STOCK AS A PERCENTAGE OF THE TOTAL POPULATION BY SELECTED COUNTRIES, 1960–2010

Country	*Percentage*	
	1960	*2010*
Australia	16.5	21.9
Austria	11.5	15.6
Denmark	2.1	8.8
France	7.7	10.7
Germany	—	13.1
Ireland	2.6	19.6
Italy	0.9	7.4
Norway	1.7	10.0
Spain	0.7	14.1
Sweden	4.0	14.1
Switzerland	13.4	23.2
The Netherlands	3.9	10.5
United Kingdom	3.2	10.4
United States	5.8	13.5

Source: U.N., Department of Economic and Social Affairs, Population Division, "Trends in International Migrant Stock: The 2008 Revision," U.N. Doc. POP/DB/MIG/Stock/Rev.2008, 2009.

Note: There are other countries in which there was a large increase of net migration. Examples are the Gulf states (Bahrain, Kuwait, Oman, Qatar, Saudi Arabia, and United Arab Emirates), European states (Andorra, Cyprus, Iceland, Luxembourg, and Portugal), Caribbean Islands (Aruba, Cayman Islands, and Martinique), and Polynesia.

On the national level, migration has dramatically increased in most of the developed regions. In Ireland, international migrant stock as a share of the total population jumped from 2.6 percent (1960) to 19.6 percent (2010); in Italy—from 0.9 percent (1960) to 7.4 percent (2010); in Denmark—from 2.1 percent (1960) to 8.8 percent (2010); and in Spain—from 0.7 percent (1960) to 14.1 percent (2010) (see Table 1.2).

Migration also plays an important role in total population growth in developed regions. In 2005–2010, in countries such as Austria, Belgium, Canada, Greece, Italy, Luxembourg, Spain, Sweden, and Switzerland, the contribution of net migration to national population growth was slightly higher than the contribution of natural increase (births minus deaths).[14]

[14] International Organization for Migration, *World Migration 2005: Costs and Benefits of International Migration* (Geneva: IOM, 2005): pp. 383, 398; U.N., "World Population Prospects: The 2006 Revision," p. xii (n 13); U.N., "International Migration Report 2009," p. 23 (n 12).

It is difficult to predict demographic trends fifty years ahead. Five decades ago, most demographers did not foresee the demographic decline in the West. Instead, they predicted a demographic explosion. One of the best-sellers in 1968 was Paul Ehrlich's book, *The Population Bomb*, which warned against overpopulation and advocated actions to limit Western population growth in order to prevent mass starvation. Nevertheless, demographic predictions should not be entirely ignored. Existing indicators show that net migration will continue to grow. In their thought-provoking book, *Exceptional People*, Ian Goldin, Geoffrey Cameron, and Meera Balarajan present nine interrelated factors that are likely to bring about migration pressures—both an increase in the supply of migrants and a demand for migrants.[15] In the near future, people will have more reasons to move to the developed world and more resources to do it. Six factors are likely to increase the supply of migrants: intercountry inequality and disparity, economic growth in developing countries (higher incomes allow more people to migrate), urbanization, increased education in developing countries, a growing working-age population in developing countries, and climate changes producing larger numbers of climate refugees. At the same time, the demand for migrants is likely to increase due to three factors: population decline in developed countries, growing demand for low-skilled migrants, and global competition for high-skilled migrants. Other push and pull factors that may influence the volume of migration are political transitions, technological innovations, and an increase in the number of natural disasters in developing regions. It is not surprising that a Gallup World Poll of 119 countries found that 14 percent of the world's adult population wished to move permanently to a different country, while 26 percent wished to move to a new country for temporary work.[16]

In 2011, the European Union published population projections for the EU. The report embraces four models. Model 1 projects that the share of "persons with a foreign background" in the total EU population, which was 10.4 percent in 2011, will reach 17.9 percent by 2031 and 24.0 percent by 2051 (the report does not distinguish, however, between EU and non-EU migrants). Unlike the other models, Model 1 is "modest" because it includes some contestable assumptions: (a) it assumes that the fertility rates of native-born persons and persons with a foreign background are identical; (b) it excludes irregular migrants from the calculation; (c) for

[15] Ian Goldin, Geoffrey Cameron, and Meera Balarajan, *Exceptional People: How Migration Shaped Our World and Will Define Our Future* (Princeton: Princeton University Press, 2011): pp. 219–258.

[16] Julie Ray and Neli Esipova, "More Adults Would Move for Temporary Work Than Permanently," Gallup, March 9, 2012.

Table 1.3 Persons with a foreign background as a percentage of the total population by selected countries and years (Model 1)

Area	*Percentage*		
	2011	*2031*	*2051*
European Union	10.4	17.9	24.0
Austria	16.8	28.4	38.5
Belgium	14.8	23.7	29.6
Denmark	9.8	19.2	26.8
France	11.8	14.4	15.6
Germany	13.6	23.0	32.1
Ireland	17.6	29.8	34.6
Italy	8.2	17.7	26.2
Spain	16.2	29.0	36.2
Sweden	15.1	23.3	28.0
The Netherlands	11.6	17.3	21.5
United Kingdom	11.9	21.8	28.8

Source: Giampaolo Lanzieri, "Fewer, Older and Multicultural? Projections of the EU Populations by Foreign/National Background," Eurostat, 2011: pp. 6–7, 27–30.

Note: "Persons with a foreign background" are defined as foreign-born persons ("first-generation") plus native-born persons of a foreign-born mother ("second-generation").

methodological reasons, it considers a person born to a foreign-born father a native, not a migrant; and (d) it regards third-generation migrants as natives. And still, in spite of these arguable assumptions, EU projections indicate a fast and consistent increase in the percentage of the foreign-born population in the European Union (see Table 1.3).

The European Union predicts that, based upon even the most modest projections, in 2051 more than ten states will comprise large groups of people (25 percent or more of the population) with a foreign background. When other models are included, there are a number of states in which the current majority becomes a minority. These states include Austria, Belgium, Cyprus, Germany, and Spain. The report considers the growing diversity of the European population to be one of Europe's biggest challenges.

It is not just the scale of migration that has changed—the *character* of migration has changed as well. In general, until the 1950s, international migration remained largely within the boundaries of the so-called Western world; for example, European migration to America at the turn of the nineteenth century and the early twentieth century. Migrants might have been foreigners in the target states, but generally they were not total strangers to Western political ideas—with the exception of Asian migrants. Goldin, Cameron, and Balarajan observe that "between 1800 and 1860, two-thirds of migrants to the United States were from Britain, and a further 22 percent were from Germany. From 1860 to 1920, most of the 30 million migrants to the United States came from Scandinavia, Ireland, Italy, Spain, and Eastern Europe."[17] Today, however, particularly in Europe, most international migrants come from non-Western countries.

Compared to the past, the character of migration is different today in yet another aspect—the type of migration. Until the mid-twentieth century, international migration consisted mainly of labor migrants who, particularly in Europe, were perceived as temporary. Even in the United States, the leading immigration country, about one-third of the migrants between 1860 and 1910 either returned to their home country or relocated to a different country.[18] Today, however, family, rather than labor migration, characterizes the vast majority of migrants. In 2005, family migration constituted 70 percent of total migration to the United States, 62 percent to New Zealand, 61 percent to France, 60 percent to Canada and Norway, 58 percent to Italy, 57 percent to Australia and Sweden, 47 percent to Switzerland, 46 percent to the Netherlands, 45 percent to Germany, and 31 percent to the United Kingdom.[19] When excluding refugees and asylum seekers, family migration constitutes about 70 percent of total migration in some parts of the developed regions. Compared to labor migration, family migration is different for three main reasons: (a) it is usually not temporary; (b) it is more difficult to restrict family migration because citizens have a right to family life; and (c) it is likely to increase migration. Empirical studies show that family ties in a different country are among the most important factors in an individual's decision to move to a new country—more important than wages and human development.[20]

[17] Goldin, Cameron, and Balarajan, p. 59 (n 15). It should be noted that migrants from Eastern and Southern Europe were not regarded at that time as "Western" in America, but alien to democracy and Western political ideas. See William P. Dillingham, U.S. Immigration Commission, *Abstracts of Reports of the Immigration Commission, with Conclusions and Recommendations and Views of the Minority*, vol. I, *Reports of the Immigration Commission* (Washington: Government Printing Office, 1911).

[18] Goldin, Cameron, and Balarajan, p. 60 (n 15).

[19] International Organization for Migration, *World Migration 2008: Managing Labour Mobility in the Evolving Global Economy* (Geneva: IOM, 2008): p. 157.

[20] Goldin, Cameron, and Balarajan, pp. 102–103 (n 15); Timothy B. Gravelle et al., "What Makes 700 Million Adults Want to Migrate," Gallup, February 18, 2010.

Contemporary migration is relatively homogeneous in nature. In some countries migration not only means that more people of a different cultural background staying on a permanent basis, but also more people who are not of the same ethnicity or religion as the native population. In France, to take an extreme example, Muslims composed 68.5 percent of all new migrants in 2010.[21] In Europe, when excluding intra-regional migration, a large percentage of migrants are Muslims. In EU Member States, Muslim migrants constitute 27 percent of total migration and 39 percent of total migration when intra-EU movement is excluded from the calculation.[22] In addition, a large percentage of Muslim migration to Europe is nationally homogeneous; for instance, Algerian and Moroccan migrants in France, Turks in Germany, Turks and Moroccans in the Netherlands and, to a lesser extent, Pakistanis in the United Kingdom.[23] On the other side of the ocean, in the United States, 41 percent of the migrants in 2000–2009 arrived from Latin America, mostly from one country—Mexico. Indeed, in 2012, 64 percent of the Hispanic-origin population in the United States was of Mexican origin.[24]

The composition of migration has demographic effects. Take the United States, for example. The number of Hispanics is expected to triple—from 47 million in 2010 (16 percent of the population) to 133 million in 2050 (30 percent of the population) (see Table 1.4).[25] According to the U.S. Census Bureau, minorities—mainly Asians, Hispanics, and Blacks—comprised 36.6 percent of the U.S. population in 2011. However, most children younger than one-year of age (50.4 percent) and almost half of the children younger than five-years old (49.7 percent) were "minorities." Hispanics are the most populous and the fastest growing group. In three states—California, New Mexico, and Texas—the non-Hispanic White population has already become a minority. The 2012 National Population Projections estimate that the non-Hispanic White population will become a national minority by 2043.[26]

[21] Pew Research Center, "The Future of the Global Muslim Population: Projections for 2010–2030," 2011: pp. 20, 134.

[22] Pew Research Center, "Faith on the Move: The Religious Affiliation of International Migrants," 2012: p. 54.

[23] Peter Stalker, "Migration Trends and Migration Policy in Europe," *International Migration* 40, no. 5 (2002): pp. 151–179 at 174.

[24] Philip Martin and Elizabeth Midgley, "Immigration in America 2010," U.S. Population Reference Bureau, 2010: p. 3; Pew Hispanic Center, "Statistical Profile: A Demographic Portrait of Mexican-Origin Hispanics in the United States," 2013: p. 5.

[25] U.S. Census Bureau, "2008 National Population Projections," 2008. "Minorities" are defined as people who have a race other than white alone or Hispanic; "the majority," thus, constitutes non-Hispanic Whites.

[26] U.S. Census Bureau, "Most Children Younger than Age 1 are Minorities, Census Bureau Reports," May 17, 2012; U.S. Census Bureau, "Methodology and Assumptions for the 2012 National Projections," 2012: p. 33.

TABLE 1.4 PROJECTIONS OF THE U.S. POPULATION BY RACE, 2010–2050

Race	*Percentage*		
	2010	*2030*	*2050*
Non-Hispanic White	64.7	55.5	46.3
Hispanic	16.0	23.0	30.2
AIAN	1.0	1.2	1.2
Asian	4.6	6.3	7.8
Black	12.9	13.0	13.0
NHPI	0.2	0.2	0.3
Two or more races	1.8	2.6	3.7

Source: Jennifer M. Ortman and Christine E. Guarneri, "United States Population Projections: 2000 to 2050," U.S. Census Bureau, 2009: p. 17.

Notes: (a) AIAN: American Indian and Alaska Native; (b) NHPI: Native Hawaiian and Other Pacific Islander; (c) People of "Hispanic" origin may be of any race.

The relatively homogeneous character of contemporary migration may lead to changes in the electoral map. Hence, for example, according to projections by the Pew Hispanic Center, 40 percent of the growth in the eligible electorate in the United States from 2012 to 2030 will be Hispanic—even without including an increase in naturalization rates or legalization of about 11 million irregular migrants presently living in the United States.[27]

Due to the current character of migration, the challenge it poses is substantially different from the one posed by past migration flows. In numbers, past waves of migration from Europe to North America and Australia were sometimes higher.[28] However, one needs to look beyond mere numbers to understand the current challenge of migration. Looking beyond numbers, one may identify differences, for example, between the cases of Cyprus, Israel, and Qatar versus those of Austria and Germany. According to EU projections, the share of the population with a foreign background in Cyprus, 18.8 percent in 2011, is projected to reach 53.3 percent by 2050 under the most modest estimate.[29] But numbers are deceptive; the largest sending-country to Cyprus is Greece.[30]

[27] Pew Hispanic Center, "An Awakened Giant: The Hispanic Electorate is Likely to Double by 2030," 2012: pp. 5–7.

[28] U.N., Department of Economic and Social Affairs, Population Division, "World Economic and Social Survey 2004: International Migration," U.N. Docs. E/2004/75/Rev.1/Add.1, 2004: pp. vii–viii, 9–10.

[29] Giampaolo Lanzieri, "Fewer, Older and Multicultural? Projections of the EU Populations by Foreign/National Background," Eurostat, 2011: p. 28.

[30] Panayiotis Gregoriou, Zenon Kontolemis, and Maria Matsi, "Immigration in Cyprus: An Analysis of the Determinants," *Cyprus Economic Policy Review* 4, no. 1 (2010): pp. 63–88 at 67.

Migrants, in the main, join an already existing group and enhance, rather than deplete, the majority. Similarly, in 2010 Israel had a 40.4 percent migrant stock, yet most migrants are Jews, who are not even considered as migrants by Israel, but rather as repatriates (*olim*). Jewish newcomers do not undermine Israel's Jewish majority but have the opposite effect. Likewise, although 86 percent of the population in Qatar consisted of migrants in 2010, most of those migrants were noncitizens (out of Qatar's 1.75 million inhabitants, only 14 percent are citizens) and, generally, will never be granted citizenship unless they are Muslims who are married to a citizen of Qatar. Had most migrants to Qatar been Jews, most migrants to Cyprus been Turks, and most migrants to Israel been Palestinians, the challenge of migration would have been different. This is, however, not the case in countries such as Austria or Germany in which many international migrants do not identify with the majority group but, rather, join an already existing minority group.

Changes in the character of migration come in three categories and can be identified by the composition of both the migrants and the host societies. The first category is related to migrants who join an already existing majority, such as Jewish migrants to Israel or ethnic German repatriates to Germany. The second category concerns migrants who are not generally perceived as part of either the majority or the minority group, such as non-Jewish yet non-Muslim/Arab migrants to Israel, or Polish migrants to Germany. The third category relates to migrants who join an already existing minority, such as Palestinian migrants to Israel or Turkish migrants to Germany. The data of the United Nations and the European Union does not distinguish between these categories. For instance, EU statistics consider intra-European movements as "foreign-born" population. But even though Polish migrants are often viewed differently in some Member States than, say, Swedish migrants, they both belong to the same category (category 2) and are not considered as having joined a large minority group. This typology explains why Luxemburg, which has the largest foreign-born population percentage in Europe—mostly Europeans—raises different issues compared with those of countries such as Germany and Austria.

The alleged homogeneous character of contemporary migration is not really homogeneous. Neither Islam nor Muslims are a unified category. Among Muslims, there are different groups based upon ethnicity (Asians, South Asians, Berbers, Arabs, etc.);

nationality (Algerians, Pakistanis, Turks, etc.); and denominations (Sunni, Shia, etc.), alongside individual differences based upon culture, outlook, and lifestyle. Similarly, Hispanic migrants are diverse, and even Mexicans are diverse and include various groups. In fact, the very category of "non-Hispanic Whites" in the U.S. Census Bureau is odd. It means that migrants from Spain and Portugal are "whites" but, if they happen to arrive from Puerto Rico, they are considered "Hispanics." Still, even though people are diverse, demographic characteristics are not meaningless. Just think of Israel as a Jewish-majority state versus an Arab-majority state, or of Germany as a Christian-majority state versus a Muslim-majority state. In other words: we should be suspicious of categories such as "foreign-born population" and avoid grouping people into one group, yet we should not completely ignore them.

Contemporary migration is not just different because of its scale and character—the *intensity* of migration plays a key role as well. The pace of migration today is fast. In the United States, the size and character of the population is rapidly changing. According to the U.S. Census Bureau, in the next four decades the population will grow by 129 million—a 42 percent increase; much of the increase will result from migration (newcomers and their descendants).[31] An addition of 129 million people, in just a four-decade period, is almost equivalent to the migration of both the Mexican and Canadian populations together (114 and 35 million, respectively). In Europe, in only five decades, Member States have turned from countries of emigration to countries of large-scale migration. The intense pace of migration is more visible in relatively small countries—such as Austria, Denmark, the Netherlands, and Switzerland—in which rapid demographic changes are easier to observe. While data does not support the popular claim that Muslims in Europe are likely to become a majority by 2030—there is no official data on Europe's religious composition and estimates vary widely according to different methodologies and definitions—Muslims will indeed become a sizeable religious (and often national) minority in some European states; salient examples are Austria, Belgium, France, Sweden, Switzerland, and the United Kingdom (see Table 1.5).

[31] U.S. Census Bureau, "Table 1. Projections of the Population and Components of Change for the United States: 2010 to 2050," 2008.

TABLE 1.5 PERCENTAGE OF MUSLIM POPULATION BY SELECTED COUNTRIES, 1990–2030

Country	*% of Muslim Population*		
	1990	*2010*	*2030*
Austria	2.1	5.7	9.3
Belgium	2.7	6.0	10.2
Denmark	2.1	4.1	5.6
France	1.0	7.5	10.3
Germany	3.2	5.0	7.1
Ireland	0.4	0.9	2.2
Italy	1.5	2.6	5.4
Spain	0.7	2.3	3.7
Sweden	1.7	4.9	9.9
Switzerland	2.2	5.7	8.1
The Netherlands	2.3	5.5	7.8
United Kingdom	2.0	4.6	8.2
United States	0.6	0.8	1.7

Source: Pew Research Center, "The Future of the Global Muslim Population: Projections for 2010–2030," 2011: pp. 158–163.

In major cities the growth of minority populations is faster. In the United States, Los Angeles is experiencing the fastest growth of Hispanic population. In Europe, large foreign-born communities (noncitizens only) exist in Amsterdam (11 percent), Antwerp (16 percent), Copenhagen (13 percent), Frankfurt (25 percent), and Vienna (19 percent).[32] When citizens with dual citizenship and second-generation migrants are included, the percentage is much higher: 49 percent in Amsterdam, 30 percent in Antwerp, 20 percent in Copenhagen, 38 percent in Frankfurt, and 31 percent in Vienna. And still, the share of the Muslim population is relatively low. According to estimates of the Open Society Foundation, 12 percent of the population in Amsterdam is Muslim, 6.4 percent in Berlin, 8.5 percent in Copenhagen, 8.5 percent in London, and 13 percent in Rotterdam.[33] Muslims are far from becoming a majority in European cities.

[32] Doris Lüken-Klaßen and Friedrich Heckmann, "Intercultural Policies in European Cities," European Foundation for the Improvement of Living and Working Conditions, 2010: pp. 15–16. Other cities with a large foreign-born population are Birmingham, Brussels, Cologne, Malmo, Marseilles, Oslo, Rotterdam, and Stockholm.

[33] Open Society Foundations, "Muslims in London," 2012: p. 32; Open Society Foundations, "Muslims in Copenhagen," 2011: pp. 36–38; Open Society Foundations, "Muslims in Amsterdam," 2010: pp. 29–30;

To sum up, migration patterns are rapidly changing: the *number* of migrants and their share of the total population is increasing tremendously in both absolute and relative terms on the global level, regional level (the developed world), and national level (in Europe and North America). The increasing number is related to fundamental changes in the *character* of migration—the cultural background of migrants (mainly in Europe), the type of migration (family, rather than labor migration), and its more homogeneous character. The *intensity* of these changes—in terms of pace, geographic dispersal, and socio-demographic implications—contributes to the sense of majority groups that they are losing control of their borders.

Demographer David Coleman observes that the ratio between majority groups and minority groups in various regions and countries is changing in a manner that "would be an ultimate 'replacement migration' of a kind not previously seen over large geographic areas without invasion or force."[34] Coleman asserts that even before the majority loses its strength and may become the minority in provinces and cities, two social consequences may occur: first, regarding minorities, "With larger numbers, populations of foreign origin may feel less need to adapt to local norms, instead becoming more confident in extending their own values, language, or laws." And second, regarding majorities, as the numerical balance changes, "majority values and shared identity may cease to be tenable."[35]

THE CHANGING FACE OF THE WEST

The second transformation is related to the West: its population is in decline, Western values and lifestyles are transforming, and human rights law is changing. Let us focus on each of these factors. To begin with, *Western population is declining*. The institution of marriage, which governed the world for thousands of years, has lost its appeal. Fewer people are getting married and the divorce rate is unprecedented—in some countries, it has increased by 40 percent over the past few decades and it stands above 50 percent.[36] True, the divorce rate has risen all over the

Open Society Foundations, "Muslims in Berlin," 2010: pp. 38–39; Open Society Foundations, "Muslims in Rotterdam," 2010: pp. 32–34.

[34] David Coleman, "Immigration and Ethnic Change in Low-Fertility Countries: A Third Demographic Transition," *Population and Development Review* 32, no. 3 (2006): pp. 401–446 at 402–403.

[35] Coleman, p. 426 (n 34).

[36] U.N., Department of Economic and Social Affairs, Population Division, "World Marriage Data 2008: Annual Number of Divorces and Crude Divorce Rate," U.N. Doc. POP/DB/Marr/Rev2008, 2009; U.N., Department of Economic and Social Affairs, Population Division, "World Marriage Patterns 2000," 2000.

world; nevertheless, it is significantly higher in the developed regions. And although the number of children is not necessarily dependent on the status of marriage, high divorce rates negatively affect family size.[37]

In almost all Western countries, the Total Fertility Rate (TFR)—the number of children that a woman bears over her lifetime—has dropped below the "replacement rate" of 2.1, which is the fertility rate required for demographic stability. The TFR is plunging worldwide; it fell from 4.95 (in 1950) to 2.45 (in 2010). Yet it is much higher in developing regions compared to developed regions. With very few exceptions—in OECD countries: Israel, Mexico, and New Zealand—there are no Western countries in which the TFR is above the replacement rate.[38] In 2010, the TFR in the United States was 2.07, among the highest in the developed world, and the average European level was much lower, 1.53. Interestingly enough, in 1960, there were only two countries throughout the world in which the TFR was *lower* than the replacement rate—Estonia and Latvia. Five decades later, in 2010, there was only one country in the developed region (not including Israel and Mexico) in which the TFR was slightly *higher* than the replacement rate—New Zealand (other countries that were at, or close to the replacement rate were France, Ireland, Iceland, and the United States (see Table 1.6)).

The decline of the TFR is countered by the relatively high TFR of migrants. The TFR of migrants in developed regions is declining over time and is approaching the TFR of the native population; yet, differences still exist between first and second-generation migrants and the native-born. In Europe, the Muslim population in twenty-five European states has a TFR that is higher by 68 percent on average than that of the overall population. In 2010, in Austria, the TFR of Muslims was 2.4 compared to 1.3 of non-Muslims; in Denmark—2.7 compared to 1.8; in France—2.8 compared to 1.9; in Germany—1.8 compared to 1.3; in the Netherlands—2.7 compared to 1.6; and in the United Kingdom—3 compared to 1.8.[39] Hence, in spite of the convergence of fertility rates of migrants and the native population, considerable gaps still exist. On the other side of the globe, in the United States, the Hispanic population had a TFR of 2.35 in 2010 (it was 2.91 in 2008), while the non-Hispanic

[37] U.N., Department of Economic and Social Affairs, Population Division, "World Fertility Report 2009," U.N. Doc. ST/ESA/SER.A/304, 2011: pp. 13–19.

[38] OECD, *Pensions at a Glance 2011: Retirement-Income Systems in OECD and G20 Countries* (Paris: OECD Publishing, 2011): pp. 162–163.

[39] Pew Research Center, "The Future of the Global Muslim Population," p. 131 (n 21); Lanzieri, p. 14 (n 29).

White population had a TFR of 1.79 (it was 1.83 in 2008).[40] A recent study demonstrates two interesting findings. First, TFR in Europe is not identical across religions and sects. In Austria, for example, TFR of Roman Catholics was 1.32 in 2001, Protestants—1.21, and Muslims—2.34. Second, TFR is not identical among Muslims in Europe. In the Netherlands, for example, the TFR of Moroccan-born women was 2.87 in 2005, compared to 1.88 of Turkish-born women.[41]

Low fertility rates are linked to an aging population. People live longer today than ever before and the percentage of the young population is in decline. In Europe, life expectancy was 75 years of age in 2010, and in the United States it was 78.[42] In countries such as Japan and Switzerland, people reach 83 to 84 years of age on average.[43] The changes in life expectancy affect the "old-age support ratio," which measures the number of people of working age (15 to 64) in relation to the number of people of retirement age (65 +). In 2012, the old-age support ratio was particularly low in Germany, Italy, Japan, and Sweden—only three working-age persons for every retired person (see Table 1.6). With one exception—Japan—*all* of the twenty countries with the lowest old-age support ratio are European; *all* of them have fewer than five working-age persons for every retired person. By contrast, *all* of the twenty countries with the highest old-age support ratio are in Asia and Africa; *all* of them have more than 20 working-age persons for every retired person.

High life expectancy combined with a low fertility rate means fewer people of working age and more people in need of welfare stipends, pensions, and healthcare. In other words, the percentage of working-age persons, who are capable of providing economic support for older persons, is declining. Public spending on pensions, particularly in Europe, is projected to expand significantly. Europe will need a substantial number of foreign workers in the near future. Goldin, Cameron, and Balarajan estimate that "To keep dependency ratios constant between 2000 and 2050, Europe would have to admit more than 1.3 *billion* migrants by 2050," an incredible number which, if it takes place, will affect Europe's

[40] Brady E. Hamilton, Joyce A. Martin, and Stephanie J. Ventura, "Births: Preliminary Data for 2010," *National Vital Statistics Report* 60, no. 2 (November 2011): pp. 1–26 at 8.

[41] Charles F. Westoff and Tomas Frejka, "Religiousness and Fertility among European Muslims," *Population and Development Review* 33, no. 4 (2007): pp. 785–809 at 788–795.

[42] U.N., Department of Economic and Social Affairs, Population Division, "World Population Prospects: The 2010 Revision," U.N. Doc. POP/DB/WPP/Rev.2010/01/F05-1, 2011.

[43] U.N., Department of Economic and Social Affairs, Population Division, "World Mortality 2011," U.N. Doc. ST/ESA/SER.A/308, 2011.

TABLE 1.6 TOTAL FERTILITY RATE AND OLD-AGE SUPPORT RATIO BY SELECTED COUNTRIES AND YEARS

Country	*Total Fertility Rate*		*Old-age support ratio*	
	1955–60	*2005–10*	*2012*	*2050*
Austria	2.50	1.38	4	2
Belgium	2.50	1.79	4	2
Denmark	2.55	1.85	4	2
France	2.70	1.97	4	2
Germany	2.30	1.36	3	2
Ireland	3.58	2.10	5	2
Italy	2.29	1.38	3	2
Japan	2.16	1.32	3	1
Norway	2.84	1.92	4	2
Spain	2.70	1.41	4	2
Sweden	2.23	1.90	3	2
Switzerland	2.39	1.46	4	2
The Netherlands	3.10	1.75	4	2
United Kingdom	2.49	1.83	4	3
United States	3.71	2.07	5	3

Sources: (a) U.N., Department of Economic and Social Affairs, Population Division, "World Population Prospects: The 2010 Revision," U.N. Doc. POP/DB/WPP/Rev.2010/01/F01, 2011; (b) U.N., Department of Economic and Social Affairs, Population Division, "Population Ageing and Development 2012," U.N. Doc. ST/ESA/SER.A/323, 2012.

demographic composition.[44] The United Nations projects that, in order to keep its demographic stability ("constant total population"), the European Union would have to admit almost one million migrants every year for a fifty-year period (2000–2050); in order to maintain its labor force ("constant age group 15–64"), the European Union would have to admit 1.6 million migrants every year; and in order to maintain its potential support ratio ("constant ratio 15–64/65 years or older"), the European Union would have to admit 13.5 million migrants every year.[45] In order to achieve the same goals, the United States would have

[44] Goldin, Cameron, and Balarajan, p. 248 (n 15).

[45] U.N., Department of Economic and Social Affairs, Population Division, "Replacement Migration: Is It a Solution to Declining and Ageing Populations?," U.N. Doc. ST/ESA/SER.A/206, 2001: p. 2. All projections are based upon a medium variant of fertility rate. They refer to the EU in 2002 (15 Member States).

to admit, respectively, 1.3 million, 3.6 million, and 11.8 million migrants every year. Similar estimates are shared by the European Commission.[46] As a result, and to the extent that countries wish to keep their potential support ratio, further migration is inevitable.

But it is not just population decline—*Western values and lifestyles have changed* too. The West is much more permissive, liberal, and secular today than before. Studies reveal that, particularly in Europe, migrants and native Europeans often hold opposing values and lifestyles on five issues.

The first issue is related to core liberal values—topics such as freedom of speech, gender equality, and gay rights. Thus, for example, one study has found that 55 percent of Muslims in Britain believe that "wives should always obey [their] husbands" and that 68 percent believe that "people who insult Islam should be arrested and prosecuted."[47] Another study indicates that 61 percent of Muslims in Britain hold that homosexuality is wrong and should be illegal.[48] When asked if homosexual acts are "morally acceptable," none of the Muslims in Britain agree, as opposed to 58 percent of the overall population.[49] Only a small percentage of Muslims in France (18 percent) and Germany (26 percent) believe that homosexual acts are morally acceptable, compared to a much higher percentage of the overall population (81 percent and 68 percent, respectively).[50]

The second issue is related to sexual openness—topics such as sex before marriage, extra-marital affairs and nudity, which, although they may not be the core of liberalism, are often a litmus test for liberalism. Thus, for example, 3 percent of Muslims in the United Kingdom believe that sex between unmarried people is "morally acceptable" compared to 82 percent among the general public.[51] Different attitudes

[46] European Commission, "Europe's Demographic Future: Facts and Figures on Challenges and Opportunities," 2007: pp. 99–104.

[47] Gfk NOP, "Attitudes to Living in Britain: Topline Findings," 2006: pp. 45, 18, respectively.

[48] Munira Mirza, Abi Senthilkumaran, and Zein Ja'far, "Living Apart Together: British Muslims and the Paradox of Multiculturalism," Policy Exchange, 2007: p. 47.

[49] Gallup, "The Gallup Coexist Index 2009: A Global Study of Interfaith Relations: With an In-Depth Analysis of Muslim Integration in France, Germany, and the United Kingdom," 2009: p. 31.

[50] Pippa Norris and Ronald Inglehart, "Islam & the West: Testing the 'Clash of Civilization' Thesis," Harvard Kennedy School of Government, Faculty Research Working Paper Series RWP02-015, 2002: pp. 19–22; John L. Esposito and Dalia Mogahed, *Who Speaks for Islam? What a Billion Muslims Really Think* (New York: Gallup Press, 2007): pp. 87–91, 105–122; NFO GmbH and Liljeberg Research International, "Erste Internationale Studie zur Wertewelt der Deutschen, Deutsch-Türken und Türken," 2009.

[51] Gallup, "The Gallup Coexist Index 2009," p. 32 (n 49).

toward issues such as premarital sex are only a symptom of a deeper controversy. Sexual permissiveness, perceived by some as a sign of progress, is seen by others as immodest and immoral.[52] So, although it is viewed as a dispute on the "periphery" of liberalism, sexual liberation, for some, is part of the "core" of liberalism, as it symbolizes human liberation and gender equality.

The third issue is related to the rule of law and the authority of Western constitutions as the supreme law of the land. For instance, 47 percent of Muslims in Germany and 72 percent of the Turkish population in Austria state that the Koran's commandments are more important to them than democratic principles.[53] In the Netherlands, a majority of Muslim students declared that in a case of an irreconcilable conflict, they would choose loyalty to Allah over loyalty to the Dutch Constitution.[54] Persons who believe that religious commands are superior to human decisions challenge one of the greatest achievements of Western civilization—the idea of the social contract, namely, that the law is legitimate because it is based upon freely-consented man-made laws, rather than religious orders.

The fourth issue is related to the legitimacy of the use of violence in political conflicts. One study has found that 32 percent of Muslim students in Britain believe that killing in the name of religion is justified, while just a slight majority (53 percent) believes that it is never justified (15 percent are "not sure"). In comparison, among non-Muslim students in Britain, 2 percent believe that killing in the name of religion is justified (94 percent believe that it is never justified and 4 percent are "not sure").[55] Another study has shown that 22 percent of Muslims in Britain agree that the 7/7 London bombings were justified.[56] In France, 16 percent of Muslims agree that "suicide bombing of civilian targets to defend Islam" can sometimes be justified. Support for suicide bombings as a justified tactic is occasionally greater among the younger generation.[57]

[52] Esposito and Mogahed, pp. 131–132 (n 50).

[53] Katrin Brettfeld and Peter Wetzels, "Muslime in Deutschland: Integration, Integrationsbarrieren, Religion und Einstellungen zu Demokratie, Rechtsstaat und Politisch-religiös Motivierter Gewalt," Bundesministerium des Inneren, 2007: p. 141; Peter A. Ulram, "Integration in Österreich: Einstellungen, Orientierungen, und Erfah- Rungen von MigrantInnen und Angehörigen der Mehrheitsbevölkerung," GfK-Austria GmbH, 2009: p. 45.

[54] Ian Buruma, *Murder in Amsterdam: Liberal Europe, Islam, and the Limits of Tolerance* (New York: Penguin Books, 2006): pp. 94–95.

[55] John Thorne and Hannah Stuart, "Islam on Campus: A Survey of UK Student Opinions," Centre for Social Cohesion, 2008: p. 43.

[56] Gfk NOP, p. 32 (n 47).

[57] Pew Research Center, "Muslim Americans: Middle Class and Mostly Mainstream," 2007: pp. 53–54.

The fifth issue is related to the centrality of religion to public life. Religious freedom is a central tenet of liberal theory. A person should be able to practice, or not practice religion—free of coercion. Yet, surveys indicate that a sizeable percentage of Muslims in Europe supports the idea that a religious lifestyle should dominate daily life, especially with regard to women—beliefs such as only men should vote and that women must wear a veil. Furthermore, a majority supports the idea that restrictions on freedom of speech are legitimate to protect religion. For instance, 68 percent of British Muslims state that people who insult Islam should be arrested and prosecuted and 62 percent hold that freedom of speech should not be allowed if it offends religious groups.[58] In addition, a decent percentage of Muslims would prefer living in a country governed by *Sharia* law, either as a source of law or as the only source of law, instead of living by democratic principles—14 percent in Norway,[59] 30 percent in the United Kingdom,[60] and 54 percent in France.[61]

The challenge to freedom from religion is taking place in a continent that is more secular today than in the past. Cultural clashes are not just about Islam, but about *the role of religion in the public sphere*. In Germany, 87 percent of Muslim students characterize themselves as religious. By contrast, only 19 percent of the non-Muslim German population consider themselves religious.[62] A large majority of Muslims in Berlin, London, and Paris state that "religion is an important part of their daily lives," compared to a much lower percentage of the general population in these countries.[63] Muslims in Britain, France, and Germany identify more with their religion than with their country, unlike the general population in these countries, which identify more with their country than with their religion.[64]

[58] Gfk NOP, p. 18 (n 47). Similar findings exist in other countries. See, e.g., Capacent, "Muslimer I Danmark: Resultater," DR, 2009.

[59] TNS Gallup, "Holdninger til Integrasjon og Internasjonale Konflikter Blant Muslimer I Norge og den Norske Befolkning Generelt," TV 2, 2006: p. 9.

[60] Gfk NOP, p. 14 (n 47); Mirza, Senthilkumaran, and Ja'far, p. 46 (n 48); ICM Research, "Muslims Poll—February 2006," *Sunday Telegraph*, 2006: p. 14; Thorne and Stuart, pp. 40–41 (n 55).

[61] CSA Opinion Institutionnel, "Islam et Citoyenneté," *Le Monde des Religions*, 2008: p. 9.

[62] Brettfeld and Wetzels, pp. 242, 262 (n 53).

[63] Zsolt Nyiri, "Muslims in Berlin, London and Paris: Bridges and Gaps in Public Opinion," Gallup, 2007: p. 2; Mirza, Senthilkumaran, and Ja'far, pp. 5, 37 (n 48); Gfk NOP, p. 3 (n 47).

[64] Dalia Mogahed and Zsolt Nyiri, "Reinventing Integration: Muslims in the West" *Harvard International Review* 29, no. 2 (2007): pp. 14–18 at 15; Gallup, "The Gallup Coexist Index 2009": pp. 16–19 (n 49).

A long standing proposition asserts that, over time, migrants integrate into the new society. So, even if the number of migrants is high and different in nature, at the end, according to the theory, a Pakistani migrant becomes British, French, or German. Interestingly, numerous studies have found that second and third-generation Muslim migrants living in Europe are sometimes more religious than their parents and grandparents. For example, a higher percentage of young Muslim Britons (ages 16 to 24) prefer to live under *Sharia* law, rather than British law, as compared to British Muslims aged 55 and older (37 percent compared to 17 percent).[65] Even more interesting is that they identify more strongly with Islam than do Muslims living in their country of origin.[66] And even more striking is that their TFR is often higher than the TFR in their country of origin—for instance, people of Turkish and Moroccan descent in Europe sometimes tend to have a higher TFR than the TFR in Turkey and Morocco.[67]

Cultural gaps on such a scale do not exist in America. There are a few possible explanations for this variance. First, American identity may be more inclusive than European national identities. Second, the composition of migration to America is slightly different to that of its European counterpart—Hispanics mostly belong to Christian denominations. Third, the United States has longer experience than Europe in the absorption of newcomers. Fourth, American society may be more tolerant toward different ways of life and lifestyles. And fifth, the American population is generally more religious than the European population. Thus, while in Europe there is a discrepancy between Muslims and non-Muslims over the importance of religion in life, in the United States Muslims and Christians attribute approximately equal importance to religion.[68] Moreover, while in Europe churches are almost unattended and mosque attendance is higher than church attendance,[69] in the United States, church and mosque attendance rates are fairly equal.[70] In a largely secular Europe, a growing religious

[65] Mirza, Senthilkumaran, and Ja'far, p. 46 (n 48).

[66] Mirza, Senthilkumaran, and Ja'far, pp. 5, 21 (n 48); Thorne and Stuart, pp. 36–37 (n 55).

[67] Westoff and Frejka, p. 795 (n 41).

[68] Pew Research Center, "Muslim Americans: No Sign of Growth in Alienation or Support for Extremist," 2011: p. 25; Pew Research Center, "U.S. Religious Landscape Survey: Religious Affiliation: Diverse and Dynamic," 2008: p. 1.

[69] The World Values Survey Association, "World Values Survey 2005–2008: Official Data File," 2009, results of question V186 of the WVS questionnaire on religious service attendance. See also Robert Manchin, "Religion in Europe: Trust Not Filling the Pews," Gallup, September 21, 2004; Gallup, "The Abu Dhabi Gallup Forum: Research, Dialogue, and Solutions," 2011: pp. 165–166. Data varies significantly, however, between religious denominations and EU Member States.

[70] Pew Research Center, "Muslim Americans: No Sign of Growth," p. 10 (n 68).

faith—not just Islamic faith, but any religious faith—accelerates social tensions.

Cultural gaps similar to those in Europe are not visible in America for another reason. American society is relatively more conservative on issues such as homosexual rights, abortions, and nudity, which are at the core of current disputes in Europe. For example, when asked about the acceptance of homosexuality, 39 percent of American Muslims state that it should be "accepted by society," compared to 58 percent of the general U.S. population which holds that belief.[71] The gap in the acceptance of homosexuality—39 percent versus 58 percent in the United States—is considerably narrower than, say, the gap in France (18 percent versus 81 percent) and in Germany (26 percent versus 68 percent).

It is not just population decline and changing lifestyles—*human rights law has changed* as well. Until roughly the 1970s, there were few legal obstacles to migration control. The power to restrict entry to the territory and, to a lesser extent, to citizenship, was largely plenary. The International Court of Justice ruled that "international law leaves it to each State to lay down the rules governing the grant of its own nationality."[72] This ruling reflected the prevailing wisdom of that time that nations have an inherent right to control their borders. Today, however, human rights law, in particular with respect to family migration, limits plenary power doctrines.

Human rights law affects migration in another important aspect. Due to the legal rights of refugees and family migrants, the vast majority of migration is not discretionary. Liberal democracies do not really "select" humanitarian and family migrants; they arrive after fulfilling conditions on the basis of humanitarian needs and family ties. Labor migrants are those who are really "selected" according to skills and merits. However, although labor migrants constitute the largest share of migration in a few countries—such as Australia, Canada, and Switzerland—in most countries, including the United States, labor migrants do not constitute the largest share of migration. An OECD report has found that "most immigrants enter not because they have been specifically selected... but because they are entitled to do so."[73] The report has further indicated that "Even the OECD countries that make greatest use of immigrant selection, such as Canada and Australia, directly select no more than one

[71] Pew Research Center, "Muslim Americans: No Sign of Growth," p. 59 (n 68).

[72] Nottebohm Case, *Liechtenstein* v. *Guatemala*, I.C.J. Rep. 1955: p. 23, April 6, 1955.

[73] Brian Keeley, *International Migration: The Human Face of Globalisation* (Paris: OECD Publishing, 2009): p. 49.

in four of all newcomers."[74] Non-selective migration means less control over its scale and composition. All of this is without considering irregular migration, which is obviously not "selected" and, occasionally, is granted amnesty.

In addition to changes in immigration law, recent decades have witnessed the rise of multiculturalism and group rights. Some authors, well represented by Brian Barry, consider multiculturalism to be a betrayal of the classic theory of liberalism. Their concern is that multicultural policies encourage groups to live in a "parallel society," rather than as part of a society, and impede integration by restricting the (legal) option of forcing migrants to adopt the local way of life.[75] The combined effect of the fact that countries no longer enjoy absolute sovereignty in making immigration decisions and minorities' increasing demands for political recognition and cultural preservation accelerates the anxiety of majorities.

Although much exaggerated, and with weak ties to reality, majority groups hold increasing subjective fears that geographically-concentrated ethnic and religious immigrant groups could become "national minorities," and thereby demand self-governing powers. One point, nevertheless, deserves the spotlight. When Will Kymlicka, the guru of multiculturalism, began developing liberal justifications for cultural group rights, he clearly distinguished between "indigenous peoples" and "national minorities"—groups that were incorporated into states, such as the American Indians, native Hawaiians, or Puerto Ricans—and "immigrant groups," groups that voluntarily arrived in a new land. Kymlicka emphasized that "national minorities typically have the sort of societal culture that should be protected, while immigrants typically do not." Unlike national minorities, who often cannot choose between different ways of life without special cultural privileges, migrants can choose, and they indeed choose by moving to a new country. Voluntary migration is exactly this: a choice to leave one way of life and adopt another way of life. What has happened since is that Kymlicka's theory, developed for national minorities, is now embraced by immigrant groups. This was not the original idea. In *Multicultural Citizenship*, Kymlicka asserted that it would not be unjust if liberal states "decided not to give immigrants the legal status and resources needed to become national minorities." He further claimed that "The expectation of integration is not unjust" inasmuch as "immigrants had the option to stay in their original culture

[74] Keeley, p. 50 (n 73).

[75] Brian Barry, *Culture and Equality: An Egalitarian Critique of Multiculturalism* (Cambridge: Harvard University Press, 2001).

[their country of origin]....In deciding to uproot themselves, immigrants voluntarily relinquish some of the rights that go along with their original national membership."[76] Today, however, Kymlicka's empirical proposition, under which "there is little evidence that immigrants are seeking national rights,"[77] does not fully apply.

Human rights law has changed in another field—social rights. If the rise of multiculturalism creates fewer incentives for *cultural* assimilation, the structure of the welfare state creates fewer incentives for *economic* assimilation. Welfare states provide a platform allowing people to live on welfare stipends and remain out of the job market. For different reasons, EU Member States demonstrate considerable discrepancies in unemployment rates between migrants and the native population.[78] The existence of generous stipends may only be one source of high unemployment rates—others relate to dissimilar work ethics and discrimination against migrants in the job market—but whatever the main reason is, unemployment rates enhance cultural challenges by slowing the process of cultural assimilation and contributing to cultural alienation. The welfare state affects migration in another aspect: it is built upon a model that requires a constantly growing young population in order to sustain it.

To sum up, changing migration patterns have been merging with the changing character of Western societies. The West faces an unprecedented *population decline*. For the first time in history, some countries are edging closer to a point in which the elderly will outnumber the young. Western populations are rapidly declining and migrants are being called upon to increase the national TFR, lower aging populations, balance the old-age support ratio, and replenish the labor force. Due to demographic and economic needs, Western countries have become more dependent on migration. However, migrant and native groups sometimes have different attitudes, values, and lifestyles. Some of these *cultural gaps* touch upon the core of liberalism—issues of gender equality, freedom of speech, and religious freedom—yet other issues may be more peripheral, though still central, such as sexual openness, extra marital affairs, or nudity. Different attitudes also exist regarding the centrality of religion

[76] Kymlicka, *Multicultural Citizenship*, pp. 94–96 (n 9). Under the assumption that the majority culture is welcoming to migrants, allowing them to retain some elements of their identity, and providing them with some exemptions to accommodate cultural differences. See pp. 96–97, 114–115.

[77] Kymlicka, *Multicultural Citizenship*, p. 97 (n 9).

[78] European Commission, pp. 112–138 (n 46).

in daily life, loyalty to the law when in conflict with religious norms and rules, and the use of violence in political conflicts. Some of these gaps have grown even wider in the second and third-generations of migrants. The crossroads between the changing face of Western societies, mainly in Europe, and the changing nature of migration, yields cultural gaps. As a result, Western countries have tried to reconcile the demographic and economic benefits of migration with its cultural outcomes, yet *human rights law*—legal barriers, the rise of multiculturalism and group-based identities, and the increase in social rights and welfare states—creates a variety of obstacles, making it relatively difficult for majorities to impose assimilation policies.

Wide cultural gaps have caused people to emigrate from their home country. In a few countries, emigrants have outnumbered migrants. In Ireland and Spain, for instance, the main reason for emigration is the economic crisis. But in other countries, cultural diversity has been a major trigger for emigration. A survey among Dutch emigrants has found that the main reason they leave the Netherlands is due to their low opinion of the country's economy and welfare institutions. The second main reason, however, relates to societal issues, such as the mental outlook of the people and ethnic diversity. "A faltering process of immigrant integration, reflected by segregation in schools and neighborhoods," the survey concludes, "leads people to perceive ethnic diversity negatively."[79] The survey reveals that, for some, quality of life is not only a function of housing and high income, but also of having a homogenous cultural environment.

GLOBAL CHANGES

The third transformation is related to geopolitical, technological, and global changes. Let us elaborate on each of these changes beginning with *geopolitics*. According to estimates of the United Nations, the world population numbered 300 million at the birth of Christ. This number increased only slightly over the next several centuries. In 1804, the global population reached one billion and advanced due to medical discoveries.[80] In 1927, the population doubled and reached 2 billion. Since then the population has continued to grow rapidly, mainly because of significant

[79] Hendrik P. Van Dalen and Kène Henkens, "Longing for the Good Life: Understanding Emigration from a High-Income Country," *Population and Development Review* 33, no. 1 (2007): pp. 37–65 at 53.

[80] Karoly Lorant, "The Demographic Challenge in Europe," European Parliament, 2005: p. 6.

advances in health services. In 1999, the world population tripled and reached six billion, but this growth has not been equal across regions.

The last century has witnessed dramatic geopolitical changes. The European population has shriveled from 25 percent of the global population in 1900 to 12 percent in 2000 and, if current trends continue, only 7 percent of the world population will be "European" by 2050. In contrast, the African population was 8 percent of the total world population in 1900; it climbed to 13 percent in 2000 and is poised to grow to 20 percent by 2050 (see Table 1.7). Geopolitics has changed not only geographically, but also religiously. Islam is the rising demographic star. The Muslim population made up 19.9 percent of the world population in 1990. It reached 23.4 percent of the world population in 2010 and is expected to be more than a quarter (26.4 percent) in 2030. A Pew Research Center study has found that "Globally, the Muslim population is forecast to grow at about twice the rate of the non-Muslim population over the

TABLE 1.7 CHANGES IN THE WORLD POPULATION, 1900–2050 IN MILLIONS AND AS A PERCENTAGE OF THE TOTAL

Area	*1900*	*1950*	*2000*	*2050*
World	1,650	2,519	6,071	9,191
More developed	539	813	1,194	1,245
	(33%)	(32%)	(20%)	(14%)
Less developed	1,111	1,706	4,877	7,946
	(67%)	(68%)	(80%)	(86%)
Africa	133	221	796	1,803
	(8%)	(9%)	(13%)	(20%)
Asia	904	1,399	3,680	5,222
	(55%)	(56%)	(61%)	(59%)
Europe	408	547	728	632
	(25%)	(22%)	(12%)	(7%)
Latin America and the Caribbean	74	167	520	768
	(4%)	(7%)	(9%)	(9%)
North America	82	172	316	448
	(5%)	(7%)	(5%)	(5%)
Oceania	—	13	31	46
	—	(>1%)	(>1%)	(>1%)

Sources: (a) U.N., Department of Economic and Social Affairs, Population Division, "World Population to 2300," U.N. Doc. ST/ESA/SER.A/236, 2004: p. 22; (b) U.S. Population Reference Bureau, "Transitions in World Population," *Population Bulletin* 59, no. 1 (March 2004): pp. 1–41 at 5.

Note: Data for Asia in 1900 includes Oceania.

next two decades."[81] In 2030, "nearly three-in-ten of the world's youth and young adults—29.1 percent of people aged 15–29—are projected to be Muslims."[82] The turning point at which Muslims will outnumber Christians, 32 percent of the world population in 2010,[83] may occur before 2050.

Changes in the world population are also evident on the national level. In 1950, European states such as Germany, the United Kingdom, Italy, France, and Spain were among the top twenty most populated countries worldwide. Five decades later, in 2000, only Germany and France remained among the top twenty countries. In 2050, not even one EU Member State will remain on the list. By contrast, rapid population growth exists mainly in developing countries.[84] The comparison between Italy and Egypt is striking. In 1950, the Italian population was more than double that of the Egyptian population—47 million versus 21 million. A century later, in 2050, the Italian population is expected to be only one-third of the size of the Egyptian population—44 million versus 127 million.[85] These rapid demographic changes, occurring in a relatively short period, contribute to the subjective demographic and cultural fears held by majority groups.

Geopolitics is one factor; *technology* is another. Cultures seldom intermingled in the past, mainly due to the large geographic distances between, say, India and America. Today, due to technology and easy mobility, satellite television and the Internet, there is an unprecedented trans-cultural diffusion. It's a small world. A Turkish migrant in Berlin can easily stay culturally "Turkish": she can read *Hürriyet*, watch *TRT International*, and speak with Turkish relatives on Skype. The modern world enables people to live in a host country while retaining close ties with their home country and preserving their original identity. Technology indirectly facilitates migration by making it easier to live physically in Germany, for example, yet culturally remain Turkish. Cheap air transport and communications facilitate the existence of transnational communities—communities that retain their economic

[81] Pew Research Center, "The Future of the Global Muslim Population," pp. 13, 172 (n 21).

[82] Pew Research Center, "The Future of the Global Muslim Population," p. 18 (n 21).

[83] Pew Research Center, "Global Christianity: A Report on the Size and Distribution of the World's Christian Population," 2011: p. 9.

[84] U.N., Department of Economic and Social Affairs, Population Division, "World Population to 2300," U.N. Doc. ST/ESA/SER.A/236, 2004: pp. 41–45.

[85] U.N., "World Population to 2300," pp. 42, 199 (n 84).

and political stance in both the receiving country and the country of origin. While living transnationally is not new, Peggy Levitt has shown that its current frequency and intimacy are historically unique.[86] Dual citizenship, once an exception in international law, has become common.

The emergence of diasporas and transnational migrant networks brings opportunities, but at the same time creates concerns. It enhances solidarity with kin-states and contributes to the involvement of foreign governments in the interests of expatriate populations. In 2008, in his speech in Cologne, the Turkish Prime Minister Erdogan called upon Turks in Germany to retain their Turkish identity and condemned assimilation as "a crime against humanity." In his speech in Düsseldorf in 2011, Erdogan similarly stated: "Yes, integrate yourselves into German society but don't assimilate yourselves. No one has the right to deprive *us* of *our* culture and *our* identity.... *Our* children must learn German but they must first learn good Turkish."[87] In the United States, the Mexican President Felipe Calderón declared in 2007 that "Mexico does not stop at its border... wherever there is a Mexican, there is Mexico."[88]

It is not just geopolitics and new technology—*globalization* influences global migration as well. It is too early to determine whether globalization dilutes national identity or enhances it, but it certainly affects public perceptions of migration. Globalization undermines concepts of borders, territory, and sovereignty.[89] This is even more apparent in European Member States, whose identities have also been challenged by EU institutions. The combined effect of a bottom-up mass migration and a top-down globalization challenges the traditional concept of sovereignty.

Geopolitical transitions are a time for reflection. About a decade ago, in a thought-provoking article, Samuel Huntington cautioned that America was ignoring the cultural challenge posed by large-scale Hispanic migration. "Continuation of this large immigration (without improved assimilation) could divide the United States into a country of two languages and two cultures," he warned. Huntington attempted to provoke a

[86] Peggy Levitt, *The Transnational Villagers* (Berkeley: University of California Press, 2001): pp. 21–27.

[87] Daryl Lindsey, "Turkish Prime Minister Erdogan Wants to Be the Father," *Spiegel*, March 1, 2011 (emphasis added).

[88] James C. Mckinley Jr., "Mexican President Assails U.S. Measures on Migrants," *New York Times*, September 3, 2007.

[89] Linda Bosniak, "Multiple Nationality and the Postnational Transformation of Citizenship," *Virginia Journal of International Law* 42, no. 4 (2002): pp. 979–1004 at 982–991.

debate on the essence of Americanism before American society would significantly change. "The transformation of the United States into a country like these [Belgium and Canada] would not necessarily be the end of the world; it would, however, be the end of the America we have known for more than three centuries," he argued. Huntington was obviously aware that sooner or later countries change. He probably thought that it would be important to point this out as a wake-up call: "Americans should not let that change happen unless they are convinced that this new nation would be a better one."[90] While Huntington's plea was to adopt a stricter immigration policy, his point was aimed at the larger picture: the interwoven relationship between immigration policy and national identity, citizenship and the Constitution.

CITIZENSHIP AND THE CONSTITUTION

States are legal entities. Their character and identity, destiny and aspirations, are defined by peoples. "What is the city but the people?...The people are the city," writes Shakespeare.[91] When the people change, the city changes as well. It may be the same geography with the same city hall, but its character will be different. In referring to ancient Greek cities, Aristotle observes, "Every state is a community of some kind, and every community is established with a view to some good."[92] This community of some kind, which shares a view of some good, is established through a social contract—a partnership of citizens in a constitution. For Aristotle, a "constitution" is not a formal legal document; rather, it is the community's essential way of life and its form of government. When the defining principles of the constitution change, the city changes; in Aristotle's words:[93]

> When the form of government changes and becomes different, then it may be supposed that the state is no longer the same, just as a tragic differs from a comic chorus, although the members of both may be identical.... the sameness of the state consists chiefly in the sameness of the constitution, and may be called or not called by the same name, whether the inhabitants are the same or entirely different.

[90] Samuel P. Huntington, "The Hispanic Challenge," *Foreign Policy*, no. 141 (March/April 2004): pp. 30–45 at 44–45.

[91] William Shakespeare, *The Oxford Shakespeare: Coriolanus*, R.B. Parker, ed. (Oxford: OUP, 2008): p. 257.

[92] Aristotle, *Politics*, Benjamin Jowett, trans. (New York: Dover Publications, 2000): p. 25 (Book I, I).

[93] Aristotle, p. 105 (n 92) (Book III, III).

The city can be composed of "unlikes"—that may even be desirable—yet people should share a bond that keeps them together, a common goal. On a sailing ship, Aristotle argues, sailors have different functions. One is a rower, another is a pilot, and a third is a look-out man. But in spite of their different functions, they all have one common goal—the safety of the ship. In a city, Aristotle analogizes, "one citizen differs from another, but the salvation of the community is the common business of them all." The essence of the community "is the constitution" and "the virtues of the citizen must therefore be relative to the constitution of which he is a member."[94]

There are plenty of unresolved questions: for example, what is this bond or common object? Who shall decide and according to which criteria? But the most puzzling question is how legitimate is it to protect fundamental changes in the city's character by controlling its gates; can the city preserve its character by setting selective rules of admission? Aristotle replies to this question in the affirmative. He argues that citizenship law can be used to preserve the character of the city. "The law is relaxed when there is a dearth of population," he declares, "but when the number of citizens increases," the rules have to be changed by restricting the option of becoming a citizen, for example, by granting citizenship only to a person "who shares in the honours of the state."[95] Indeed, when the number of non-Athenians who settled in Athens following the Greco-Persian Wars sharply increased, Pericles, the Greek statesman, changed Athenian law so as to grant citizenship only to children whose mother and father were both Athenians (the previous law was content to grant citizenship to every child, provided his father was Athenian). Pericles' citizenship law was a means of constitutional design in order to preserve the identity of Athens.[96] One may hold a different view, but the question is worth pondering as it goes to the heart of the most fundamental issues of politics: who are "We" and in what type of city do "We" want to live?

* * *

Migrants have long ceased to be merely an immigration issue. They shape global politics and redefine national identity. "International migration," Stephen Castles and Mark Miller note, "has changed the face of societies.... [migration] may become so entrenched and resistant to

[94] Aristotle, p. 106 (n 92) (Book III, III).

[95] Aristotle, p. 111 (n 92) (Book III, III).

[96] Aristotle, *The Athenian Constitution*, Peter J. Rhodes, trans. (New York: Penguin Books, 2004): p. 70; Peter J. Rhodes, *A Commentary on the Aristotelian Athenaion Politeia* (Oxford: Clarendon Press, 1981).

governmental control that new political forms may emerge."[97] Indeed, managing global migration is one of the greatest challenges facing liberalism today.

Currently, there is not even one case among the countries discussed in which there is an imminent risk that a national majority would become a minority in times to come (cities raise a different case). And even if a national majority becomes a minority, it will still be the largest group in the state since, in most cases, there is no solid unified minority that could take over. In addition, by the time a minority becomes a majority, it may be unnoticeable as it is likely that the minority will have merged itself into the majority group, just as Chinese and Italian Americans are all Americans now.

Current data does not support the popular view that the majority is likely to become a minority in EU states due to migration. Interestingly, perhaps the closest case we have is the United States. The U.S. Census Bureau projects that the non-Hispanic White population will become a national minority by 2043. Yet this case, as Chapter 2 describes, is the least challenging from a cultural perspective. However, there are cases in which the existing national majority could face a significant demographic decline in one to two generations. The most salient examples in Europe are Austria and Germany. From the perspective of the majority group, the "tipping point" may be before it becomes the minority group.

The purpose of this chapter is descriptive—bringing together recent trends that, combined, challenge one of the most fundamental premises in liberal thought under which majority groups "can take care of themselves" by using immigration law to perpetuate their culture. My conclusion is modest. I do not argue that majority groups can no longer take care of themselves; even though this premise is still valid, I argue that it has been jeopardized, both subjectively and objectively. The changes described in this chapter accelerate subjective fears of majorities that part of their culture is under "threat." However, some fears, mainly of losing control, and some claims, mainly that majority groups cannot take care of themselves solely by using immigration law and policy, are not merely subjective; they are also objective—they are empirically-grounded and connected to reality.

Is our case really new? Almost every mass migration in recent history has been perceived as *sui generis*, a new case. Is the situation really

[97] Stephen Castles and Mark J. Miller, *The Age of Migration: International Population Movements in the Modern World*, 4th ed. (New York: Palgrave Macmillan, 2009): pp. 1, 3–4.

different this time? The answer is disputable. Some would argue that the current changes are not historically unique. Maybe. If we single out each of the nine changes described here, we may find historical precedents for each one. Yet, the combination of all of them at one point in history has no precedent. And even if our case is not entirely new to the United States, it is certainly new to other Western societies. Current debates on migration go beyond classic debates on migrants as individuals. Contemporary migration touches upon nation-states, sovereignty, and self-determination. Goldin, Cameron, and Balarajan predict that future migration will progress "in a manner not experienced since our evolutionary origins in Africa" and that this new reality calls for "new approaches to managing migration."[98] They advocate a more open policy due to the economic gains brought by migrants, yet leave unsettled the cultural challenge associated with open migration policies. This challenge is explored in greater detail in the next chapters.

[98] Goldin, Cameron, and Balarajan, pp. 213, 215 (n 15).

2

Demographic Anxiety

Let us deal wisely with them; lest they multiply.

—Exodus 1:10

Shifting demographics have always been a source of concern. History is full of such examples, but perhaps the first notable case occurred in ancient Egypt. Modern reading of the Bible tells us that the children of Israel were "economic refugees" who fled from Canaan due to a severe famine and settled in the land of Goshen in Egypt. Following their arrival, they assured Pharaoh, the ruler of Egypt, that their stay would be temporary, lasting until the dearth of food in Canaan was over ("For to sojourn in the land are we come"). The Bible tells us that Pharaoh welcomed the children of Israel and gave them the best land in Egypt. However, as the years passed, they grew, multiplied, and became a great nation: "The children of Israel were fruitful, and increased abundantly, and multiplied, and waxed exceeding mighty." Pharaoh felt threatened by the growing number of Israelites. "Let us deal wisely with them," he advised his people, "lest they multiply, and it come to pass, that, when there falleth out any war, they join also unto our enemies, and fight against us." In order to address the changing demographics, Pharaoh first enslaved the children of Israel, making their life bitter and hard. He incorrectly assumed that this would cause the Israelites to have fewer children. Yet, according to the story, "the more they afflicted them, the more they multiplied and grew." Since slavery turned out to be ineffective, Pharaoh ordered the Hebrew midwives, Shiphrah and Puah, to kill every male newborn, but they did not comply with his command and saved the Hebrew children. In light of that, Pharaoh adopted a draconian policy, charging all his people: "Every son that is born ye shall cast into the river, and every daughter ye shall save alive."[1]

[1] Robert Carroll and Stephen Prickett, eds., *The Bible: Authorized King James Version with Apocrypha* (Oxford: OUP, 2008). For the quotations see, respectively, Genesis 47:4, Exodus 1:7, 1:10, 1:12, 1:22.

This biblical story is remarkable and rich. First, the story depicts demographic hysteria when it comes to aliens and minorities. The Israelites were a minority in Egypt, but in Pharaoh's mind they had already grown to be a powerful nation ("the people of the children of Israel *are* more and mightier than we"). Second, the story illustrates the short path between demographic changes and perceptions of a threat. Pharaoh believed that the large number of Israelites posed a threat to Egypt's security and stability.[2] Third, the story indicates just how slippery the demographic slope can be. Pharaoh began with a policy of penal labor, moved to enslavement, continued with a plan of mass-execution of Israelite babies by the Hebrew midwives, and ended with a brutal order to kill every Hebrew son born in Egypt. Finally, the story presents an interesting dialectic. Pharaoh tried to have it both ways—keeping the Hebrew workers due to their economic value (he refused to let the Israelites go free) while attempting to maintain the demographic status quo.

Incorrect facts, false conclusions, and slippery slopes continue to characterize contemporary immigration debates. In recent history, new waves of immigrants have normally been accompanied by exaggerated feelings of threat to national identity and unity. Furthermore, they have quite often prompted an extreme and disproportionate response. This is the case in traditional immigration countries, such as the United States. And this is the situation in more recent immigration destinations, such as Europe and Israel. By analyzing three cases—Hispanics in America, Muslims in Europe, and Palestinians in Israel—this chapter demonstrates a modern disproportionate reaction to immigration. The cases are radically different one from the other, as briefly explained in the following sections, but they nevertheless have a common denominator—"demographobia."

The purpose of this chapter is threefold. The first purpose is to present a typology of demographic concerns—civic, cultural, and ethnic—which have characterized the United States, Europe, and Israel in different periods. The second purpose is to show how demographic concerns are frequently accompanied by exaggerated facts, false conclusions, and public hysteria. The third purpose is to demonstrate how demographic

[2] Carroll and Prickett, Exodus 1:9 (n 1). There are various explanations for Pharaoh's fear. One interpretation is rooted in the ongoing war that existed between the King of Egypt and the King of Canaan; the Israelites, who migrated from Canaan to Egypt, were perceived as a "fifth column." See R.H. Charles, ed., *Pseudepigrapha*, vol. II, *The Apocrypha and Pseudepigrapha of the Old Testament* (Oxford: Clarendon Press, 1913), The Book of Jubilees 46:1–16.

concerns are reflected in immigration policy. Immigration law functions as a kind of "gatekeeper." It has been crafted and designed to "deal wisely" with migrants—that is, to include only the desirable people and exclude the undesirable ones. Generally speaking, the chapter illustrates how states want to have it both ways—enjoying the economic benefits of migration, while not willing to fully accommodate the cultural changes brought by it.

WHAT ARE "WE" AFRAID OF?

Demographic anxiety is a catch-all phrase. There are different sorts of (and reasons for) anxieties. One reason is related to national security; majorities may seek to keep out migrants who are regarded as security risks. A second reason relates to the economy; majorities may seek to keep out migrants who are likely to become a financial burden and overload the welfare system. A third reason is associated with community cohesion; majorities may seek to keep out migrants who are viewed as a threat to social cohesion. A fourth reason touches on civic participation; majorities may seek to keep out migrants who, they believe, will not positively contribute to the healthy functioning of a democratic society (voting, serving on a jury, participating in public life, etc.). A fifth reason concerns population density; majorities may seek to keep out migrants per se, irrespective of their characteristics, due to natural population growth and environmental issues. A sixth reason, the focus of this chapter, involves culture. Majorities may seek to keep out migrants who are seen as a challenge to the "liberal culture" (liberal values and institutions); "national culture" (language, national symbols, common destiny); or "popular culture" (dress code, folklore, social mores). Reality is more nuanced. Demographic anxiety often involves a combination of reasons rather than one single reason. Moreover, majority groups are not homogeneous; different groups may have different concerns. For instance, poor people may object to low-skilled migration, while affluent people may support it.

THE UNITED STATES

The development of America's demographic concerns reflects the transformation in the essence of Americanism and in the meaning of belonging to America. The following pages briefly describe the transformation of America's demographic anxieties since the infancy of the nation in an attempt to better understand the contemporary challenge.

A history of demographic distrust

The debate over immigration goes back to the colonial period. In *America as a Land of Opportunity*, Benjamin Franklin expressed doubts as to whether America would remain an Anglo-Saxon society. Franklin was concerned that foreigners would overwhelm the American cultural fabric. "The Number of purely white People in the World is proportionably very small," he worried, as "All *Africa* is black" and "*Asia* [is] chiefly tawny." This tone sounds racist today, but Franklin was more concerned with preserving American culture than with racial impurity. He was particularly anxious about the growing number of Germans in Philadelphia: "Why should *Pennsylvania*, founded by the *English*, become a Colony of *Aliens*, who will shortly be so numerous as to Germanize us instead of our Anglifying them, and will never adopt our Language or Customs?"[3]

About five years prior to the adoption of the Naturalization Act of 1790, Thomas Jefferson expressed his views on immigration in the *Notes on the State of Virginia*. Jefferson supported an open immigration policy and appreciated the positive contribution of immigrants to America. He doubted, however, whether the U.S. government should encourage a large-scale immigration of a different character—specifically, monarchists and Catholics. Jefferson's words, considered classic, illustrate a dilemma:[4]

> Every species of government has its specific principles. Ours perhaps are more peculiar than those of any other in the universe. It is a composition of the freest principles of the English constitution, with others derived from natural right and natural reason. To these nothing can be more opposed than the maxims of absolute monarchies. Yet, from such, we are to expect the greatest number of emigrants. They will bring with them the principles of the governments they leave, imbibed in their early youth.... These principles, with their language, they will transmit to their children. In proportion to their numbers, they will share with us the legislation. They will infuse into it their spirit, warp and bias its direction, and render it a heterogeneous, incoherent, distracted mass.

[3] Benjamin Franklin, "Observations Concerning the Increase of Mankind, Peopling of Countries, etc," in *The Writings of Benjamin Franklin*, vol. III, Albert Henry Smyth, ed. (New York: The Macmillan Company, 1905): pp. 63–73 at 72.

[4] Thomas Jefferson, *Notes on the State of Virginia* (London: John Stockdale, 1787): pp. 141–142.

Jefferson's dilemma was not choosing between open or closed borders—two options he rejected. Rather, the *Notes on the State of Virginia* questioned how to admit immigrants, who were vital to the future prosperity of America, while minimizing the risk of a large influx of people who might not believe in American liberties and freedoms.

In referring to Jefferson's notes, Alexander Hamilton expressed similar concerns over uncontrolled admission of foreigners. He invoked history to demonstrate the risk in changing demographics: "It is known, that hardly any thing contributed more to the downfall of Rome, than her precipitate communication of the privileges of citizenship to the inhabitants of Italy at large." Hamilton's fear should be viewed in its historical context. In the infancy of the United States, its strengths and stability were far from secure. Hamilton valued the contribution of aliens to national prosperity, yet supported a selective migration policy whose scale and disposition could be monitored. He found the key element of nation-building in a common sentiment: "The safety of a republic depends essentially on the energy of a common National sentiment; on a uniformity of principles and habits ... and on that love of country." Echoing Jefferson's concerns, he asserted:[5]

> Foreigners will generally be apt to bring with them attachments to the persons they have left behind; to the country of their nativity, and to its particular customs and manners.... how extremely unlikely is it that they will bring with them that *temperate love of liberty*, so essential to real republicanism?

Jefferson and Hamilton were both pro-immigration provided that immigrants would become Americans. The debate has always been about the meaning of "becoming an American." Throughout American history, there have been different approaches and views on the essence of Americanism and the process of becoming American. However, with a few exceptions, mainly during wars and crises, the prevailing view has been that becoming an American means conforming to American ideals (whatever they are).

Franklin, Jefferson, and Hamilton's concerns have continued to drive the immigration debate throughout the nation's history. At times, Americanism was an enterprise associated with race (a whites-only country), religion (Protestantism), nationality (national-origin quotas), and ideology (anti-anarchists, anti-communists, etc.)—but all along,

[5] Harold C. Syrett, ed., *July 1800–April 1802*, vol. XXV, *The Papers of Alexander Hamilton* (New York: Columbia University Press, 1977): pp. 494, 496–497.

American immigration policy has been largely shaped by varying cultural anxieties.

Cultural anxiety is not always empirically false, but U.S. history is rich in disproportionate reactions that were grounded on false beliefs. Perhaps the most infamous example is the *Chinese Exclusion* case. In May 1882, Congress passed the Chinese Exclusion Act, which authorized the executive branch to exclude persons of Chinese descent. Chae Chan Ping was a Chinese-born laborer who had lived in California for many years. Before he departed the United States for a brief visit to China, he had obtained a certificate that would entitle him to return to the United States. During his absence, Congress amended the law to ban the entry of people of Chinese descent—including those with validly-issued certificates—and, subsequently, Chae Chan Ping was barred from re-entering. In 1889, he challenged his exclusion before the U.S. Supreme Court. In its judgment, the Supreme Court upheld the Chinese Exclusion Act and set ground rules for the plenary power of the political branches over immigration.

Justice Field, writing for a unanimous Court, ruled that the Chinese were culturally different. They "remained strangers in the land, residing apart by themselves, and adhering to the customs and usages of their own country. It seemed impossible for them to assimilate with our people or to make any change in their habits or modes of living." Justice Field went even further to stress a political concern: "As they grew in numbers each year," they would present a "great danger that at no distant day that portion of our country would be overrun by them unless prompt action was taken to restrict their immigration." The Court considered Chinese arrivals to be invaders: "Their immigration was in numbers approaching the character of an Oriental invasion.... It matters not in what form such aggression and encroachment come, whether from the foreign nation acting in its national character or from vast hordes of its people crowding in upon us."[6]

The Chinese Exclusion Act was motivated by demographic fear of a large influx of Chinese immigrants, who were perceived to be culturally different (they "remained strangers in the land") and incapable of integration (they "constituted a Chinese settlement within the State"). These assumptions led to the hysterical reaction motivating the Chinese exclusion. Notably, some 130 years later, the U.S. House of Representatives apologized for the passage of the Chinese Exclusion Act.[7]

[6] *Chae Chan Ping* v. *United States* 130 U.S. 581: pp. 595–596, 606 (1889).

[7] House Resolution 683, 112th Congress (2012).

The Chinese Exclusion was a precursor to similar concerns that existed throughout the first half of the twentieth century. Almost all new arrivals—Germans, Irish, Italians, Jews, Russians—were first perceived as a cultural threat. Some came from countries having a recent history of extremism and fascism, such as Italy, Ireland, and Spain. This reality led to claims that certain migrants were disloyal, incapable of assimilation, and therefore would create parallel societies. A similar experience characterized other migrant groups, such as Southern and Eastern Europeans at the end of the nineteenth century and at the turn of the twentieth century. It was a period when nativism turned into racism in America. The "science" of eugenics, holding that there are "scientific" differences between races, became an influential force. A main concern was that the United States was in jeopardy due to a large admission rate of people from "inferior" races.[8]

The history of U.S. immigration law reflects various forms and levels of demographic anxiety. Historians have documented how racial and cultural concerns triggered policies aimed at perpetuating a white, English-speaking, Anglo-Saxon, Protestant majority.[9] Among the means designed to preserve the Anglo-Saxon superiority were, one, the extension of the Chinese Exclusion to the so-called "Asiatic Barred Zone"[10] and, two, the adoption of immigration quotas based on race and nationality.[11] Racial restrictions were eased after World War II, but were not completely removed until the passage of the Immigration and Nationality Act of 1952.

American history shows that none of these concerns was ultimately realized. It is an important historical lesson. Jefferson and Hamilton were probably correct in presuming that foreigners would bring with them customs and manners from their country of origin—and some of these customs and manners were indeed passed on to American youth—yet, in retrospect, it is likely that they enriched, rather than diluted, American society, making it stronger and wealthier. Millions of Europeans brought their outlooks and attitudes that were rooted in feudalism, monarchism,

[8] Patrick Weil, "Races at the Gate: A Century of Racial Distinctions in American Immigration Policy (1865–1965)," *Georgetown Immigration Law Journal* 15, no. 4 (2001): pp. 625–648.

[9] James H. Kettner, *The Development of American Citizenship, 1608–1870* (Chapel Hill: University of North Carolina Press, 1978); John Higham, *Strangers in the Land: Patterns of American Nativism, 1860–1925* (New Brunswick: Rutgers University Press, 2002); Aristide R. Zolberg, *A Nation by Design: Immigration Policy in the Fashioning of America* (Cambridge: Harvard University Press, 2008).

[10] Immigration Act (1917); Emergency Quota Act (1921).

[11] Immigration Act (1924) includes two Acts: National Origins Act and Asian Exclusion Act.

fascism, and Marxism—indeed, some communist and fascist movements popped up occasionally—but, overall, newcomers did not pose a threat to American liberties. Rather, they blended smoothly into American society, largely dissolving the historic differences that had existed among Russians, Irish, and other immigrants from cultures that did not value assimilation.

The 1965 immigration reform

In 1965, at the height of the Civil Rights Movement, Congress abolished the National Origins Quota System (racial quotas were largely eliminated in 1952) and adopted a new immigration system.[12] This system, the basis of the current immigration policy, is founded on three main admission categories: (a) family-based migration; (b) employment-based migration; and (c) humanitarian-based migration, principally refugees and asylum seekers. These categories are relatively neutral because they select migrants by using "universal" criteria: family ties, skills and merits, and humanitarian needs. Family-based migration, the largest category, does not include quotas for immediate relatives of U.S. citizens—that is, parents, spouses, and unmarried minor children. Yet, numerical limits exist in all other admission categories, including that of the "family preference system" (brothers and sisters of U.S. citizens and other family relatives).

The initial expectation in giving preferences to family ties was to promote European migration. The prevailing wisdom was that Americans of European ancestry would bring their immediate relatives to join them. Or, as George Borjas notes, it was meant to preserve the demographic status quo, but wisely—"without having to resort to explicit racial or national-origin restrictions."[13] In this sense, the 1965 reform was not a complete departure from the history of demographic distrust. Demography, however, was only one reason for the reform. Influences of the Civil Rights Movement were central too—concepts of liberty and equality for all were incorporated into the immigration law. And, as some scholars demonstrate, historical evidence shows that Congress did expect a slight increase in Asian, and not just European

[12] Immigration and Nationality Act (1965). The preference system was first established, in a slightly different form, in the Immigration and Nationality Act (1952). The 1965 reform changed and tweaked those preferences.

[13] George J. Borjas, *Friends or Strangers: The Impact of Immigrants on the U.S. Economy* (New York: Basic Books, 1990): p. 32.

migration.[14] Nevertheless, the prevailing view was that preferences for family relationships would primarily benefit Europeans.[15] Senator Ted Kennedy, a key player in the 1965 immigration reform, promised that "the ethnic pattern of immigration under the proposed measure is not expected to change [sharply]"; he also stated that there would be no mass immigration from "one country or area."[16]

Contrary to initial expectations, the 1965 immigration reform brought about the most significant demographic change in U.S. history.[17] The foreign-born population increased from 5.4 percent (1960) to 12.9 percent (2010). But the increase of the foreign-born population was not the main change. Rather, the main change related to the regions from which the migrants arrived. In 1960, European-origin immigrants composed 75 percent of the foreign-born population in the United States; by 2010, European-origin immigrants only equaled 12 percent. In sharp contrast, the Hispanic share of the U.S. foreign-born population rose from 9 percent (1960) to 53 percent (2010); the Asian share increased from 5 percent (1960) to 28 percent (2010) (see Table 2.1).

TABLE 2.1 FOREIGN-BORN POPULATION BY REGION OF BIRTH IN THE UNITED STATES

Region	*Percentage*	
	1960	*2010*
Europe	75	12
North America	10	2
Latin America	9	53
Asia	5	28
Other	1	5

Source: Elizabeth M. Grieco et al., "The Size, Place of Birth, and Geographic Distribution of the Foreign-Born Population in the United States: 1960 to 2010," U.S. Census Bureau, 2012: pp. 19–22.

Note: "Foreign born" is anyone who is not a U.S. citizen at birth, such as naturalized citizens, legal permanent residents, temporary migrants, and humanitarian migrants.

[14] Gabriel J. Chin, "The Civil Rights Revolution Comes to Immigration Law: A New Look at the Immigration and Nationality Act of 1965," *North Carolina Law Review* 75, no. 1 (1996): pp. 273–346 at 303–321.

[15] Roger Daniels, *Coming to America: A History of Immigration and Ethnicity in American Life*, 2nd ed. (Princeton: Perennial, 2002): pp. 338–344; Nathan Glazer, "The Closing Door," *The New Republic* 209, no. 26 (December 1993): pp. 15–20 at 16; Peter H. Schuck, "The Emerging Political Consensus on Immigration Law," *Georgetown Immigration Law Journal* 5, no. 1 (1991): pp. 1–34 at 7.

[16] Oscar M. Trelles and James F. Bailey, eds., "Immigration: Hearings Before the Subcommittee on Immigration and Naturalization of the Committee on the Judiciary United States Senate, on S. 500. 89th Congress, 1st Session" (February 10, 1965), in *Immigration and Nationality Acts: Legislative Histories and Related Documents*, vol. 11 (Buffalo: Hein, 1979): pp. 1–41 at 2.

[17] Peter H. Schuck, *Diversity in America: Keeping Government at a Safe Distance* (Cambridge: Harvard University Press, 2003): pp. 75–76, 87–94.

Demographic changes are evident in more than migration statistics. Table 2.2 presents American demographics according to race and years. The data is striking. In 1960, White Americans composed 89 percent of the general U.S. population; in 2010, they formed 65 percent; by 2050 they are expected to be a minority. In contrast, Hispanic Americans, a tiny minority in 1960, constituted 16 percent of the general U.S. population in 2010, and are expected to reach 30 percent of the population by 2050. Asian Americans, 0.5 percent of the general U.S. population in 1960, reached 5 percent in 2010, and are expected to comprise 8 percent by 2050.

TABLE 2.2 U.S. POPULATION BY RACE, 1960–2050

Race	*Percentage*					
	1960	*1980*	*1990*	*2010*	*2030*	*2050*
Non-Hispanic White	88.6	79.6	75.6	64.7	55.5	46.3
Hispanic	—	6.4	9.0	16.0	23.0	30.2
Asian	0.5	1.5	2.9	4.6	6.3	7.8
Black	10.5	11.7	12.1	12.9	13.0	13.0

Sources: (a) Campbell Gibson and Kay Jung, "Historical Census Statistics on Population Totals By Race, 1790 to 1990, and By Hispanic Origin, 1970 to 1990, for The United States, Regions, Divisions, and States," U.S. Census Bureau, 2002; (b) Jennifer M. Ortman and Christine E. Guarneri, "United States Population Projections: 2000 to 2050," U.S. Census Bureau, 2009: p. 17.

Notes: (a) "Asian" for 1960, 1980, and 1990 includes "Asian and Pacific Islander"; (b) the data on "non-Hispanic White" in 1960 (88.6%) refers only to "White"; (c) for the sake of convenience, Table 2.9 focuses only on the four major categories of the U.S. Census Bureau: Non-Hispanic White, Hispanic, Asian, and Black; (d) The percentage of Hispanics among the U.S. population in 1960 is unspecified because the U.S. Census Bureau fully introduced a separate category of "Hispanic" only in 1980.

The changing demographics of America are not only due to the 1965 immigration reform. European migration to America would have declined in any event, mainly for two reasons. First, emigration from Eastern Europe to the United States declined dramatically due to the Cold War; and second, after World War II some European countries themselves became a magnet for migration. Economic demands in America were largely met by increasing the volume of migrants from other regions, principally Latin Americans, who were not prohibited from entering the U.S. by the quota system that had preceded the 1965 reform (the quota system did not apply to migrants from the Western Hemisphere).[18] Thus, while the effect of the 1965 reform in generating the changes in U.S. demography should not be underestimated, it was not the sole contributor.

One aspect of America's changing demographics relates to national origin. Contrary to Senator Kennedy's expectation that there would be no mass migration from "one country," since the enactment of the 1965 reform a large percentage of newcomers has arrived from one country—Mexico. In 1960, Mexicans formed 6 percent of the foreign-born population in America; in 2010, they reached 29 percent. Of the entire U.S. Hispanic population, 64 percent are Mexicans.[19] If one considers undocumented aliens, the share of Mexicans among the U.S. foreign-born population would be higher (55 percent of the undocumented aliens are Mexicans).

The changing demography of America has stirred up the old debate about the essence of Americanism and belonging to America. The focus this time is not on Chinese or Catholics, but mainly on Mexicans.

Creedal nation

In the nineteenth century, the American poet and diplomat, James Russell Lowell, was asked how long he believed the American Republic would endure. His reply: "So long as the ideas of the men who founded it continue dominant."[20] Indeed, from its establishment, the United States was founded on belief in certain ideas. These ideas were drafted by Thomas Jefferson on July 4, 1776, in the Declaration of Independence: "We hold these Truths to be self-evident, that all Men are created equal, that they are endowed by their Creator with certain unalienable Rights, that among these are Life, Liberty, and the Pursuit of Happiness." America's nationalism has since been built upon civic and political ideas that, at least in theory, are open to all people who demonstrate a commitment to them (albeit in practice, for almost two centuries, American freedoms

[18] Douglas S. Massey, "The New Immigration and Ethnicity in the United States," *Population and Development Review* 21, no. 3 (1995): pp. 631–652 at 637–640.

[19] Pew Hispanic Center, "A Demographic Portrait of Mexican-Origin Hispanics in the United States," 2013: pp. 5–7 ("Worldwide, 9% of people born in Mexico live in the U.S. In addition, the U.S. has more immigrants from Mexico alone than any other country has immigrants").

[20] James Russell Lowell, *Literary and Political Addresses*, vol. VI, *The Writings of James Russell Lowell* (Boston: Houghton, Mifflin and Company, 1890): p. 207.

and liberties were not open to all people).[21] Given this arguable proposition, why should ethnic demographic changes in the United States matter at all?

The changing demographics of America raise the issue of the so-called "American creed." A creed is a term rooted in religious belief. It is a statement of belief shared by a religious group. Affirmation of the creed by a concise statement is considered the test of orthodoxy for believers. While Americanism may have a specific creed, its character has various versions. One version, represented by the late Harvard University Professor Samuel Huntington, holds that America's creed includes liberty, equality, private property, democracy, the rule of law, egalitarian values, Protestant values, individualism, the English language, English traditions of law and justice, and limits on government power. Huntington argues that there is a broad consensus on these ideas in America.[22] For him, adherence to these ideas is the ultimate test in becoming an American citizen.

Huntington asserts that America's creed has been fading since the 1950s because, among others, Mexicans challenge the Anglo-Protestant culture. Without a Protestant culture, he notes, America would not be the same nation since the creed is the product of the Anglo-Protestant culture.[23] Huntington sees Mexican migration as a "serious problem" and a "[disturbing] challenge to our cultural integrity, our national identity, and potentially to our future as a country."[24] In his view, the Anglo-Protestant culture is not part of the creed, but a prerequisite for its existence. "There is no Americano dream," Huntington contends, "there is only the American dream created by an Anglo-Protestant society. Mexican Americans will share in that dream and in that society only if they dream in English."[25]

Huntington's writings illustrate fundamental difficulties in: (a) defining a core bond (tie, glue, attachment) holding a people together;

[21] Gerald L. Neuman, *Strangers to the Constitution: Immigrants, Borders, and Fundamental Law* (Princeton: Princeton University Press, 1996): pp. 19–43, 139–164; Rogers M. Smith, *Civic Ideals: Conflicting Visions of Citizenship in U.S. History* (New Haven: Yale University Press, 1999): pp. 14–15.

[22] Samuel P. Huntington, *American Politics: The Promise of Disharmony* (Cambridge: Harvard University Press, 1982): pp. 4, 14–15.

[23] Huntington, *American Politics*, pp. 22–27, 229 (n 22).

[24] Samuel P. Huntington, "Reconsidering Immigration: Is Mexico a Special Case?," Center for Immigration Studies, 2000.

[25] Samuel P. Huntington, "The Hispanic Challenge," *Foreign Policy*, no. 141 (March/April 2004): pp. 30–45 at 45.

(b) deciding who does or does not belong by setting admission and exclusion criteria; (c) deciding the level of compatibility between (a) and (b), that is, in what sense joining a new community (b) requires confirmation of its creed (a).

Defining a national project is a lofty goal. Huntington's prescription raises some puzzling issues associated with any attempt to define a creed. First, methodologically, Huntington's method for defining a creed is to look at the past. Looking at the past ("who we were") to define the present ("who we are") is a limited method. Huntington's plea is that newcomers embrace "America's Anglo-Protestant culture and political values," not necessarily because it is its current identity, but because it *was* its original identity and should continue to prevail.[26] This method offers a static concept of identity, which leaves very little room for fundamental changes.

Second, empirically, even if one accepts the method of defining the present by looking merely or mainly at the past, some disputes remain. It may be that current integration is slower than past integration (this is an open debate), yet it does not necessarily mean that Mexican migrants are not capable of integration. Mexican integration may be different but contemporary America is also different. The world is different. Globalization and technological developments have dramatically altered concepts of belonging and integration (see Chapter 1). Measuring integration in 2015 by criteria applied in the 1920s offers a static conception of integration.

Third, conceptually, Huntington discusses "identity," but intertwines it with "creed,"[27] as if these are overlapping concepts. Nevertheless, national identity is not the same as national creed. National identity is not fixed, solid, and eternal; it is not permanent and static. It is dynamic. Values, ways of life, customs, traditions, lifestyles, folkways, conventions, and mores—are all changeable. In a sense, national identity is largely a myth. There is hardly one fixed "Israeli identity" (consider Jerusalem versus Tel Aviv), "European identity" (France versus Germany), or even "American identity" (Wisconsin versus Arizona). Creed, however, is a less fungible concept. It is a statement of the most fundamental beliefs of a group, its *raison d'être*. Israel's creed, for instance, might be "Jewish and democratic State"; France's might be *"Liberté, Égalité, Fraternité."*

[26] Samuel Huntington, "One Nation, Out of Many: Why 'Americanization' of Newcomers is Still Important," *The American Enterprise* 15, no. 6 (September 2004): pp. 20–25 at 21, 24.

[27] Samuel P. Huntington, *Who Are We? The Challenges to America's National Identity* (New York: Simon & Schuster, 2004): pp. 21–27.

The content of the creed is arguable, yet it is not equivalent to identity. A creed can be a source of identity, but not its sole source. It has often preceded national identity, because it is the reason for establishing a new political community.

Returning to Jefferson's and Hamilton's fears, it seems that they were more concerned with America's creed, its most fundamental liberties and freedoms, than with America's identity in the sense of its Protestant values. Their anxiety was about a threat to the love of liberty. They were afraid of foreigners who would not be attached to principles of "Life, Liberty, and the Pursuit of Happiness" and to the truths of the Declaration of Independence.

Reconquista

Some people claim that the demographic challenge facing America is not cultural or creedal, but territorial. In 2008, Mark Krikorian, the executive director of the Center for Immigration Studies, a conservative think-tank in Washington, D.C., published a book that advocates strict immigration restrictions. His concern is a Mexican "*reconquista*." This term means to recapture and it refers to two historical events. The first is *reconquista* in Middle Ages Europe when Christian kingdoms re-established Christian rule in the Iberian Peninsula by conquering Islamic kingdoms. The second is *reconquista* in colonial Spanish America when several Spanish colonies in Latin America gained autonomy. The use of this term in the context of Mexican migration is odd. It refers to an unrealistic scenario in which, in the future, Mexico will take over territories in Southwest America, annexed during the U.S.–Mexican War. Krikorian does not assert that this is a realistic scenario. Instead, he claims that Mexican migration is a new form of *reconquista*: "What we are seeing right now is the gradual development of a new constitutional order of shared sovereignty in which the nominal borders stay the same but, through an accumulation of seemingly small American capitulations, the Mexican government gradually acquires more and more authority over the decision making" in the United States.[28]

Krikorian's assertion is not unusual; there are a growing number of *reconquista* believers.[29] The most prominent is Samuel Huntington. In *The Hispanic Challenge*, Huntington asserts that the continuing movement

[28] Mark Krikorian, *The New Case Against Immigration: Both Legal and Illegal* (New York: Sentinel, 2008): pp. 46–59.

[29] See, e.g., David M. Kennedy, "Can We Still Afford to Be a Nation of Immigrants?," *Atlantic Monthly* 278, no. 5 (November 1996): pp. 52–68 at 54, 68; John J. Miller, *The Unmaking of Americans: How*

of Hispanics to America "threatens to divide the United States into two peoples, two cultures, and two languages." More specifically, he argues that Mexican migration differs from past migration due to a combination of six factors: scale (unprecedented number of migrants), persistence (it is likely to continue), regional concentration (in the Southwest), contiguity (a neighbor country), illegality (high number of undocumented aliens), and historical presence (historical claims to U.S. territories). To these six factors, Huntington adds a further one—changes in self-perception: "Mexican Americans no longer think of themselves as members of a small minority who must accommodate the dominant group and adopt its culture." The combination of these factors allows Mexicans to become a majority in the Southwest: "The *reconquista* (re-conquest) of the Southwest United States by Mexican immigrants is well underway.... by 2080 the southwestern states of the United States and the northern states of Mexico will form *La República del Norte* (The Republic of the North)."[30]

A note of clarification: until the U.S.–Mexican War, 1846–48, most of the southwestern United States was part of Mexico. Arizona, California, Nevada, New Mexico, Texas, and Utah—were all formerly northern Mexican lands that had been taken by force from Mexico during the war. Their incorporation into America did not, however, happen soon after the war. Historical evidence shows that President James Polk and some Congressmen worried about the demographic consequences of the incorporation of former Mexican territories into the Union. These fears led them to amend the Treaty of Guadalupe Hidalgo, the peace agreement between the United States and Mexico. Revisions were inserted into the treaty, stating that the incorporation of the annexed territories into the Union would be "at the proper time." The original language provided that the incorporation shall be "as soon as possible." The revised treaty gave Congress the discretion when to incorporate the lands. Juan Perea found that, in reality, "Congress deemed the admission of former Mexican territories 'proper' only when the immigration of whites to the territories created a majority white population."[31] New Mexico, for

Multiculturalism Has Undermined America's Assimilation Ethic (New York: The Free Press, 1998): pp. 5–7, 145–146, 236–239; Peter Brimelow, *Alien Nation: Common Sense About America's Immigration Disaster* (New York: Harper Perennial, 1996): pp. 59, 168, 193–195; Patrick J. Buchanan, *State of Emergency: The Third World Invasion and Conquest of America* (New York: Thomas Dunne Books, 2006): pp. 5, 12, 49, 107, 125, 132, 135–136.

30 Huntington, "The Hispanic Challenge," pp. 30, 33–36, 44, 42, respectively (n 25). See also Huntington, "Reconsidering Immigration" (n 24); Huntington, *American Politics*, pp. 221–256, 316–324 (n 22).

31 Juan F. Perea, "A Brief History of Race and the U.S.-Mexican Border: Tracing the Trajectories of Conquest," *UCLA Law Review* 51, no. 1 (2003): pp. 283–312 at 293–300.

instance, was not incorporated into the Union for almost sixty years, until a predominantly white-populated majority was present in its territory. Likewise, California and Texas were incorporated only after White Anglos became the majority.

Contemporary debates about Mexican migration are not free of historical context. Non-Hispanic Whites have already become a minority in California, New Mexico, and Texas. Yet, conspiracy theories of a Mexican government-led plan to take over the Southwest are implausible.[32] Even if the majority in the Southwest becomes Mexican, the scenario of an American-version of a Quebec-like secession movement seems far-fetched.

Lessons from the United States

In modern history, there is no better example of an immigration country than the United States. More than two hundred years of U.S. experience in absorbing immigrants holds some lessons. One obvious lesson is that anxiety is likely to erupt when the following four factors combine: a growing number of foreigners, possessing a character (religion, ethnicity, culture, ideology) which differs to that of the existing majority, and which affects the numerical proportions between the native population and newcomers, over a short period of time. Another lesson relates to the response to almost every wave of culturally distinct migration. From Chinese to Mexican immigrants, U.S. history provides multiple examples of false demographic alarms. In immigration debates, there is a tendency to overstate facts, infer wrong conclusions, and adopt extreme policies.

In numbers, America is witnessing the most drastic demographic change in its history. However, contemporary concerns are less alarming and visible compared to those of the past. Despite the persistence of anti-immigrant groups, demographic concerns are not part of mainstream politics in America and are not front-page news. Current immigration debates focus on economy and border security, not on culture and national identity (with the exception of the English language as a possible cultural issue). Huntington and other like-minded scholars[33]

[32] For such claims see, e.g., Huntington, *Who Are We?*, p. 208 (n 27).

[33] *Comprehensive Immigration Reform: Becoming Americans—U.S. Immigrant Integration: Hearing Before the Subcommittee on Immigration, Citizenship, Refugees, Border Security, and International Law of the Committee on the Judiciary, House of Representative, 110th Congress, 1st Session* (Washington: Government Printing Office, 2007): pp. 57–65 (prepared statement of John Fonte).

are an exception. Unlike past experiences, in which immigrant groups were seen as a challenge to American democracy and identity, there are no similar serious claims nowadays. Historian John Higham rightly observes that the nativist movements have largely disappeared; "the twenties have not returned."[34]

Some explanations for the relaxing response to migration are related to the migrants. Mexicans are mostly Christians, in the main Catholics, and they are not perceived as a challenge to American democracy or identity. Other explanations are a function of the American society. Some people claim that America is less demanding today in its integration requirements than in the past because it has lost confidence in its identity. Perhaps. But it may also be that America is less demanding of its migrants precisely because it has more confidence in its values and political institutions. Other explanations pertain to the contemporary world. Due to technological changes, such as the Internet and satellite TV, cultural differences between Mexicans and Americans are narrower today than the cultural differences that existed in the past between, say, Chinese or Irish and Americans. Numbers matter, but so do other factors.

EUROPE

Demographic concerns in Europe are different from those in the United States. First, the experience is different. Europe has been facing a rapid growth in the number of migrants since the 1960s, while the United States has been confronting similar issues for more than two centuries. Recent immigration debates in Europe had long been addressed, and largely resolved, in America. Second, demographic changes are different. Religious diversity is not a major issue in the United States the way it is in Europe. Third, the type of concern is different. While American concern largely relates to the American creed, Europe's concerns include a blend of multiple creeds—both of the developing European identity and of the national identities of Member States. Fourth, the anxiety is of a different kind. While in the United States the demographic change does not bring up feelings of substantial threats to its democratic nature, in Europe there are subjective fears that democracy and liberty are at stake. Fifth, the scope is different. While demographic anxiety is not widely shared in the United States, it is mainstream in

[34] Higham, p. 332 (n 9).

some European states. Finally, the historical context is different. It is impossible to analyze the current situation in Europe without considering the ghosts of World War II.

It seems that Europe is developing its own version of nativism and moral panic is spreading across the continent. The following pages briefly describe Europe's cultural concerns, show how they are partly followed by a high level of public hysteria, and investigate their origins.

European nativism

In October 2010, Angela Merkel, the German Chancellor, declared that the policy of multiculturalism has "utterly failed" in Germany.[35] It has created an illusion that natives and migrants can "live happily side by side." A few years earlier, in 2004, Merkel had made clear: "Anyone coming here must respect our constitution and tolerate our Western and Christian roots.... A democracy cannot tolerate lawless zones or parallel societies.... [immigrants must] acknowledge our democratic ways of doing things."[36]

In February 2011, David Cameron, the British Prime Minister, put forward a similar view and pronounced the death of multiculturalism. In his view, multiculturalism leads to "the weakening of our collective identity." Cameron did not explain what British identity means, but he did point out the outcome. "Under the doctrine of state multiculturalism," he argued, "we have encouraged different cultures to live separate lives, apart from each other and apart from the mainstream.... We've even tolerated these segregated communities behaving in ways that run completely counter to our values." "At stake," Cameron warned, is "our way of life."

Cameron advocates a policy termed "muscular liberalism." Liberalism is not only about obeying the law, he contends. This is its passive element. "A genuinely liberal country," Cameron asserts, "*believes* in certain values." This is the active element of liberalism. Which values? Cameron has a clear prescription: "Freedom of speech, freedom of worship, democracy, the rule of law, equal rights." Britain should tell migrants "this is what defines us as a society: to belong here is to *believe* in these things."[37]

[35] Jess Smee, "The World from Berlin: Merkel's Rhetoric in Integration Debate is 'Inexcusable'," *Spiegel*, October 18, 2010.

[36] Ray Furlong, "Germans Argue Over Integration," BBC News, November 30, 2004.

[37] GOV.UK, "PM's Speech at Munich Security Conference," February 5, 2011 (emphasis added).

A few days after Cameron's speech, Nicolas Sarkozy, the former French President, denounced multiculturalism. "It is a failure," he claimed, since it has led to a reality in which "communities coexist side by side." "If you come to France," Sarkozy stated, "you accept to melt into a single community, which is the national community, and if you do not want to accept that, you cannot be welcome in France." In Sarkozy's view, France has "been too busy with the identity of those who arrived and not enough with the identity of the country that accepted them."[38] Sarkozy's Chief of Staff and the Minister of the Interior, Claude Guéant, made an even more astonishing observation. Civilizations are not equal, he said. There are superior civilizations, those which believe in *Liberté, Égalité, Fraternité*, and there are inferior civilizations, those which do not accept those ideas.[39]

Anti-immigrant sentiment is more blatant in Europe's rising right-wing parties. In Denmark, a campaign launched by the Danish People's Party in the 2007 elections showed veiled women under the slogan "follow the country's customs or leave" (*Skik følge eller land fly*). There are many other examples, including slogans that were disqualified due to concerns of racism in Austria and France, but one of the most notorious examples came from Switzerland. During the 2007 election campaign, the Swiss People's Party (SVP) hung posters advocating the deportation of criminal migrants. The poster showed three white sheep standing on the Swiss flag, while one of the sheep kicked out a black sheep under the caption "to create security" (*Sicherheit schaffen*). These are not marginal voices. The SVP is currently (2015) the largest party in the Federal Assembly. In 2010, a federal referendum was successfully passed in support of its deportation initiative.

Anti-immigrant sentiments are mushrooming across Europe not just in politics, but also in scholarly studies and popular books. In *Eurobia*, Bat Ye'or argues that Europe is transforming itself from an enlightened Judeo-Christian civilization to a "civilization of dhimmitude" in which non-Muslims are subjugated to Islamic rule "to avoid enslavement or death." Because of lax immigration policies, Europe will soon become "Eurabia," a mix and match of Euro-Arab culture.[40] In *While Europe Slept*,

[38] "Nicolas Sarkozy Joins David Cameron and Angela Merkel View that Multiculturalism Has Failed," *Daily Mail*, February 11, 2011; Soeren Kern, "France's Tottery Effort to Reverse Creeping Islamization," Gatestone Institute, January 2, 2012.

[39] "French Minister Slammed for 'Unequal Civilisations' Comment," France 24, February 5, 2012.

[40] Bat Ye'or, *Eurabia: The Euro-Arab Axis* (Cranbury: Fairleigh Dickinson University Press, 2005): pp. 9–11, 36.

Bruce Bawer asserts that migrants in the Netherlands are more like diplomats—emissaries who do not adopt the local ways of life. Bawer is afraid of an Islamist plot to take over. When Muslims are the majority, he asks, "can we still wear shorts in the summer?" Europe is at "a Weimar moment."[41]

In *America Alone*, Mark Steyn is worried that a new war is imminent. It is a war without warfare. Nations no longer need to invade other nations. These are old strategies. Rather, he claims, "if you frame the issue in terms of multicultural[ism]. . . . [you will have] everything you want." According to Steyn, it may be just too late to save Europe as a liberal society: "Much of what we loosely call the Western world will not survive the twenty-first century, and much of it will effectively disappear within our lifetimes, including many if not most European countries."[42]

In *Reflections on the Revolution in Europe*, Christoper Caldwell holds that Europe is facing a revolution. It is a demographic revolution triggered by a large influx of migrants. The book's key question is "Can you have the same Europe with different people?" Caldwell's answer is "no." Muslims are only a minority in Europe, he admits, but "words like 'majority' and 'minority' mean little. When an insecure, malleable, relativistic culture meets a culture that is anchored, confident, and strengthened by common doctrines, it is generally the former that changes to suit the latter."[43]

One should not underestimate the influence of these books. Most of them were best-sellers. When a German or French citizen wishes to read an analysis of European immigration law, or of Muslims in Europe, he does not usually read Christian Joppke's instructive articles in the *European Journal of Sociology*. He reads Caldwell, Bawer, Steyn, and Bat Ye'or—who, along with others, create an image that Europe is under a large-scale cultural invasion; that Muslims are becoming a majority; that Muslims pose a threat to liberalism and the national culture; and that migration is one of the most troubling issues on the agenda. If a visitor from Mars reads these books or daily European newspapers, he or she might think that Saladin and his troops are moving into London and Paris.

[41] Bruce Bawer, *While Europe Slept: How Radical Islam is Destroying the West from Within* (New York: Doubleday, 2006): pp. 188, 233.

[42] Mark Steyn, *America Alone: The End of the World as We Know It* (Washington: Regnery Publishing, 2006): pp. xxx, xiii, 61, 74.

[43] Christopher Caldwell, *Reflections on the Revolution in Europe: Immigration, Islam, and the West* (New York: Doubleday, 2009): pp. 24, 349.

Myth or reality?

Europe's cultural challenge is obviously not a myth. Even the most optimistic studies cannot deny that Europe is confronting a serious challenge. Considerable cultural gaps exist on five key issues: liberal values, the rule of law, the legitimacy of the use of violence in political conflicts, the role of religion in the public sphere, and sexual openness (as detailed in Chapter 1). Findings are particularly troubling since studies indicate that these gaps are often wider in second and third generation immigrants. Perhaps more troubling is that attitudes do not remain without actions. Practices such as honor killing, female circumcision, and forced marriages reveal the existence of patriarchal norms in Europe. Riots in Paris and Stockholm, terrorist acts in Madrid and London, and social clashes in Copenhagen and Rotterdam—have made the issue of Muslims in Europe central and visible. But like other immigration debates, this debate, too, is followed by exaggerated descriptions and false normative conclusions.

Popular claims fail in at least two aspects. The first failure touches on the empirical validity of some *premises*. A good example is "Eurabia," the widespread claim that Muslims will soon become a majority. This claim is empirically false. The largest Muslim community in the European Union, located in France, constituted 7.5 percent of the population in 2010 and is expected to reach 10.3 percent by 2030. As detailed in Chapter 1, by 2030, Muslims will remain a relatively small minority—up to ten percent—in *all* EU states. This hardly indicates "Eurabia." If one considers the falling fertility rates of Muslims, despite the existing gaps between the Muslims and the host population, and the fact that Christian migrants outnumber Muslim migrants even if one excludes intra-EU movements (in 2010, 42 percent of all migrants to Europe were Christians and 39 percent were Muslims),[44] it is unlikely that Muslims will become a majority in the near future.

The second failure relates to false *conclusions* inferred from empirically-valid premises. A good illustration is burial. In some Member States, a vast majority of citizens of Muslim faith are not buried in Europe. Instead, their bodies are sent back to their country of origin. These figures are often brought to support the assertion that Muslims are not interested in integration. A closer look, however, reveals barriers to Islamic funerals. Take Denmark: in 2015, it only had one Muslim

[44] Pew Research Center, "Faith on the Move: The Religious Affiliation of International Migrants," 2012: pp. 17, 54.

cemetery. Section 4 of the Constitutional Act of Denmark provides that "The Evangelical Lutheran Church shall be the Established Church of Denmark, and as such shall be supported by the State." Funerals are open to all people yet the Lutheran Church possesses exclusive jurisdiction to oversee funerals. And while Catholics and Jews have historical arrangements and own private lands for religious cemeteries, Muslims, mainly due to financial hurdles, do not enjoy the same benefits. They are either buried in a separate section for non-members and thus must pay a fee, unlike the members-section cemetery in which plots are free, or be buried in a different country. Other issues touch upon religious ceremonies. Islam obliges Muslims to be buried with their heads facing Mecca, which is not always possible in Danish cemeteries given the preexisting designs. Hence, the fact that Muslims opt for an overseas funeral is not necessarily because they reject integration, but often ensues from substantial barriers to Islamic funerals.

These examples are not rare. Demographic concerns are frequently based on false facts and wrong conclusions. Combined with the discourse characterizing immigration debates, which very often plays on fears, this is a perfect environment to cultivate moral panic. I turn to this issue now.

Moral panic

Following are three examples of public hysteria in Europe: handshaking, swimming lessons, and minarets. These examples emphasize three points: first, some conflicts are just a symptom of a broader debate over the public sphere; second, some policies violate the same values Europe seeks to protect; and third, some cases leave little room for cultural diversity. While politicians speak about the failure of multiculturalism, these cases show that multiculturalism is not always an available option for migrants.

The first example is handshaking. In *Murder in Amsterdam*, Ian Buruma recalls the story of an imam from Tilburg who refused to shake hands with Rita Verdonk, the former Dutch Minister of Integration. Buruma says that "The sturdy figure of Rita Verdonk facing the bearded imam became a prime symbol of the Dutch crisis, of the collapse of multiculturalism."[45] In the following years, Samira, a female Muslim teacher, was suspended from teaching at a public school after she refused to

[45] Ian Buruma, *Murder in Amsterdam: Liberal Europe, Islam, and the Limits of Tolerance* (New York: Penguin Books, 2006): p. 8.

shake hands with men due to her religious beliefs. The school, Vader Rijn College in Utrecht, had three claims: first, as a teacher, she was a role model for students and a ban on handshaking based on gender was incompatible with her profession. Second, schools had to be free of religious influences; religious beliefs had to remain in the private sphere. After the Utrecht District Court rejected her claim,[46] Samira appealed to the Central Appeals Court for Public Service and Social Security Matters, which upheld the suspension, holding that handshaking was a "standard greeting form that is compatible with common good manners in the Netherlands."[47] In another case, the City Council of Rotterdam refused a Muslim candidate the position of a client manager after he refused to shake hands with women, albeit he was willing to greet women in an alternative respectful manner. The candidate sued for discrimination, but a Dutch court in The Hague ruled against him, holding that the job of client manager involves shaking hands with people. The Court further added that shaking hands is an accepted form of greeting in the Netherlands and a refusal to do so is inappropriate behavior.[48]

A second example is swimming lessons. In some EU states, swimming lessons are a compulsory part of the curriculum. In Germany, parents of a nine year-old female Muslim student requested her exemption from mixed swimming lessons with boys in a public school. The case was brought to a court in Münster, which rejected the parents' request. The Court held that since the girl was before puberty, there was no risk of sexual temptation; if the lessons were deemed immoral, the girl could protect her modesty by wearing a *burkini*, a swimsuit that covers the body.[49] In similar cases, Muslim girls aged 12, who had already reached maturity, were not exempted from mixed swimming lessons. The courts ruled that girls could swim in a *burkini* and, in any event, swimming takes place underwater and hence the girls would remain covered. The courts added that mixed swimming lessons are a social norm in Germany and part of the daily life; migrants "*have to deal with it*."[50] After all, pupils may see bare-chested men even on the street.[51]

46 Rechtbank Utrecht, L.J.N. BB2648, August 30, 2007.

47 Centrale Raad van Beroep, L.J.N. BI2440 para. 7.8, May 7, 2009.

48 Gerechtshof's-Gravenhage, L.J.N. BW1270 paras. 3, 15, April 10, 2012.

49 OVG Nordrhein-Westfalen, Az. 19 B 1362/08 paras. 6–9, May 20, 2009.

50 VG Düsseldorf, Az. 18 K 301/08 paras. 20, 34–40, 50–52, May 7, 2008 (emphasis added); BVerfG, 1 B.v.R. 436/03, April 29, 2003; VG Düsseldorf, Az. 18 K 74/05, May 30, 2005; BVerwG, 6 C 25.12, September 11, 2013.

51 Hessischer VGH, Az. 7 A 1590/12 para. 21, September 28, 2012.

In Switzerland, the Federal Supreme Court exempted female Muslim students from mixed swimming lessons in 1993.[52] Fifteen years later, when the number of Muslims in Switzerland had increased, the Court overruled its decision and held that mixed swimming classes were mandatory. In justifying this reversal, the Court explained that in 1990 there were 152,220 Muslims in Switzerland, while in 2008 the number had reached 400,000. Amazingly, to support this claim, the Court cited a blog post titled "Switzerland is on its way to become an Islamic State" (*Schweiz auf dem Weg zum Islam-Staat*) published by an Israeli Jew on his blog (IsraSwiss.ch), a very uncommon judicial practice. It ruled that swimming lessons are needed for "integration," "social cohesion," and a "harmonious society." Immigrants in a foreign country "must regularly accept changes and limitations to their own ways of life." Indeed, boys see partially naked female co-students in swimming lessons but, according to the Court, this "cannot be prevented." In Switzerland, people daily see girls on the streets wearing short skirts and the immigrants "*should learn to deal with it.*"[53]

A third example is the minaret ban. On November 29, 2009, 57.5 percent of Swiss voters approved a referendum to ban the building of minarets in Switzerland. Consequently, the ban has been incorporated into the Federal Constitution. Article 72(3) of the Constitution provides that "the building of minarets is prohibited." Amending the Constitution is possible through a mechanism of direct democracy; one such popular mechanism, a popular initiative, grants 100,000 voters—about 2 percent of the electorate—the right to propose an amendment to the Federal Constitution.

In 2009, when the ban was passed, minarets were rare; there were only four minarets at the time in Switzerland: in Zurich, Geneva, Winterthur, and Wengen. After the ban was passed, the Isopublic Institute conducted a poll to investigate the reasons for the vote. It found that minarets were perceived as a symbol of Islam; the vote was against an Islamic symbol. As historian Jean-François Mayer explains: "The four main reasons for voting Yes appeared to be the conviction that minarets do not belong in Swiss landscape or culture; the belief that Islam is intolerant and hampers the building of churches in the country; fear of Islam's excessive influence and expansion; and the idea that Muslims should adapt and integrate."[54]

[52] BGer, 119 B.G.E. Ia 178, June 18, 1993.

[53] BGer, 135 B.G.E. I 79 para. 7.2, October 24, 2008 (emphasis added).

[54] Jean-François Mayer, "In the Shadow of the Minaret: Origins and Implications of a Citizens' Initiative," in *The Swiss Minaret Ban: Islam in Question*, Patrick Haenni and Stéphane Lathion, eds., Tom Genrich, trans. (Fribourg: Religioscope Institute, 2011): pp. 10–16 at 16.

Demographic concerns lie at the center of these three examples. In Switzerland, a demographic change was found to be a key reason for the "Yes" vote in an *ex-post* analysis of electoral behavior. In Germany and Switzerland, the judicial decisions on mixed swimming lessons in public schools should be seen within the context of the growing number of Muslim communities. And in the Netherlands, the issue of handshaking, which has never been at the core of liberalism, cannot be separated from the demographic context.

It seems that Europe has internalized the fact that Muslims are not about to "disappear" and focuses on their visibility in the public sphere. As Olivier Roy states, "It is no longer the physical presence of immigrants which is considered problematic, but the visibility of Islam as a religion."[55] John Bower rightly notes that, to be counted as "Europeans," Muslims are expected to "pretend to be something other than Muslims."[56] In other words, Muslims are accepted, as long as they are *invisible* in the public sphere.

Christian heritage

The "Muslim question" in Europe is interwoven with a broader debate over European identity. Due to various reasons—globalization, the creation of the European Union, the declining European population, the economic crisis, etc.—"There is an angst over identity in Europe," argues Vincent Geisser, "There's a feeling that Europe is becoming smaller and less important. Europe is like an old lady, who whenever she hears a noise thinks it's a burglary." In this reality, Islam is "a box in which everyone expresses their fears."[57] Islam crystallizes Europe's anxiety over its past and its future; it steps into the ongoing debate over European identity.[58]

Europe's cultural conflicts over Islamic symbols hide deeper conflicts over the role of religion in the public sphere: how religiously neutral should the public sphere be? While Islamic symbols, the *burqa* or the

[55] Olivier Roy, "Islam in Europe: An Ordinary Religion Like Any Other," in *The Swiss Minaret Ban* (n 54): pp. 90–95 at 90; Olivier Roy, *Globalized Islam: The Search for a New Ummah* (New York: Columbia University Press, 2004): pp. 26–29.

[56] John R. Bowen, *Can Islam Be French? Pluralism and Pragmatism in a Secularist State* (Princeton: Princeton University Press, 2010): p. 5.

[57] Cited in Steven Erlanger, "French Mosque's Symbolism Varies With Beholder," *New York Times*, December 27, 2009.

[58] Anne Norton, *On the Muslim Question* (Princeton: Princeton University Press, 2013): pp. 23–24.

minaret, are new in Europe, Christian symbols *are already there*; they have been part of Europe's landscape for centuries. "Parisians may not notice a cross or a church," John Bowen notes, but "they certainly notice a headscarf or a minaret."[59] Unlike Jews, whose history as a widely dispersed people is acknowledged nowadays and whose "Europeanness" no longer constitutes a "problem," the Europeanness of Muslims is still contentious.

At stake, however, is more than the role of religion in the public sphere; it is Christian heritage and tradition. Europe's Christian heritage is easy to observe. One just needs to examine national constitutions, which in many cases include archaic "Christian clauses," as well as national anthems, symbols, and holidays. Indicating that Christianity is part of the constitutional identity of Member States does not necessarily refer to Christianity as a religion. Europe is largely secular. Churches are sparsely attended and the religious identity of many Christian Europeans is relatively weak (see Chapter 1). In this regard, constitutional "Christian clauses"[60] tell more about a country's past and its heritage, than its present-day society. Christian clauses and symbols have become a cultural icon. Susanne Baer neatly terms it the "culturalization of religion."[61]

The "culturalization of religion" is best illustrated by the *Lauti* case. On March 18, 2011, the Grand Chamber of the European Court of Human Rights issued its judgment as to whether the display of crucifixes on the walls of public classrooms in Italy violates the European Convention for the Protection of Human Rights and Fundamental Freedoms. The issue was brought before the Court by Soile Lautsi, a Finnish-born atheist citizen who had moved to Italy and appealed on behalf of her minor children. The Italian government, which defended the use of the crucifix, argued that the crucifix is "a historical and cultural symbol." The crucifix, it claimed, is part of Italy's "national particularity" and keeping it hanging on the walls in schools is a "matter of preserving a centuries-old tradition." While the majority did not directly rule on this matter, it held that, whatever other meanings the crucifix may have, it is "above all a

[59] Bowen, p. 3 (n 56).

[60] Alexander Yakobson, "God and Religion in Modern Democratic Constitutions," in *Contemporary Challenges to the Nation State: Global and Israeli Perspectives*, vol. II, *The Nation State and Religion: The Resurgence of Faith*, Anita Shapira, Yedidia Z. Stern, and Alexander Yakobson, eds. (Eastbourne: Sussex Academic Press, 2013): pp. 1–13.

[61] Susanne Baer, "A Closer Look at Law: Human Rights as Multi-Level Sites of Struggles Over Multi-Dimensional Equality," *Utrecht Law Review* 6, no. 2 (2010): pp. 56–76 at 58–61.

religious symbol" that "undoubtedly refers to Christianity." In spite of the religious connotation, the Court ruled that, as long as there is no indoctrination, states enjoy a wide "margin of appreciation"[62] in setting their curriculum.[63]

In a concurring opinion, Judge Bonello discussed the tension between secularism and religion, cultural symbols and state neutrality: "A court of human rights cannot allow itself to suffer from historical Alzheimer's. It has no right to disregard the cultural continuum of a nation's flow through time, nor to ignore what, over the centuries, has served to mould and define the profile of a people." In Judge Bonello's view, as long as the crucifix remains a voiceless badge on the wall with no religious indoctrination, its presence does not infringe upon freedom from religion; removing the crucifix is "a major act of cultural vandalism."[64] What is so interesting in Judge Bonello's opinion is that it does not sweep the challenge of Italian identity under the carpet, but candidly addresses it.

The Muslim issue should be viewed in light of Europe's broad debate over its identity. Handshaking, mixed swimming lessons, and minarets are only the tip of the iceberg. Paradoxically, Muslim migrants have pushed Europeans to reaffirm, even if symbolically, their Christian heritage.

The European experience

Compared to the United States, the share of international migration in Europe is low. And yet, Europe's challenge seems more acute. This reality is the outcome of various factors, including a sharply different culture (and religion) brought by migrants over a short period, which is followed by integration difficulties even in the third generation. To this one should add social tensions, violence, and discrepancies in perceptions of human rights and liberal values. But as serious as these challenges are, Europe is far from facing a "cultural invasion" or a "demographic revolution." The examples of handshaking, swimming lessons, and minarets represent moral panic. To a large extent, they are a symptom of a broader debate over European (and national) identity and over the role of religion in the public sphere. Interestingly, they show

[62] Under the "margin of appreciation doctrine" the Court defers to the national level on controversial topics in which no European consensus exists.

[63] *Lautsi* v. *Italy*Application 30814/06 (E.Ct.H.R., March 18, 2011): paras. 15, 36, 66, 71, 69, respectively.

[64] *Lautsi*, paras. 1.1, 1.4 (n 63).

how Member States violate the same values they seek to protect (see Chapter 4) and leave little room for cultural diversity. These examples reveal that, while Member States declare the failure of multiculturalism, the option of a multicultural way of life is not fully viable for migrants and minorities. Talks about "moderate Islam" hide a desire for a liberal Islam, a kind of "Islam-lite," which is friendly to homosexuals and sexual permissiveness.

ISRAEL

Israel is among the countries with the highest percentage of migrants in the world. Nonetheless, it is conspicuously absent from most migration studies. Until the beginning of the twenty-first century, with very few exceptions, Israel admitted only Jewish migrants and spouses of Jews. This reality has changed with an increasing wave of non-Jewish migration. Israel's changing demographics present a case of "cultural defense," which is different from the American and European cases. The following pages briefly describe Israel's demographic concerns in the immigration context.

Becoming an immigration country

Aliyah—immigration of Jews and their families to Israel—was the main source of population growth outside the natural population growth for the newly established Jewish state. Immigration was not on Israel's agenda at the time of the country's foundation for three reasons: first, Israel's borders were defined by the armistice lines established after the War of Independence; second, beleaguered by security and economic problems, Israel was not a magnet for migrants; and third, Israel did not have an economic need for a foreign labor force, particularly given the large pool of workers among new Jewish arrivals and local Arab citizens. All these factors changed after the Six-Day War in 1967. The occupied territories included a large and poor population, offering new labor opportunities. Israel's economy grew significantly; and the consistent drop in the number of Jewish migrants increased the demand for a non-Israeli labor force, which was initially supplied from the occupied territories.

Since the late 1990s, three significant processes have occurred: first, the number of Palestinian family immigrants has increased. Following the 1993 "Oslo Accord"—the peace agreement between Israel and the Palestine Liberation Organization—tens of thousands of Palestinians from the West Bank and the Gaza Strip entered Israel to reunite with their Palestinian Israeli families. Second, the number of non-Jewish workers has increased. Israel has become an attractive destination for labor migrants. It has encouraged foreign migration to replace the Palestinian labor force, which, for security reasons, is no longer a stable source of labor following the outbreak of the "Second Intifada" in 2000. Many migrants have remained in Israel, some have had children, and their temporary stay has often become permanent. Third, the number of asylum seekers has increased. Due to its geographical location and economic prosperity, Israel has become a preferred destination for asylum seekers. The genocide in Darfur and other ethnic and national conflicts have attracted a large number of asylum seekers to Israel, arriving at its southern border after a grueling journey from east Africa via Egypt.

Taken together, these processes have changed the face of non-Jewish immigration to Israel. In two decades (1993–2013), the number of non-Jewish immigrants—family members, foreign workers (both documented and undocumented workers), and asylum seekers—has increased to a total of approximately 400,000 people, about 5 percent of Israel's population.[65] The exact number is unknown because, despite the changing reality, Israel does not maintain reliable immigration statistics. It continues to deny that it has changed from an "*aliyah* country" to an "immigration country" that absorbs a considerable number of non-Jewish migrants. The Supreme Court of Israel even ruled that "Israel's character is essentially perceived an 'aliyah country,' namely, a repatriation country, rather than an 'immigration country'... migration appears to be a concept of 'all other nations' that is incompatible with Israel's unique entity and its Zionist vision."[66]

Immigration and a Jewish state

The growing number of non-Jewish migrants has led to anti-immigrant sentiment. Prime Minister Benjamin Netanyahu stated that "Israel is being flooded by waves of refugees who threaten its Jewish character" and argued that "infiltrators are conquering Tel Aviv." This is not a rare statement. On different occasions, Netanyahu asserted that "undocumented African migrants threaten the identity of the Jewish State."

[65] This figure includes around 300,000 foreign workers (including undocumented aliens and infiltrators) and 100,000 family migrants. For data, see Israel Population and Immigration Authority, "Data About Aliens in Israel," 2013.

[66] AdminA 1644/05, *Frieda* v. *Ministry of the Interior*, June 29, 2005.

"If we do not stop this," he said, "60,000 infiltrators may become 600,000 and possibly bring about the end of Israel as a Jewish democracy." Former Minister of the Interior, Eli Yishai, was even more dramatic: "Infiltrators along with Palestinians would quickly bring the Zionist dream to an end. Since the destruction of the Second Temple the Jewish People has not faced such a tangible threat." Yishai, a former member of the ultra-Orthodox Shas Party, held that Israel, a country of "the white men," should not "import problems from Africa." In a similar line, former Minister of Justice, Yaakov Neeman, declared: "Saying that the situation is catastrophic is an understatement. It is an existential threat... we have a right to preserve Israel as a Jewish and democratic state."[67] On national politics, anti-immigrant sentiments are not just nativist, but often racist.

Israel's immigration challenge must be viewed in the larger context of its demographic situation. According to predictions of the Central Bureau of Statistics, in 2034, about 23 percent of Israel's population will be Arabs, and an additional 17 percent will be ultra-Orthodox Jews (*Haredim*). Combined, these two communities are likely to become a majority by 2059 (see Table 2.3). In 2017, 44 percent of the students in Israel's education system aged 6 to 18 will study in a separate publicly-subsidized education system, *Haredi* schools and Arab schools, while 56 percent of the students will study in public schools.[68] This is a challenge to Israel's liberal character. Large parts of these communities hold different views on family values, women's rights, and freedom of religion. A growing *Haredi*/Arab group presents another challenge. Economically, these communities are the poorest in Israel, and their share in welfare spending is relatively high. They are exempt from military service and their combined majority means that only a minority of citizens would be called upon to serve their country at a decisive moment. Israel faces, therefore, a domestic demographic challenge, even before considering additional non-Jewish immigration.

In order to cope with the immigration challenge, the Israeli government decided to draft an immigration law that would "assure Israel's

[67] Eli Bernstein, "Netanyahu: To Exclude the Infiltrators, They Threaten National Identity," *Maariv*, May 20, 2012; Shalom Yerushalmi, "Eli Yishai in a Special Interview: It's We or They," *Maariv*, June 1, 2012; Noam Sharvit, Kalman Libeskind, and Harel Segal, "Loyal to His Approach: The Minister of Justice Talks," *Maariv*, February 17, 2012.

[68] Israel Central Bureau of Statistics, "Back to School: Selected Data from 'Society in Israel—Report No. 5' and CBS Data," 2012.

TABLE 2.3 POPULATION PROJECTIONS BY TYPE AND YEAR FOR ISRAEL

Group	*percentage (medium variant)*			
	2009	2019	2034	2059
Jews and "others" (without Haredim)	70	66	60	50
Haredim	10	12	17	27
Arabs	20	22	23	23

Source: Ari Paltiel et al., "Long-Range Population Projections for Israel: 2009–2059," Israel Central Bureau of Statistics, 2012: pp. 46–47.

Notes: (a) "Arabs" include Muslim Arabs, Christian Arabs, and Druzes; (b) "Others" include non-Arab Christians and not-religiously affiliated.

existence as a Jewish and democratic state."[69] Israel's Jewish and democratic character is anchored in the Basic Laws, its informal constitution. The idea of a Jewish state contains different meanings yet, legally, in the context of immigration law, it entails maintaining a solid Jewish majority by giving a preference to Jewish immigration. Maintaining a solid Jewish majority is perceived to be essential for the existence of a Jewish state in which the Jewish people's right to a state-based self-determination is achieved.

In spite of the plan to redesign its immigration policy, Israel has not yet codified an immigration law outside the framework of the Law of Return.[70] The ability to join the Jewish-Israeli society is still largely determined by ethnic and religious criteria. Apart from rare exceptions, it is practically impossible to become a naturalized Israeli unless the person is:

(a) A Jew: The Law of Return provides that "Every Jew has the right to come to this country [Israel]." It embraces the *halakhic* religious definition of a Jew—a "person who was born of a Jewish mother or has become converted to Judaism and who is not a member of another religion." Eligibility under the Law of Return is further granted to "a child and a grandchild of a Jew," namely, persons of partly Jewish descent.

(b) A close relative of a Jew: the right of a Jew is vested in a "spouse of a Jew, the spouse of a child of a Jew and the spouse of a grandchild of a Jew."

(c) A spouse of an Israeli citizen, either Jewish or non-Jewish.[71]

[69] Resolution 3805, 30th Government (2005).

[70] Ministry of the Interior, "Advisory Committee for the Review of Israel's Immigration Policy 2006," 2006.

[71] Law of Return (1950): arts. 1, 4A(a), 4B.

What is the reason for Israel's demographic anxiety? The answer to this question varies. For some, Jewish character is an end in itself. It should be preserved due to the intrinsic value of a Jewish state. Within this group, there are those who believe that a Jewish state means Jewish culture; those who believe that a Jewish state requires a religious Jewish majority; and those who believe that a Jewish state is an ethnic project (Jewish blood). For others, a Jewish state is a means to an end. Some people believe that in the Middle East, a Jewish state is a prerequisite for a democratic state. This claim is grounded in the empirical proposition that among countries with a Muslim majority, not even one is a liberal democracy. There are other versions of this claim. Some people hold that a Jewish state is a means to guarantee the safety and security of Jews; only a state-based Jewish majority can effectively protect Jews in the Land of Israel.

Israel's concerns are quite different from those of America and Europe. There is a broad consensus in Israel regarding the need to maintain a solid Jewish majority. But unlike America and Europe, in which migrants are largely accepted as long as they are (culturally, economically, politically) integrated into the society (in spite of different concepts of integration), Israeli citizenship is generally not open to people who are not at least partially ethnically Jewish, even if they are willing to become cultural Israelis. Thus, *Haredi* Jews can easily become Israeli citizens, even if they do not speak Hebrew, have different views of liberal values, do not serve in the army, study in a separate education system, rarely marry a secular Jew, live in separate neighborhoods, and participate on a limited basis in the national labor force. Similarly, people of Jewish descent have a right to migrate to Israel, even if their mother is not Jewish. They are socially accepted by the non-Orthodox Jewish population and undergo a process labeled "sociological conversion."[72] At the same time, children of non-Jewish foreign workers can rarely become citizens, even if they were born and educated in Israel, speak Hebrew, serve in the army, identify with the country, pledge allegiance to Israel, learn its history, and adopt its culture.

Immigration and the Israeli-Palestinian conflict

The Israeli case has some distinguishing features. One is rooted in Palestinian migrants. Generally, migrants do not create or join an already

[72] Alexander Yakobson, "Joining the Jewish People: Non-Jewish Immigrants from the Former USSR, Israeli Identity and Jewish Peoplehood," *Israel Law Review* 43, no. 1 (2010): pp. 218–239 at 226–227.

existing large minority group in the receiving country. Palestinian newcomers to Israel, however, join a large Palestinian minority—about 17 percent of the citizenry. Hence, their migration raises issues of the relationship between majority and minority. It touches upon the Jewish concern that Palestinian citizens will become a majority group in Israel.

The Jewish demographic anxiety and the case of Palestinian migration are rooted in the core of the Israeli-Palestinian conflict. In one aspect, the conflict is, at least partially, a "demographic contest" over sovereignty and self-determination in the same land. Both Jews and Palestinians view Israel/Palestine as their homeland and seek self-determination in at least part of it. The Partition Plan for Palestine, adopted by U.N. Resolution 181 on November 29, 1947, meant that the two groups in Palestine, Jews and Arabs, would have their own states—a Jewish-majority state alongside a Palestinian-majority state. This was supposed to be a political solution that would allow two peoples with intense attachments to the same land to live side by side. In this context, a large volume of Palestinian migrants is perceived by the Jewish majority as undermining the "two-state solution" since it may lead to a Palestinian majority in Israel, thereby undermining the idea of a Jewish-majority state alongside a Palestinian-majority state. This concern is not without historical precedent. If there is one people in recent history that should clearly understand the power of a demographic change and its potential consequences, it is the Jewish people. The mass Jewish migration to Palestine, motivated by the Zionist movement, created a new reality that could hardly be ignored by the international community. In fact, the U.N. Partition Plan was grounded upon recognition of this reality.

The demographic anxiety of the Jewish majority is intensified by five other factors. First, Israeli-Palestinian relations are followed by a high level of hostility and ongoing armed conflict. Thus, Palestinian migration to Israel raises national security considerations that do not usually exist in ordinary cases of migration. Second, Palestinians have historical claims over lands in Israel, according to which lands were unjustly taken from them by the Jews. Some consider themselves as repatriates, not as migrants, in the same way as Jews in the Diaspora view themselves. Third, Israel and the Palestinian territories are neighboring entities. Contiguous territory, especially when associated with wide economic gaps between the two territories, makes migration easier. Moving from one place to another is not "migration," but more like "relocation." Fourth, a subjective perception by each side that it is the victim: The Holocaust and the history of the Jews as a "battered nation," alongside the Palestinians history as an oppressed people, accelerate mutual fears. And fifth, each side perceives itself to be a fragile nation: Jews are a large majority in Israel, yet a tiny minority in a predominantly-Arab area; in contrast, Arabs are a minority in Israel, yet a majority in the Middle East. Combined, these factors place the issue of Palestinian migration at the center of a fierce political conflict.

THE GATEKEEPERS

People have always moved from one place to another to find new jobs, improve their lives, join their families, and escape conflicts. Their movement has very often been met by suspicion and fear in the host society. From ancient Egypt to contemporary liberal democracies—demographic anxiety has always characterized the political reaction to migrants and minorities.

Understanding the demographic concern is essential, especially if one assumes, reasonably I believe, that it will continue to be interwoven with national politics and international relations. Throughout history, demographic anxiety has displayed similar features—exaggerated facts that have often led to incorrect conclusions, resulting in disproportionate policies. In retrospect, demographic fears have often been proven to lack merit. Is there a reason to believe that contemporary concerns are better-grounded?

Immigration laws are the gatekeepers. They are designed to "deal wisely" with migrants—to allow acceptance of the desirable people while excluding the undesirable. An examination of immigration laws reveals national choices. Recent immigration laws mirror the choices made by the United States, European states, and Israel. This subject is presented in Chapter 3.

3

Cultural Defense

We are a Nation with the duty to survive.

—The U.S. Supreme Court (1931)[1]

Douglas Macintosh moved from Canada to the United States in 1916 and became a professor of theology at Yale University. He hoped to receive American citizenship, but his application was rejected. Macintosh was a selective pacifist. He was willing to pledge allegiance to the U.S. Constitution—even to fight for it in a morally justified war—but refused to make a blanket promise to bear arms: "I am willing to do what I judge to be in the best interests of my country, but only in so far as I can believe that this is not going to be against the best interests of humanity."[2] Macintosh's allegiance, however, was limited. In his court hearing, he declared that he would be loyal to the U.S. Constitution, but his prime loyalty would be to God.

In one of the most fascinating cases in the corpus of American constitutional law, the U.S. Supreme Court denied Macintosh's petition. The Court regarded his statement as undermining the very essence of Americanism—the rule of law and the supremacy of the U.S. Constitution. In America, the Court ruled, the power to decide what is a morally justified war belongs to "the wisdom of Congress," not to individual discretion. When Macintosh made "*his own interpretation* of the will of God the decisive test" for his actions, he became unfit to be an American. In a rare judicial statement, the U.S. Supreme Court noted that "We are a Christian people," acknowledging "with reverence the duty of obedience to the will of God." Nevertheless, the Court added, "we are a Nation with the duty to survive," requiring "unqualified allegiance to the Nation."[3]

[1] *United States* v. *Macintosh* 283 U.S. 605, p. 625 (1931).

[2] *Macintosh*, p. 618 (n 1).

[3] *Macintosh*, pp. 624–625 (n 1).

These are strong words. Judges do not usually speak this way. The Court apparently found important interests at stake. Macintosh provoked a debate on the essence of Americanism and the core meaning of belonging to America. His statements, according to the majority, were un-American. The dissenting opinion, by contrast, found the essence of Americanism to be slightly more diverse. Macintosh could qualify for citizenship, in spite of his conscientious objections, because there are other "important methods of defense, even in time of war, apart from the personal bearing of arms."[4]

Immigrants encourage nation-states to define themselves. Immigration law serves as a means for immigrants to subscribe to the tenets of the community. In order to design immigration requirements, however, the community must first define its tenets. The substance of the requirements "we" demand of "them" is about "us." Immigration policy thus echoes constitutional identity, by mirroring not only the qualities that "we" value in others, but also by reflecting what defines "us" as a nation. In a sense, drafting immigration requirements is a form of nation-building. A political community, whose members are linked through a common project, is engaged in an attempt to determine the nature of the common project, the essence of the social contract, and the bond (glue, tie, attachment) that binds the people together.

Chapter 3 aims to identify recent responses to migration as translated into law and policy in the immigration context. The chapter shows that immigration policies have increasingly taken a restrictive course, mainly in Europe. This includes a process that I label "cultural convergence," under which liberal democracies define the essence of their citizenship, and thereby the rules for joining the community, in cultural terms. The analyzed cases—Europe, America, and Israel—vary one from the other. While in Europe admission and naturalization criteria are largely culturally thickening, they have been gradually thinning in the United States. The two cases of Europe and the United States represent a different philosophy of naturalization, as does Israel, the third case discussed in this chapter. In Israel, becoming a citizen is not a matter of knowledge of civic political culture, or acceptance of national culture, but one of birthright.

"Cultural defense" takes place by using five legal mechanisms: (a) citizenship tests, (b) language requirements, (c) loyalty oaths, (d) attachment

[4] *Macintosh*, p. 631 (n 1). The Court overruled the Macintosh case in *Girouard* v. *United States* 328 U.S. 61, pp. 64–65 (1946) (discussed in Ch. 4).

requirements, and (e) integration contracts. Together with other means involved in the naturalization process, such as citizenship ceremonies, immigration law provides a unique platform to reflect on three issues: defining the "we," setting criteria for identifying the desired "they," and finding the core to which "they" should subscribe to become part of "us."

The first issue concerns the question of who "we" are. For the first time in history, nation-states have attempted to legally define their collective identity. In so doing, the immigration process mirrors not only who "we" are (or think "we" are), and what kind of nation "we" want to be, but also spells out what "we" want other people to think "we" are. The second issue relates to the "other." Setting admission criteria helps clarify who is, in the state's view, a "good citizen," and the current understanding of what it means to become a citizen in a liberal state. For example, is citizenship like a bar exam—one can *learn* how to become a citizen by memorizing knowledge of a country's civics and history and learning its language; or, is citizenship about values with which a citizen should *identify*; or, is citizenship about demonstrating patterns of good *behavior*? The third issue is related to the level of compatibility between the first two issues—in what sense does joining a new community require confirmation of its essentials.

EUROPE

The following pages briefly describe counter-reactions to immigration in Europe, focusing on four Member States: France, Germany, the Netherlands, and the United Kingdom. Although these are limited examples, they provide a clear picture of current trends in Europe. On the whole, these cases demonstrate a process of "culturalization" under which culture increasingly becomes a dominant factor in immigration selection.

The French Communauté

Faiza Silmi was lawfully admitted into France. She married a French citizen and gave birth to three French-born children. She did everything necessary to become a French citizen, but her application for citizenship was nonetheless rejected. Her traditional headdress, the *niqab*, was incompatible with French values, claimed the French officials. Silmi filed a petition in court to reverse the decision, but lost. She did not give up and challenged the lower court's decision in the highest French administrative court, le Conseil d'Etat. On June 27, 2008, the Conseil d'Etat upheld the denial of her citizenship based on "insufficient assimilation" into the French Republic. It ruled that Silmi adopted a "radical religious practice," incompatible with the "values essential to the French *communauté*, notably the principle of gender equality."[5] The Conseil d'Etat invoked a provision in the French Civil Code according to which "the government may, on grounds of indignity or lack of assimilation other than linguistic, oppose the acquisition of French nationality by the foreign spouse," and that "no one may be naturalised unless he proves his assimilation into the French community."[6] It was the first time in French history that a citizenship application had been officially rejected on this ground.

The exact reasons for the Conseil d'Etat's decision are not clear. It is uncertain whether Silmi was denied citizenship due to her belief, her conduct, or both. Silmi arrived at the immigration interview wearing a *niqab*. She refused to remove it for identification or for a passport photo, even after she was offered the opportunity to be interviewed by a woman. She told the officials that she was not interested in voting because "only men should vote." She was ignorant of *laïcité*—the French concept of secularism—and declared that she was a Salafi—an adherent of a radical Sunni sect. Most of these facts do not appear in the decision. Instead, they are found in the conclusions of the Government Commissioner.[7] Thus, it is unclear what the case stands for. Is the ruling based on wearing a *niqab* or refusing to vote? Is it because Silmi expressed no sense of belonging to the French Republic or because she was unwilling to participate in French political life? If the decision stands for what Silmi had inside her head, rather than what she wore on top of it, then it should not matter whether she wore a *niqab* or a thong. In addition, contrary to what was implied by the press,[8] the ruling is not based on the principle of *laïcité*, but on the principle of gender equality. The Conseil d'Etat found that Silmi's lifestyle and clothing reflected submission to her husband, thereby indicating gender inequality, and consequently insufficient assimilation. And still, this vague statement leaves unclear what is held in the case. Is the *niqab* the only religious headscarf indicating the

[5] Conseil d'Etat, N° 286798, June 27, 2008.

[6] Code Civil, arts. 21–24.

[7] Conclusions du Mme Prada Bordenave, Commissaire du Gouvernement, May 27, 2008.

[8] Stéphanie Le Bars, "Une Marocaine en Burqa se Voit Refuser la Nationalité Française," *Le Monde*, July 11, 2008; Katrin Bennhold, "A Veil Closes France's Door to Citizenship," *New York Times*, July 19, 2008.

absence of gender equality, or do other head-coverings transmit a similar message? Moreover, the case refers to "values essential of the French *communauté*," yet it does not specify what these values are. Is it the French *communauté*, or French *nationalité*? What exactly is being defended in the French Civil Code?

The Conseil d'Etat's decision is typical of an emerging trend. As of January 2007, every migrant must sign a "Reception and Integration Contract" (*Contrat d'accueil et d'intégration*) in order to receive a permanent residence permit.[9] By signing the contract, the migrant promises to respect the "fundamental values of the Republic," take French language lessons, and participate in a one-day civic training course. During the training session, the person learns about French values by watching a film entitled *Living Together in France*, which exposes the migrant to the French motto *Liberté, Égalité, Fraternité*, and is followed by a personal interview to test his or her knowledge and language skills. Noncompliance with the contract's terms can lead to a refusal to issue a residence permit, non-renewal of the permit, and a fine. Recently, France has adopted a new policy of "pre-departure integration" (or "integration from abroad"). According to this policy, newcomers, including spouses of French citizens, have to participate in French language classes and orientation courses covering fundamental values of the Republic even before entering France for the first time.[10] The purpose of the policy is to familiarize people with the French language and values before being admitted into France.

The *Contrat d'accueil et d'intégration* is an interesting exercise in nation-building. The contract seeks to reflect the core of French identity and its fundamental essentials. It explains that the "French are attached to a history, a culture, and fundamental values"; that living together means knowing and respecting French values; that the Republic is indivisible, secular, democratic, and social; that sovereignty belongs to the people; and that religion is a private matter. The contract puts an emphasis on gender equality. Migrants must sign that parents are jointly responsible for their children and that women are not subject to the authority of their husbands.

[9] Décret n° 2006-1791 du 23 décembre 2006 relatif au contrat d'accueil et d'intégration et au contrôle des connaissances en français d'un étranger souhaitant durablement s'installer en France et modifiant le code de l'entrée et du séjour des étrangers et du droit d'asile (partie réglementaire); L-311-9-1 du code de l'entrée et du séjour des étrangers et du droit d'asile; Loi n° 2006-911 du 24 juillet 2006 relative à l'immigration et à l'intégration, art. 5 (Loi n° 2006-911).

[10] Loi n° 2006-911, art. 7.

The integration contract is followed by another contract, "The Charter of Rights and Duties of a French Citizen" (*Charte des droits et des devoirs du citoyen français*), which must be signed as part of the naturalization process. The Charter is a kind of "social contract" specifying the terms for joining the French community. The migrant must promise to respect French values (*Liberté, Égalité, Fraternité*), principles (a secular, democratic, and social Republic), and symbols (the Marseillaise, the Tricolore, Marianne), and be loyal to the Republic. "In return," France recognizes him or her as a citizen.[11] Reading the Charter, one gets a sense of French constitutional essentials. It is like a quasi-constitution summarizing the essence of Frenchness from a wide range of sources. Putting them together in one document is not a simple task. But in so doing, France tells migrants—here are "our" essentials and what is most important to "us." These are the fundamental values of the Republic—the "values essential to the French *communauté*," to use the language of the Conseil d'Etat—that non-French must embrace to become French citizens.

In 2012, the French government decided that applicants for citizenship would have to demonstrate sufficient knowledge of French history, culture, and society by passing a citizenship test.[12] In October 2012, however, the new government announced that it was abandoning the implementation of the test. Manuel Valls, the new Minister of the Interior, declared: "You do not become French by answering a quiz."[13] While the formal quiz has been abandoned, assimilation is still tested by answering questions about French history, culture, and society during the immigration interview.[14] Questions are cognitive and relatively simple; issues include the Constitution of the Fifth Republic, the French Revolution, the Edict of Nantes, colonialism, World War II, the Marseillaise, secularism, taxes, and the European Union. The topics were revised during 2012 to include French culture: the Eiffel Tower, the Louvre, Brigitte Bardot, Edith Piaf, Auguste Rodin, Molière, and the like. In order to become French, it is apparently insufficient to cite principles from the Declaration of the Rights of Man and of the Citizen

[11] Décret n° 2012-127 du 30 janvier 2012 approuvant la charte des droits et devoirs du citoyen français prévue à l'article 21-24 du code civil.

[12] Décret n° 2012-126 du 30 janvier 2012 relatif au niveau et à l'évaluation de la connaissance de l'histoire, de la culture et de la société françaises requis des postulants à la nationalité française au titre de l'article 21-24 du code civil.

[13] Ministère de l'Intérieur, "Accueil des Nouveaux Citoyens Français," October 19, 2012.

[14] Décret n° 2013-794 du 30 août 2013 portant modification du décret n° 93-1362 du 30 décembre 1993 relatif aux déclarations de nationalité, aux décisions de naturalisation, de réintégration, de perte, de déchéance et de retrait de la nationalité française.

and be familiar with French history; one must know something about French culture. "The Frenchman," writes Sanche de Gramont, "is not someone who possesses a navy blue passport and speaks the language of Descartes, but someone who knows who broke the Soissons vase, what happened to Buridan's donkey, why Parmentier gave his name to a hash, and why Charles Martel saved Christendom."[15] Gramont's concept of Frenchness may be too broad—it includes French folkways—but the question is worth pondering: who is (legally) French and how should one become French?

The questions "Who is a Frenchman?" and "What are the qualities one should possess to become French?" are puzzling. In November 2009, President Sarkozy launched a nationwide discussion over the meaning of being French. "What is French?" he asked the public.[16] The three-month public debate sparked a heated discussion, both over the wisdom of such a debate and over the essence of being French. Sarkozy's question, "For you, what does it mean to be French?" yielded hundreds of public meetings and newspaper articles.[17] Whether the campaign was a political ploy or a real exercise in nation-building, it was an interesting move. It shows that when nations start to examine what holds a people together, they often conclude that there are more sources of division than unity. As Patrick Weil shows in a detailed study of French citizenship, becoming French is a dynamic concept that changes frequently. "Since the Revolution," Weil explains, "France has changed its [nationality] laws more often and more significantly than any other democratic nation has."[18]

The national debate over the essence of French identity provides a rare opportunity to get a sense of the French's perception of themselves and their expectation of the process of becoming French. Thousands of citizens engaged in an attempt to conceptualize a definition of French identity. The finding, as one study points out, is that "it is impossible to

[15] Cited in Karl E. Meyer, "Who Gets to Be French?," *New York Times*, April 11, 2012.

[16] Circulaire IMIK0900089C du 2 novembre 2009 relative l'organisation du grand débat sur l'identité nationale.

[17] Ministère de l'Intérieur, "Intervention de M. Eric Besson Lors de la Conclusion de la 1ère Étape du Grand Débat sur l'Identité Nationale, le Vendredi 5 Février 2010," February 5, 2010; InfraForces and Obea, "Francais et l'Identite Nationale," *20 Minutes*, 2010; TNS Sofres, "Les Français et l'Identité Nationale," *La Croix*, 2009.

[18] Patrick Weil, *How to Be French: Nationality in the Making since 1789*, Catherine Porter, trans. (Durham: Duke University Press, 2008): p. 3.

provide a single definition of what constitutes the French national identity." Nevertheless, if one wishes to extract from the process France's collective psyche, one may identify three main tenets. The first tenet is French history and culture. For many citizens, being French means pride in French heroes and heroines: statesmen such as de Gaulle and Napoleon; philosophers such as Montesquieu, Rousseau, and Voltaire; writers such as Hugo, Molière, and Zola; composers such as Debussy and Ravel; and artists such as Monet and Picasso. Being French means sharing in France's greatness, its history (the French Revolution, the Enlightenment), symbols (the Marseillaise, the Tricolor), popular culture (wine, cheese), and manners (gallantry, elegance, romanticism). The second tenet is the French language; being able to speak French is central to French identity. The third tenet is loyalty to French values—*Liberté, Égalité, Fraternité, Laïcité.*[19]

The debate over the essence of Frenchness was widely criticized. After all, it was not an academic exercise, but a government-led initiative to define the boundaries of French identity. For some, it was seen as a way to distinguish the "real French" from the "other." The discussion quickly became a debate over compatibility between Islam and French values. The disagreement in French society over its identity shows how difficult it is to define a national identity. It also raises the question whether the very idea of publishing a list of "French values" is not, in and of itself, un-French.[20]

If it is difficult to define "what is French?" perhaps it is easier to find "what is un-French?" Among the first candidates is the Islamic veil. In 2004, France passed a law banning the wearing of headscarves and all other conspicuous religious symbols in public schools. In 2010, France passed another law banning the wearing of veils in *all* public places: banks, post offices, hospitals, public transportation, shopping centers, and even streets.[21] The law was passed by an overwhelming majority—a 335:1 vote in the National Assembly and a 246:1 vote in the Senate—and was upheld

[19] Jean-François Caron, "Understanding and Interpreting France's National Identity: The Meanings of Being French," *National Identities* 15, no. 3 (2013): pp. 223–237 at 224–226.

[20] Jonathan Laurence and Gabriel Goodliffe, "The French Debate on National Identity and the Sarkozy Presidency: A Retrospective," *The International Spectator: Italian Journal of International Affairs* 48, no. 1 (2013): pp. 34–47 at 43.

[21] Loi n° 2010-1192 du 11 octobre 2010 interdisant la dissimulation du visage dans l'espace public. For a discussion of the law, see Christian Joppke and John Torpey, *Legal Integration of Islam: A Transatlantic Comparison* (Cambridge, Harvard University Press, 2013): pp. 21–47.

by the Constitutional Council.[22] It was widely endorsed by the public,[23] which even supported expanding the ban on religious symbols to private companies.[24] While police officers are not authorized to order the removal of the veil, they can issue a fine and impose citizenship lessons on those who violate the law. Presenting the bill, Jean-François Copé, the political leader of the Union for a Popular Movement, called the ban "a law of liberation."[25] Previously, President Sarkozy had said that a *burqa* was "not welcome in France" and called it a symbol of "submission." Officially, the *burqa* ban is justified mainly due to gender equality and human dignity. French law, to be clear, makes no explicit reference to Islam. It forbids face coverings in public places subject to a few exceptions, such as for health reasons or for motorcycle helmets. Éric Raoult, the rapporteur of the commission that recommended banning the *burqa*,[26] probably revealed too much by saying "we want to fight Islamic fundamentalism.... the burqa is a manifestation of that fundamentalism."[27]

France's "cultural defense" is related to its immigration challenge. In absolute and relative terms, France has the largest Muslim community in Europe. In 2010, 11.1 percent of its population was foreign-born: 7.8 percent in a non-EU state and 3.3 percent in EU states.[28] Failed integration policies directed at migrants from the Maghreb, mainly Algerians and Moroccans, together with social tensions that culminated in the 2005 civil unrest spearheaded by young migrants, signified that something was not working well. France has never been (or claimed to be) a multicultural society. The expectation has always been that migrants would become French by assimilating into French society. French scholar Olivier Roy says that "the French consider Anglo-Saxon multiculturalism either as the destruction of national unity or as an instrument of ghettoization." Roy claims that Muslims challenge French identity, not necessarily because of Islam, but since Muslims tend to display religious

[22] Décision n° 2010-613 DC du 7 octobre 2010.

[23] Pew Research Center, "Most Americans Disapprove: Widespread Support for Banning Full Islamic Veil in Western Europe," 2010: p. 1; LH2, "L'Observatoire de l'Opinion," *Le Nouvel Observateur*, 2010, p. 10.

[24] BVA, "La Démission de Jérôme Cahuzac—La laïcité," i>TELE, 2013: p. 12.

[25] "France to Ban Full Face Veil, Says Ruling Party Chief", RFI, December 16, 2009.

[26] Assemblée Nationale, "Rapport d'Information: Au Nom de la Mission d'Information sur la Pratique du Port du Voile Intégral sur le Territoire National," 2010: p. 13.

[27] Kyle James, "French Commission Recommends Banning the Burqa," Deutsche Welle, January 26, 2010.

[28] Katya Vasileva, "6.5% of the EU Population are Foreigners and 9.4% are Born Abroad," *Eurostat Statistic in Focus* 34 (2011): pp. 1–7 at 2.

symbols in the public sphere: "We have nothing against immigrants (at least for now), but we want secular Muslims.... The problem is not Islam but religion." Roy explains that "Islam seems to call into question the very identity of the country," mainly *laïcité*, the sacred French concept. Thus, France has adopted a policy of "militant *laïcité*." But, Roy wonders, "Is Islam such a threat, or has French identity reached such a crisis point that a few hundred veiled girls and bearded preachers can overwhelm it?"[29]

Back to Silmi: in 2008, Silmi's actions were compatible with French law. However, her beliefs or actions were found to be incompatible with the "values essential to the French *communauté*." Silmi contravened an accepted way of life. The Conseil d'Etat, however, did not offer guiding standards of what she should do, or avoid doing, in order to assimilate into the French way of life, nor did it provide a definition of those "values essential to the French *communauté*." In 2013, Silmi divorced and removed the *niqab*. Nevertheless, she stated "my faith in God remains the same; it's only this piece of cloth that has changed."[30] One may wonder whether, in spite of her statement, Silmi will finally obtain French citizenship. Silmi's belief and action may be incompatible with the "values essential to the French *communauté*," but, to a great extent, her case puts these values to the test.

The German Kulturnation

In September 2005, Baden-Württemberg's Minister of the Interior, Heribert Rech, introduced new guiding questions to assess the loyalty of migrants requesting naturalization to the liberal constitutional order. Under this policy, loyalty was assessed in an interview examining the applicant's beliefs and moral judgments. Let's take a look at a few examples:

- Imagine that your adult son comes to you and declares that he is a homosexual and would like to live with another man. How would you react?
- Your daughter applies for a job in Germany but she is rejected. Later, you discover that a black African from Somalia got the job. How would you react?

[29] Olivier Roy, *Secularism Confronts Islam*, George Holoch, trans. (New York: Columbia University Press, 2007): pp. x, 31, 102, 1, 2, respectively. See also pp. 16–22.

[30] Stéphanie Le Bars, "Vivre sans Voile Intégral, le Nouveau Départ de Faiza," *Le Monde*, December 22, 2010.

- Your adult daughter or your spouse would like to dress like other German girls and women. Would you try to prevent this?
- Some people accuse the Jews of being responsible for all the evil in the world, and even state that they were behind the September 11 attacks? Do you believe in such statements?

The Baden-Württemberg questionnaire is unusual in its intrusive questions—thirty in total—about gender equality, religion, politics, promiscuity, and marital relations—all in a two-hour oral exam. The *Land*'s Minister of the Interior explained the test's rationale: "Until now, we have always asked what the immigrants know about our constitution.... But there's a big difference between what one knows and what one believes or identifies with."[31] Amazingly, the questions were originally posed only to applicants from one of the fifty-seven Member States of the Organization of the Islamic Cooperation (OIC), or other applicants *"appearing to be Muslim."*[32]

The Baden-Württemberg questionnaire is not about law, but about morals. It does not ask whether the candidate would accept that certain norms are lawful in Germany. Instead, it focuses on personal beliefs and preferences. The questions are personal; they are about "your daughter," "your spouse," "your son." Some questions delve into the core of the private sphere and intimate familial relationship. One question asks a female applicant "what would you do if your daughter wishes to dress like other German girls" but "your husband is against it"? The right answer is "I would explain to my husband that our daughter at this age enjoys fundamental rights, such as the right to free development of her personality, which includes a right to dress according to her taste." And even when the questionnaire focuses on more neutral issues, such as gender equality and human dignity, it does not center on law but on morals; it asks, for instance, "are these principles according to your *personal* preferences?"

In March 2006, another *Land*, Hessen, announced a new naturalization test. This test is less intrusive and contains questions on ethics, politics, and culture. The Hessen test was never implemented due to the introduction of a replacement federal test, yet it provides a unique opportunity to understand the Hessian concept of being German. The applicant

[31] Charles Hawley, "Muslim Profiling: A German State Quizes Muslim Immigrants on Jews, Gays and Swim Lessons," *Spiegel*, January 31, 2006.

[32] Islamic Human Rights Commission, "The Über-Citizen and German Kulturkampf—s.10 German Naturalisation Law: A Front?," 2007: pp. 3–4.

first has to list three reasons for wanting to become a German citizen. Then he or she has to explain—it is not a multiple choice exam—the concepts of Reformation, the Holocaust, and constitutional principles, such as freedom of religion, freedom of speech, and equality. Next, the applicant has to explain "which measures are permitted and which are forbidden" when educating children, and whether "a woman should be allowed to be seen in public without being accompanied by a close male relative." In the next part, the applicant is asked to name German composers, poets, philosophers, athletes, and painters. The applicant needs to be familiar with symphonies of Beethoven and poems of Goethe and Schiller, name Nietzsche and Kant as German philosophers, mention Oliver Kahn and Michael Schumacher as German athletes, and refer to the *Chalk Cliffs on Rügen* as the inspiration for a painting by Caspar David Friedrich. Some questions require a high degree of social knowledge, for example, "To which sport event does the film 'The Miracle of Bern' refer?" (The 3:2 victory of Germany over Hungary in the 1954 World Cup Final in Bern).

The *Länder* tests do not necessarily mirror German identity, but rather what some Germans imagine or want it to be. They indicate an ideological concept of *Kulturnation*. By adopting these tests, some *Länder* embrace a strict policy of cultural assimilation. The rationale for this can be explained by Chancellor Angela Merkel: "Anyone coming here must respect our constitution and tolerate our Western and Christian roots.... Immigrants must respect our laws and acknowledge our democratic ways of doing things."[33] And yet, in searching for the German "ways of doing things," some *Länder* ended up with a romantic concept of being German.

Since September 2008, a federal test has replaced the *Länder* tests. The federal test includes thirty-three multiple choice questions selected randomly from a catalogue of 310 questions, from which the applicant must correctly answer seventeen (the *Länder* can pick and choose questions from the catalogue). It is a less intrusive test, focusing on history, constitutional principles, geography, economy, practical issues relating to life in Germany, and German customs, such as "what do Germans traditionally do at Easter?" (Paint eggs). One question asks "what should parents of a 22-year-old girl do if they do not like her boyfriend?" (They must respect her decision), but this question is an exception. The novelty of

[33] Ray Furlong, "Germans Argue Over Integration," BBC News, November 30, 2004.

the federal test is to apply a knowledge-based test. It is cognitive—one can *learn* how to be German.

Passing the test is not the sole criterion for becoming German. Every applicant must demonstrate an adequate knowledge of the German language by taking integration courses, which include 600 hours of language training and an additional sixty hours of orientation training. Every applicant must also possess "knowledge of the legal system, society and living conditions in Germany,"[34] and "confirm his or her commitment to the free democratic constitutional system" by a written "declaration of loyalty."[35] Foreign spouses of German citizens may be naturalized *only if* "it is ensured that they will conform to the German living conditions."[36] A sufficient knowledge of the German language and basic knowledge of the legal and social order and the living conditions in Germany are also prerequisites for obtaining a settlement permit (*Niederlassungserlaubnis*).[37]

What, then, is German identity, and what are the qualities one should possess to become German? Is German identity a set of moral values and ethical beliefs, as implied by Baden-Württemberg, or is it a wide range of knowledge about German composers, philosophers, and poets, as implied by Hessen? Is there a "German identity" shared by the *Länder*? These questions, rarely discussed in the decades after World War II, are now being openly debated. The journey to define "Germanness" demonstrates that there are more sources of division than unity. Of course, most Germans share some commonalities. They speak the German language, share German heritage, and are expected to be loyal to the German Constitution. Yet, are there elements of identity that are *intrinsically* German?

The debate over German identity was brought to the fore in 2000 with the introduction of the concept *Leitkultur*. Friedrich Merz, the previous Chairman of the Christian Democratic Union Party (CDU), turned the term *Leitkultur* into a topic of national debate. Literally, *Leitkultur* means dominant or leading culture. According to a Position Paper published by the CDU, Germany has dominant cultural values to which migrants must adhere. Germany should not hide its values because integration

[34] Staatsangehörigkeitsgesetz (1913), § 10 (StAG).

[35] Allgemeine Verwaltungsvorschrift zum Staatsangehörigkeitsrecht (2000), § 85.1.1.1 (StAR-VwV); StAG, § 10(1)(1).

[36] StAG, § 9(1)(2); StAR-VwV, §§ 8.1.2.1, 8.1.2.5.

[37] Aufenthaltsgesetz (2004), §§ 9(2)(7), 9(2)(8), 9a(2), 30(1)(2), 43.

can only succeed in a nation that is confident of its identity. Integration means becoming part of the "German cultural and social living conditions."[38] The very existence of the term "German living conditions" raises the question what is German? Yet, the *Leitkultur* debate reveals a relatively thin version of Germanness in which the decisive factors are mainly the values enshrined in the German Basic Law—the rule of law and basic principles of democracy. Germany, ultimately, cannot clearly articulate what its *Leitkultur* is, and cannot really agree about what it means to be German.

But perhaps the search for a common German ground should not focus on lofty ideas, but on more practical customs characterizing daily life in Germany. Guides on "How to be German" do not focus on romantic notions of German identity, yet include valuable, practical information. One can learn about the three German P's (planning, preparation, process), the need to obey rules—including the "red man" at a pedestrian crossing—and the importance of recycling. Germans, we are told, usually have a long breakfast, drink *Apfelschorle*, use fake identities on Facebook, speak freely about sex, and watch popular German TV series.[39] There is no glory in these details, but they may offer a practical sense of life in Germany.

Muslims are at the center of the national identity debate. In 2010, Muslims constituted 5 percent of the German population.[40] Although a relatively small share of the general population, Muslims have become a target of hostility. One study found that the hostility toward Muslims in Germany ranks among the highest in Europe.[41] In 2010, a board member of the Deutsche Bundesbank, Thilo Sarrazin, published a book, arguing that Muslims pose a threat to German culture. But Sarrazin did more than raise the usual claims. He advocated ideas of racial superiority according to which Muslims are intellectually inferior and are "dumbing down" the German intelligence. According to Sarrazin, intelligence is not nurtured, but inherited. There are genetic differences between the

[38] CDU, "Arbeitsgrundlage für die Zuwanderungs-Kommission der CDU Deutschlands," 2000; CDU and CSU, "Umfassendes Gesetz zur Steuerung und Begrenzung der Zuwanderung sowie zur Förderung der Integration jetzt vorlegen," 2001.

[39] See, e.g., Adam Fletcher, *How to Be German in 50 Easy Steps: A Guide from Apfelsaftschorle to Tschüss*, Ingo Herzke, trans. (Munich: C.H. Beck, 2013).

[40] Pew Research Center, "The Future of the Global Muslim Population: Projections for 2010–2030," 2011: p. 124.

[41] Andreas Zick, Beate Küpper, and Andreas Hövermann, "Intolerance, Prejudice and Discrimination: A European Report," Meredith Dale, ed. and trans., Friedrich-Ebert-Stiftung, 2011: pp. 61–63, 171.

IQs of Muslims and those of ethnic Germans and, given that Muslims have a higher fertility rate than ethnic Germans, Germany is becoming a less intelligent society.[42] A marginal view? Not really. A public opinion poll showed that one-third of ethnic Germans agreed with Sarrazin's main thesis.[43] Perhaps more striking is the fact that some politicians demanded the imposition of IQ tests on migrants.[44] This idea and Sarrazin's book were quickly condemned as racist. Nevertheless, the book was a bestseller in Germany.

The eruption of national patriotism may not be an anomaly in most countries, yet in Germany it is quite unusual. In post-World War II Germany, open and lively debates on national identity were "forbidden fruit."[45] German nationalism was a source of shame, not pride. Talk about biological superiority was taboo, and jargon of "bad" and "good" Germans was associated with right-wing tendencies. Interestingly, migrants—more than any other factor (the unification of Germany, the establishment of the European Union, etc.)—have urged German society to rethink its identity in an attempt to reconstruct the essence of being German.

Until 2000, German citizenship law was based on blood (*jus sanguinis*) rather than place of birth (*jus soli*). A non-ethnic German could reside in Germany for decades without being permitted to become German, while people of German ancestry living in Eastern Europe could be freely admitted under repatriation laws. This rule has been changed. The initial expectations were that non-ethnic Germans would culturally become Germans by long residence in Germany. The residency requirement is currently eight years (it was fifteen in the past) and it is designed to facilitate integration. However, integration has not fully occurred.

The debate over the qualities required to become German has ended so far with the imposition of minimal threshold requirements. Non-Germans must demonstrate an adequate knowledge of the

[42] Thilo Sarrazin, *Deutschland Schafft sich ab: Wie wir unser Land aufs Spiel setzen* (Munich: Deutsche Verlags-Anstalt, 2010): pp. 24, 286–287, 348–360.

[43] Institut für Demoskopie Allensbach, "Meinung zu Sarrazins Thesen," 2010: p. 3; Consumerfieldwork GmbH, "Meinungsumfrage zur Buchveröffentlichung von Thilo Sarrazin: Hat Sarrazin Recht, oder Hat Sarrazin nicht Recht?," 2010.

[44] "Germany's Immigration Debate: Politician Demands IQ Tests for Would-Be Immigrants," *Spiegel*, June 28, 2010.

[45] Cynthia Miller-Idriss, *Blood and Culture: Youth, Right-Wing Extremism, and National Belonging in Contemporary Germany* (Durham: Duke University Press, 2009): pp. 46–92.

language, measured by a language exam; possess basic knowledge of the German legal system, society, and living conditions, measured by a citizenship test; and confirm commitment to the liberal constitutional order, measured by a written declaration of loyalty. The eruption of nationalism, as displayed by the Baden-Württemberg and Hessen tests, is the exception rather than the rule. With a 98 to 99 percent pass rate of the federal test, and a low level of German language proficiency, it is relatively easy to become German. However, the debate is still a work-in-progress and it is too early to predict how it will evolve.

The Dutch Inburgering

Dutch naturalization requirements were minimal until 1998. It was sufficient to have a clean police record and pass a short interview. During recent years, however, the Dutch tradition of openness and diversity has shifted. Current policy resembles a process of acculturation under which, in order to become Dutch, migrants have to subscribe to Dutch values.

The first immigration reform occurred in 1998 with the passage of the Civic Integration (Newcomers) Act.[46] The Act requires migrants already in the country to take integration courses on Dutch language and society. In 2005, more restrictions followed with the adoption of the Integration Abroad Act.[47] This Act incorporates a brand new concept worldwide—"*Integration from Abroad*." Every individual aged between 16 and 65 wishing to enter the Netherlands on a non-visitor visa must apply at the Dutch Embassy in his or her country of citizenship (or country of residence) and enroll in a language course and civic training. At the end, he or she must pass two tests: an oral exam testing elementary knowledge of Dutch language proficiency, and a computer-based exam testing basic knowledge of Dutch society. Passing the tests does not guarantee citizenship, but merely admission. After being admitted, and before gaining a permanent residence permit, the applicant must attend further courses and pass additional exams, testing a higher level of knowledge of the Dutch language and society. In other words, the applicant faces two stages of testing: before entry (*Basisexamen inburgering in het buitenland*) and before receiving a permanent residence permit (*Inburgeringsexamen*). Failing to pass the *inburgeringsexamen* within

[46] Wet Inburgering Nieuwkomers (1998). This process is currently regulated by the Nieuwe Wet Inburgering (2006) (Civic Integration Act).

[47] Wet Inburgering in het Buitenland (2005).

a timeframe of three years—there is a strict time limit—may result in administrative fines of up to €1,000—and rejection of the application. Integration-from-abroad policies, however, do not apply to EU citizens nor to citizens of Australia, Canada, Japan, New Zealand, South Korea, Switzerland, and the United States.

In spite of the title "*civic* integration examination abroad," the Dutch policy is culture-based. The applicant has to watch a two-hour film, *Coming to the Netherlands* (*Naar Nederland*), which gives the impression that it would be better to stay out. It treats the migrant as a Martian who will have to contend with the "complexity" of escalators and computers. The film contains statements such as "it's too cold here," "my goodness, they really are white," "Dutch people really have very little patience," and "people suffer from culture shock here." A migrant from Turkey advises foreigners not to move to the Netherlands: "If someone from abroad was planning to come here, I would tell them, think hard about what you are doing." One of the controversial scenes shows homosexuals kissing and topless women, and no exemption from viewing is made for religious scholars, such as Jewish rabbis or Muslim imams.[48] A Dutch woman in the film explains its rationale: "It has taken us five hundred years to get this far and I would like to put a plea to keep it like that for a very long time."

Naar Nederland provides a glimpse into the Dutch perception of themselves and their sense of "Dutchness." The film, for the most part, is descriptive. It contains basic information on Dutch history, demography, geography, and the legal system. The film also explains Dutch cultural habits. We can learn that the Dutch like to cycle, love birthday gifts, feel comfortable with nudity, say goodbye loudly, and are very direct. They do not show up uninvited to parties, plan everything in advance, and leave house curtains open. Nevertheless, descriptive as it is, *Naar Nederland* takes a moral position. One can see that in the Netherlands, according to the film, women are dominant and men are often in the kitchen, people talk freely about sex and sexuality, and handshaking is a common custom. Dutch people are presented as a homogenous entity, as if all Dutch are the same.

The content of the exams about Dutch society is kept secret, and there is no official handbook to prepare for the exam (an exam sample exists,

[48] These scenes appear only in the unedited version. However, the film has an edited version omitting scenes with sexual connotations. This is because it is prohibited to show some of these scenes in certain countries and it might even be considered a crime.

but not the actual exam). This is because the Dutch citizenship philosophy is that "One cannot study to be Dutch, one has to feel Dutch."[49] In order to feel Dutch, however, one must ask "what is Dutch?" Judging from the film, which is the only preparatory material available for the citizenship test to be taken abroad, "Dutchness" is a mix and match of customs and mores. The film focuses on social behavior and how one should act in everyday situations. The message is that there is a "correct" way to behave in social interactions. Some test questions do not have a right or wrong answer and, often, do not have a right answer at all. For example, how "wrong" is it when a person visits a widow of a deceased neighbor instead of sending a condolence card, or does not keep the front yard tidy (these are two test questions). Other questions are peculiar. An example is the question "Is tea made with cold or hot water?" Or, take the following question: "Zara works in a retirement home. The director of the home walks into the coffee room. What is the best thing Zara can do? (a) shake his hand and tell him her name; (b) continue to work and wave at him; or (c) wait until he says something to her." The right answer is (a)—Zara should shake the director's hand, though, for some, including religious Jews and devout people of Japanese descent, a wave would be a more appropriate manner of saying hello. Whatever the "correct" answer may be, the message is that there is a fixed Dutch way of life and migrants should fit in.

The Dutch require applicants to integrate in advance—before receiving a temporary residence permit. Yet, it is quite difficult to learn to speak Dutch and become familiar with Dutch society by watching movies in the Dutch Embassy in Pakistan. As Joan Scott rightly notes, this is like "asking them to pass final exams at the beginning of the course."[50] Under the new policy, the applicant, while still *abroad*, has to pass a test about Dutch society. This policy applies to non-exempted family members, a reality that can lead to harsh results. If a Dutchman falls in love with a Moroccan woman, he must wait until she is able to speak Dutch and pass tests on Dutch society before they can live together in the Netherlands.

In adopting the policy of "integration from abroad," the Netherlands has drastically swung from one extreme to the other. After World War II, the Netherlands welcomed the migration of temporary guest workers from former Dutch colonies. The workers were expected to return to

[49] Cited in Ricky van Oers, Betty de Hart, and Kees Groenendijk, "The Netherlands," in *Country Analyses*, vol. 2, *Acquisition and Loss of Nationality: Policies and Trends in 15 European Countries*, Rainer Bauböck et al., eds. (Amsterdam: Amsterdam University Press, 2006): pp. 391–434 at 415.

[50] Joan Wallach Scott, *The Politics of the Veil* (Princeton: Princeton University Press, 2007): p. 103.

their country of origin and thus no integration policy was implemented; they were even encouraged to maintain their culture since diversity was seen as an advantage. However, the fact that the workers remained in the Netherlands and the ensuing integration difficulties led to the adoption of a new policy of *inburgering*. The term *inburgering*, which has no equivalent in English, means to become like the native-born, "autochthonous."[51]

One reason for the change in Dutch immigration philosophy is related to Muslims. Like France and Germany, the Netherlands has a growing Muslim community, comprising 5.5 percent of the population in 2010. Social segregation, cultural clashes, a high level of unemployment, and social unrest—culminating in the political assassination of the Dutch filmmaker Theo van Gogh—have all contributed to the sentiment that the multicultural dream is over. In contemporary politics, a large percentage of the public feels wronged (*Verongelijktheid*) about multiculturalism. A memo written by the Labor Party President, Lilianne Ploumen, suggests making a u-turn regarding multiculturalism: "The mistake we can never repeat is stifling criticism of cultures and religions for reasons of tolerance."[52] A public opinion poll indicates that 57 percent of the Dutch population believes that allowing migration has proven "the biggest mistake in Dutch history."[53] This view was articulated by Paul Scheffer, a prominent Dutch scholar, in his essay *Het Multiculturele Drama* (the Multicultural Drama). Scheffer warned that an alienated foreign population undermines the social cohesion of Dutch society and called for a new policy based on shared language and norms.[54]

What, then, is "Dutchness"? It is difficult to grasp the essential elements of Dutch identity. Besides Dutch history and language, what is *uniquely* Dutch? Dutch identity is diverse. There are regional differences; Randstad versus Bible Belt and Limburg. One province, Friesland, has its own language (Fries), national anthem (*De âlde Friezen*), and traditional sport (*Fierljeppen*). And yet, Dutch immigration law sets up qualifications

[51] Leonard F.M. Besselink, "Integration and Immigration: The Vicissitudes of Dutch '*Inburgering*'," in *Illiberal Liberal States: Immigration, Citizenship and Integration in the EU*, Elspeth Guild, Kees Groenendijk, and Sergio Carrera, eds. (Burlington: Ashgate, 2009): pp. 241–257.

[52] John Vinocur, "From the Left, a Call to End the Current Dutch Notion of Tolerance," *New York Times*, November 29, 2008.

[53] Peter Giesen, "Nederlander heeft Weinig Kaas Gegeten van Historie," *de Volkskrant*, March 26, 2008.

[54] Paul Scheffer, "Het Multiculturele Drama," *NRC Handelsblad*, January 29, 2000.

for becoming Dutch that create an image of a *fixed* identity and way of life.

In 2007, in an attempt to better understand the Dutch identity, the Scientific Council for Government Policy released a special report titled *Identification with the Netherlands*. The Council advised changing the focus of the national identity debate from identity to identification. It noted that insisting on assimilation into a fixed Dutch identity may lead to the marginalization of migrants, who often do not share these identities. Instead, the Netherlands should cause the migrants to identify with the country in three spheres: functional identification (shared interests), normative identification (shared norms), and emotional identification (a shared sense of belonging).[55] The Council is clear in its recommendations, but leaves their meaning vague. What are Dutch norms? Perhaps we can learn something about these issues from a government report that was published a few months earlier. In 2006, the government published a list of Dutch Canon that all young children (aged 8 to 14) must learn in school. The Dutch Canon contains a list of fifty topics (events, persons, texts, etc.), such as the Dutch East India Company, Surinam and the Netherlands Antilles, the Constitution, Anne Frank, Hugo Grotius, Rembrandt, Spinoza, and William of Orange.[56]

The Canon of the Netherlands is formative; it seeks to form identification. Canons, as Moshe Halbertal indicates, set boundaries for a community: "Canons are both exclusive and inclusive. They create monopolies and define who is worthy of being heard and who is not."[57] Still, the concept of Dutchness, as depicted in the Dutch Canon, embodies history and society, rather than ways of life and social mores. Comparing the content of the Canon of the Netherlands with the Dutch immigration requirements shows two different concepts of Dutchness. It demonstrates the ambiguity displayed by the Netherlands toward its national identity.

[55] Wetenschappelijke Raad voor het Regeringsbeleid, *Identificatie Met Nederland* (Amsterdam: Amsterdam University Press, 2007).

[56] Committee for the Development of the Dutch Canon, *A Key to Dutch History: Report by the Committee for the Development of the Dutch Canon* (Amsterdam: Amsterdam University Press, 2007).

[57] Moshe Halbertal, *People of the Book: Canon, Meaning, and Authority* (Cambridge: Harvard University Press, 1997): p. 4.

UK Britishness

In a thought-provoking article, published in *Prospect Magazine*, the editor, David Goodhart, states that Britain has become too diverse to sustain a good society. Too many migrants from too many backgrounds erode British common culture. Britain, he claims, "has long since ceased to be Orwell's 'family'" and is approaching a turning point where it may be "difficult to sustain the legitimacy of a universal risk-pooling welfare state." Diversity threatens solidarity, and solidarity is necessary for social cohesion. Goodhart lays the blame on the British concept of citizenship. He notes that "modern liberal societies cannot be based on a simple assertion of...the rule of law, [and] of equal legal treatment for everyone." Rather, citizenship must arise "out of a shared history, shared experiences, and, often, shared suffering." Goodhart is clear about what Britain needs—more people of "our own kind," that is to say, "people who think and behave like us."[58] Only thus, he asserts, can Britain survive.

Goodhart is not alone. The Denham Report on *Building Cohesive Communities*—aimed at investigating the causes and implications of the 2001 violent riots in Bradford, Burnley, and Oldham—found that a key cause for the riots was "lack of a strong civic identity or shared social values to unite diverse communities." It pointed out that British youths grow up "ignorant of other cultures and lifestyles" and that this reality is a source of conflict. It then recommended promoting an idea of citizenship that gives citizens a shared sense of belonging and "expresses common goals and aspirations." Shared identity, the Report found, is needed to unite diverse people and create community cohesion. It does not mean cultural uniformity, but it does include mastering the English language and "recognition of and adherence to fundamental rights and duties."[59] The Report held that this vision has to be developed by the communities; the government may lead the process, but should not impose values. The Report thus introduced community cohesion as a state goal that should be achieved by developing a concept of "shared values." Similar conclusions appear in the Cantle Report, published by the Home Office. The Report found the lack of a meaningful concept of British citizenship to be a key factor of the riots and recommended the government to develop "values which focus on what it means to be a citizen of a modern multi-racial Britain."[60] In 2003, after a

[58] David Goodhart, "Too Diverse?," *Prospect Magazine* 95 (February 2004): pp. 30–37 at 30–32.

[59] Home Office, "Building Cohesive Communities: A Report of the Ministerial Group on Public Order and Community Cohesion," 2001: pp. 11–12, 19–20.

[60] Home Office, "Community Cohesion: A Report of the Independent Review Team Chaired by Ted Cantle," 2001: p. 9.

long debate on the essence of being British, the Home Office published its own version of what it means to be British:[61]

> To be British seems to us to mean that we respect the laws, the elected parliamentary and democratic political structures, traditional values of mutual tolerance, respect for equal rights and mutual concern; and that we give our allegiance to the state (as commonly symbolised in the Crown) in return for its protection. To be British is to respect those over-arching specific institutions, values, beliefs and traditions that bind us all, the different nations and cultures, together in peace and in a legal order.

The Home Office's prescription of British identity is basically shared by most liberal democracies. Respecting democratic political structures is British just as it is French and German. Christian Joppke rightly points out the interesting paradox of trying to have specific national identities, while ending up with universal principles. "The British state . . . is caught in the paradox of universalism," Joppke observes, "it perceives the need to make immigrants and ethnic minorities parts of *this* and not of *any* society, but it cannot name and enforce any particulars that distinguish the 'here' from 'there' . . . . [British values] are nationally anonymous."[62]

What is *Britishness*, then? In 2007, the Smith Institute published a thick volume directed at defining the concept of Britishness.[63] The discussion is instructive. There is an agreement among the contributors that Britishness does not connote British folklore, but "British values." The hard question is which values, and whose? Most of the contributors specify values that are universal: social justice, tolerance, the rule of law, diversity, egalitarianism, and the like; the only particular items are language and history. But are English language and Commonwealth history intrinsically "British"? Redefining Britishness is a lofty idea. While the government searches for a British version of the French motto *Liberté, Égalité, Fraternité*, no British set of values has yet been found. When *The Times* sponsored a motto-writing contest, the slogan favored by most readers was "No Motto please, we're British."[64] In the Smith Institute's volume, Trevor Phillips asserts that although British values are not

[61] Home Office, "The New and the Old: The Report of the 'Life in the United Kingdom' Advisory Group," 2003: p. 11.

[62] Christian Joppke, *Citizenship and Immigration* (Malden: Polity Press, 2010): p. 130.

[63] Nick Johnson, ed., "Britishness: Towards a Progressive Citizenship," Smith Institute, 2007.

[64] Greg Hurst, "Maverick Streak Makes Mockery of Hunt for a British Motto," *The Times*, November 22, 2007.

unique to Britain, the way the British express them is British. Phillips has no answer to what values are British, but he is sure that "We would never do anything as French as set this down on paper so that everyone could read it."[65]

Phillips is right—Britain does not set down its values on paper as France does. However, it has set them down on a computer program. Starting in 2005, every migrant must demonstrate "sufficient knowledge of the English, Welsh or Scottish Gaelic language," as well as "sufficient knowledge about life in the United Kingdom."[66] Demonstrating this knowledge is satisfied by passing the *Life in the UK Test*. The test is taken before a foreigner can settle in the United Kingdom (a settlement permit grants permission to stay in the United Kingdom indefinitely). The applicant must answer eighteen out of twenty-four questions correctly in forty-five minutes.[67]

The *Life in the UK Test* suggests an interesting philosophy of how to become British. Until 2013, the test excluded references to British history. To become British, one did not need to know anything about the Magna Carta, the 1689 Bill of Rights, the Petition of Right, the birth of Parliament, or common law tradition. One only had to be familiar with British geography, national holidays, constitutional institutions and principles, and a long list of practical knowledge of healthcare, housing, employment, bank accounts, taxes, insurance, and everyday needs.[68] A person had to know what people do on Valentine's Day (lovers exchange gifts and cards), what is the Grand National (an annual steeplechase), and whether the Queen may marry someone who is not Protestant (she cannot).[69] The applicant had to know the legal minimum age for buying alcohol and tobacco, how to buy a ticket for the Underground, and that dogs in public places must wear a collar that shows the name and address of the owner. This might not be surprising because the test was not about fundamentals of British history, but about *Life in the UK*.

The first edition (2005) and the second edition (2007) of the official guide of the *Life in the UK Test* were peculiar—"the funniest book currently

[65] Trevor Phillips, "Britishness and Integration," in "Britishness: Towards a Progressive Citizenship" (n 63), pp. 37–46 at 42–45.

[66] British Nationality Act (1981), Sch. 1.

[67] Borders, Citizenship and Immigration Act (2009), Pt. 2, s. 40(3); Home Office, "Knowledge of Life in the UK Settlement Q&A," 2007.

[68] Home Office, *Life in the United Kingdom: A Journey to Citizenship*, 2nd ed. (London: TSO, 2007).

[69] Henry Dillon, *How British Are You? Questions from the British Citizenship Test* (London: Red Squirrel Publishing, 2008).

available in the English language," as described by the *London Review of Books*.[70] The first edition contained some factual errors, such as assuming that Northern Ireland is part of Great Britain, rather than Britain (or the UK).[71] Bernard Crick, who wrote parts of the handbook, had to admit that "There are errors" in the test, yet explained that "it [is] because it was done fairly quickly."[72] The test, to be clear, was generally not intrusive, but it did ask about sports (horse racing, rugby, and cricket) and other features of daily life, such as "how might you stop young people playing tricks on you on Halloween?" The applicant also had to provide an answer to questions such as: "Suppose you spill someone's pint in the pub. What, according to the book, usually happens next?" Other questions focused on religious myths, such as "where does Father Christmas come from?" The essence of Britishness under the test was, as Trevor Phillips pointed out, "what people do [in Britain].... 'British is as British does'."[73]

The *Life in the UK Test* downgraded British identity to daily life issues. British historical icons and cultural symbols received little attention. This may not be accidental. In *Londonistan*, Melanie Phillips contends, among other things, that Britain has increasingly privatized its identity. Instead of preserving its values, Britain "was apologizing for those values." The British "majoritarian culture is viewed as illegitimate.... and any attempt to impose majoritarian values is held to be discriminatory." Britain no longer has an identity, because the very idea of having a national identity is found to be discriminatory and prejudicial.[74]

In 2007, the Institute for Public Policy Research suggested downgrading British national symbols to improve race relations. Many of the "symbols and stories that once bound this country together have to be recast and new ones need to take a place alongside them," the Report claimed, and added: "We can no longer define ourselves as a Christian nation." The Report recommended removing the seats for bishops in the House of Lords and updating the Union Jack Flag that has three crosses on it. It also suggested revising the content of the Pledge of Allegiance to focus on loyalty to the state rather than to the Queen, who is the

[70] Andrew O'Hagan, "Short Cuts," *London Review of Books* 28, no. 22 (November 2006): p. 22 (referring to the first edition of 2005).

[71] Home Office, *Life in the United Kingdom: A Journey to Citizenship*, 1st ed. (London: TSO, 2005): p. 17.

[72] Lee Glendinning, "Citizenship Guide Fails Its History Exam," *The Guardian*, April 29, 2006.

[73] Phillips, pp. 42, 46 (n 65).

[74] Melanie Phillips, *Londonistan* (New York: Encounter Books, 2006): pp. xv–xvi, xx. See also pp. xi, xx, 59–63, 169.

Head of the Church of England. If Britain wants to keep Christmas as a national holiday, "public organisation should mark other major religious festivals too." British tradition becomes a barrier to integration, the Report found.[75]

In March 2013, Britain revised its national identity, as reflected in the *Life in the UK Test* and, for the first time, incorporated British history. The government published an updated handbook of how to prepare for the test. Britain, it is evident, has a long tradition of architecture, art, theater, literature, and poetry. The handbook is like a renaissance of British identity. One of the most detailed parts of the handbook relates to sports. It contains a long list of notable British sportsmen and detailed explanations on cricket, rugby, and football. Composers, too, are a source of British pride. The handbook notes that the "German-born composer *George Frederick Handel (1695–1759)* spent many years in the UK and became a British citizen in 1727." Even issues such as shopping, cooking, and gardening have become uniquely British ("The countries that make up the UK all have flowers which are particularly associated with them."). The British also have a unique cuisine: roast beef with potatoes, Yorkshire pudding, Welsh cakes, haggis, and Ulster fry. The British have a unique film industry that exerts a "major influence on modern cinema" ("Lawrence of Arabia," as well as "Four Weddings and a Funeral") and have a very British-style comedy ("comedy and satire, and the ability to laugh at ourselves, are an important part of the UK character"). The British are also cool and modern. They use Facebook and Twitter and go out to pubs and nightclubs (pubs "are an important part of the UK social culture"). And they also like to gamble, especially on sports. In Britain, there are "places of interest" that every newcomer should be familiar with: Big Ben, the Eden Project, Edinburgh Castle, the Giant's Causeway, the London Eye, Snowdonia, the Lake District, and the Tower of London.[76]

Following the revisions in the handbook, the current *Life in the UK Test*, which took effect in March 2013, includes a new set of questions. One has to know, for instance, "Who was Mary, Queen of Scots' son?" (James VI of Scotland and James I of England.); "What is Maiden Castle in Dorset an example of?" (An Iron Age hill fort); and "Who was King of England at the time of the Norman invasion in 1066?" (Harold).[77] Other questions address

[75] Ben Rogers and Rick Muir, "The Power of Belonging: Identity, Citizenship and Community Cohesion," Institute for Public Policy Research, 2007: pp. 36, 33, respectively. See also pp. 42–43, 49–52.

[76] George Sandison and Henry Dillon, eds., *Life in the UK Test: Study Guide: The Essential Study Guide for the British Citizenship Test*, 7th ed. (London: Red Squirrel Publishing, 2013): pp. 35, 45–47, 49.

[77] Sandison and Dillon, pp. 64–66 (n 76).

The Canterbury Tales, Shakespeare's *Romeo and Juliet*, Blake's poem, *The Tyger*, Lord Byron's poem, *She Walks in Beauty*, John Constable, Charles Dickens, Jane Austen, Adam Smith, David Hume, Isaac Newton, the Beatles, and British soap operas.[78] Perhaps the most significant change is related to history. Britain has rediscovered its history. Topics include the Vikings, the Magna Carta, the Spanish Armada, the Restoration, World War II, and a very long list of English kings and queens. To become British, one has to find his or her way in a royal maze: John, Henry V, Henry VII, Elizabeth I, Charles I, and Henry VIII, not to mention a long list of Henry VIII's wives—and he had six! Other questions focus on St. Patrick's Day, the Proms at the Royal Albert Hall, Churchill, and Admiral Nelson. The questions about practical daily life, such as how to buy a ticket for the Underground, have largely disappeared. The test, however, keeps some "essential" knowledge. One should know that "pool" and "darts" are "traditional pub game[s] in the UK," and whether it is true or false that "pantomimes are plays based on fairy stories" (It's true).[79]

Unsurprisingly, the new design of the *Life in the UK Test* has been criticized. British journalist Mehdi Hasan claims that the test reflects the identity of only part of the society: "Who decides what is and isn't relevant to British 'culture and history'?" The test, he adds, is also not religiously neutral—"God save the Queen? I was convinced from a young age that He has far more important things to do with His time."[80] Thom Brooks, a British law professor, argues that the test is a form of entertainment. Brooks is not against a citizenship test but prefers a test that reflects practical knowledge—"contact[ing] an ambulance or report[ing] a crime"—and not impractical points, such as the "approximate age of Big Ben . . . and height of the London Eye in both feet and metres."[81] The third edition of the test largely omits these practical issues. There are only a few items in the current exam about bank accounts, job interviews, and credit cards.[82]

Compared to other European states, the UK policy is far less rigid. First, unlike the Dutch citizenship test, the *Life in the UK Test* is taken in the United Kingdom. However, unlike the French and German tests, which are part of the naturalization process, the UK test is a prerequisite

[78] Michael Mitchell, *Life in the United Kingdom: Official Practice Questions and Answers* (London: TSO, 2013).

[79] For the quotations, see Mitchell, pp. 167, 170, 13, respectively (n 78).

[80] Mehdi Hasan, "Testing Makes a Mockery of Britishness," *New Statesman*, July 4, 2012.

[81] Thom Brooks, "The 'Life of the United Kingdom' Citizenship Test: Is It Unfit for Purpose?," Durham University, 2013: pp. 23–24.

[82] GOV.UK, "New Life in the UK Test Goes Live," March 25, 2013.

for obtaining a permanent residence permit. Second, unlike the Dutch policy, which has two tests—one on the Dutch language and another on Dutch society—the United Kingdom only requires one test. Passing the *Life in the UK Test* means that the migrant proves sufficient knowledge of the language as well. Third, unlike the Dutch, who keep the content of their test secret, the British publish a detailed handbook on how to prepare for the test. Fourth, unlike the Dutch case, where the test results are only valid for one year after which the test must be retaken, the UK test has no time-limit. And finally, unlike the Dutch exemptions for people arriving from Western societies, the United Kingdom—although it exempts EEA citizens seeking settlement in Britain due to EU laws on freedom of movement—asks EEA citizens seeking British citizenship to pass the test.

Current immigration reforms in the United Kingdom have a broader reach than language and citizenship tests. Beginning in 2004, naturalized persons have to attend a citizenship ceremony in which they pledge loyalty: "I will *give* my loyalty to the United Kingdom and *respect* its rights and freedoms. I will *uphold* its democratic values. I will *observe* its laws faithfully and *fulfil* my duties and obligations as a British citizen." In addition to the Pledge of Loyalty, applicants have to take the traditional Oath of Allegiance in which they must swear to "be faithful and bear true allegiance to Her Majesty Queen Elizabeth the Second, Her Heirs and Successors."[83] As part of the debate on the meaning of Britishness, a government committee found that there had been a diminution in British identity. In order to foster social cohesion, it proposed a third loyalty oath, an American-style pledge of allegiance to be recited in public schools.[84]

The debate over British identity yields fascinating insights. The Britons resemble a nation in search of identity. So far, the journey has led to peculiar results. Back in 1990, Lord Norman Tebbit coined the term the "cricket test" to test whether a migrant cheers for England in a cricket match against the team of his or her country of origin; "Cheer for the English cricket team and you will be fine!"[85] Tebbit probably had something deeper in mind—that there are some patterns of behavior

[83] British Nationality Act (1981), Sch. 5 (emphasis added).

[84] Lord Goldsmith Q.C., "Citizenship: Our Common Bond," Ministry of Justice, 2008: pp. 84, 97–98.

[85] Amartya Sen, *Identity and Violence: the Illusion of Destiny* (London: Penguin Books, 2006): pp. 153–154. See also Dan Fisher, "Split Between Britain, U.S. Seen as 'Inevitable': Foreign Policy: The Conservative

that make a person English (or British), namely, that the test of belonging to the United Kingdom is not ethnicity or nationality, but culture. Interestingly, Tebbit picked up an odd issue, a "cricket test," to specify what loyalty to Britain means. Two decades later, in 2010, Phil Woolas, the then Minister for Immigration, offered a different test for being British, the "queuing test"—the "British practice of forming an orderly line." According to Woolas, "The simple act of taking one's turn is one of the things that holds our country together."[86] What is interesting is not just the fact that Woolas finds queuing to be a "British" practice, but that he finds it necessary to hold the British nation together.

A restrictive turn?

By means of immigration laws, states create an image of a culturally homogenous group that speaks the same language, shares the same values, celebrates the same holidays, and dresses in the same way—as if all people are the same. They offer an imagined description of who they are by romanticizing who they were (or want to be). Then, they impose part of this prescription on immigrants in order to promote cohesion and unity.

There is much to learn from recent immigration law in Europe. Whatever we call it—a thick version of civic nationalism, a thin version of cultural nationalism, muscular liberalism, militant liberalism, or cultural defense—culture has become increasingly dominant in keeping the gates. Surely, there are nuances. In some states, cultural defense policies apply to naturalization processes only; in others, they exist as a pre-arrival entry. In some states, cultural defense applies to all sorts of migrants; in others, there are exemptions for family members. In some states, cultural defense focuses on cognitive knowledge; in others, the process is not just cognitive, but requires understanding and acceptance of some values and, rarely, identification with them. As always, legal formalism never tells the whole story. Local pragmatism often deviates from formal law and, in reality, actual policies may be narrower (or broader) than legal rules. But, on the whole, the restrictive turn in Europe can hardly be denied.

Empirical research supports the proposition that there is a restrictive cultural turn in Europe. In 2002, only four out of fourteen European states had a compulsory language requirement (29 percent); in 2007,

Party Chairman Fears that a 'Less European' America Will Provide the Wedge," *Los Angeles Times*, April 19, 1990.

[86] Melissa Kite, "Immigrants to Be Taught How to Queue," *Daily Telegraph*, February 13, 2010.

eleven out of eighteen states had a compulsory language requirement (61 percent); and, in 2010, seventeen out of twenty-three European states had a compulsory language requirement (71 percent), including eight states with a language requirement to be met *abroad*.[87] Similarly, a citizenship test, which two decades ago was largely associated with U.S. law, has become common in Europe. In 1999, only four EU states had a formal test; in 2010, the number tripled to twelve.[88] Likewise, integration pacts, almost unknown a decade ago, exist nowadays in many Member States, among them Austria, Denmark, France, Germany, and The Netherlands. Loyalty oaths, too, have become widespread.[89] These changes show that the culturalization of immigration and citizenship policies in European states is broader than the above four cases.

In spite of these findings, scholars find the restrictive turn in Europe to be an exception. Christian Joppke, one of the leading scholars in the field of comparative immigration policy, finds that, globally, there is a process of universalization of citizenship. In his view, recent laws are only an exception to the general liberalization in access to citizenship.[90] Joppke dismisses the rising power of culture as an immigration criterion by arguing that, at the end, the "state culture" resembles the universal concept of political liberalism: "The national particularisms that immigrants and ethnic minorities are asked to accept across European states are but local versions of the universalistic idiom of liberal democracy."[91]

The findings presented in this chapter somehow deviate from this prevailing view. First, they show that, at the very least, there are more and more exceptions to the general process of universalization of citizenship until the point at which the "exceptions" almost become the rule. Second, they demonstrate that, although European states attempting to find

[87] Claire Extramiana and Piet Van Avermaet, "Language Requirements for Adult Migrants in Council of Europe Member States: Report on a Survey," Council of Europe, 2011: pp. 8, 12. Four EU states were not analyzed: Bulgaria, Croatia, Portugal, and Romania.

[88] Sara Wallace Goodman, "Naturalisation Policies in Europe: Exploring Patterns of Inclusion and Exclusion," European University Institute, 2010: p. 17. See also Ricky van Oers, Eva Ersbøll, and Dora Kostakopoulou, eds., *A Re-definition of Belonging? Language and Integration Tests in Europe* (Leiden: Martinus Nijhoff, 2010).

[89] Liav Orgad, "Liberalism, Allegiance, and Obedience: The Inappropriateness of Loyalty Oaths in a Liberal Democracy," *Canadian Journal of Law & Jurisprudence* 27, no. 1 (2014): pp. 99–122.

[90] Christian Joppke, "The Role of the State in Cultural Integration: Trends, Challenges, and Ways Ahead," Migration Policy Institute, 2012: p. 4.

[91] Joppke, *Citizenship and Immigration*, p. 137 (n 62); Christian Joppke, "Exclusion in the Liberal State: The Case of Immigration and Citizenship Policy," *European Journal of Social Theory* 8, no. 1 (2005): pp. 43–61 at 44–45, 48.

"muscular" national identities often end up with universal political concepts, some identities are essentially particular—either institution-based, as in the case of the monarchy in England, or value-based, as in the case of France's *laïcité*. Other examples are languages and the so-called national "way of life" and "way of doing things." And third, universal values have a particularistic meaning due to their local cultural understanding and legal interpretation. Universal concepts, such as freedom of speech, equality, and freedom of religion, have more than one application; their meaning is understood in a particular culture and national constitution.

Cultural defense policies suggest that the retreat from multiculturalism in Europe, at least in the context of immigration and naturalization policy, is real; it is not merely rhetoric, but has become law and policy. Multiculturalism may be still alive in the West,[92] but, in the domain of immigration law, the commitment to it is weakening.[93] This is the case in the Netherlands and the United Kingdom (France has never claimed to be multicultural), but it would be fair to say that it is also the case in other European states, such as Austria, Denmark, and Switzerland.

THE UNITED STATES

The United States has long experience in absorbing immigrants. Unlike past periods of demographic hysteria, current American experience illustrates that European states are more suspicious of immigration and more obsessed with imposing values. In contemporary America, with a few exceptions, the "Europeanization" of citizenship is not even political rhetoric, not to mention law and policy. During the last decade, America significantly downgraded its cultural immigration requirements. Focusing on two naturalization requirements—the U.S. naturalization test and the "attachment requirement"—the following pages briefly show the consistent dilution of the cultural essence of the U.S. naturalization process.

[92] Will Kymlicka, "Multiculturalism: Success, Failure, and the Future," Migration Policy Institute, 2012; Keith Banting and Will Kymlicka, "Is There Really a Retreat from Multiculturalism Policies? New Evidence from the Multiculturalism Policy Index," *Comparative European Politics* 11, no. 5 (2013): pp. 577–598.

[93] Sara Wallace Goodman, "Integration Requirements for Integration's Sake? Identifying, Categorising and Comparing Civic Integration Policies," *Journal of Ethnic and Migration Studies* 36, no. 5 (2010): pp. 753–772; Christian Joppke, "The Retreat is Real—But What is the Alternative? Multiculturalism, Muscular Liberalism, and Islam," *Constellations* 21, no. 2 (2014): pp. 286–295.

Creating new Americans

The U.S. Constitution grants Congress the power to set naturalization requirements.[94] The Naturalization Act of 1790, among the first acts of Congress, permitted the naturalization of a "free white person" of "good character" following two years of U.S. residency and subject to taking an oath to "support the constitution of the United States."[95] In 1795, Congress extended the residency period to five years and added a requirement that the applicant be "attached to the principles of the constitution."[96] These laws granted foreigners a chance to become U.S. citizens at a time in which the option of becoming a citizen was rare or did not even exist in most countries. From 1795 until 1905—except for the restrictions following the hysteria of the XYZ Affair,[97] which triggered the infamous Alien and Sedition Acts of 1798, and the restrictions on Asian immigrants—there was little federal immigration regulation.[98]

At the turn of the nineteenth century, the process of becoming an American citizen started to take on greater significance in national politics. President Theodore Roosevelt turned Americanization into a national obsession. Roosevelt asserted that immigrants "must learn to celebrate Washington's birthday rather than that of the Queen or Kaiser, and the Fourth of July instead of St. Patrick's Day," and "must learn to talk and think and *be* United States."[99] Americanization programs were established in order to train newcomers in how to become "good Americans." The prevailing view was that there is a solid concept of the American way of life that must be adopted by immigrants. In the patriotic fervor of World War I, Louis Brandeis explained the essence of Americanization: "The adoption of our language, manners and customs is only a small part of the process.... The immigrant is not Americanized unless his interests and affections have become deeply rooted here.... He must be brought into complete

[94] U.S. Constitution, art. I, § 8, cl. 4.

[95] Naturalization Act (1790), § 1.

[96] Naturalization Act (1795), § 1.

[97] The XYZ Affair was a diplomatic incident between the United States and France that led to the Quasi War.

[98] Gerald L. Neuman, "The Lost Century of American Immigration Law (1776–1875)," *Columbia Law Review* 93, no. 8 (1993): pp. 1833–1901.

[99] Theodore Roosevelt, "True Americanism," in *True Americanism: Four Essays* (New York: Kessinger Publishing, 2006): pp. 27–57 at 51–52, 45–54.

harmony with our ideals and aspirations and cooperate with us for their attainment."[100]

The thickening of the cultural dimension of American citizenship was more than political rhetoric; it became law. From the beginning of the twentieth century until the 1950s, Congress made a few changes in the naturalization process increasing quite significantly the requirements for becoming a citizen. First, the English language became a trademark of Americanization. In 1906, Congress passed a bill providing that no alien shall be naturalized if he cannot speak the English language.[101] Second, in 1917, a literacy test was adopted. The test was a means to filter out the entry of "aliens over sixteen years of age, physically capable of reading, who can not read the English language, or some other language or dialect."[102] Third, during the McCarthy era, Congress listed as potentially excluded, people who supported communism, anarchism, and other subversive ideologies.[103] Finally, in 1950, Congress adopted a new requirement—demonstration of "knowledge and understanding of the fundamentals of the history, and the principles and form of government, of the United States."[104]

In order to become an American citizen, under current law, one should go through a threefold process: meeting admission requirements, overcoming grounds of inadmissibility, and satisfying the naturalization requirements. The naturalization requirements include: (a) minimum age of 18; (b) minimum period of continuous residence and physical presence in the United States; (c) possession of good moral character; (d) basic English language proficiency; (e) knowledge and understanding of fundamental U.S. history and civics; (f) attachment to the principles of the U.S. Constitution; and (g) taking an oath of allegiance.[105] In addition, the applicant should not be disqualified by grounds of inadmissibility, such as the opposition to government and membership of a totalitarian party.[106]

[100] Solomon Goldman, ed., *Brandeis on Zionism: A Collection of Addresses and Statements by Louis D. Brandeis* (Washington: Zionist Organization of America, 1942): p. 4.

[101] Naturalization Act (1906), § 8.

[102] Immigration Act (1917), § 3.

[103] Internal Security Act (1950), § 25.

[104] Immigration and Nationality Act (1952), § 312(2) (INA) (codified as amended at 8 U.S.C. § 1423(a) (2006)).

[105] See, respectively, INA, §§ 334(b)(1), 316(a), 316(d) and 316(e), 312(1), 312(2), 316(a)(3), 337(a) (codified as amended at 8 U.S.C. §§ 1445(b), 1427(a)(1), 1427(a)(3), 1423(a)(1), 1423(a)(2), 1427(a)(3), 1427(f)(2) (2006)).

[106] INA, § 313 (codified as amended at 8 U.S.C. § 1424 (2006)).

During recent decades, U.S. naturalization requirements have been narrowed, not so much in formal law as in administrative policy and practice. The following pages briefly demonstrate this trend by focusing on two naturalization requirements: the naturalization test, requirement (e), and attachment to the principles of the Constitution, requirement (f).

Naturalization test

At the beginning of the twentieth century, the Bureau of Naturalization began to develop the concept of "good Americans" by introducing immigrant education programs.[107] These programs were the beginning of the idea that new citizens needed to be "created." Their official purpose was orientation: to supply the knowledge required for examination in a naturalization court. But the real purpose was to instill American values and ways of life. It was assumed that compelling people to learn civics would shape their attitudes: "Genuine citizenship is primarily a state of inward feeling and only secondarily one of knowledge."[108] Hence, citizenship handbooks intended to teach migrants how they should behave, think, and were even supposed to feel in America. They taught migrants how they should dress, cook, decorate the home, and behave in society.

Immigrant education programs were rich in information on daily life situations: how to protect the home from fire, get meals ready, keep clothes clean and mended, or slice vegetables and cook eggs. Immigrants were taught about American culture and directed to love America, even more than their country of origin.[109] Making Americans out of immigrants was seen a matter of heart and soul.[110] The education programs were further developed during World War II. "Good Americans" were described as persons who work all day, speak English well, buy a house, learn how to prepare American food, watch baseball, love to vote, belong

[107] John Higham, *Strangers in the Land: Patterns of American Nativism, 1860–1925* (New Brunswick: Rutgers University Press, 2002): pp. 234–263; Noah Pickus, *True Faith and Allegiance: Immigration and American Civic Nationalism* (Princeton: Princeton University Press, 2007): pp. 107–123.

[108] Cited in Susan M. Gordon, "Integrating Immigrants: Morality and Loyalty in US Naturalization Practice," *Citizenship Studies* 11, no. 4 (2007): pp. 367–382 at 376.

[109] Raymond F. Crist, U.S. Department of Labor, Bureau of Naturalization, *Student's Textbook: A Standard Course of Instruction for Use in Public Schools of the United States for the Preparation of the Candidate for the Responsibilities of Citizenship* (Washington: Government Printing Office, 1918): pp. 23, 109–110 ("When I become a citizen of the United States.... I may love my native land, but I love the Government of America better.... This is not only a law of man but it is a law of God.").

[110] Edwin W. Adams, *A Community Civics: A Text-book in Loyal Citizenship* (New York: Charles Scribner's Sons, 1920): p. 3.

to community clubs, obey the law, share responsibilities, show loyalty, believe in the U.S. Constitution, and are familiar with the community.[111]

The turning point came in the 1950s, when the programs became less about the American way of life and more about U.S. history and civics.[112] In 1950, at the height of hysteria over the threat of communism, Congress introduced a civic knowledge requirement, according to which no person shall be naturalized as a citizen if he or she cannot demonstrate:[113]

> A knowledge and understanding of the fundamentals of the history, and of the principles and form of Government, of the United States.

In 1952, there was no federal procedure to assess the knowledge and understanding of the applicant. Immigration officials in different districts applied disparate evaluation standards and tended to ask different questions. It was only in 1986 that the federal government established a standard citizenship test. Since 1986, the test has been taken in English during a short face-to-face interview. Every applicant must pass an English language proficiency test alongside a test on U.S. history and civics in which the applicant must correctly answer six out of ten random questions chosen from a closed list of ninety-six pre-published questions and answers.

The original questions were formulated in 1986 and remained in effect until October 1, 2008. The test included questions on the Bill of Rights, the U.S. form of government, and American history. Applicants were required to identify the author of "Give me liberty or give me death" and know who penned the Star-Spangled Banner. The only skill necessary to pass the test was an ability to memorize relatively easy civic information. The applicant could memorize, for example, that the basic beliefs of the Declaration of Independence are equality and the right to life, liberty, and the pursuit of happiness without even understanding what these beliefs mean.

[111] U.S. Immigration and Naturalization Service, *Federal Textbook on Citizenship: The Gardners Become Citizens: A Supplementary Literacy Reader* (Washington: Government Printing Office, 1943); U.S. Immigration and Naturalization Service, *Federal Textbook on Citizenship: The Business of Our Government* (Washington: Government Printing Office, 1944).

[112] U.S. Immigration and Naturalization Service, *Federal Textbook on Citizenship: Laws for the Nation* (Washington: Government Printing Office, 1959); U.S. Immigration and Naturalization Service, *Federal Textbook on Citizenship: Our Constitution and Government*, Catheryn Seckler-Hudson, ed. (Washington: Government Printing Office, 1969).

[113] INA, § 312(2) (codified as amended at 8 U.S.C. § 1423(a)(2) (2006)).

In 1997, the U.S. Commission on Immigration Reform published a report on immigration policy calling for a renewed commitment to Americanization of immigrants in the sense of "*the cultivation of a shared commitment to the American values of liberty, democracy and equal opportunity.*" It declared that "American unity depends upon a widely-held belief in the[se] principles and values" and found that immigrants "truly become Americans when they give allegiance to these principles and values." The Commission recommended making the naturalization process, including the citizenship test, more meaningful. It noted that the test "relies on memorization of discrete facts rather than on *substantive understanding* of the basic concepts of civic participation." The Commission called for the development of a new test, which would "assess whether applicants understand the basic principles of U.S. government."[114]

In September 2007, after seven years of a redesign process, the U.S. Citizenship and Immigration Services (USCIS) released the new test. It announced that the test—which entered into force on October 1, 2008—better assesses whether applicants have "a meaningful understanding of U.S. government and history."[115] The test structure remains the same—the applicant must answer correctly six out of ten questions from a list of 100 pre-published questions and answers. The topics are mainly civic: American government (system of government, rights and responsibilities), American history (the colonial period and independence, the 1800s, recent American history), and civics (geography, national symbols, holidays). This test is more multicultural than the preceding one; it represents the diversity of U.S. society. For instance, one question asks the candidate to "name *one* American Indian tribe"; another question addresses slavery.[116]

The new naturalization test demonstrates the cultural transformation in the process of becoming American. The test began as an ambitious project, which included asking immigrants to adopt American mannerisms and cultural characteristics. It has been downgraded since to focus on memorizing relatively easy information. Making the test more meaningful and substantive was a central motive for the redesign of the test. And yet, the new test includes very few questions requiring a substantive

[114] U.S. Commission on Immigration Reform, *Becoming an American: Immigration and Immigrant Policy* (Washington: Government Printing Office, 1997): pp. 26, 25, 47, respectively. See also pp. 27–29, 54–55.

[115] U.S. Citizenship and Immigration Services, "USCIS Introduces New Naturalization Test," *USCIS Monthly* (October 2007): pp. 1–8 at 2.

[116] U.S. Citizenship and Immigration Services, "Civics (History and Government) Questions for the Redesigned (New) Naturalization Test," 2008.

understanding of American liberties. Moreover, because the questions and answers are published in advance, all the applicant needs to do is to memorize the information (one might ask whether it is really a "test"). In addition to the U.S. Constitution, applicants should be familiar with geography ("name *one* of the two longest rivers in the United States"), provide answers to technical questions such as "how many justices are on the Supreme Court?," and answer esoteric questions such as "where is the Statue of Liberty?" Applicants are not obliged to participate in integration courses and can easily pass the test without even opening the handbook. Indeed, the handbook itself advises migrants to skip reading most of it because "*you will not be tested on the additional information.*"[117]

Compared to citizenship tests in Europe, the United States has a low expectation of its citizenship test. First and foremost, the U.S. test is about knowledge of history and civics. This is not the case in other countries, where tests also focus on ways of life and social mores. Unlike America, in which passing the test is a requirement at the end of the naturalization process, in other countries it is a prerequisite for entry (the Netherlands) or obtaining a residence permit (Britain). As for the test format, the United States is the only surveyed country that pre-publishes its questions and answers, and where the questions always remain the same. For better or for worse, the United States has adopted a test that is very relaxed. From a comparative view, no other country asks so little in its naturalization test.

Attachments to the Constitution

In the Naturalization Act of 1795, Congress provided that no person shall be naturalized unless he is "a man of a good moral character, attached to the principles of the constitution of the United States, and well disposed to the good order and happiness of the same." The attachment requirement has been left vague: first, what does "attachment" mean: is it about legal acceptance of a norm, or about moral identification with it? Second, what does the "Constitution" mean: is it only the formal document we call a "constitution," or does it include other sources, such as the Declaration of Independence, statutory law, and case-law? And third, what are the "principles" of the Constitution to which should one be attached?

[117] U.S. Citizenship and Immigration Services, "Learn About the United States: Quick Civics Lessons for the New Naturalization Test," 2013.

U.S. case-law reveals three approaches to attachment to the Constitution. The first approach focuses on *knowledge* and suggests that attachment to the Constitution is equivalent to knowledge about its essentials, for instance, the reasons for the enactment of the Constitution, the rights and duties of an American, and the form of government of the United States. A person "cannot be attached to principles of which he is entirely ignorant,"[118] or swear allegiance to some principles that he or she does not even know. Consequently, the applicant should show, even if not in detail, "some general comprehension of what the constitution is."[119]

The second approach focuses on *behavior*; a person is attached to the Constitution, even without knowing its essentials, by acting according to its spirit. *Re Rodriguez* provides an example. In 1896, Ricardo Rodriguez, a natural-born Mexican citizen, applied for U.S. citizenship. He was illiterate and could not understand American constitutional principles. Rodriguez could not even name the U.S. President. In a court hearing, Fisk, a character witness, testified: "I know the man. I know that he is a good man, and know that if, whatever the principles of the constitution of the United States might be, that he would uphold them if he knew what they were." Based on Fisk's testimony, the Court admitted Rodriguez to American citizenship, noting that he "is a very good man, peaceable and industrious, of good moral character, and law abiding to a 'remarkable degree'."[120] The possession of certain traits allowed the judge to accept Rodriguez's appeal and made him eligible to become a citizen.

Another example is the *Hansen* case, in which Marius Hansen was granted U.S. citizenship in spite of the fact that he knew almost nothing about the U.S. Constitution. In a court hearing, Hansen was found to believe that the U.S. President was Washington; that Duluth is the capital of the United States; and that Roosevelt (then the U.S. President) was the Governor of Minnesota. Nevertheless, he was admitted to citizenship since he showed good citizenship. The Court offered a functional test of "whether the evidence, considered as a whole, justifies the conclusion that the applicant will make a good citizen." Hansen had married an American woman, had fathered four American-born children, had resided in the country for twenty-four years, had held a decent job, and had spoken English fairly well.[121]

118 *Re Meakins* 164 F. 334, p. 335 (E.D. Wash. 1908).

119 *Re Bodek* 63 F. 813, p. 815 (E.D. Pa. 1894).

120 *Re Rodriguez* 81 F. 337, pp. 338, 355 (W.D. Tex. 1897).

121 *State ex rel United States* v. *District Court* 107 Minn. 444, p. 448 (Minn. Sup. Ct. 1909); *Re Pisciattano* 308 F. Supp. 818 (D. Conn. 1970).

The criterion of behavior has proved useful not only for admission, but also for exclusion. Courts have denied citizenship petitions filed by people who possessed knowledge about the Constitution, yet could not promise in advance to perform civic duties. Under this view, a naturalized citizen must be a "citizen in fact as well as in name."[122] Notable examples are the cases of Jehovah's Witnesses, who refused to pledge under oath that they would vote in elections, serve on a jury, or bear arms. American courts hold that a person who "refuses to vote, serve on juries or otherwise participate in government is not attached to the principles of the Constitution"; the attachment requirement is not theoretical, but practical.[123] While "we must accept our natural-born citizens as we find them, we can scrupulously select those aliens upon whom to confer the privilege of United States citizenship. More is demanded of an alien than a native-born citizen."[124]

Can a person who seeks to amend the U.S. Constitution be considered attached to it? American courts have ruled that a person should be attached to the basic structure of the U.S. government, not to each constitutional provision. The principles to which a person should be attached are arguably: (a) representative government; (b) a dual form of government; (c) distribution of governmental authorities by a separation of powers; (d) the right to life, liberty, and private property; and (e) due process of law. According to some courts, these principles, to which applicants for American citizenship must be attached, are "the political philosophy of the Constitution."[125] In one case, a court held that complete abolition of the U.S. form of government is more than an "amendment of the Constitution"; it is a "destruction" of the Constitution. There is nothing wrong in seeking to amend the Constitution, but it is not an "amendment" if a person seeks to "abolish" the Constitution's basic structure,[126] its political philosophy.[127]

The third approach focuses on *inner devotion*; attachment to the Constitution is evident in a positive feeling toward its values and principles. At the beginning of the twentieth century, courts ruled that

[122] *Luria* v. *United States* 231 U.S. 9, p. 23 (1913).

[123] *Re Petition of Matz* 296 F. Supp. 927, p. 929 (E.D. Cal. 1969).

[124] *Matz*, p. 930 (n 123).

[125] *Re Saralieff* 59 F. 2d. 436, pp. 436–437 (E.D. Mo. 1932).

[126] *Saralieff*, p. 437 (n 125). The Court overruled this decision in *Schneiderman* v. *United States* 320 U.S. 118, p. 122 (1943) (discussed in Ch. 4).

[127] *Petition of Sittler* 197 F. Supp. 278 (S.D. N.Y. 1961). See also *Stasiukevich* v. *Nicolls* 168 F. 2d. 474 (1st Cir. 1948); *Re Ramadass* 445 Pa. 86 (Pa. Sup. Ct. 1971).

knowledge of constitutional essentials is not sufficient for U.S. citizenship if one is not emotionally attached to the U.S. Constitution. One court ruled that attachment refers to "the mental attitude of the petitioner toward this country.... a depth of conviction which would lead to active support of the principles in question." A second court held that the attachment requirement should serve to exclude "persons disbelieving in our form of government." A third court noted that attachment means "affection for" constitutional principles and sustaining them "by moral force." A fourth court held that attachment "requires ascertainment of his [the applicant's] state of mind."[128] This approach was overruled in the 1940s,[129] yet for years the U.S. naturalization process continued to include a question on constitutional faith. One question in Form N-400, which every applicant had to file, was: "Do you *believe* in the Constitution and form of government of the U.S.?"[130] In only about the year 2000 was the question revised to "Do you support the Constitution and form of government of the U.S.?"[131]

The attachment requirement has never been clearly defined. Congress left this elastic formula for judicial interpretation. U.S. courts, however, have usually been reluctant to provide a consistent and clear definition of what attachment to the principles of the U.S. Constitution means. Perhaps the whole point of choosing a catch-all term was to remain vague.[132]

Historically, the attachment requirement served as a means for immigration selection. This goal is not its current focus. Contrary to the thickening of the naturalization requirements in Europe, the United States has gradually downgraded its naturalization requirements and, especially, its cultural requirements. The U.S. citizenship test, to quote Peter Spiro, "is a joke," which "measures only rote memorization."[133] The process of redesigning the test, aimed at creating a more meaningful test, has ended up with a test that offers a very thin version of Americanism; one may wonder whether it is really a "test," given that the questions and answers are published in advance. The attachment

128 See, respectively, *Re Shanin* 278 F. 739, p. 740 (D. Mass. 1922); *Saralieff*, p. 436 (n 125); *Re Siem* 284 F. 868, p. 871 (D. Mont. 1922); *Sittler*, p. 280 (n 127).

129 *Schneiderman* (n 126); *United States* v. *Rossler* 144 F. 2d. 463, p. 465 (2nd Cir. 1944).

130 56 Federal Register 20448, p. 20452 (May 3, 1991) (emphasis added).

131 64 Federal Register 1221, p. 1236 (January 8, 1999).

132 Frank George Franklin, *The Legislative History of Naturalization in the United States from the Revolutionary War to 1861* (Chicago: University of Chicago Press, 1906): pp. 40–41.

133 Peter J. Spiro, *Beyond Citizenship: American Identity After Globalization* (Oxford: OUP, 2008): p. 43.

requirement is almost non-existent. In order to show attachment to the Constitution, the applicant should nowadays take the oath of allegiance and mark "Yes" in question number 47 of the application for naturalization (Form N-400): "Do you support the Constitution and form of government of the United States?" The oath, too, is technical. And the requirement of "good moral character" is currently satisfied by checking police records and governmental databases and answering a few questions on the application form. Even the English language requirement is very simple. In practice, not much cultural substance has been left in U.S. naturalization policy.[134]

In 1997, the U.S. Commission on Immigration Reform called to make the U.S. naturalization policy more meaningful. The Chair, Barbara Jordan, admitted that Americanization had "earned a bad reputation when it was stolen by racists and xenophobes in the 1920s," yet added that, "it is our word, and we are taking it back." The Commission found the core of Americanization to be "a shared commitment to the American values of liberty, democracy, and equal opportunity."[135] About a decade later, a task force of the Department of Homeland Security repeated these words by advocating "patriotic assimilation."[136] Thus far, the cultural core of Americanism, as reflected in U.S. naturalization policy, remains minimal. American policy is pluralistic and diverse; diversity is even an official immigration policy—the Diversity Visa Program, which distributes visas by lottery.[137] Noah Pickus characterizes the existing American philosophy of immigrant integration as "don't invest, don't expect." Under this approach, the United States does not invest much effort in immigrant integration but, at the same time, it "does not expect that newcomers will learn much about [its] history and values."[138]

[134] Peter H. Schuck, "The Reevaluation of American Citizenship," in *Citizens, Strangers, and In-Betweens: Essays on Immigration and Citizenship* (Boulder: Westview Press, 1998): pp. 176–206 at 194.

[135] U.S. Commission on Immigration Reform, p. 6 (n 114).

[136] U.S. Department of Homeland Security, Task Force on New Americans, *Building an Americanization Movement for the Twenty-first Century: A Report to the President of the United States from the Task Force on New Americans* (Washington: Government Printing Office, 2008): pp. ix, 44.

[137] Stephen H. Legomsky, "Immigration, Equality and Diversity," *Columbia Journal of Transnational Law* 31, no. 2 (1993): pp. 319–336; Peter H. Schuck, *Diversity in America: Keeping Government at a Safe Distance* (Cambridge: Harvard University Press, 2003): pp. 75–133.

[138] Noah Pickus, "Laissez-Faire and Its Discontents: US Naturalization and Integration Policy in Comparative Perspective," *Citizenship Studies* 18, no. 2 (2014): pp. 160–174 at 164–165.

ISRAEL

Jewish homeland

Israel does not have citizenship tests, nor does it have attachment requirements or integration contracts, because Israel does not consider itself an immigration country. The Supreme Court of Israel ruled that "Israel's character is essentially perceived [as]... a repatriation country, rather than an 'immigration country'."[139] Therefore, every Jew, or a close relative of a Jew,[140] has a right to enter Israel and become naturalized. These immigration preferences reflect the idea that Israel is the homeland of the Jewish people. Limitations are only imposed on the migration of Jews in cases of a Jewish applicant who: (a) "is engaged in an activity directed against the Jewish People"; (b) "is likely to endanger public health or the security of the State"; (c) has a criminal record and is "likely to endanger public order."[141] Nonetheless, in reality, denying entry to Jews is rare.

In order to receive Israeli citizenship through naturalization, a non-Jewish applicant must reside in Israel when applying, reside in Israel at least three out of five years prior to applying, be eligible for permanent residency, possess some knowledge of the Hebrew language, renounce previous citizenship, and pledge to be a "loyal citizen of the State of Israel."[142] These naturalization requirements do not apply to Jews, close relatives of Jews, and non-Jewish spouses of Israeli citizens. In theory, a non-Jewish immigrant can become a naturalized Israeli. In practice, however, there are not many successful applications because only a very few non-citizens are eligible for a permanent resident status in Israel.

Although Israel does not generally offer naturalization for non-Jews, two recent cases illustrate the tension between the state's Jewish and democratic identity. In many ways, the whole dilemma of Israel's nationhood can be seen in these two cases.

Love and war

Israel's War of Independence caused the separation of Palestinian extended families who lived together in Mandatory Palestine. Palestinians who currently live in the Palestinian Authority have close family ties to Palestinian citizens living in Israel. However, the outbreak of armed

[139] Admin A 1644/05, *Frieda* v. *Ministry of the Interior*, June 29, 2005.

[140] Law of Return (1950), arts. 1, 4A(a) (Law of Return).

[141] Law of Return, art. 2(b).

[142] Nationality Law (1952), art. 5.

conflict in late September 2000 between Israel and the Palestinians placed a severe burden on these ties. During Passover 2002, a suicide bomber blew himself up in a restaurant in Haifa, killing dozens of people. The terrorist was a Palestinian from the West Bank who held an Israeli ID following his migration, which had been sponsored by an Israeli citizen. In the following months, twenty-six Palestinian family migrants were involved in terror attacks in Israel. Because of the Security Fence, which prevents easy incursion of terrorists from the Palestinian territories, family migration has become the main legal path for entering the State of Israel.

In May 2002, the Israeli government adopted a new policy on family migration. Previously, every applicant requesting family migration had to apply for temporary residence status and could be naturalized after a period of four-and-a-half years. Under the new policy, the government banned family migration of persons residing in the Palestinian Authority. This policy became law: The Citizenship and Entry into Israel Act (Temporary Order) 2003. The Act provides that, with a few exceptions, "the Minister of the Interior shall not grant an inhabitant of an area citizenship" and "shall not give him/her a license to reside or to stay in Israel." The term "area" refers to the West Bank and the Gaza Strip.

In May 2006, the High Court of Justice (HCJ) delivered its ruling on the constitutional validity of the Act. In a 6 to 5 decision, not a typical event in Israel, the HCJ sustained the Act.[143] Justice Mishael Cheshin, for the majority opinion, upheld the Act on the basis of three premises: first, there is an armed conflict between Israel and the Palestinians; second, people living under Palestinian Authority rule resemble "enemy aliens"; and third, in time of conflict, states may ban migration of enemy aliens. Hence, his conclusion was that Israel may ban family migration of people residing in the Palestinian Authority. Justice Cheshin added that replacing the blanket ban with individualized inspections "is likely to lead to quite a high probability of an increase in terror activities in Israel; to the killing and wounding of residents of the state; to a real and tangible weakening of the feeling of stability; and . . . to the undermining of democracy itself."[144]

President of the Supreme Court, Aharon Barak dissented. In his view, every Israeli citizen has a constitutional right to form a family with

[143] HCJ 7052/03, *Adalah* v. *the Minister of Interior*, P.D. 61(2), May 14, 2006.

[144] *Adalah*, paras. 79, 109 (n 143).

persons whom they love *and* to establish that family in Israel, where they have cultural and societal roots. Justice Barak ruled that the Act's impact is discriminatory; the burden of the ban falls mostly on Israeli-Palestinian citizens. He was willing to assume that no intentional discrimination existed, yet held that the controlling factor is not intent but effect. As for the security risks, Justice Barak ruled that "the additional security that the blanket prohibition achieves is not proportionate to the additional damage caused to the family life and equality of the Israeli spouses. Admittedly, the blanket prohibition does provide additional security; but it is achieved at too great a price [in human rights]."[145] According to Barak, banning family migration can only be lawful following individual checks on a case-by-case basis.

A Jewish majority

In the *Family Migration* case, national security was at stake, but below the surface there was more. For some, at stake was the constitutional character of Israel. Large-scale Palestinian migration is perceived by the Jewish majority as undermining the "two-state solution," because it may gradually lead to a Palestinian majority in Israel. Thus, the *Family Migration* case strikes at the very root of the Israeli-Palestinian conflict.

Justice Cheshin does not merely consider in his opinion the individual, the one Israeli Palestinian citizen who fell in love with a Palestinian from the West Bank. Rather, he looks at the picture as a whole and the potential consequences of the case: "We are obliged to cast a glance from side to side, above and below. Concentrating our gaze on the individual tree, while ignoring the forest around it, is tantamount to ignoring reality. By protecting the individual tree we may harm the forest, and thus we unintentionally harm the tree itself, since the tree exists only within the limits of the forest." The "trees" in Justice Cheshin's ruling are individual human rights; the "forest around" is probably the broad picture of the conflict and Jewish sovereignty in Israel.[146] In Justice Cheshin's words:[147]

> A state is made up of its residents. The residents of the state are the persons who shape the nature of the society, and the 'state' serves as a framework for the society and its residents. The entry of a foreign national into the state as a permanent resident thereof means a change of the *status quo ante* in the relationship of the citizens and residents *inter se*.... this

[145] *Adalah*, para. 92 (n 143). [146] *Adalah*, para. 43 (n 143). [147] *Adalah*, paras. 54–55 (n 143).

> way the nature of the society and [of] the state changes. Where we are speaking of an individual resident or citizen, the change is infinitesimal. But this is not the case with a massive incursion of foreign residents and citizens whose joint influence on the state may significantly change its nature.

The question whether Palestinian family migration endangers Israel's character is both empirical and normative. On the empirical level, there is a debate as to the number of Palestinians who have entered Israel via family-based migration. Numbers count, but numbers are disputed. On the normative level, the debate concerns the number of family reunifications that may significantly affect Israel's character and, importantly, whether it is legitimate to restrict migration for this purpose. To a great extent, this question, which was not explicitly addressed by the Court, is *the* question.

Israeli peoplehood

The State of Israel maintains a population registry database, primarily for statistical purposes, in which it records demographic data, such as a person's previous citizenship, religious affiliation, and nationality.[148] "Nationality" here has a different meaning than the Anglo-American meaning of citizenship. Instead, it signifies an ethno-cultural affiliation, or peoplehood. In cases of natural-born citizens, it is determined by the nationality of the father or the mother: Jewish, Arab, Buddhist, Greek, etc.

In 2013, the Israeli Supreme Court had to decide a "hot" topic—whether an Israeli nationality exists. The petitioners asked to change their status in the population registry database to a new status of "Israeli nationality." Because the registry is mainly statistical, the petition was seemingly procedural. And yet, it was a hot potato. The main categories of the Central Bureau of Statistics include "Jews," "Arabs" (Muslims, Christians, Druzes), and "others" (non-Arab Muslims/Christians and people who have no religious affiliation). The recognition of a new nationality would mean a new sub-nationality of "Israelis," Jews and non-Jews.

The Supreme Court of Israel rejected the petition, ruling that no "Israeli nationality" in the sense of peoplehood shared by all citizens, Jews, and non-Jews, has been created thus far. Justice Vogelman viewed the petition as asking the Court to decide between two conflicting

[148] Population Registry Law (1965), art. 2.

models of nationality: civic nationality, in which citizenship and nationality overlap, and ethno-cultural nationality, in which citizenship is not identical to nationality. He noted that, inasmuch as civic Israeli nationality has been created in Israel, petitioners had not proved the point by empirical evidence. While Justice Vogelman left open both the factual and normative questions—whether there is or ought to be an Israeli nationality—Justice Meltzer went one step further. He dismissed the idea that there is an Israeli nationality, as well as the claim that an Israeli nationality is desirable—"at this stage, the separated nationalities living in Israel should not be legally united to one 'Israeli nationality' because it would conflict with the character of Israel as a Jewish and democratic state." The petitioners, Justice Meltzer found, had asked the Court to rewrite the Israeli Declaration of Independence by recognizing the creation of "an Israeli people." However, Justice Meltzer observed, "Israel was established as a Jewish and democratic state for the Jewish people."[149]

The issue of Israeli nationality is perceived as central to Jewish sovereignty. One point that most Jews and Arabs in Israel agree upon is that they belong to different nationalities: Jewish and Palestinian. Unlike European nation-states, where the migration debates persistently seek a common sense of British or French identity, the identity debate in Israel is grounded on the premise that there is no single nationality shared by all. The decision on Israeli nationality, as in the *Family Migration* case, characterizes the closure of the Jewish state. Israel designs its immigration policy to protect not a common culture and way of life, nor a commitment to civic and political principles, but the preservation of its Jewish majority.

A NATION WITH A DUTY TO SURVIVE

Every sovereign, according to Rousseau, has an unavoidable end: "The body politic, as well as the human body, begins to die as soon as it is born." Governments do not survive forever. Their death is an inevitable destiny. After all, "if Sparta and Rome perished, what State can hope to endure for ever?" And yet, the body politic differs from the human body. The death of the human body is a matter of nature, but the death of the body politic is a matter of constitutional design: "It is not in men's power

[149] Civil Appeal 8573/08, *Ornan* v. *The Minister of Interior*, paras. 20–21, 25 (Justice Vogelman) and paras. 4–5, 12 (Justice Meltzer), October 6, 2013.

to prolong their own lives; but it is for them to prolong as much as possible the life of the State, by giving it the best possible constitution."[150]

Recent immigration policies in Europe and Israel, as in the United States in the past, reveal subjective fears that important national interests are under "threat." The exact interests are not always clearly defined. They may be a culture, a way of life, a political idea, a liberal institution, or an ethnic majority—whatever they are, they generate a counter-reaction that I term "cultural defense of nations." This results in forced cultural integration, rather than its encouragement—integration is mandatory, sanctioned, and test-based. It is expressed in the extension of culture-based selection to the requirement for entry—as a pre-arrival integration (or integration from abroad). It applies to most types of migrants, including family members. And it is usually more invasive than the classic requirements of familiarity with a country's history and civics.

The development of cultural defense policies is of dual nature. On the one hand, it affirms the identity crisis in modern nation-states. Nation-states seek to protect their identity, but cannot clearly specify what that identity is. National identities are undermined, and there is no better illustration for that than the very idea of searching their content and attempting to redefine them. The domain of immigration shows that even firmly established nation-states—Britain, France, and Germany—have been affected by a national identity crisis. On the other hand, there is a revival of national identity debates. Nation-states try to formulate their identities in order to strengthen their solidarity and unity. In this regard, regulating immigration is a form of nation-building. National identities require canons, real or imagined: historical events, languages, myths, traditions, symbols, and ways of life. It is in the immigration context that the national identity debate is conducted and in which "we" find a revival of concepts such as the "Dutch way of life," "German way of doing things," and "values essential to the French *communauté*."

A comparative review helps us to understand the differences and similarities between various sorts of defenses. There are differences in the anxieties of the United States, European states, and Israel. The cultural suspicion that prevailed in U.S. immigration law in the first half of the twentieth century no longer exists. Current policy, even

[150] Jean-Jacques Rousseau, *On the Social Contract*, G.D.H. Cole, trans. (Mineola: Dover Publications, 2003): p. 60 (Book III, Ch. XI).

in light of the resentment against Mexicans, has not led to cultural defense policies. American naturalization policy contains a thin, perhaps overly thin version of cultural defense, focusing on mastering basic English language, passing an easy test, taking an oath to support the U.S. Constitution, and showing good moral character. In Europe, however, the main concern is that immigrants do not share common national cultures and undermine liberal democratic structures. Europe's concerns are largely of a different kind. Israel presents a third case in which the demographic concerns do not focus on political values or national cultures, but on the existence of a Jewish majority. In Israel, one cannot just learn to be like the majority by acquiring the language and adopting the culture. There is no citizenship test because the actual test is birthright. In spite of these differences, a common denominator exists: the relationship between immigration policy and constitutional identity. Immigration laws are gatekeepers. They are designed to prolong the constitutional identity of a society. But, in so doing, they reveal the difficulties of defining exactly what should survive. Put differently, the resurgence of national identities seems to make hollow the meaning of national identity. It presents a deep disagreement over the essence of national identity that should be preserved.

Cultural defense policies raise a set of normative questions. Two simple but important questions are: (a) Is the cultural continuity of majority groups a legitimate *purpose* to restrict migration and access to citizenship? and (b) Is culture a legitimate *criterion* to restrict migration and access to citizenship? In other words: can a liberal state legitimately encourage or restrict migration of people of a specific cultural background? If some forms of cultural defense can be justified, what may be the legitimate scope of this defense—when is cultural defense justified; what does cultural defense justify; and which culture, and whose? These questions are thoroughly analyzed in the second part of the book, in Chapters 4 to 6.

PART II

LEGITIMATE AND ILLEGITIMATE DEFENSE

4

Illiberal Liberalism

> If there is any principle of the Constitution that more imperatively calls for attachment than any other it is the principle of free thought—not free thought for those who agree with us but freedom for the thought that we hate. I think that we should adhere to that principle with regard to admission into . . . this country.
>
> —The U.S. Supreme Court (1929)[1]

Cultural defense policies create a *Paradox of Liberalism*. Liberal democracies, in order to protect what they perceive as a liberal regime, resort to illiberal means that violate the same values they seek to protect. Herein lies the paradox. Either the liberal should tolerate illiberal practices, or turn to illiberal means in order to "liberate" the illiberal. Either choice undermines liberalism. The idea that one should adopt a liberal way of life as a prerequisite for living in a liberal society is, in itself, illiberal. This is because liberalism contains the freedom to choose *not* to hold liberal beliefs or live a liberal way of life as long as a person's way of life complies with law and order.

The purpose of this chapter is threefold. The first purpose is to present two opposing approaches to naturalization. One approach—represented by current U.S. policy—does not engage in an investigation of a person's belief in liberal values and institutions; the other approach—represented by current policy in some European states—emphasizes belief in liberal values and institutions. While both approaches have pros and cons, the chapter argues that, from a liberal perspective, the second approach has gone too far and is approaching the point of becoming illiberal. This is due to three reasons: state neutrality, liberal tolerance, and policy motivation. The second purpose is to show that joining a liberal state is frequently followed by a requirement to adopt a constitutional "story" in

[1] *United States* v. *Schwimmer* 279 U.S. 644, pp. 654–655 (1929).

the sense of accepting its "truths." The third purpose is to demonstrate several difficulties in evaluating normative aspects relating to cultural defense policies: their purpose is not clear, their effectiveness is a conundrum, and their lawfulness is yet to be clarified. Overall, the chapter illustrates risks involved in immigration and citizenship policies which, in order to protect liberal values, embrace illiberal means that violate those very same values.

AMERICA: THE END OF CONSTITUTIONAL FAITH

Attachment to the Constitution

In the Naturalization Act of 1795, the U.S. Congress provided that no person shall be naturalized unless he is "of a good moral character, attached to the principles of the constitution of the United States, and well disposed to the good order and happiness of the same." The content of the attachment requirement has been left vague. American courts have been reluctant to define what it means to be attached to the principles of the U.S. Constitution. Throughout American history, attachment has implied three meanings (see Chapter 3). The first is knowledge. One is attached to the Constitution when one possesses a minimum level of knowledge about its tenets, history, and function. The second is behavior. One is attached to the Constitution when one acts according to the spirit of the Constitution (whatever that means). The third is inner devotion. One is attached to the Constitution when one feels positively toward its tenets. These three meanings do not always apply at the same time or in the same way. U.S. policy shows how diverse the attachment requirement may be.

The interpretation of the attachment requirement changed significantly during the twentieth century. The change in the judicial interpretation reflects a fundamental alteration to the U.S. naturalization philosophy—from excluding people because of their beliefs, to tolerating practically any belief. Arguably, the turning point came at the height of World War II.

On June 21, 1943, the U.S. Supreme Court issued one of the most interesting decisions in American constitutional law. The case, *Schneiderman* v. *United States*, discusses whether Schneiderman, a Russian-born citizen who became an American citizen in 1927, should be denaturalized. In 1939, about twelve years after his naturalization, the government sought to denaturalize him because, in its view, his citizenship had been procured illegally. At the time of his naturalization, Schneiderman believed in Communism and was a member of Communist organizations which, according to the government, espoused ideas opposed to the U.S. form of government.[2] The government claimed that Schneiderman was not attached to the Constitution and declared his naturalization to be flawed.

Justice Murphy, writing for the majority, reversed Schneiderman's denaturalization on the merits of the evidence. He found that the U.S. government had not proved by clear, unequivocal, and convincing evidence that Schneiderman was not attached to the principles of the Constitution at *the time of his admission*. The interesting aspect of the case lies in the fact that Justice Murphy found that the Communist Party indeed opposed the U.S. form of government, but that Schneiderman was nonetheless attached to the U.S. Constitution. Justice Murphy admitted that the Communist Party of the United States advocated "the abolition of the Senate [and], of the Supreme Court," yet ruled that one can be attached to the Constitution even if one supports the abolition of the judicial branch, to which Justice Murphy belonged: "It is true that this Court has played a large part in the unfolding of the constitutional plan... but we would be arrogant indeed if we presumed that a government of laws, with protection for minority groups, would be impossible without it." In Justice Murphy's own words:[3]

> These would indeed be significant changes in our present governmental structure... but whatever our personal views, as judges we cannot say that a person who advocates their adoption through peaceful and constitutional means is not in fact attached to the Constitution—those institutions are not enumerated as necessary in the Government's test of "general political philosophy", and it is conceivable that "ordered liberty" could be maintained without them.... it is possible to advocate such changes and still be attached to the Constitution.

How can one be attached to the U.S. Constitution while advocating the abolition of the U.S. form of government? According to Justice Murphy, such a scenario is possible when a person shows unqualified attachment to "the guaranties of the Bill of Rights and especially that of freedom of thought." Attachment should be to the "general political philosophy" of the Constitution, rather than to each constitutional principle. The First Amendment "refute[s] the idea that attachment to any particular

[2] *Schneiderman* v. *United States* 320 U.S. 118, pp. 121–122 (1943). For a legal analysis of the case see Sanford Levinson, *Constitutional Faith* (Princeton: Princeton University Press, 1988): pp. 122–154; Patrick Weil, *The Sovereign Citizen: Denaturalization and the Origins of the American Republic* (Philadelphia: University of Pennsylvania Press, 2013): pp. 111–123.

[3] *Schneiderman*, pp. 143–144 (n 2).

provision or provisions is essential, or that one who advocates radical changes is necessarily not attached to the Constitution." Justice Murphy went further, stressing the sanctity of freedom of thought. He cited with approval a quotation of Thomas Jefferson that, "If there be any among us who would wish to dissolve this Union or to change its republican form, let them stand undisturbed as monuments of the safety with which error of opinion may be tolerated where reason is left free to combat it." Applying this rationale to Schneiderman, Justice Murphy found that, although he had different views on constitutional issues, his beliefs at the time of his admission were not entirely against the "general political philosophy" of the U.S. Constitution.[4]

The idea that one can seek to change the U.S. form of government through peaceful means, yet be attached to the Constitution, was criticized by Chief Justice Stone in his dissenting opinion. Justice Stone found that the Communist Party of the United States supported the establishment of an entirely new form of government in which "the freedoms guaranteed by the Bill of Rights were to be ended."[5] On May 31, 1943, three weeks before the decision was released, Justice Frankfurter, who joined the dissenting opinion, wrote a personal note to Justice Murphy: "I think it is only fair to state, in view of your general argument, that Uncle Joe Stalin was at least a spiritual co-author with Jefferson of the Virginia Statute for Religious Freedom." The U.S. Constitution "ain't got no principles. The Communist Party don't stand for nuthin'. The Soopreme Court don't mean nuthin'."[6]

The *Schneiderman* case downgrades the attachment requirement to the bare minimum. It implies that, in the main, a person should be attached to two principles. The first is freedom of speech, which allows advocating almost any idea inasmuch as it is not incompatible with the "general political philosophy" of the Constitution. The second is peaceful legal change, which enables the promotion of even radical political changes as long as they are promoted according to the amendment procedure. In other words: a person should essentially be attached to the substantive ideas enshrined in the First Amendment (freedom of speech and of thought) and to the legal procedure of Article V (the constitutional amendment procedure).

[4] *Schneiderman*, pp. 144, 137, 139, 141, respectively (n 2).

[5] *Schneiderman*, pp. 193–194 (n 2).

[6] Cited in Weil, p. 118 (n 2).

Oath of allegiance

The years after the *Schneiderman* case witnessed one of the greatest battles for freedom of speech in U.S. history. In 1944, the U.S. Supreme Court decided the *Baumgartner* case. Baumgartner was a German-born citizen who became a naturalized American in 1932. Ten years later, in 1942, the government sought to denaturalize him due to fraud. It claimed that when Baumgartner had taken the oath of allegiance in 1932, he had not truly renounced his allegiance to Germany. Baumgartner was devoted to Adolf Hitler and the Nazis and hostile to the U.S. form of government.[7]

In 1944, while the United States was at war with Nazi Germany, the Supreme Court confirmed Baumgartner's naturalization. Justice Frankfurter, who had affirmed the denaturalization of a Communist believer just a year earlier (Schneiderman), was surprisingly unwilling to strip a Nazi activist of his citizenship. Writing for the majority, Justice Frankfurter admitted that Baumgartner praised Hitler, but added that Americanism was all about the "freedom to speak foolishly and without moderation."[8] Baumgartner, however, did more than just praise Hitler and the Nazi regime; his *actions* undoubtedly showed active support for Hitler. In order to escape this conclusion, Justice Frankfurter found that, at the time of his admission in 1932, Baumgartner had merely renounced his allegiance to the Weimar Republic and not to Hitler, who came to power only a year later, in 1933.

The tone of the Court was similar even in cases in which the outcome was different. In 1946, the Court approved the denaturalization of a native-born German, Knauer, who had become a citizen in 1937. Justice Douglas found solid and convincing evidence that Knauer was a Nazi *before* his naturalization, and continued to be an active follower of Hitler after becoming a U.S. citizen. Justice Douglas repeated that citizens can "promote changes in our laws *including the very Charter of our Government*," yet affirmed the denaturalization on the grounds that the oath of allegiance "is a promise of future conduct," and Knauer broke his oath.[9] Justice Rutledge dissented. He refused to take away the citizenship of a Nazi activist because "No native-born American's birthright could be stripped from him for such a cause." If Knauer had committed a crime, the government had to prosecute him, but not strip him of his citizenship. According to Justice Rutledge:[10]

[7] *Baumgartner* v. *United States* 322 U.S. 665 (1944). [8] *Baumgartner*, p. 674 (n 7).

[9] *Knauer* v. *United States* 328 U.S. 654, pp. 658, 671 (1946) (emphasis added).

[10] *Knauer*, pp. 676–679 (n 9).

> Naturalized citizens are no more free to become traitors or criminals than others and may be punished as they are when they commit the same offense.... Unless it is the law that there are two classes of citizens, one superior, the other inferior, the status of no citizen can be annulled for causes or by procedures not applicable to all others.... If this means that some or even many disloyal foreignborn citizens cannot be deported, it is better so than to place so many loyal ones in inferior status.

The Court affirmed the denaturalization based on fraud, rather than on limitations on freedom of speech. It found clear evidence to indicate that, at the time of taking the oath of allegiance to the U.S. Constitution in 1937 (Hitler was already in power at that time), Knauer was a faithful follower of Hitler and the Nazis, and actively promoted Nazism in America.[11]

If *Knauer* and *Baumgartner* were limited cases, because they were about denaturalization, the Court adopted a similar line in naturalization cases. In 1946, the Supreme Court granted citizenship to Girouard, a Canadian citizen who was willing to pledge allegiance to the United States, but refused to give a positive answer to the question: "If necessary, are you willing to take up arms in defense of this country?" Girouard agreed to serve in the army as long as it was not in a combat unit. The Court held that without explicit Congressional authority, it was not permitted to exclude a person merely due to a refusal to bear arms: "The bearing of arms, important as it is, is not the only way in which our institutions may be supported and defended.... The nuclear physicists who developed the atomic bomb, the worker at his lathe, the seamen on cargo vessels, construction battalions, nurses, engineers, litter bearers, doctors, chaplains—these, too, made essential contributions."[12] The *Girouard* case, read together with the previous cases, implies that a person can disbelieve in some constitutional ideas, even object to fundamental principles, and still be attached to the "general political philosophy" of the Constitution.

Flag salute

At the height of World War II, another battle took place in the U.S. Supreme Court—on the role and function of the pledge of allegiance

[11] *Knauer*, p. 660 (n 9).

[12] *Girouard* v. *United States* 328 U.S. 61, pp. 62, 64 (1946). Following the *Girouard* case, Congress amended the oath of allegiance requiring newcomers to pledge to bear arms on behalf of the United States when it is required by the law.

and the flag salute in high schools. In the first decision, the *Gobitis* case, two children were expelled from a public school due to their refusal to salute the flag and recite the pledge of allegiance. Their dedication to Jehovah's Witnesses precluded them from pledging allegiance to the flag, in view of their belief that only God is the supreme authority. Justice Frankfurter, for the majority, adopted a patriotic stance. He found the flag and the pledge to be symbols of national unity ("We live by symbols") and essential for evoking the "unifying sentiment without which there can ultimately be no liberties." In order to foster national unity, there had to be "unconscious feelings" and a sense of patriotism. Chief Justice Stone dissented. In his view, compelling a person to recite the pledge of allegiance and salute the flag would be the end of liberty. The right to liberty "is the freedom of the individual from compulsion as to what he shall think and what he shall say."[13]

Following the *Gobitis* case, West Virginia's Board of Education adopted a resolution ordering that the pledge of allegiance become a regular part of the curriculum. This time, the U.S. Supreme Court overruled its previous decision. Justice Jackson ruled that requiring a child to pledge allegiance when the pledge offends his or her conscience is unlawful *precisely* because it "requires affirmation of a belief and an attitude of mind." For Justice Jackson, "Those who begin [with] coercive elimination of dissent soon find themselves exterminating dissenters. Compulsory unification of opinion achieves only the unanimity of the graveyard." Allegiance means the freedom to dissent, even from the most fundamental constitutional ideas. Echoing Justice Holmes in the *Schwimmer* case, Justice Jackson ruled: "If there is any fixed star in our constitutional constellation, it is that no official, high or petty, can prescribe what shall be orthodox in politics, nationalism, religion, or other matters of opinion or force citizens to confess by word or act their faith therein."[14]

The flag-salute cases were another signal that, however good the government's cause is, it is impermissible to interfere with a person's state of mind, whether this person is a natural-born citizen, a naturalized citizen, or a candidate for citizenship. The flag-salute cases are the third angle in a triangle of cases on this matter—cases about denaturalization (mainly *Schneiderman*), admission to citizenship (mainly *Girouard*), and

[13] *Minersville School District* v. *Gobitis* 310 U.S. 586, pp. 596–597, 600, 598, 604, respectively (1940).

[14] *West Virginia State Board of Education* v. *Barnette* 319 U.S. 624, pp. 633, 641–642 (1943). The Court did not rule that it is unconstitutional to require children to pledge allegiance but, rather, that a child has a right not to pledge *if* it offends his/her conscience.

the essence of citizenship as manifested in public education in the United States.

In spite of judicial rhetoric, policy and practice may be different. First, a significant part of the screening process is conducted by visa procedures at the U.S. consulates abroad. It may be that the admission regulations are quite different. Second, U.S. naturalization policy still contains grounds of inadmissibility based on affiliation with Communist and other totalitarian parties. Third, the Policy Manual used by the United States Citizenship and Immigration Services explains that attachment requires "a depth of conviction, which would lead to active support of the Constitution"; it clarifies that attachment means "a mental attitude" and "An applicant who is hostile to the basic form of government of the United States, or who does not believe in the principles of the Constitution, is not eligible for naturalization."[15] And fourth, in actual practice different forms ideological exclusion continued to dominate U.S. immigration policy even in the aftermath of the *Schneiderman* case.[16]

Nonetheless, the *Schneiderman* case has signified the end of *actual* investigation into whether a person believes in the Constitution. In practice, the immigration officer does not second-guess formal acceptance of the U.S. Constitution demonstrated by reciting the oath of allegiance, and marking "No" to some questions in the application for naturalization (Form N-400), such as: "Do you support the Constitution and form of government of the U.S.?"[17] In reality, the United States has abandoned its investigation into people's beliefs when admitting them to the citizenry.

EUROPE'S PARADOX OF LIBERALISM

Immigration and naturalization policies in Europe are slightly different to those in America. Perhaps the best description of this reality was coined by the British Prime Minister David Cameron when referring to "muscular liberalism." The idea of muscular liberalism (see Chapter 2) contains an inherent tension: the more "muscular" (aggressive, coercive,

[15] USCIS Policy Manual, vol. 12: Citizenship & Naturalization, Part D: General Naturalization Requirements, 2014.

[16] Gerald L. Neuman, "Justifying U.S. Naturalization Policies," *Virginia Journal of International Law* 35, no. 1 (1994): pp. 237–278 at 253–263; Gerald L. Neuman, *Strangers to the Constitution: Immigrants, Borders, and Fundamental Law* (Princeton: Princeton University Press, 1996): pp. 40–41, 149–164.

[17] 64 Federal Register 1221, p. 1236 (January 8, 1999).

defensive, militant) liberalism is, the less liberal it becomes. To be clear, the manifestation of muscular liberalism in Europe's immigration context has not yet reached the point of being completely illiberal (obviously, there is a great deal of variation in Member States' policies). However, the tone of the public discourse, the language of some laws, their political motivation, and their discriminatory impact—all create a troubling atmosphere that threatens liberal values in the name of their protection. As Christian Joppke and John Torpey argue, the growing appeal to "'muscular liberalism' is perhaps the more serious threat to liberalism than Islam could ever be."[18]

Liberalism has different meanings and variations. According to John Gray, one version views liberalism as a *modus vivendi* allowing plural ways of life. There is no true or ideal way of life, but "many forms of life in which humans can thrive." *Modus vivendi*, however, is "far from being the idea that anything goes"; it recognizes only ways of life that "seek peaceful coexistence." A second version views liberalism as an ethical project. There is a true or ideal way of life that ought to be promoted in a liberal democracy; liberalism is a moral project that holds universal truths.[19]

The following sections briefly describe three concerns relating to cultural defense policies: state neutrality, liberal tolerance, and policy motivation. The general claim is that Europe's challenge is dual. On the one hand, liberal states should not ignore challenges to liberal values and institutions posed by global migration (as detailed in Chapter 1). It is close to impossible to maintain a liberal democracy if a significant part of the population does not have faith in liberalism—they must not just strictly obey the law, but truly believe that liberalism is good. On the other hand, coping with this predicament is a challenge in and of itself. In protecting liberal values, liberal democracies should refrain from violating the very values they wish to protect. In other words, liberal democracies should confront the challenge to liberalism, but shall never forget to live up to their own ideals.

State neutrality

The first concern is the ideological nature of cultural defense polices. Immigration rules are often not content with applicants' knowledge of

[18] Christian Joppke and John Torpey, *Legal Integration of Islam: A Transatlantic Comparison* (Cambridge: Harvard University Press, 2013): p. 14.

[19] John Gray, *Two Faces of Liberalism* (New York: The New Press, 2000): pp. 5, 20.

the host society's history and civics, but explore their moral judgments and psychological attitudes. They investigate the applicant's reactions to ideas like homosexuality, nudism, children's education, social mores, and the political agenda. The relative weight of each question in the overall assessment is hard to measure. However, as long as these questions are given some weight, they may be an expression of ideological exclusion.

Consider a question that appeared in the first edition of the *Life in the UK Test*: "Suppose you spill someone's pint in the pub. What, according to the book, usually happens next?" The possible answers are: (a) You would offer to buy the person another pint; (b) You would offer to dry the wet shirt with your own; and (c) You may need to prepare for a fight. While the "correct" answer is (a)—one may conceivably choose (b) and ask whether this choice is morally or legally wrong—the question raises a fundamental concern: why is the British government interested in private interactions in bars? Spilling pints of beer in a bar is generally not illegal behavior and, as long as the reaction to such an act is not unlawful, as may be the case with answer (c), one might ask what business the government has with this issue. Should not the response be learnt by daily life interactions, rather than a governmental code of how to behave in bars?

Or consider the question in the citizenship test previously adopted by the *Land* of Baden-Württemberg: "Imagine that your adult son comes to you and declares that he is a homosexual and would like to live with another man. How would you react?" The "right" answer, according to the test, is to tell the son that, as an adult, he can live as he likes in his intimate relationship. But this question is tricky. A person may dislike the fact that his or her son is gay, or dislike homosexuality in general, and yet accept that people in Germany can live according to their sexual preferences and that same-sex marriages are legally permitted in Germany. As it stands, the question may represent an invasion of privacy, which may also be illegal because it violates the German concept of human dignity and the right of free development of personality, enshrined in the *Grundgesetz*.[20]

If these two examples are an exception—both questions were quickly abandoned and the current naturalization process in Germany and the United Kingdom is generally not invasive—the Dutch naturalization

[20] Rüdiger Wolfrum and Volker Röben, "Gutachten zur Vereinbarkeit des Gesprächsleitfaden für die Einbürgerungsbehörden des Landes Baden-Württemberg mit Völkerrecht," 2006.

policy embraces a set of questions about ways of life. Take the following question: "Zara works in a retirement home. The director of the home walks into the coffee room. What is the best thing Zara can do? (a) shake his hand and tell him her name; (b) continue to work and wave at him; or (c) wait until he says something to her." The "right" answer is (a), but is it morally or legally wrong to wave at the director, rather than to shake his hand?

Cultural defense is best reflected in the Dutch philosophy that "One cannot study to be Dutch, one has to feel Dutch" (see Chapter 3). In order to achieve the goal of "feeling Dutch," an effort is made to teach migrants to think and behave in a manner similar to a "typical" (or imagined) Dutch citizen. Migrants are expected to know how they should behave in daily life situations. This is allegedly cognitive, yet the fact that the content of the exam is undisclosed, and given that there is no official handbook for exam preparation, it is not purely cognitive. In addition, a person can fail the test even if the answers to the daily life situations are all reasonable and lawful, if they are incompatible with the Dutch "way of doing things."

Do these policies contradict the principle of neutrality? State neutrality is an elusive concept. One view of neutrality is "neutrality of impact"; the state should avoid policies that result in favoring one way of life. Another view of neutrality is "neutrality of justifications"; this view focuses on the policy's intention. A policy is neutral—even when it burdens some people more than others—if its justifications are neutral. In practice, neutrality is largely a myth that cannot possibly be achieved (in particular "neutrality of impact," because all policies unavoidably favor some groups). Samuel Scheffler rightly notes that "Where culture is concerned, neutrality is not an option."[21] In the real world, states are never neutral, no matter how they should be in theory.[22] Instead, it is a matter of degree: how much non-neutrality should be implemented, in what fields, and for what purposes?

In a stimulating book about civic education in America, Stephen Macedo argues that liberal democracies need *not* be neutral toward what he calls basic "civic liberalism." In order to protect freedoms, liberal states should promote shared citizenship based upon basic civic morality

[21] Samuel Scheffler, "Immigration and the Significance of Culture," *Philosophy and Public Affairs* 35, no. 2 (2007): pp. 93–125 at 114.

[22] See, generally, Brian Barry, *Culture and Equality: An Egalitarian Critique of Multiculturalism* (Cambridge: Harvard University Press, 2001); Veit Bader, *Secularism or Democracy? Associational Governance of Religious Diversity* (Amsterdam: Amsterdam University Press, 2007).

and common civic culture. To "keep Sydney from becoming Sarajevo, or Boston from becoming Beirut," liberalism should be transformative ("liberalism with spine") in an attempt to mold people "in a manner that helps ensure that liberal freedom is what they want." Citizens should support liberal principles and institutions because, in the end, "Citizens, not courts or legislatures, are the ultimate custodians of our public morality." Liberalism should not be taken for granted and must not assume that people who live in a liberal democracy are "good liberal democrats."[23]

Macedo's argument is powerful. But even those who agree with the idea that liberalism must not be neutral toward its own truths—namely, that a liberal way of life should have preference over a nonliberal way of life and even become "muscular" when it faces an imminent threat—may have a different view about the implications of this approach. On the empirical level, one question is whether liberal states are indeed under threat, the character of that threat, its severity, and whether cultural restrictions might help minimize it. As previously discussed, there are good reasons to believe that the reaction to contemporary migration is exaggerated and disproportionate (see Chapter 2). On the normative level, one might ask *what degree of threat justifies what measures and for what purpose*. The first face of liberalism, as a *modus vivendi* allowing plural ways of life, contains the freedom to choose not to hold liberal views, or even live a liberal way of life, as long as a person's way of life is lawful, democratic, and does not challenge the peaceful coexistence of the society.

But even the second face of liberalism, which views liberalism as an ethical project that should be promoted, as Macedo asserts, might reject some cultural defense policies. First, some policies exclude patterns of behavior or forms of thinking that are not necessarily illiberal; at most, they are incompatible with the real or imagined way of life of the majority. For example, it would not be illiberal if, in the Dutch case, Zara does not shake the director's hand but, instead, waves or bows to him, or just ignores him. At most, her behavior would be impolite. Second, liberal democracies, especially multicultural societies, are characterized by ongoing social tensions. Immigration laws are not the appropriate means for resolving these tensions or teaching people how to behave in society, because other, less intrusive alternatives exist, such as social

[23] Stephen Macedo, *Diversity and Distrust: Civic Education in a Multicultural Democracy* (Cambridge: Harvard University Press, 2003): pp. 26, 5, 15, 164–165, 5, respectively.

institutions, educational systems (public schools are the state institutions intended to create "good citizens"), and civic and criminal sanctions.

To sum up, muscular liberalism is not an illiberal idea per se, yet some of its recent uses and applications are close to the point of being illiberal. It transmits a message that people arriving in a liberal society must subscribe to the "right" national way of doing things and adopt the national form of life. It opens a door to a slippery slope that compels people to adopt a liberal way of life in order to become a member of a liberal society. In so doing, muscular liberalism is at risk of becoming theological and deviating from its own values for the sake of their protection.

Liberal tolerance

The second concern relates to liberal tolerance. Existing literature deals with a case where liberal tolerance, which is friendly to intolerant ideas, may undermine tolerance itself. In order to avoid this situation, some people claim that liberal tolerance must not tolerate the intolerant. In a sense, this might be the justification for cultural defense policies, which are aimed at excluding intolerant practices. In other cases, however, cultural defense policies reveal a case of intolerance to *tolerant* practices, which, although seen as wrong by the majority group, are not intolerant as such.

Take the decisions about handshaking in the Netherlands in which employees who were fired from their job, or who rejected a job, due to their refusal to shake hands with a person of the opposite gender (as described in Chapter 2). These decisions are peculiar. If a person refuses to shake hands on grounds of hygiene, skin disease, or for some other non-religious reason, would he or she be fired or rejected from a job? No doubt, a refusal to shake hands is impolite, especially if the reason for the refusal is grounded on a belief that shaking hands with women is impure. And, of course, there are certain jobs that are almost impossible to perform if one refuses to touch another human being. There are other nuances. It is one thing not to accept a candidate for a new job, yet quite another thing to dismiss an existing employee. There may be different legal rules applying to government services compared to the private sector. Yet there is another consideration—religious tolerance. It requires religious believers to tolerate non-religious manners but, similarly, it requires non-religious people to tolerate religious manners as long as these manners are not unlawful. Requiring a man to shake hands with a woman contrary to his religious beliefs, especially when he is willing to greet her in an alternative respectful manner, is also not an expression of liberal tolerance.

In identifying the boundaries of national culture, states tend to equate the citizenry with the majority, as if the two are the same. Take the Netherlands. The country has large Moroccan and Turkish communities. Had the Dutch wanted to preserve their culture, they should have taken into account Moroccan and Turkish cultures. Ignoring minority cultures might be regarded as "un-Dutch" since diversity and pluralism are central elements of Dutch culture. In a different context, Joseph Weiler observed:[24]

> The "be one of us", however well intentioned, is often an invitation to the alien to be one of us, by being us. Vis-à-vis the alien, it risks robbing him of his identity. Vis-à-vis oneself, it may be a subtle manifestation of both arrogance and belief in my superiority as well as intolerance. If I cannot tolerate the alien, one way of resolving the dilemma is to make him like me, no longer an alien.... it is still a form of dangerous internal and external intolerance.

As long as a liberal state prioritizes ways of life of the dominant majority, it should tolerate other ways of life, which, although not necessarily according to the majority's taste, are not unlawful or contrary to basic democratic principles. The cases discussed in Chapters 2 and 3—the ban on the construction of minarets in Switzerland, the handshaking decisions in the Netherlands, France's blanket prohibition of wearing the *burqa* in a public place,[25] compulsory mixed swimming lessons in Germany, and social expectations relating to sexual freedom and nudity—leave little room for liberal tolerance. In multicultural societies, the line between liberty and oppression is not always clear-cut. What one considers as liberty, the other views as oppression; what one sees as sexual freedom, the other regards as a moral breakdown. Judicial approaches such as "this is our norm and migrants must deal with it"—adopted by courts in Germany, Switzerland, and the Netherlands—are

[24] J.H.H. Weiler, "In Defence of the Status Quo: Europe's Constitutional *Sonderweg*," in *European Constitutionalism Beyond the State*, J.H.H. Weiler and Marlene Wind, eds. (Cambridge: Cambridge University Press, 2003): pp. 7–23 at 19.

[25] Following this law, women were fined for covering their faces. See Jean-Louis Bianco, "Point D'étape sur les Travaux de l'Observatoire de la Laïcité," Premier Ministre, 2013; Cour de cassation, chambre criminelle, N° 12-80891, March 5, 2013; Cour de cassation, chambre criminelle, n° 12-81518, April 16, 2013; Cour de cassation, chambre criminelle, n° 12-83965, April 3, 2013.

an "invitation to the alien to be one of us by being us," to repeat Joseph Weiler's words.

Policy motivation

The third concern derives from discriminatory intent. Some policies were introduced and designed to exclude certain groups of immigrants. This is the case of Baden-Württemberg, whose citizenship test originally applied only to applicants from one of the fifty-seven Member States of the Organization of the Islamic Cooperation.[26] This is arguably the case of the Dutch admission policy, which is seemingly "universal" yet does not apply to Western countries: EU states, Australia, Canada, Japan, New Zealand, South Korea, Switzerland, the United States and, more recently, Turkey.[27]

The appeal to cultural defense may be a form of discrimination even when the cultural background of the migrant is not explicitly used as a selection criterion. States can design criteria in a more neutral way, say, by setting an income requirement, as exists in European Member States, or a minimum age of 24 for admission of a foreign spouse, as exists in Denmark.[28] These criteria can have a non-cultural purpose, such as to protect the welfare system. However, they can also be designed to deal wisely with migrants. They may be a form of "*legal white lie*"—the law does not tell the truth because it is legally impermissible and thus offers a different story. For example, the law can seek to reduce the scale of migration by setting an income requirement based on the assumption that migrants from developing countries have a low income level. Similarly, the law may set up a minimum age of 24 for admission of a foreign spouse based on the assumption that women in some countries are likely to get married before the age of 24. These legal constraints are "legal white lies."

Illiberal liberalism?

The challenge of liberalism has always been how to promote belief in liberal values and institutions without crossing the line into

[26] Islamic Human Rights Commission, "The Über-Citizen and German Kulturkampf—s.10 German Naturalisation Law: A Front?," 2007: pp. 3–4.

[27] Following a ruling of the Administrative High Court (*Centrale Raad van Beroep*), Turkish immigrants are exempted from the integration process abroad. See Centrale Raad van Beroep, L.J.N. BR4959, August 16, 2011.

[28] Stephen H. Legomsky, "Rationing Family Values in Europe and America: An Immigration Tug of War Between States and their Supra-National Associations," *Georgetown Immigration Law Journal* 25, no. 4 (2011): pp. 807–858 at 810–825.

indoctrination. There is a blessing in liberalism, yet also a risk. The danger of liberalism has its roots in what Philip Hamburger calls "liberal theology." Liberal theologists expect people to think alike, behave alike, and arrive at similar conclusions about the good life. Hamburger explains that "when pursued by a powerful majority," liberalism can itself "become a threat to freedom" and, ironically, may become theologically intolerant.[29]

There is a growing body of literature regarding the question as to whether Europe has reached the point of being illiberal toward migrants. Christian Joppke, the leading author in this field, observes that except for rare examples, mainly the citizenship test previously adopted in Baden-Württemberg and some elements of Dutch policies, Europe's immigration and naturalization policies are largely liberal. The controlling factor, for a citizenship test, is whether the test requires cognitive knowledge that can be learned, in this case it is not illiberal, or inquires into a candidate's moral perceptions, in this case it is illiberal.[30] While this criterion focuses on the substance of the test, another criterion is procedure: the level of difficulty of the test, the required test fees, and the availability of preparatory materials. Joppke argues that, overall, citizenship tests in Europe are not illiberal, mainly because they are cognitive and learnable.[31]

I tend to agree with Joppke's observation subject to a few reservations. First, there are cognitive issues that are learnable and still it may not be justified to test migrants on them. Math and physics are also cognitive. Second, we should not hastily dismiss the eruption of cultural nationalism in places like the *Land* of Baden-Württemberg. True, it was ultimately abandoned, but it is not unreasonable to expect that similar trends will return in the near future. There are political powers advocating migration restrictions for the purpose of the protection of national identity. The result of the European Parliament election in 2014 has demonstrated the rise of right-wing anti-immigration parties in Europe, a reality that

[29] Philip Hamburger, "Illiberal Liberalism: Liberal Theology, Anti-Catholicism, & Church Property," *Journal of Contemporary Legal Issues* 12, no. 2 (2002): pp. 693–726 at 694.

[30] Christian Joppke, "How Liberal are Citizenship Tests?" and "How Liberal are Citizenship Tests? A Rejoinder," in *How Liberal are Citizenship Tests?*, Rainer Bauböck and Christian Joppke, eds., EUI Working Paper RSCAS 2010/41, 2010: pp. 1–4 at 1–2 and pp. 39–41 at 39–40, respectively.

[31] Christian Joppke, "The Retreat is Real—But What is the Alternative? Multiculturalism, Muscular Liberalism, and Islam," *Constellations* 21, no. 2 (2014): pp. 286–295.

already exists at the national level. Third, even less suspicious measures, such as loyalty oaths, may be illiberal. Is it liberal to coerce a Jewish spouse of a British citizen to publicly pledge allegiance to Queen Elizabeth the Second, Head of the Church of England? Fourth, the liberal line is not only a function of content and form. Characterization of a policy as liberal is a product of other factors, such as its motivation. We must review cultural defense policies in the broader context of anti-immigration sentiment in Europe. And finally, the message of some of the policies is that there is a "right" way of life. However, a liberal state should let citizens freely choose their own way of life without compelling them to identify with a particular way of life, even when the individual's choice is incompatible with the mainstream, provided that it is lawful and fundamentally democratic.[32] Hence, while cultural defense policies across Europe are not entirely illiberal, some are badly managed to the extent that they are almost illiberal.

CONSTITUTIONAL STORIES

Naturalization policies often require migrants to accept a story. This is a different demand from the one focusing on liberal values because the story includes *particular* narratives. The following sections briefly present cases in which migrants are required to subscribe to a "story" in the sense of accepting its "truths." Inasmuch as they are not asked to believe in the story, this, too, is not illiberal per se. However, when the demand is to share the story's truths, it resembles a form of constitutional worship. In addition, when the story is not shared by, or known to, most natural-born citizens, migrants are being asked to accept an imagined story, one which does not reflect the actual collective conscience of the dominant majority.

Finding a national story

The art of storytelling is the ability to collect all relevant details—events, heroes, and characters—and convey them in a powerful way. Once there is a story, one should choose a method in which to convey it. Artists tell a story in paintings and statues. Writers tell a story in novels and poems. And directors tell a story in plays and films. Some stories are written,

[32] John Rawls, "Justice as Fairness in the Liberal Polity," in *The Citizenship Debates: A Reader*, Gershon Shafir, ed. (Minneapolis: University of Minnesota Press, 1998): pp. 53–72 at 63–70.

while others are delivered orally. Some stories are based on facts, others are fiction, and a few fall in the gray area between fiction and non-fiction.

Stories are told not only by people, but also by religions and nations.[33] The Bible tells that God created the world in six days and rested on the seventh day; this is the "creation story." It further tells that the Jews were designated by God as the "chosen people." God delivered the Israelites from slavery in Egypt, gave them the Ten Commandments, and brought them into the land of Canaan. This is the story of Exodus. Nations have stories too. Their story is usually told in constitutional documents—the declaration of independence, the preamble, the anthem—and by constitutional conventions that are not written in a formal text.

In *Constitutional Redemption*, Jack Balkin discusses the importance of constitutional stories. Balkin contends that "Fidelity *to* the Constitution requires faith *in* the Constitution." The level of faith "depends on the story that we tell ourselves about our country, about our constitutional project.... To believe in the constitutional project is to believe in a story." Constitutional stories proclaim the national aspirations of a people, the tenets of a political community, the essence of a social contract, and the constitutional understandings of the founding fathers. Stories have an *informative* part—they explain "who we are, where we came from, what we have done, what we have yet to do, what we stand for, what promises we made to ourselves, what we hope for, what we fear, [and] what we said we must never let happen again."[34] But stories are not just descriptive; they are also *normative*—they seek to create a sense of shared history,[35] teach values, and instill moral lessons about good behavior in society.

Constitutional stories are not neutral. They are rooted in ideologies. The Americans tell themselves that "America began with a break from tyranny, established a free government under a wise Constitution, and ever since then has been getting better and better, more just and more free."[36] The Jews in Israel tell themselves that the land of Israel is the historical homeland of the Jewish People, from which they

[33] See, generally, Rogers M. Smith, *Stories of Peoplehood: The Politics and Morals of Political Memberships* (Cambridge: Cambridge University Press, 2003).

[34] Jack M. Balkin, *Constitutional Redemption: Political Faith in an Unjust World* (Cambridge: Harvard University Press, 2011): pp. 2, 17, 26.

[35] Rainer Bauböck, "Sharing History and Future? Time Horizons of Democratic Membership in an Age of Migration," *Constellations* 4, no. 3 (1998): pp. 320–345.

[36] Balkin, p. 3 (n 34).

were forcibly exiled, and that they have a justified right to re-establish themselves in at least part of this land. Most parts of national stories have some historical evidence, but other parts are disputed on factual grounds, or by reason of the normative consequences that the story seeks to entail.

Constitutional stories tell a partial tale. Take the U.S. naturalization test, which is supposed to include the essence of U.S. civics and history. One salient feature of the story, as delivered in the test and recorded in the handbook, is that it contains selective recollections of American history. It excludes some groups and infamous historical events. Except for the Pilgrims, the test does not directly address the contribution of immigrant groups to American history nor does it address Hispanic or Asian figures or events. It largely hides America's notorious history, such as the 1882 Chinese Exclusion Act, or the World War II internment of Japanese Americans.[37]

Constitutional stories are shaped by historical experiences and traumas. History talks. "We do this now because we did that then," Balkin asserts, and "we do not do this now because we promised ourselves we would never do that again or let it be done to us again." The Jewish story, for instance, is interwoven with the Holocaust—the killing of six million Jews in Europe and the urgency of the re-establishment of a Jewish state to solve the problem of Jewish homelessness. It is also rooted in a long history of a persecuted people who formed an exiled diasporic group throughout most of its history. In referring to the American story, Balkin observes that "We respect religious conscience because our Pilgrim forefathers left persecution in Europe. We guarantee racial equality because of Lincoln, the Civil War, [and] Martin Luther King.... We guarantee rights of criminal defendants because of the actions of King George and his imperial government."[38] For better and for worse, historical experience shapes national perceptions of what is good and what is just.[39]

Historical experiences and traumas are part of constitutional stories even when they are not directly written in constitutional sources. Thus, the field of comparative constitutional law requires deep understanding of national histories and cultural legal structures. The Israeli *Family*

[37] Liav Orgad, "Creating New Americans: The Essence of Americanism Under the Citizenship Test," *Houston Law Review* 47, no. 5 (2011): pp. 1227–1298 at 1253–1257.

[38] Balkin, p. 3 (n 34).

[39] Charles Taylor, *Sources of the Self: The Making of the Modern Identity* (Cambridge: Harvard University Press, 1989): p. 47.

Migration case (see Chapter 3) should be read in light of the Jewish history of a persecuted nation and the Jewish anxiety of another exile. Similarly, the German decision on abortion, in which the Court invalidated a liberal abortion law due to the fetuses' right to life, should be read in light of World War II and the memories of the Final Solution. In both cases, the justices did not directly refer to collective histories and traumas, but it is clear that history talks. Formal legal arguments, about the fetus' right to life or Israel's right to self-defense, do not tell the whole story.[40]

What are the elements of a national story? Three elements exist. The first part of a story includes facts, attributes of who "we" actually are. It includes details about geography and demography: population size, rivers, mountains, etc. This is non-fiction. The second part of the story includes "imagined" facts, attributes that "we" ideally hope to possess. This part includes romantic conceptions of ourselves, such as the German image of its identity as including poems of Goethe and Schiller, writings of Nietzsche and Kant, paintings of Caspar David Friedrich, and symphonies of Beethoven. This is not to say that these heroes are not part of the German story. They certainly are. However, they represent a romantic ideal of the German identity, the good old days. This is a blend of fiction and non-fiction of the contemporary "we." The third part of the story includes "ought-to-be facts," attributes that are not the best description of the "we" but, rather, what "we" want other people to think that "we" possess. This part includes details aimed at deterring people from coming to our state, or conversely, encouraging them to come.

Think of online dating as an analogy. Persons who subscribe to the service go through a process of defining their "self." A person should specify physical information (hair color, height, weight), personal background details (education, occupation, date of birth), and lifestyle (smoking, drinking, willingness to relocate). While these details are factual, similar to details about demography or geography, other details are more complex: "my life ambitions are…", "my personality is best described as…", "the things I could never live without are…", "for fun, I like to…". Studies show that persons who subscribe to online dating websites define their identity by referring to three aspects of their self.[41] The

[40] For the German case, see BVerfG, 1 B.v.F. 1/74; 1 B.v.F. 2/74; 1 B.v.F. 3/74; 1 B.v.F. 4/74; 1 B.v.F. 5/74; 1 B.v.F. 6/74, February 25, 1975.

[41] See, e.g., Nicole Ellison, Rebecca Heino, and Jennifer Gibbs, "Managing Impressions Online: Self-Presentation Processes in the Online Dating Environment," *Journal of Computer-Mediated Communication* 11, no. 2 (2006): pp. 415–441.

first is the *actual self.* People write factual details about their weight and height. The second is the *ideal self.* People write details that they believe to be factual. A person can describe his "body style" as muscular and athletic, even though his real body style is plump and flabby. A person may choose a wrong description of his self not because he lies, but because he indeed believes that he has an athletic body style; this is an imagined "self." The third is the *ought-to-be self.* People write details that are fiction because, for various reasons, they want others to believe that they possess certain attributes. For instance, a woman may say that she likes classical music, even though she really likes techno music, because she believes that classical music will further impress her targeted audience.

While it may be legitimate to require migrants to know the "actual self," studies show that most citizens would fail a citizenship test should they be required to take one. If this is the case, liberal states do not ask migrants to be "like us," but *better* than us. The tests focus on an imagined self; not what Germans/French/Dutch are, but what they think they are (the "ideal self"). Take the United States. Studies have found that most Americans fail a civics test similar to the naturalization test. In a test presented to college freshmen and seniors at fifty colleges nationwide, freshmen scored on average 51.4 percent; the seniors' average score was 54.2 percent. Only 24 percent of college graduates knew that official religion is prohibited by the First Amendment, and only 21 percent knew that the phrase "government of the people, by the people, for the people" is rooted in Lincoln's Gettysburg Address. While only 21 percent of American pupils could recognize a phrase from the Gettysburg address, two-thirds knew that Paula Abdul was a judge on the TV show *American Idol.* The data is much more striking regarding office-holders, whose average score was 44 percent—even less than freshmen students.[42]

These findings, which are likely to exist in other countries, raise doubts as to whether citizenship tests reflect a society's actual bond. The fact that a large percentage of the population, including college students and civil servants, fails the test, indicates that the story we tell ourselves about shared identity and culture has a fictional element. Clearly, if citizens were to study for the test, as migrants do, they would obtain better

[42] Intercollegiate Studies Institute, "Our Fading Heritage: Americans Fail A Basic Test on Their History and Institutions," 2008: pp. 6–9, 15, 19; David S. Broder, "One Nation No More?," *Washington Post,* July 3, 2008.

results; still, the findings show that a decent percentage of citizens do not possess the level of knowledge required from migrants.

Furthermore, in some cases even the "ideal self" that appears in the test is mistaken. Take question 100 of the U.S. naturalization test: "Name two national U.S. holidays." Alongside Independence Day, Veterans Day, Columbus Day, and Memorial Day, the answer includes Christmas. Although it is widely celebrated by non-Christians, Christmas is a religious holiday, not a "national" U.S. holiday; legally, it is a "public holiday."[43] Not less embarrassing is the grammar and syntax of the test. One question asks "who does a U.S. Senator represent?"; another asks "who did the United States fight in World War II?" Both questions should use "whom," not "who." And this is the result of a seven-year redesign process, evaluated by ELS specialists, with an investment of seven million dollars. Perhaps the most peculiar case is Denmark. The government asked migrants in the citizenship test a question that seems to be fundamental—"When did the word 'Denmark' appear for the first time?"—but offered three different answers that were all false. It is odd that the Danish government, after consulting with social scientists and historians, could not even provide a correct answer to the origin of the country's name.[44]

Constitutional fidelity

Liberal democracies ask migrants to accept their story. They tend to believe that by accepting their story, migrants would accept their values.[45] Take a migrant who is willing to obey the U.S. Constitution yet believes that the U.S. Founding Fathers committed an act of treason against George III. Or think of a person who comes to the immigration interview with an empirical study according to which the U.S. Constitution is an archaic document of declining global influence.[46] The applicant rationally explains that, upon becoming a citizen, he will

[43] 5 U.S.C. § 6103.

[44] Eva Ersbøll, "On Trial in Denmark," in *A Re-definition of Belonging? Language and Integration Tests in Europe*, Ricky Van Oers, Eva Ersbøll, and Dora Kostakopoulou, eds. (Leiden: Martinus Nijhoff, 2010): pp. 107–152 at 143, 145–146; Danish Immigration Service and Danish Agency for Labour Market and Recruitment, "Ombedømmelse af Indfødsretsprøven Spørgsmål 10," Nyidanmark.dk, February 24, 2009.

[45] See, e.g., U.S. Citizenship and Immigration Services, "USCIS Announces New Naturalization Test," September 27, 2007 ("We believe, through study, that the applicants will understand and attach themselves to those principles.").

[46] David S. Law and Mila Versteeg, "The Declining Influence of the United States Constitution," *New York University Law Review* 87, no. 3 (2012): pp. 762–858.

devote his life to calling for a new "Philadelphia Convention" because the current document is badly formulated. Will or should he be admitted? Or take a migrant who accepts Israel's Basic Laws and its character as a Jewish state, but rejects the story of salvation and believes that historically the land of Israel belongs to the Palestinian people, or that Israel's founding fathers were land robbers—will or should Israel accept that migrant?

Imagine that the immigration officer asks an applicant question number 86 of the U.S. naturalization test: "What major event happened on September 11, 2001, in the United States?" Imagine that the applicant does not provide the "correct" answer, which is "terrorists attacked the United States," but instead replies "the Great Satan was humiliated by the greatest Muslim freedom fighters." Or imagine that the applicant knows that, according to the handbook, the right answer is "terrorists attacked the United States," but adds that she personally does not believe in this interpretation, or at least has no conclusive evidence to support it. If the migrant is a philosopher, she may cite Nietzsche by saying "there are no truths, only interpretations." If she is a lawyer, she may claim that there is no commonly-accepted legal definition of terrorism in international law. What should the officer do? Should the officer reply "wrong" answer and move forward to the next question? Or should the officer disqualify the applicant just for that? More importantly, do we want migrants to be philosophers or lawyers, or just parrots who repeat words we teach them?

Cases of viewpoint-based restrictions are always difficult for a liberal democracy. On the one hand, those who support a politically-neutral naturalization process, or hold that ideology does not necessarily indicate future actions, may reach the conclusion that a test aimed at exploring an applicant's intolerant attitudes and utterances is inappropriate. On the other hand, those who think that beliefs are indicative of future wrongdoing and that states must take a stance in extreme cases may reach the conclusion that beliefs should be taken into account. In the latter case, two options exist. One extreme option is to ask applicants directly about their beliefs. A second option is to refrain from intrusive questions, but take into account beliefs when the applicant voluntarily declares them. Even those who oppose viewpoint-based restrictions may hold that some words express sentiments so reprehensible that society could, or should, deny a citizenship petition based on those views, whatever they may be. Here, too, two options exist. One option is to exclude applicants due to hateful beliefs on the assumption that people who hold such beliefs are undesirable for that reason alone. A second option is to tolerate such beliefs, but nevertheless exclude applicants who hold them on the ground that intolerant beliefs are likely to lead to intolerant behavior. In the latter case, exclusion is based on a concern of future intolerant behavior.

The idea that one should accept national stories as a prerequisite to joining a community has religious origins. Take Jewish conversion as an analogy. Think of a person who accepts the authority of God and divine law as the supreme law of the land yet rejects the theological stories and premises. The Orthodox Jewish view would disqualify that person in a conversion process; he or she would not be able to convert in the absence of religious belief. However, one view, expressed by the Jewish philosopher Yeshayahu Leibowitz, finds the essence of Jewish religion in Jewish law (the *mitzvoth*—the dos and don'ts of Jewish religious laws), rather than belief. In Leibowitz's view, a devoted Jew must adhere to Jewish law, even if he or she does not believe in Jewish mystical or theological stories. Having faith in God is not a function of a state of mind, but a commitment to a particular way of life—the Jewish mode of life. It requires no religious consciousness, but only commitment to Jewish law. For Leibowitz, Judaism is "the religion of Mitzvoth" and apart from it "Jewish faith does not exist."[47] Belief in God is commitment to its law—external devotion in the form of obedience to religious (*halachic*) laws.[48]

How can one be committed to Jewish law without having a belief in God? The idea is that practicing Jewish law may create the conditions that *lead* to belief in God. In psychology, for example, if a person smiles enough—that is, adopts the act of smiling—studies show that, in the end, the person will feel joy. A similar rationale may apply to love—one cannot love on demand. Instead, one can adopt a suitable way of life that may lead to love.[49] A man can date a woman and hope that, after a few dates, he will feel something toward her; it is an indirect way of encouraging love.

Following the analogy between naturalization and religious conversion it is possible to offer two constitutional approaches. One is

[47] Yeshayahu Leibowitz, *Judaism, Human Values, and the Jewish State*, Eliezer Goldman, ed. and Eliezer Goldman et al., trans. (Cambridge: Harvard University Press, 1992): p. 38.

[48] Leibowitz, *Judaism, Human Values, and the Jewish State*, p. 27 (n 47); Yeshayahu Leibowitz, *On Just About Everything: Talks with Michael Shashar* (Jerusalem: Keter Publishing House, 1987): p. 97.

[49] Avishai Margalit, "Revisiting God's Authority," *Social Research* 80, no. 1 (2013): pp. 77–100 at 81–82.

"orthodox constitutionalism"; another is "non-orthodox constitutionalism." Orthodox constitutionalism requires belief in constitutional essentials, either in the "basic structure" of the constitution (a narrow view), or in the basic structure together with some principles and stories (a wide view). Non-orthodox constitutionalism asks whether a person is willing to adopt a liberal-democratic way of life that, eventually, may lead to belief in liberal-democratic values and institutions. Under this approach, it is not belief or a will to believe that is important, but instead the *will* to adopt a way of life that may indirectly lead to belief. If, for example, a person says "I am willing to be loyal," that would not be enough. The desire to be loyal does not in itself create loyalty but, rather, a *will to adopt a suitable way of life* that, in the end, may/can lead to the mental attitude of loyalty.

Take the question "Do you believe in the Constitution and form of government of the U.S.?" which, for decades, dominated the U.S. naturalization process. Under a wide view of orthodox constitutionalism, a person may be disqualified if he disbelieves that the September 11 attack was "an act of terror." A narrow view of orthodox constitutionalism would require more than that to disqualify a person; for instance, lack of belief in the basic structure of the Constitution—its "general political philosophy." Under non-orthodox constitutionalism, however, a person may be disqualified only if he refuses to obey the law, regardless of whether he believes in the law or believes that the law is morally good. Belief may hopefully emerge as a result of continuous residence in the United States.[50] A difficult question, which is discussed in Chapter 6, is whether the liberal state can make some predictions about who is likely to obey the law, or whether it should regard the immigrant's statement as decisive.

THREE PUZZLES

In order to better assess the legitimacy of cultural defense policies, it is essential to clarify their purpose, function, and legality. These aspects, however, are still a conundrum, probably due to the newness of the policies. This part briefly describes three puzzles that still have to be clarified. First, it is not always clear what purpose each of these policies (loyalty oaths, citizenship tests, etc.) has. Second, whatever the purpose is, it is unclear whether the policies are an effective means of

[50] The analogy is imperfect as Leibowitz discusses natural-born, rather than converted Jews.

achieving that purpose. Third, the lawfulness of each of these policies is not always clear.

Normative goal

What is the purpose of cultural defense: is cultural integration the ultimate end, or is it only a means to an end? This question has no simple answer. One possible goal can be related to national security. Culture can serve as a pretext to keep out certain kinds of migrants who are seen by the host society as potential terrorists and as a security risk. A second goal relates to the use of culture to control migration. Under this explanation, states do not want large-scale migration, irrespective of its composition, and culture is just another means of reducing the number. A third explanation relates to protection of the welfare system, that is, culture is used to keep out certain migrants who are seen as a potential financial burden on the state. The assumption is that there is a link between culture and chances of participation in the job market. A fourth goal can be the promotion of social cohesion, that is, culture is used on the premise that a culturally homogeneous society is more stable. The assumption here is that a society that is too diverse may lose its solidarity and hence face the danger of fragmentation. A fifth goal can be to encourage democratic participation. Under this explanation, citizens in liberal democracies are expected to participate in public life and monitor elected officials. To carry out social and political responsibilities, migrants need to speak the local language, develop relevant competencies required for active citizenship, and not be culturally-alienated. The assumption here is that people of a certain culture find it easier to fulfill civil duties. A sixth goal can be orientation—helping migrants to prepare for their life in the new state by enriching their civic experience. Cultural integration is perceived as good for the migrants.

While in all these cases culture serves as a means of achieving a non-cultural end, there can be another explanation according to which cultural preservation is an end in itself. Under this explanation, cultural defense policies are implemented in order to preserve the cultural hegemony of the majority, whose members have an interest in adhering to their culture and sustaining it. The value of culture is intrinsic, not just instrumental. Consider the English language requirement in Britain. One way to view it is to say that English is an essential element of British identity, a value that has to be preserved. Another view is instrumental—mastering English is a functional competence necessary for daily life in Britain. This distinction has implications. If culture is only a means to promote civic or economic ends, states must try to find less intrusive ways to achieve them. Restrictions can only be justified to the extent they promote these ends.

Culture, thus, can be a means, or an end in itself (cultural preservation). Four cases can be distinguished. In the first case, a state seeks to achieve a *cultural purpose* (say, cultural solidarity) by using *cultural criteria* (namely, the cultural background of the migrant). In the second case, a state seeks to achieve a *cultural purpose* by using *non-cultural criteria* (skills, education, income), which are strategically designed in order to achieve a cultural purpose. In the third case, a state seeks to achieve a *non-cultural purpose* (protecting the welfare system, national security, etc.) by using *cultural criteria*. The assumption here is that there is a connection between the non-cultural purpose and the cultural background of the migrant. In the fourth case, a state seeks to achieve a *non-cultural purpose* by using *non-cultural criteria*; states may use non-cultural criteria—education, income, skills, etc.—for civic purposes, such as increasing economic efficiency.

Cultural defense policies have various purposes depending on the specific state, the means (tests, oaths, pacts, etc.), and the government in power. And yet, even when focusing on a particular case, the purpose is often unknown. Identifying a purpose is essential for the legal analysis of a certain policy—examining whether the policy has a legitimate aim as well as checking whether a chosen means effectively serves the purpose and whether other, less intrusive means exist (the test of proportionality).

Empirical conundrum

We have little knowledge of where cultural defense policies lead. As long as their goal is to reduce the number of migrants, they may be effective. However, it is unclear if such policies, in one format or another, are also an effective predictor for the applicant's adherence to certain values. Take citizenship tests: does a list of disconnected events and values really create a sense of belonging to the society? It is naive to assume that a person who can quote Goethe or Nietzsche is ipso facto integrated into German society. He may be more educated, but is he more integrated? In addition, there is little evidence to suggest that a "Blitzkrieg-style" of integration, in which applicants are asked to participate in hundreds of hours of integration lessons, or a "contract-based" model, in which integration is a contractual liability, indeed foster integration. Similarly, social science provides no evidence to support the efficiency of loyalty oaths and citizenship ceremonies. We do not know what transformation occurs in the hearts and minds of people taking a loyalty oath or participating in a citizenship ceremony. The empirical effects of cultural defense policies on the individual and the society are largely unknown.[51]

Forced integration may be counterproductive and lead to radicalization among migrants and minority groups as a reaction to what they regard as a threat to their own culture.[52] Olivier Roy notes that radical Islamism in Europe is not a product of Islam, but a byproduct of the collision between tradition and modernity; the demand to subscribe to liberal ideas so alien to the migrants' tradition produces a crisis in Muslim identity.[53] Likewise, Joseph Raz asserts that "multicultural society often makes cultural groups more repressive."[54] These findings beg the question: do cultural defense policies resolve a "problem," or just exacerbate it?

The empirical puzzle is more complex in Europe. Under EU laws, freedom of movement for EU citizens exists within Member States. The Netherlands, for example, cannot prevent a Swedish citizen from moving and resettling in its territory. Therefore, it is harder to preserve cultural sameness if culturally-diverse EU citizens can freely move from one Member State to another. Moreover, under the current European regime—in which there is no unified EU citizenship law and the requirements differ among Member States—a person wishing to become European can be naturalized in a more permissive state, for instance Sweden, and then resettle in a state with a stricter migration regime, for instance Denmark. This creates a sort of "forum shopping" where a migrant can choose the state with the most lenient requirements and, once a citizen, move to a different state. Without common *European* standards for acquiring citizenship in the European Union, different policies of the Member States continue to affect the whole Union.[55] In this reality, the effectiveness of cultural defense policies is at least doubtful.

[51] Sara Wallace Goodman and Matthew Wright, "Does Mandatory Integration Matter? Effects of Civic Requirements on Immigrant Socio-economic and Political Outcomes," *Journal of Ethnic and Migration Studies* 41 no. 12 (2015): pp. 1885–1908.

[52] Will Kymlicka, "Multicultural Citizenship," in *The Citizenship Debates* (n 32), pp. 167–188 at 178.

[53] Olivier Roy, *Globalized Islam: The Search for a New Ummah* (New York: Columbia University Press, 2004): pp. 143–146, 186, 315–317.

[54] Joseph Raz, "Multiculturalism: A Liberal Perspective," in *Ethics in the Public Domain: Essays in the Morality of Law and Politics* (Oxford: Clarendon Press, 1996): pp. 170–191 at 185–186.

[55] Rainer Bauböck, "Civic Citizenship: A New Concept for the New Europe," in *Managing Integration: The European Union's Responsibilities Towards Immigrants*, Rita Süssmuth and Werner Weidenfeld, eds. (Washington: Migration Policy Institute and Bertelsmann Stiftung, 2005): pp. 122–138 at 127–128.

Legal discipline

Another issue yet to be clarified, is the lawfulness of cultural defense policies. The law puts limits on state powers to restrict migration in general and based on culture in particular. Three legal disciplines exist.

Under general principles of constitutional law, it is not easy to disqualify cultural defense policies. Constitutions generally do not apply extraterritorially to noncitizens outside the territory and do not provide substantive constitutional protection in admission cases.[56] Nevertheless, a constitution can impose some limits on admission policies. An example is the case of family migration, an issue that touches not only upon the interests of noncitizens, but also upon the rights of citizens, such as equal protection and family life. As for citizenship requirements, constitutions apply within a particular state's territory and provide some protection in cases of violations of constitutional rights. Still, to date, with a few exceptions, cultural defense policies have not been declared unconstitutional in liberal democracies. This may be attributed to the newness of the policies or to the deference shown by courts toward the legislature on immigration. All in all, constitutional law leaves little room for invalidating immigration criteria.

A second discipline is international law. International law provides states with broad discretion to regulate immigration rules and rarely interferes on issues of immigration. In 1955, in the *Nottebohm* case, the International Court of Justice held that "international law leaves it to each State to lay down the rules governing the grant of its own nationality."[57] More specifically, in 1984, the Inter-American Court of Human Rights ruled that preferences in naturalization criteria in Costa Rica for nationals of Central American countries, Spaniards, and Ibero-Americans are compatible with the American Convention on Human Rights. The Court justified the naturalization preferences for Central American nationals by noting that they have "closer historical, cultural and spiritual bonds with the people of Costa Rica.... [and are likely to] identify more readily with the traditional beliefs, values and institutions of Costa Rica, which the state has the right and duty to preserve."[58] Recent developments in international human rights law impose greater restrictions on states in

[56] For American law, see generally Neuman, *Strangers to the Constitution* (n 16).

[57] Nottebohm Case, *Liechtenstein* v. *Guatemala*, I.C.J. Rep. 1955: p. 23, April 6, 1955.

[58] *Proposed Amendments to the Naturalization Provisions of the Constitution of Costa Rica*, Advisory Opinion OC-4/84, Inter-Am.Ct.H.R. Series A no. 4, January 19, 1984.

regulating immigration, mainly regarding anti-discrimination norms,[59] but they seem unlikely to disqualify most forms of cultural defense policies.

The invocation of cultural criteria to filter out migrants is tricky. On the one hand, international human rights law allows states to select migrants by means of "universal" criteria, such as education, wealth, skills, and family ties. On the other hand, the use of racial and ethnic criteria is impermissible when it discriminates against a "particular nationality."[60] Culture is not explicitly included in either category and its lawfulness is vague. The Committee on the Elimination of Racial Discrimination noted that discrimination in the immigration context occurs only if the criteria "are not applied pursuant to a legitimate aim, and are not proportional to the achievement of this aim."[61] It seems unlikely that international law would outlaw cultural restrictions on admission, though it may outlaw some forms of culture-based discrimination in access to citizenship.

A third legal discipline is EU law. EU bodies are not clear on the issue of integration criteria into the European Union. In 2004, Member States decided to develop a common integration policy for newcomers to the Union.[62] Soon after, they agreed upon *Common Basic Principles for Immigrant Integration Policy*. These principles are not binding, yet they guide Member States in forming policies. They start with the premise that integration is a "two-way process of mutual accommodation," but emphasize that it entails "respect for the basic values of the European Union," including "basic knowledge of the host society's language, history, and institutions," as well as the "values of the European Union."[63] In 2008, the Union adopted the *European Pact on Immigration*, a French-led initiative directed at formulating principles for integration.

[59] Peter J. Spiro, "A New International Law of Citizenship," *American Journal of International Law* 105, no. 4 (2011): pp. 694–746 at 720–733; Kay Hailbronner, "Nationality in Public International Law and European Law," in *Comparative Analyses*, vol. 1, *Acquisition and Loss of Nationality: Policies and Trends in 15 European Countries*, Rainer Bauböck et al., eds. (Amsterdam: Amsterdam University Press, 2006): pp. 35–104 at 42–45.

[60] International Convention on the Elimination of all Forms of Racial Discrimination (New York, March 7, 1966, 60 U.N.T.S.), Art. 1(3).

[61] Committee on the Elimination of Racial Discrimination, "General Recommendation 30: Discrimination Against Non-Citizens," Committee Doc. CERD/C/64/Misc.11/rev.3, 2004: p. 2.

[62] The Hague Programme: Strengthening Freedom, Security and Justice in the European Union [2005] O.J. C53/1, points 1.2 (Asylum, migration and border policy) and 1.5 (Integration of third-country nationals).

[63] Council of the European Union, "2618th Council Meeting: Justice and Home Affairs," Council Doc. C/04/321, 2004: pp. 12–13.

The pact requires migrants to learn the local language and respect the "identities of the Member States" and the fundamental values of democracy and human rights.[64] While the pact is not binding, a binding document is the Treaty of Lisbon. The Treaty provides that the European Union may establish measures to support the integration of foreigners in the Member States, yet leaves open the question of permissible and impermissible measures.[65]

It is difficult to evaluate cultural defense policies under EU law because, in spite of these guidelines—which offer a window into the EU understanding of integration, yet leave a wide range of discretion to the Member States—the European Union has not yet established clear admission and naturalization criteria. A set of admission criteria exists for states, the "Copenhagen Criteria"—principles that every state has to maintain before being eligible to join the European Union—but not for individual admission. Since naturalization policies are traditionally seen as part of state sovereignty, EU bodies have hesitated to interfere in this field. One exception is the EU Directive on family reunification, which is a step forward to clarifying EU law on issues of family migration.[66] The Directive permits Member States to impose "integration measures," but leaves the question of their content, format, and application unresolved. In addition, recent precedents of the European Court of Justice indicate that when the case is related to family members of EU citizens, the state power to set up admission criteria and naturalization requirements is not unlimited.[67]

In 2011, in referring to compulsory integration measures imposed on spouses of EU citizens, the European Commission provided an indefinite statement according to which integration measures must "be assessed on the basis of the accessibility of courses or tests, how they are designed and/or organised (test materials, fees, venue, etc.), and whether such measures or their impact serve purposes other than integration." It made clear that integration is "about achieving a sense of belonging" and that the understanding of the "cultural traditions and values" of the

[64] Council of the European Union, "European Pact on Immigration and Asylum," Council Doc. 13440/08, 2008: pp. 4, 6.

[65] Treaty of Lisbon [2007] O.J. C306/1, Art. 63a(4).

[66] Council Directive 2003/86/EC of September 22, 2003 on the Right to Family Reunification [2003] O.J. L251/12, Art. 7(2). In addition, Art. 17 provides that Member States can take into account "the existence of family, cultural and social ties" with the spouse's country of origin.

[67] Case C-127/08 *Metock* v. *Minister for Justice, Equality and Law Reform* [2008] E.C.R. I-6241; Case C-578/08 *Chakroun* v. *Minister van Buitenlandse Zaken* [2010] E.C.R. I-1839.

host society is central to migrant integration.[68] The coming years will be crucial for developing EU integration rules; so far, all we have is a set of inconsistent guidelines that leave a considerable margin of discretion to Member States.

* * *

Liberalism offers a blessing yet poses a risk. In human rights law, liberalism sanctifies individual freedom. In democratic peace theory, liberal democracies are less likely to conduct war against each other. "After the demise of some 20th century alternatives, which were born and sometimes ended in blood," Christian Joppke proclaims, "liberalism is all we have."[69] To maintain a liberal society, however, some level of belief in liberal values and institutions is needed; people must have faith in the blessing of liberty. The challenge has always been how to encourage belief in liberalism without crossing the line into indoctrination. But here lies the risk. When the benchmark of liberalism becomes belief rather than behavior, allegiance rather than obedience, it approaches the point of not being liberal, even if its goal is to keep liberalism alive. This is especially the case when liberalism demands conformity to a single uniform set of ideas. Back in 1967, Chief Justice Earl Warren rightly held: "Implicit in the term 'national defense' is the notion of defending those values and ideals which set this Nation apart.... It would indeed be ironic if, in the name of national defense, we would sanction the subversion of one of those liberties... which makes the defense of the Nation worthwhile."[70]

In implementing cultural defense policies, states search for a common bond that goes beyond language and territory. However, the modern nation-state, with its diverse population, cannot easily offer an actual, shared bond. At most, it can offer an imagined, "ideal self," which reflects the values, identities, and cultures of the majority group, a concept that is not identical with "peoples" or "states." What is a "majority group"? Does it have a right to protect fundamental elements of its culture? If yes, why, to what extent, and under which conditions? I now turn to these questions.

[68] European Commission, "Commission Staff Working Paper: EU Initiatives Supporting the Integration of Third-Country Nationals," Commission Doc. SEC(2011) 957, 2011: pp. 8, 23; European Commission, "Communication from the Commission to the European Parliament, the Council, the Economic and Social Committee and the Committee of the Regions: Communication on Migration," Commission Doc. COM(2011) 248, 2011: p. 13.

[69] Joppke, "How Liberal are Citizenship Tests?," p. 41 (n 30).

[70] *United States* v. *Robel* 389 U.S. 258, p. 264 (1967).

5

Majority Rights

All peoples have the right of self-determination.

—ICCPR, Article 1[1]

Persons belonging to such [ethnic, religious or linguistic] minorities... shall not be denied the right... to enjoy their own culture.

—ICCPR, Article 27

Cultural defense policies are ambiguous as to what they try to do and for whose benefit they are invoked. In public discussions and academic debates, one quite often hears a mixture of terms regarding the subject (peoples, nations, societies), the action (defense, preservation, protection), and the object (character, identity, way of life) of cultural defense policies. In Europe, the law focuses on the French *communauté*, German living conditions, Dutch society, and life in the United Kingdom; yet it does little to clarify these terms. Is the French *communauté* coincident with all citizens of the Republic? Is Dutch society equal to all Dutch people, including citizens with a foreign background? Such terms sound culturally neutral, but may be misleading. They give the impression that cultural defense policies are concerned with the culture of the entire French population, all strata of Dutch society, and Britain as a whole. But this is certainly not the case. A close review reveals that the values essential to the French *communauté* have little connection to French people of Maghrebi origin—Algerians, Moroccans, and Tunisians; Dutch society has little to do with the way of life of Moroccan-Dutch and Turkish-Dutch; and the handbook *Life in the United Kingdom* is not much concerned with the life of ethnic minorities in the United Kingdom—Indians or Pakistanis. The content of cultural defense policies, as reflected in immigration and

[1] International Covenant on Civil and Political Rights (New York, December 16, 1966, 999 U.N.T.S. 171). An identical version appears in Art. 1 of the International Covenant on Economic, Social and Cultural Rights (New York, December 16, 1966, 993 U.N.T.S. 3) (hereinafter: Common Article 1).

naturalization requirements, mainly in Europe, does not reflect a high degree of ethno-cultural diversity. The immigrants' ways of life, traditions, and values are largely absent from the characterization of what is French, Dutch, or British. Rather, at the heart of cultural defense policies, despite the politically correct language, are the ways of life, traditions, and values of non-immigrant groups, the native-born population (*autochthon, autochtonen, Français de souche*, etc.).

Broadly speaking, cultural defense policies are concerned with what may be labeled "majority groups." But who are the majorities? How can they be identified? What are their characteristics? These are puzzling issues. Identifying a majority is an exercise in classification; there is no one-size-fits-all formula for all countries. Existing demographic categories, legal rules, and sociological typologies provide little help in pinpointing the concept of a majority. But there is no doubt about the existence of a majority group. In fact, the very existence of laws protecting minorities against the power of majorities indicates that those who advocate minority rights implicitly accept the existence of a dominant majority. When the American Founding Fathers warned that the majority would abuse its power to oppress minorities,[2] they presupposed a majority of some kind. Most probably, they had in mind the protection of religious freedom of minorities against the power of a Christian and other like-minded majorities. Still, to date, neither international law nor political liberalism defines a majority.

Talking about a *liberal* theory of majority rights seems paradoxical. Liberal theorists have always been troubled with the constant threat posed to individual liberties by democratic majority rule. Democracy is a government "of the people, by the people, for the people," but "the people" is essentially a majority population expressing itself through a majority vote. In a democracy, as French thinker Alexis de Tocqueville wrote in his essay *The Tyranny of the Majority*, the majority may "do whatsoever it pleases" and tyrannize the minority.[3] In liberal political philosophy, majorities are associated with "evils against which society requires to be on its guard," to quote the English philosopher John Stuart Mill. The phrase "The will of the people," Mill argued, is deceptive because it

[2] Michael A. Genovese, ed., "Federalist No. 10" (Madison), in *The Federalist Papers: Alexander Hamilton, James Madison, and John Jay* (New York: Palgrave Macmillan, 2009): pp. 49–54; John Adams, *A Defence of the Constitutions of Government of the United States of America*, vol. III (London: John Stockdale, 1794): pp. 291, 356–358, 474.

[3] Alexis de Tocqueville, "Tyranny of the Majority," in *Democracy in America*, Henry Reeve, trans., 3rd ed. (New York: George Adlard, 1839): pp. 255–268 at 255.

"practically means, the will of the most numerous or the most active *part* of the people; the majority, or those who succeed in making themselves accepted as the majority; the people, consequently, *may* desire to oppress a part of their number; and precautions are as much needed against this, as against any other abuse of power."[4] This widely-shared view—that the power of majorities should be restrained like that of any other political authority—has become one of the most important pillars of international human rights law.

Given the infamous history of majorities, and the simple fact that a democracy is based on majoritarian politics, the idea that majorities need their rights protected seems peculiar. The majority, after all, is a majority; in most cases it can "do whatsoever it pleases" and, inter alia, perpetuate its culture by controlling entry into the community and utilizing the forces of democratic decision-making. Hence, the majority culture does not have special legal protection, nor is the concept of the majority legally recognized. The culture of the majority group is assumed to be well-off.

The changes in immigration patterns (as detailed in Chapter 1) have undermined a fundamental assumption in democratic theory—that the majority culture is protected merely by the forces of democracy. The changing reality has triggered demographic anxiety among majorities (as described in Chapter 2) and led to the adoption of cultural defense policies (as shown in Chapter 3). Compared to nineteenth- and twentieth-century nationalism, the current revival of this "majority nationalism"[5] is thin in terms of national culture, yet not insignificant (as explained in Chapter 4). If one adds to this the shift in majority-minority relations in the legal realm, as described later, we have a safe guarantee that debates concerning majority rights will continue to shape our lives in the near future.

This chapter advocates the recognition of a new concept, "majority groups"; claims that, under certain circumstances, majorities have a strong interest in protecting their "cultural rights"; and provides justifications for defending the majority culture in the immigration context. The chapter is organized as follows: the first part describes the legal background for the revival of majority rights. It shows a consistent process of large-scale upgrading of minority rights alongside

[4] John Stuart Mill, *On Liberty* (New York: Dover Publications, 2002): pp. 4, 3, respectively (Ch. I).

[5] This term is borrowed, though in a different context, from Alain-G. Gagnon, André Lecours, and Geneviève Nootens, eds., *Contemporary Majority Nationalism* (Montreal: McGill-Queen's University Press, 2011).

a converse process of downgrading the right of peoples to state-level self-determination. The second part discusses the concept of majorities. Admittedly, any attempt to group together standards that cover every majority population around the world is intellectually and politically futile. Such an attempt, however, is essential, because the legal division between "peoples" and "minorities" does not capture the new emerging reality of majority-minority relations. The chapter examines three conceptions of majorities—an ethno-cultural majority, a sociological majority, and an idea-based majority. It presents four paradigmatic cases in which majorities may need protection in the immigration context—diminishing majorities, regional-minority majorities, victimized majorities, and minoritized majorities; and offers two justifications for cultural majority rights—personal autonomy and the right to identity. On the whole, the purpose of the chapter is to bring to the fore a few cases in which majorities may be in need of protection in the immigration context and provide a primary framework for analyzing them.

MINORITIES, PEOPLES, AND SELF-DETERMINATION

The following sections briefly describe a transformation in the majority-minority discourse. The transformation has two features: greater protection of minority groups and a gradual retreat from national self-determination.

Self-determination and minority rights

The current relations between majority rights and minority rights can be summarized by referring to Article 1 and Article 27 of the International Covenant on Civil and Political Rights (ICCPR), which is a cornerstone of what is labeled the International Bill of Human Rights. These two provisions were adopted in 1966 after almost twenty years of debates in the United Nations. They provide a subtle balance between two of the most important principles of contemporary international law and international relations—self-determination of peoples and minority rights. Article 1(1) declares:

> All peoples have the right of self-determination. By virtue of that right they freely determine their political status and freely pursue their economic, social and cultural development.

Article 27 of the ICCPR, which addresses the obligations of Member States to protect rights of persons belonging to minority groups, provides:

> In those States in which ethnic, religious or linguistic minorities exist, persons belonging to such minorities shall not be denied the right, in community with the other members of their group, to enjoy their own culture, to profess and practise their own religion, or to use their own language.

The inclusion of the principle of self-determination in international human rights conventions is significant for various reasons. First, the ICCPR has explicitly turned self-determination from a political desire into a *legal* principle. Self-determination was on the agenda in international politics for almost two centuries. Propounded by the U.S. Declaration of Independence and the French Revolution, developed by the nationalistic movements in Europe during the eighteenth and nineteenth centuries, and promoted by world leaders as varied as Woodrow Wilson and Vladimir Lenin at the end of World War I, the principle of self-determination became a key player in the new international order. But it was only in the aftermath of World War II that the principle of self-determination was consecrated in international instruments. The Charter of the United Nations (1945) specifies that respect for the principle of self-determination is one of the purposes of the United Nations and an essential condition for global stability and peaceful and friendly relations among nations (Articles 1(2) and 55). However, the reference in the U.N. Charter is more declaratory than a workable legal standard. It was only the ICCPR that eventually recognized self-determination as a universal legal principle.[6]

Second, Common Article 1 recognizes self-determination not just as a legal principle, but as a *human right* (it has even been termed an "inalienable" right).[7] The debates preceding the adoption of Common Article 1 indicate that the U.N. bodies perceived self-determination as "a prerequisite and a precondition for the implementation and preservation of all other human rights and fundamental freedoms.... The right to self-determination is a fundamental right without which other rights cannot be fully enjoyed."[8] Self-determination is essentially a right relating to

[6] For an earlier recognition in the colonial context, see U.N. General Assembly Resolution 1514 (XV) of 14 December 1960 on the Declaration on the Granting of Independence to Colonial Countries and People.

[7] U.N. General Assembly Resolution 2625 (XXV) of 24 October 1970 on the Declaration on Principles of International Law concerning Friendly Relations and Co-operation among States in accordance with the Charter of the United Nations; U.N. General Assembly Resolution 50/6 of 24 October 1995 on the Declaration on the Occasion of the Fiftieth Anniversary of the United Nations.

[8] U.N., "The Right to Self-Determination: Historical and Current Development on the Basis of United Nations Instruments," U.N. Doc. E/CN.4/Sub.2/404/Rev.1, 1981 (study prepared by Aureliu Cristescu), paras. 641, 692.

self-realization and the autonomy to determine a community's political, social, and cultural status.

Third, the right of peoples to self-determination has been recognized as the only *group* right in the 1966 Human Rights Covenants. This status was not granted to "minority groups," nor was the concept of minority rights recognized. This was a political compromise. The Western countries opposed the inclusion of self-determination in the 1966 Human Rights Covenants, mainly due to their colonial interests and fears of secessionist movements. At different stages of the legislative process, Australia, Belgium, Canada, France, the Netherlands, and the United Kingdom actually voted against the inclusion of self-determination within an international human rights covenant. They were afraid that it would be misused to undermine territorial integrity and social order and might encourage secessionist movements. The developing and socialist countries were the greatest supporters of an article on self-determination. The eventual compromise drew a clear distinction between Article 1 and Article 27. Peoples—and only peoples—would have a right to self-determination, while minority groups would not be granted collective rights, although individuals belonging to these groups would be protected against discrimination and entitled to practice their religion and enjoy their culture.[9]

In the post-World War II international system, Western countries had no immediate or foreseeable need to invoke the right to self-determination to protect their identity, struggle with the question of "who we are," or search for a bond to bind them together; they had a solid sense of what was British, Italian, French, or German. Self-determination was associated with colonized and oppressed peoples and intended to help *them* develop their cultural heritage in the process of decolonization, rather than serve Western countries seeking to protect their cultural identity. But times have changed. The recent influx of refugees and asylum seekers, foreign workers, family migrants, and ex-colonials (see Chapter 1), together with flourishing minority rights and the rise of multiculturalism (see later)—as well as top-down pressure from globalization forces and transnationalism—have led to a new reality in which self-determination is currently invoked by Western peoples to protect their own cultural identity.

[9] Antonio Cassese, *Self-Determination of Peoples: A Legal Reappraisal* (Cambridge: Cambridge University Press, 1995): pp. 48–52.

The minority rights revolution

The almost fifty years that have elapsed since the enactment of the ICCPR have brought a wide range of changes in the interpretation and implementation of Article 27. These changes (or developments) have assigned a different status to minorities than was originally anticipated.

The first development relates to the shift *from individual to collective rights*. Article 27 was not designed to create or protect collective rights. The ICCPR and the Universal Declaration of Human Rights do not focus on group rights, but on the principle of non-discrimination. The original assumption was that equal protection "would safeguard the identity of the members of minority groups."[10] Cultural group rights were perceived as a challenge to national unity and the stability of national structures. Article 27 has deliberately left group rights outside its radar. It mentions the concept of minorities, but the bearers of the rights are "persons belonging to minorities"; the word "minorities," which appeared in the draft article, was intentionally replaced by the words "persons belonging to minorities."[11] However, developments in human rights law have since made it clear that the right of persons belonging to minorities to enjoy their culture can only be achieved in a meaningful way if exercised in a group.[12]

The second development touches on the shift in the type of protection: *from negative to positive rights*. Article 27 is phrased in negative terms—legal rights "shall not be denied"—and protects individuals belonging to minority groups from state interference in their cultural and religious life. However, further developments have clarified that the protection should be active and positive. The U.N. Human Rights Committee has repeatedly clarified that, "Although Article 27 is expressed in negative terms," states should take "Positive measures of protection" to ensure the exercise of minority rights. This obligation applies to "acts of the State party itself," as well as to "acts of other persons within the State party."[13]

The third development is related to the *widening of the scope of protection*. Article 27 is limited; it focuses only on "those States in which ethnic, religious or linguistic minorities exist." The idea was to confine the scope

[10] Ana Filipa Vrdoljak, "Self-Determination and Cultural Rights," in *Cultural Human Rights*, Francesco Francioni and Martin Scheinin, eds. (Leiden: Martinus Nijhoff, 2008): pp. 41–78 at 59.

[11] U.N., "Study on the Rights of Persons Belonging to Ethnic, Religious and Linguistic Minorities," U.N. Doc. E/CN.4/Sub.2/384/Rev.I, 1977 (study prepared by Francesco Capotorti), para. 171.

[12] U.N. Human Rights Committee, "General Comment No. 23: Article 27 (Rights of Minorities)," Committee Doc. CCPR/C/21/Rev.1/Add.5, 1994, para. 6.2.

[13] U.N., "General Comment No. 23," para. 6.1 (n 12); U.N., Commission on Human Rights, "Commentary of the Working Group on Minorities to the United Nations Declaration on the Rights

of protection to existing minorities. This was a compromise that would allow states to know in advance the nature of the obligation they were undertaking. However, U.N. bodies have interpreted the word "existing" to be an issue of fact, rather than law: "The existence of an ethnic, religious or linguistic minority in a given State party does not depend upon a decision by that State party but requires to be established by objective criteria." In addition, protected individuals are not confined solely to citizens or permanent residents, but may also be "migrant workers"—the new minorities—and even "visitors in a State party."[14] Moreover, while Article 27 guarantees the right of individuals "to *enjoy* their own culture," legal developments have shown that this right may be broader and include a right to "*develop* their culture, language, religion, traditions and customs," and even an obligation to "*encourage* conditions for the promotion of that identity." Similarly, the right of individuals "to *use* their own language" has turned into a state obligation "to *encourage* knowledge of the history, traditions, language and culture of the minorities."[15] The scope of minority rights has gradually become significantly wider than was originally intended by the drafters of the ICCPR.[16]

The fourth development concerns the *rise of indigenous rights.* Until the 1980s, one could not find an explicit reference to indigenous rights in international law. In the mid-1980s, global interest in indigenous rights increased. Indigenous populations opposed to their legal classification as national minorities, claimed that their case was unique due to their historical circumstances, attachment to the land, and tribal culture. In 2007, the United Nations General Assembly passed a declaration on indigenous rights. The declaration gives indigenous populations a broad set of rights: ancestral lands, cultural preservation, self-governance, and the like. Article 3 equates the right of indigenous populations to the right of peoples: "Indigenous peoples have the right to self-determination. By virtue of that right they freely determine their political status and freely

of Persons Belonging to National or Ethnic, Religious and Linguistic Minorities," U.N. Doc. E/CN.4/Sub.2/AC.5/2005/2, 2005, paras. 28–29.

[14] U.N., "General Comment No. 23," para. 5.2 (n 12).

[15] U.N. General Assembly Resolution 47/135 of 18 December 1992 on the Declaration on the Rights of Persons Belonging to National or Ethnic, Religious and Linguistic Minorities, Annex, Arts. 4(2), 1(1), 2(1), 4(4), respectively (emphasis added); U.N., "General Comment No. 23," para. 6.2 (n 12).

[16] See, generally, Sarah Joseph and Melissa Castan, *The International Covenant on Civil and Political Rights: Cases, Materials, and Commentary*, 3rd ed. (Oxford: OUP, 2013): pp. 832–866; Natan Lerner, *Group Rights and Discrimination in International Law*, 2nd ed. (The Hague: Martinus Nijhoff, 2003): pp. 5–46, 109–146.

pursue their economic, social and cultural development."[17] The declaration is not legally-binding, yet reflects some common understandings of the international community that may become binding law in the future.

When the declaration was passed in 2007, there were estimated to be 370 million indigenous people worldwide, about 5 percent of the world population.[18] An idea that started with aboriginal populations—those rare cases of original inhabitants who occupied specific lands long before their invasion by European settlers: Aboriginal Australians, American Indians, Māori in New Zealand, Sámi in Scandinavia, etc.—has ended in a growing list of groups claiming indigenous status and demanding indigenous rights. The reason for this is that, unlike laws in Western states that often equate the rights given to national minorities with those given to indigenous peoples, international law tends to provide a far more generous set of rights to indigenous peoples compared to those granted to national minorities. This creates a "race to the indigenous status" of national minorities—a growing demand to be labeled as "indigenous." Will Kymlicka describes how national minorities—Chechens, Kurds, Palestinians in Israel, and other like-minded groups—are currently acting "to define, or redefine, themselves as indigenous peoples.... After all, what homeland minority would not want the same rights—as currently formulated—that are accorded indigenous peoples?" Kymlicka warns against this development:[19]

> The net effect of such shifts in self-identification would be the total collapse of the international system of indigenous rights. Many states supported the UN draft declaration on indigenous rights only because it was seen as exceptional, relevant to a very specific and relatively small and peripheral set of groups, and not as a precedent that could be invoked by other, larger homeland groups, such as national minorities.... If more and more homeland groups adopt the indigenous label, the likely result is that the international community will retreat from its current commitment to robust accommodation rights for indigenous peoples.... *the*

[17] U.N. General Assembly Resolution 61/295 of 13 September 2007 on the United Nations Declaration on the Rights of Indigenous Peoples, Annex, Art. 3.

[18] U.N. Permanent Forum on Indigenous Issues, "Frequently Asked Questions: Declaration on the Rights of Indigenous Peoples," 2006.

[19] Will Kymlicka, "The Internationalization of Minority Rights," *International Journal of Constitutional Law* 6, no. 1 (2008): pp. 1–32 at 16–18 (emphasis added). For differences between national minorities and indigenous peoples, see Will Kymlicka, *Multicultural Odysseys: Navigating the New International Politics of Diversity* (Oxford: OUP, 2007): pp. 266–291.

development of international minority rights . . . . is in danger of becoming a victim of its own success.

The fifth development is the *expansion of national minority rights.* In the aftermath of World War I, and following the tragedies of World War II, the need to protect national minorities became a central topic in international politics. Nonetheless, international human rights documents in the following years—the Universal Declaration of Human Rights (1948), the European Convention on Human Rights (1950), and the 1966 Human Rights Covenants—did not protect national minorities (or other minorities), but only the rights of persons belonging to minority groups.[20] National conflicts in the 1990s and the collapse of the Soviet Union demonstrated that the assumption under which persons belonging to national minorities were individually well-protected had failed. In 1992, the United Nations General Assembly adopted a declaration which, arguably for the first time, granted rights directly to national minorities.[21] Europe, too, drafted legal documents protecting national minorities: the European Charter for Regional or Minority Languages (1992), which has been ratified by twenty-five countries so far (2015), and the Framework Convention for the Protection of National Minorities (1995), which so far has been ratified by thirty-nine countries.

Claims for national minority rights are advocated by groups of all kinds nowadays. Group rights are the fashion of the day; one need only look at topics of academic conferences, cases heard by international courts, and the agenda of international bodies and research institutions. The massive regulation of minority rights has produced what John Skrentny has termed a "minority rights revolution."[22] First, it relates to the expanding list of groups demanding the status of national minority—far exceeding the traditional cases, such as Puerto Ricans in the United States. Second, it concerns the widening areas of protection: cultural rights, education rights, linguistic rights, self-government rights, effective participation in public affairs, affirmative action, proportional representation, exemptions from general laws, and cultural ties with kin-states. Dozens of guides and recommendations on national minority rights have been published by the OSCE High Commissioner on National Minorities, the Venice Commission of the Council of Europe, U.N. bodies, and

20 U.N., "Study on the Rights of Persons Belonging to Ethnic, Religious and Linguistic Minorities," p. 33 (n 11).

21 U.N. General Assembly Resolution 47/135 (n 15).

22 John D. Skrentny, *The Minority Rights Revolution* (Cambridge: Harvard University Press, 2002).

international NGOs,[23] to the point where we may have reached a "minority rights inflation." While some of these guides and recommendations are not legally-binding, states often implement them voluntarily as law in action.

These five developments are connected to the rise of multiculturalism. There are various theories and forms of multiculturalism, but the core of the argument lies in the demand for equal respect and recognition of different cultures and ways of life.[24] This means that liberal states should refrain from compelling minorities to assimilate into the majority culture and instead provide them with tools to maintain their own culture. The general demand is to recognize different cultures, even if they call into question the majority culture; refrain from imposing a single national identity and way of doing things, even when this is the traditional way of doing things; and value diverse modes of life, even the nonliberal,[25] by giving them an appropriate place in the public realm (school curriculum, languages, etc.).

The rise of multiculturalism is all the more significant due to its expansion from indigenous and national minority groups to immigrant groups. Take Will Kymlicka, one of the leading theorists of multiculturalism. His original proposition that cultural group rights are limited to indigenous peoples and national minorities[26] is no longer valid in practice. Cultural group rights—demands for linguistic rights, *Sharia* law, or exemptions from general laws relating to the school curriculum and food—are invoked nowadays by immigrant groups, mainly in Europe, even if their demands are more confined than those asserted by national minorities. Kymlicka's propositions that immigrant groups are dispersed around the country, rather than geographically concentrated, seek to integrate into the national culture, rather than maintain their original cultural identities, and lack the institutional structures to form distinctive communities, are still valid in theory, but may no longer accurately describe Western reality.[27]

[23] Council of Europe, Venice Commission, "Vademecum of Venice Commission Opinions and Reports Concerning the Protection of Minorities," Council Doc. CDL-MIN(2007)001, 2007.

[24] Charles Taylor, "The Politics of Recognition," in *Multiculturalism: Examining the Politics of Recognition*, Amy Gutmann, ed. (Princeton: Princeton University Press, 1994): pp. 25–73.

[25] Bhikhu Parekh, *Rethinking Multiculturalism: Cultural Diversity and Political Theory*, 2nd ed. (New York: Palgrave Macmillan, 2006): pp. 109–113.

[26] Will Kymlicka, *Multicultural Citizenship: A Liberal Theory of Minority Rights* (Oxford: Clarendon Press, 2000): pp. 94–99, 114–115.

[27] Will Kymlicka, "The Sources of Nationalism: Commentary on Taylor," in *The Morality of Nationalism*, Robert McKim and Jeff McMahan, eds. (Oxford: OUP, 1997): pp. 56–65 at 58–60.

Back in the 1990s, in referring to multiculturalism, Nathan Glazer commented that "terms take on a life of their own, totally unexpected by their original users."[28] This description is well-suited to developments in the field of minority rights, regardless of whether they are desirable.

Peoples, nations, and self-determination

All peoples have a right to self-determination, but the precise meaning of the term "peoples" remains unclear. Common Article 1 does not provide criteria to determine who a "people" is, or how a group becomes a people. In theory, peoples have at least two meanings: (a) peoples in the civic sense of the *entire* population living permanently in a sovereign state; and (b) peoples in the ethno-cultural sense of *only a portion* of a population living permanently in a sovereign state that shares common characteristics: cultural heritage, history, language, ethnicity, and often religion. The first meaning focuses on membership in a political entity created by law and governed by law; "people" is synonymous with a state population. The second meaning focuses on membership in an ethno-cultural community; a "people" is bound together by common characteristics, real or imagined, and exists even without its members living together in a sovereign state.

International law leaves the concept of "peoples" exceedingly vague. As a result, it is difficult to identify the precise entity that possesses the right to self-determination. The absence of a legal definition was well-known to the U.N. organs. In the debates preceding the adoption of Common Article 1, it was first claimed that "Until such concepts were agreed upon, it would be premature to write into an international legal instrument an article on the 'right' of 'peoples'... to 'self-determination.'"[29] It was thus proposed to conduct a study on the meaning of the term "peoples." However, the general tone was fiercely against a solid definition: "The fact is that, whenever in the course of history a people has become aware of being a people, all definitions have proved superfluous."[30]

Legal and historical examinations indicate that the term "peoples" is associated with an ethno-cultural group. One of the most detailed legal

[28] Nathan Glazer, *We Are All Multiculturalists Now* (Cambridge: Harvard University Press, 1997): p. 19.

[29] Marc J. Bossuyt, *Guide to the "Travaux Préparatoires" of the International Covenant on Civil and Political Rights* (Leiden: Martinus Nijhoff, 1987): p. 20.

[30] U.N., "The Right to Self-Determination," paras. 274–278 (n 8).

analyses has been conducted by the United Nations Educational Scientific and Cultural Organization (UNESCO). According to UNESCO experts, peoples have some common features binding their members together, as follows: (1) common historical tradition; (2) racial or ethnic identity; (3) cultural homogeneity; (4) linguistic unity; (5) religious or ideological affinity; (6) territorial connection; (7) common economic life; and (8) self-consciousness of being a people.[31] The criteria suggested by UNESCO experts tend to emphasize the essentially ethno-cultural core of peoples.

The view that peoples have an ethno-cultural core is not only based on legal grounds, but is also supported by historical evidence. Back in 1945, when the United Nations decided to draft a human rights treaty, the holders of the right to self-determination were "peoples and nations." In the U.N. Conference on International Organization, known as the San Francisco Conference, it was stated: "surely one could use the word 'peoples' as an equivalent for the word 'states,' but in the expression 'the peoples' right of self-determination' the word 'peoples' means the national groups which do not identify themselves with the population of a state."[32] In 1950, the U.N. Commission on Human Rights presented the first draft on self-determination—"Every people and every *nation* shall have the right to *national* self-determination."[33] Two years later, in 1952, the United Nations General Assembly affirmed a draft article on the "right of peoples and nations to self-determination."[34] Indeed, the term "nations" appeared in all the drafts of Common Article 1 until the very last version.[35] Eventually, it was left out, because " 'peoples' was considered to be the more comprehensive term and was used in the Preamble to the Charter."[36] However, in a special report on self-determination, U.N. bodies clarified:[37]

> [Nations] are also holders of equal rights and the right of self-determination. Although they are not expressly mentioned in the formulation of this

[31] UNESCO, "International Meeting of Experts on Further Study of the Concept of the Rights of Peoples," UNESCO Doc. SHS-89/CONF.602/7, 1990, para. 22.

[32] U.N., *Documents of the United Nations Conference on International Organization San Francisco, 1945*, vol. VI (New York: United Nations Information Organizations, 1945): p. 300.

[33] U.N. Commission on Human Rights, "Report to the Economic and Social Council on the Work of the Sixth Session of the Commission, Held at Lake Success, New York, 27 March–19 May 1950 (E/1681)," 1950, Annex III (proposals for additional articles) (emphasis added).

[34] U.N. General Assembly Resolution 637 (VII) of 16 December 1952 on the Right of Peoples and Nations to Self-Determination.

[35] U.N., "Annotations on the Text of the Draft International Covenants on Human Rights," U.N. Doc. A/29291, 1955: pp. 13–15, 85–86; U.N. General Assembly Resolution 1803 (XVII) of 14 December 1962 on the Permanent Sovereignty over Natural Resources.

[36] U.N., "The Right to Self-Determination," para. 47 (n 8).

[37] U.N., "The Right to Self-Determination," para. 280 (n 8).

principle in the International Covenants on Human Rights, they are implied, being covered by the term "peoples."

The view that self-determination is also about nations is not surprising. In the aftermath of World War II, self-determination was associated with national groups, not state populations. The term "nations" was not adopted in Common Article 1 since, in spite of the title the United *Nations* (or the term inter-*nation*-al law), states, rather than nations, are the legal person in international law. The term "peoples" was preferred because it appeared in the Preamble to the Charter of the United Nations as the source of authority of the United Nations ("We the Peoples of the United Nations").[38]

In 2005, following the emergence of a growing number of national minorities in Europe, the Council of Europe decided to explore the concept of "nation" in Member States' constitutions. It found that "The term 'nation' is deeply rooted in peoples' culture and history," and concluded that it is "difficult, not to say impossible, to arrive at a common definition." The Council of Europe's report shows the elusive nature and diverse meanings of the term "nation." In some states, it merely designates citizenship in the civic sense of a legal status regardless of ethno-cultural differences; in other states it refers to "an organic community speaking a certain language and characterised by a set of similar cultural and historic traditions"; while in yet others, the concept of "nation" simultaneously has civic and ethnic meaning. The concept of "nation," thus, has a double meaning: an entire state population and an ethno-cultural group. The Council found the two meanings to be valid and observed that a new definition was unnecessary.[39]

The nuances between states, peoples, and nations do not fit all Western countries. In civic nations, France or the United States, all citizens are equal members of the state, nation, and people. There is no real difference between self-determination of "peoples" vis-à-vis "nations" because they are basically the same entity. This is not the case in ethno-cultural nations, where concepts of citizenship and nationality do not overlap. Croats, Czechs, Estonians, Hungarians, Jews, Macedonians, Poles,

[38] Hans Kelsen, "The Preamble of the Charter—A Critical Analysis," *The Journal of Politics* 8, no. 2 (1946): pp. 134–159 at 136.

[39] Council of Europe, Parliamentary Assembly, "The Concept of 'Nation'," Council Doc. 10762, 2005, paras. 4, 3, 5, respectively. For a theoretical and comparative analysis, see Azar Gat with Alexander Yakobson, *Nations: The Long History and Deep Roots of Political Ethnicity and Nationalism* (Cambridge: Cambridge University Press, 2013): pp. 328–379.

Romanians, Serbs, Slovaks, Slovenes, Ukrainians—all represent different versions of ethno-cultural nations. Self-determination is linked to a particular ethno-cultural group and does not coincide with the entire population/citizenry.

The ambiguity of international law as to the precise holder of the right to self-determination creates difficulties. If the right belongs to peoples in the sense of the state population, then all citizens hold that right, regardless of whether they form part of a majority or minority. If, however, the right of self-determination belongs to peoples in the sense of an ethno-cultural group—the Slovak nation or the Jewish people—then members of that group, usually the majority, hold that right (though this claim can also serve minorities and indigenous peoples). An answer to this basic question has far-reaching implications for the doctrine of self-determination.

Western countries are largely multicultural. Whether they admit it or not, they contain multiple ways of life. When society is homogenous, the culture of the majority is taken for granted. The majority hardly notices the pervasiveness of its culture in the public sphere. With the growing number of immigrants and the rise of minority rights, majority groups feel threatened that, as an American Court once stated, "In the fast-changing circumstances of our day, today's majority may be tomorrow's minority."[40] We are currently witnessing a new wave of self-determination, one which is linked to majority groups, whether we call them a "people," a "nation," a "majority," or any other umbrella category.

MAJORITY GROUPS

International legal theory is complicated enough. The concepts of "peoples," "nations," and "minorities" are among the most contentious and volatile in law and political science. Against this background, suggesting another concept, "majorities," may seem unnecessary. Nevertheless, it is worth developing because, first, existing concepts do not exactly capture the challenge to which cultural defense policies respond and the group of people who invoke them; and, second, it may be that the cultural defense of majority groups cannot be based on self-determination claims since the majority is not considered as a "people" and therefore the right to self-determination seems irrelevant. One can certainly use

[40] *Reed* v. *Jack Van Hoven* 237 F. Supp. 48, p. 51 (W.D. Mich. 1965).

other terms—majority population, majority society, majority people, and the like—to describe a similar idea. The term "majority groups" or "majorities" is preferred because it is the opposite of "minority groups."

This part starts with an introduction to the fluid nature of the concept of majorities. It then presents three conceptions of majorities and identifies four patterns of cases in which majorities may become "needy." This part ends with two justifications for cultural majority rights, which may justify cultural defense of the majority irrespective of whether it can invoke self-determination; these justifications are based on similar rationales to those invoked for cultural minority rights—personal autonomy and the right to identity.

A majority by design

Majority-minority divisions are political; "Majorities are made, not born."[41] As other communities,[42] majorities may be imagined and socially constructed, but nevertheless they are an important part of societal reality.

There are two methods of identifying a national majority:[43] formal and informal. One formal method is to look at census bureau definitions. The existence of certain categories can teach us something about the demographic interests and concerns of different states. For instance, the U.S. Census Bureau classifies the population by race. Categories include non-Hispanic White (the majority), White Hispanic, Black, Asian, American Indian or Alaska Native, and Native Hawaiian or other Pacific Islander. In Israel, the Central Bureau of Statistics divides the population by ethnicity and religion: Jews (the majority), Arabs, and others—persons who have no religious affiliation and non-Arab Christians. In the United Kingdom, classifications of the Office for National Statistics are based on race and nationality: White English/Welsh/Scottish (the majority), other White, Asian, Black, and mixed ethnic groups. In the Netherlands, Statistics Netherlands divides the population into persons of Dutch background (*autochtonen*, the majority) vis-à-vis foreign background (where

[41] Dru C. Gladney, "Introduction: Making and Marking Majorities," in *Making Majorities: Constituting the Nation in Japan, Korea, China, Malaysia, Fiji, Turkey, and the United States*, Dru C. Gladney, ed. (Stanford: Stanford University Press, 1998): pp. 1–9 at 1.

[42] Benedict Anderson, *Imagined Communities: Reflections on the Origin and Spread of Nationalism* (London: Verso, 2006).

[43] The term "national majority" is used as an umbrella-category for ethnic, religious, national, and linguistic majorities.

at least one parent was born abroad, *allochtonen*). Foreign background can be either Western—originating from Europe (except for Turkey), North America, Oceania, Indonesia, and Japan—or non-Western.

A second formal method of viewing a majority is through religious affiliation. Government databases of religious denominations present the religious composition of societies. In the United Kingdom, categories include Christian—the largest group—Buddhist, Hindu, Jewish, Muslim, Sikh, other religion, or no religion. In the Netherlands, religious divisions are Roman Catholic—the largest group—Dutch Reformed, Protestant Church in the Netherlands, Calvinist, and others. In Germany, a majority of the population declares affiliation to a Church, either Roman Catholic or Evangelical, while the rest is affiliated to other religion society or none (people may declare no affiliation, either because they do not have one or due to the Church tax that it entails).

A third formal method of perceiving the concept of majority is through the list of recognized national minorities. A majority can be a residual group—a non-minority population whose members do not see themselves, and are not seen by others, as part of a recognized national minority under national law (some countries officially recognize national minorities) or international law (international law recognizes national minorities by international legal standards, regardless of whether they are recognized on a national level).[44] Over time, a non-minority population may develop the national consciousness of a collective, yet in many cases it has no sense of being a national collective and, as a result, no claims to cultural group rights.[45]

The line between a majority and a minority is not only a function of formal criteria, but also of informal assessment, namely: who is considered part of the dominant majority by society, regardless of government classifications. This method focuses on social attitudes and common social understandings. In Israel, non-Jewish relatives of Jews and migrants from the former Soviet Union who are not considered Jewish under the legal definition in Israel—the *halakhic* religious definition under which a Jew is a person who was born of a Jewish mother or who has converted to Judaism—are seen by most Israelis as part of the Jewish majority. It is a form of "sociological conversion" where non-Jewish citizens, who moved to Israel under the Law of Return of 1950 (see Chapter 2),

[44] Council of Europe, "Vademecum of Venice Commission Opinions and Reports Concerning the Protection of Minorities," pp. 4–13 (n 23).

[45] Henri Tajfel, *Human Groups and Social Categories: Studies in Social Psychology* (Cambridge: Cambridge University Press, 1981): p. 317.

are socially considered part of the Jewish People, contrary to formal categories. The social criteria may be disputed, but arguably they stem from the fact that the non-Jewish Russian-speaking immigrants "exhibit self-identification of belonging to the Jewish society; 'they are adopting—gradually, at varying paces and in varying degrees—the behaviour patterns, culture and identity of the Jewish society,' including, 'in certain cases, aspects of Jewish tradition as practised by non-religious Jews in Israel.' "[46]

None of these categories, despite being frequently used in academic and public discourse, is appropriate when considering majorities within the context of cultural defense policies. As explained in Chapter 3, cultural defense policies, as reflected in immigration and naturalization requirements, are rarely connected to the whiteness of America, the Christian roots of Europe, or the ultra-Orthodox view of the Jewish state—though such views can be found in right-wing organizations (see Chapter 2)—but rather seek to protect different variants of "culture." These variants are not accurately reflected by formal government classifications. Informal divisions may be more accurate, yet are too vague and difficult to grasp.

The elusive nature of majorities and their blurred boundaries form one of the most fundamental challenges in discussing majority groups. In particular, it is difficult to decide how and where to draw the line between majorities and minorities. In many cases, the majority is made up of a coalition of minorities. The majority of today is composed of the minorities of yesterday. As the U.S. Supreme Court concisely phrased it:[47]

> The concepts of "majority" and "minority" necessarily reflect temporary arrangements and political judgments. As observed above, the white "majority" itself is composed of various minority groups, most of which can lay claim to a history of prior discrimination at the hands of the State and private individuals. Not all of these groups can receive preferential treatment and corresponding judicial tolerance of distinctions drawn in terms of race and nationality, for then the only "majority" left would be a new minority of white Anglo-Saxon Protestants.

[46] Alexander Yakobson, "Joining the Jewish People: Non-Jewish Immigrants from the Former USSR, Israeli Identity and Jewish Peoplehood," *Israel Law Review* 43, no. 1 (2010): pp. 218–239 at 226–227 (citing Asher Cohen, *Non-Jewish Jews in Israel* (Jerusalem: Shalom Hartman Institute and Keter Publishing House, 2006): p. 21).

[47] *Regents of University of California* v. *Bakke* 438 U.S. 265, pp. 295–296 (1978) (Justice Powell). The case discussed the constitutionality of affirmative action.

The fact that a concept is elusive does not mean that the reality to be denoted by it does not exist. Of course, there are hard cases. Certainly, there are cases in which there is no one single majority, but spheres of different majorities arrived at by applying different criteria. And surely, in some cases, majorities are presumed not to exist. In France, the idea of majorities and minorities is officially non-existent; all French citizens belong to one people with no majority-minority division.[48] However, with few exceptions—Iceland is a notable example—Western societies are heterogeneous. They contain a majority alongside one or more minorities.[49]

In an ideal civic nation, there should be no majorities and minorities, because all people are presumed to share some core civic values. Yet, in a reality where cultural minority rights dominate, this ideal does not exist. Everyone who advocates cultural minority rights should recognize their side-effect; *cultural minority rights, by definition, yield a distinctive cultural majority*. This is the inevitable outcome of multiculturalism. Indeed, where there is a minority, there is also, by definition, a majority.

Three conceptions of majorities

A majority group is a concept—similar to nations, peoples, and minorities—which has no exact definition. Any proposed definition would be under- or over-inclusive and do an injustice to a complex and subtle issue. We have a good idea of what people mean when they talk about a dominant majority, but just try to define it and you run into trouble. In a sense, majorities are connected to nations and peoples, but the boundaries between these concepts are difficult to capture and define. It is not that further study is required but rather that a legal definition may not be politically desirable or practically effective. In the debates preceding the adoption of Common Article 1, some countries proposed conducting a study on the definition of the concepts of peoples and nations. This proposal was rejected because the very idea of drafting a definition was seen as undesirable.[50] Instead, majorities can be viewed as a cluster concept that ought to be identified by referring to typical cases, then

[48] Décision n° 91-290 DC du 09 mai 1991 (*Loi portant statut de la collectivité territoriale de Corse*), para. 13; Dominique Schnapper, "The Concept of 'Dominant Ethnicity' in the Case of France," in *Rethinking Ethnicity: Majority Groups and Dominant Minorities*, Eric P. Kaufmann, ed. (New York: Routledge, 2004): pp. 90–102 at 85–87.

[49] Kymlicka, *Multicultural Odysseys*, pp. 111, 263 (n 19); Gat with Yakobson, pp. 328–329, 335, 377 (n 39).

[50] U.N., "The Right to Self-Determination," paras. 267–283 (n 8).

incorporating other cases having similar features. This method identifies different conceptions of majorities, instead of searching for an inclusive definition.

In theory, various conceptions of majorities exist. One conception is an *ethno-cultural majority*; a majority is a group that is larger than other groups in the population,[51] and is defined by one or more common ethno-cultural characteristics: descent, heritage, culture, language, religion, or way of life. Most nation-states have a dominant ethno-cultural group around which the state was originally founded—Castilians, English, Lithuanians, Poles, Russians, Serbs, etc.—alongside one or more minority groups: Basques, Catalans, Frisians, Scots, Tatars, Welsh. Anthony Smith terms them "core" and "peripheral" *ethnies*.[52] Each society has its own subtle features and there is no general basis for deciding which group would merit being called an ethno-cultural majority.[53]

A second conception is a *sociological majority*; a "majority" is a group whose members have the strongest political, economic, or cultural power in a society. A majority is measured not necessarily by the number of people, but by resources, dominance, and power. Therefore, there may be cases where a numerical minority is the actual controlling (or ruling) group. These cases ought not to exist in a democracy because a free election is unlikely to produce such an outcome, yet they exist in autocratic regimes.[54]

Sociological majorities may also be composed of groups that, in spite of being a numerical ethno-cultural minority, are seen as part of the majority due to their socioeconomic status. Take Jews in America. Are they a minority, or part of the majority? From a numerical ethno-cultural perspective, Jews are a minority. Indeed, President Truman's Committee on Civil Rights listed Jews as a religious minority

[51] The majority does not have to be more than 50% of the population. It is sufficient to establish that it is the largest of all other groups.

[52] Anthony D. Smith, *The Ethnic Origins of Nations* (Malden: Blackwell Publishing, 1988): pp. 22–32; Anthony D. Smith, *Nations and Nationalism in a Global Era* (Cambridge: Polity Press, 1995): pp. 60–62; Anthony D. Smith, *Nationalism: Theory, Ideology, History* (Malden: Polity Press, 2010): p. 109; Anthony D. Smith, "Ethnic Cores and Dominant Ethnies," in *Rethinking Ethnicity: Majority Groups and Dominant Minorities* (n 48), pp. 15–26; Anthony D. Smith, *National Identity* (Reno: University of Nevada Press, 1991): pp. 19–28, 52–68.

[53] Gat with Yakobson, pp. 328–379 (n 39).

[54] Eric Kaufmann and Oded Haklai, "Dominant Ethnicity: From Minority to Majority," *Nations and Nationalism* 14, no. 4 (2008): pp. 743–767.

that suffered discrimination.[55] During the Civil Rights Movement, when the socio-political situation of the Jews dramatically improved, a question that was debated was whether to include Jews in the EEO-1 Form on equal employment opportunities. African-American groups objected to listing Jews as a minority, arguing that they were not disadvantaged. The claim was that "from the point of view of social recognition and economic progress, Jews had done well."[56] This argument prevailed and, ultimately, Jews were not listed on the EEO-1 Form and were considered as part of the majority population for the purpose of equal employment opportunities.

A third conception is an *idea-based majority*; a majority is a group whose members share, to a high degree, certain ideas and principles that are the dominant ones in a given society. Put differently, members of the majority are those who do not differ substantively from the existing *state*'s dominant ideas and principles. This conception is broad enough to include different levels of generality and abstraction. Some ideas are common to all liberal democracies—for example, the rule of law. Other ideas are particular to a specific country: a political institution, a norm, a form of government, a principle, or a combination of ideas that, taken together, are unique to a certain country (see Chapter 6). Each society has a distinctive structure that is manifested in its fundamental ideas, principles, and institutions, what Michael Walzer terms as "*communities of character*."[57]

The essence of an idea-based majority discussed here is found in a high level of abstraction. Unlike the underlying assumption of cultural defense policies that transmits a message that there is a fixed national way of life, modern societies are multicultural; they have no single way of life but different ways of doing things—in different states, provinces, and cities (New York versus Kansas, Tel Aviv versus Jerusalem, London versus Manchester). Jeremy Waldron is right when he observes that the "assumption that the social world divides up neatly into particular distinct cultures, one to every community" is empirically false.[58] There is no fixed menu of options from which cultures can be assigned to separate

[55] President's Committee on Civil Rights, *To Secure These Rights: The Report of the President's Committee on Civil Rights* (Washington: Government Printing Office, 1947): pp. 14–15, 55–56, 68, 78.

[56] Skrentny, pp. 282–284 (n 22).

[57] Michael Walzer, *Spheres of Justice: A Defense of Pluralism and Equality* (New York: Basic Books, 1983): p. 62.

[58] Jeremy Waldron, "Minority Cultures and the Cosmopolitan Alternative," *University of Michigan Journal of Law Reform* 25, no. 3–4 (1992): pp. 751–794 at 781–782.

states. This reality, however, does not imply that states have no distinctive features. They do, but the focus here is *not* on codes of dress, tastes in food, literature, sport, poetry, and the like; rather, the focus is on the society's basic structure, its constitutive character or, to use the term coined by the U.S. Supreme Court, its "general political philosophy" (see Chapter 3).

The difference between an ethno-cultural and an idea-based majority can be illustrated by referring to Anthony Smith's distinction between normative and demographic changes. According to Smith, each society has a fundamental normative idea, a "*mythomoteur*." This refers to the constitutive character of the society, its normative core. It is what lawyers call "basic structure"—the most fundamental ideas and principles for which a society stands. "Demographic changes," Smith argues, are less important than normative ones—"There may be an influx of new populations as a ruling minority, but the vital factor is a radical discontinuity in the 'myth-symbol' complex and *mythomoteur* of the majority population."[59] The ethno-cultural composition of immigration is less of an issue when it does not radically affect the society's constitutive character. The key question is whether immigration brings with it a transformative normative change that seeks or leads to a significant departure from a society's basic structure.

The three conceptions of majorities provide a wide palette of options for viewing majority groups. In all conceptions, the majority is a collective of human beings, which typically has *three* characteristics: the bonding of a group and consciousness of a majority—collective self-identification of a distinctive group, both internally (within the group) and externally (outside the group); closeness of the members by common distinguishing features that are important for the group's sense of being distinctive (in terms of ethno-cultural character, socioeconomic character, or ideas); and the status of these characteristics in a given society as the dominant one.

The three conceptions of majorities overlap one another. In a typical case, an ethno-cultural majority constitutes a sociological majority—whose cultural, economic, and political power is the strongest in the society—and an idea-based majority, whose norms dominate the public sphere. In other cases, overlapping is less clear-cut. For instance, Jews in Israel are an ethno-cultural majority yet, sociologically, until

[59] Smith, *The Ethnic Origins of Nations*, pp. 15–16 (n 52).

roughly the 1980s, one could refer to a European Jewish (*Ashkenazi*) majority; normatively, the constitutive idea of a Jewish state is widely shared by Orthodox Jews and secular Jews, though they differ radically in their modes of life and ideas. In spite of this overlapping, the different conceptions of majorities are helpful because each group faces a different challenge.

Four cases of needy majorities

This section presents a typology of four cases in which majorities have an interest in defending their culture through immigration law: diminishing majorities, regional-minority majorities, victimized majorities, and minoritized majorities. Under certain circumstances, these cases may justify cultural majority rights in the immigration context. In other circumstances, these cases create, at most, an excuse; they are a plea to consider the existing regional, historical, and psychological circumstances of a particular group when evaluating the legitimacy of its immigration policy. It is a plea for a different interpretation of what is just, or for an exception to a general norm given the group's unique circumstances. It is analogous to a criminal defendant who asks the judge to take into account his or her unique factual circumstances, cultural background, or mental condition. When the group's regional, historical, and psychological circumstances merely relate to the past, such circumstances do not justify or excuse the majority's existing immigration policy but may, at most, mitigate the severity of its wrongfulness. The line is not clear-cut: one may think that some circumstances provide a justification, while others may regard them only as having mitigating value.

The first case concerns *diminishing majorities*; this relates to a situation in which majorities have reached a point where a fundamental feature of society faces a significant challenge due, among other things, to migration. This challenge is a function of the scale of migration and the political capacity to absorb more migrants without a reasonable likelihood that their admission would radically affect the "core" of the majority culture.

For the sake of the discussion, let us put aside decisive questions—What constitutes a society's fundamental character? What is the standard by which a risk should be measured, and how should it be measured?—and assume a hypothetical case where there is reliable evidence that additional migration endangers a fundamental idea commonly held by the majority. Under this scenario, let us further assume, if the state continues to admit migrants, the majority's ability to freely define its "self" in a state-based framework will become much weaker. Given these propositions, is it morally defensible for the majority to protect a fundamental characteristic of its "self" through immigration law and policy?

Consider the following anecdote in Bruce Ackerman's imaginary dialogue between an Eastern immigrant and a Western officer. Ackerman divides the world into two countries: a poor Eastern authoritarian dictatorship and a rich liberal Western democracy. He assumes that the Western country has an admission capacity, Z, for admitting Eastern newcomers without endangering its character and that it has reached this capacity. The imaginary conversation between an Eastern applicant, Z + 1, and the Western immigration officer at the border proceeds as follows:[60]

EASTERNER: I demand recognition as a citizen of this liberal state.

WESTERNER STATESMAN: We refuse.

EASTERNER: What gives you the right to refuse me? Do you think I would fail to qualify as a citizen of an ideal liberal state?

WESTERNER: Not at all.

EASTERNER: Do you imagine you're better than me simply because you've been born west of this frontier?

WESTERNER: No. If that were all, I would not hesitate before admitting you.

EASTERNER: Well, then, what's the trouble?

WESTERNER: The fact is that we in the West are far from achieving a perfect technology of justice; if we admit more than Z newcomers, our existing institutions will be unable to function in anything but an explicitly authoritarian manner.

EASTERNER: But why am I being asked to bear the costs of imperfection?

WESTERNER: Sorry, we're doing everything we can. But Z is the limit on immigrants.

EASTERNER: But you're not doing *everything*. Why not expel some of your native-born Westerners and make room for me? Do you think they're better than I am?

WESTERNER: Z is the limit on our assimilative capacity only on the assumption that there exists a cadre of natives familiar with the operation of liberal institutions. If some of the natives were removed from the population, even Z would be too many.

[60] Bruce A. Ackerman, *Social Justice in the Liberal State* (New Haven: Yale University Press, 1981): pp. 93–95. Ackerman's dialogue focuses on illiberal migrants and equates them with "Easterners," perhaps because it was written during the Cold War.

EASTERNER: So what am I to do? I'll be dead before I get to the front of the line of immigrants.

WESTERNER: Go back among your own people and build your own liberal state. We'll try to help you out as best we can.

Ackerman's dialogue is useful for several reasons. First, it presupposes an admission capacity, *Z*, above which additional Eastern migration "will destroy the *entire* liberal conversation that guarantees the rights of *all* existing citizens." Numbers count, especially in a democracy. Second, in certain circumstances, even the number *Z* would be too high. For example, when Westerners feel culturally alienated, they may leave their country for a different country that better fits their interests. The value of *Z* is a function of numbers and cultural gaps between the immigrants and the host group. Third, the risk to the West derives from the *entry* of illiberal migrants regardless of whether they become citizens; this is why the selection occurs at the border. Fourth, the dialogue offers some generalizations. The Westerner does not provide the Easterner with the opportunity of showing that his or her case is different—that he or she holds liberal values or would make a sincere effort to absorb them, for instance, by passing a citizenship test, participating in an integration course, or signing an integration pact. And finally, the case of a dwindling majority does not justify a complete closure of the border, but only imposition of restrictions on the *flow* of immigration.

Even those who advocate open border policies accept that migration can be restricted when there is a threat to basic liberal democratic values;[61] the controversial question is whether migration can justly be limited when it significantly affects and changes the majority culture, namely, when restrictions are seen by the majority as essential to protect its distinctive culture. Members of a majority may have an interest in restricting migration not merely to maintain liberal institutions, but also to defend their peculiar way or life, particular constitutional structure, and distinctive vision of the common good. As Ayelet Shachar convincingly observes, "One need not be a communitarian to appreciate the weight of these collective identity arguments."[62] After all, the right to self-determination does not necessarily entail only liberal democratic regimes as it also applies to peoples in non-liberal regimes. Self-determination is not only about universal values, but also about a

[61] Joseph H. Carens, "Aliens and Citizens: The Case for Open Borders," *Review of Politics* 49, no. 2 (1987): pp. 251–273 at 262.

[62] Ayelet Shachar, *The Birthright Lottery: Citizenship and Global Inequality Birthright Citizenship* (Cambridge: Harvard University Press, 2009): p. 78.

particular "self" (British, French, German, etc.). It stands for "the right of a people to claim what constitutes its originality" and for the characteristics and set of values that make a people original and unique.[63] The interests of a diminishing majority in protecting its cultural particularity are strongest when: members of the majority perceive their "culture" as worthy of protection; the culture is a key component in their collective identity; they seek to adhere to their cultural identity in the future; and there are universal justifications for protecting this culture (see Chapter 6).

The second case concerns *regional-minority majorities*; this relates to a situation in which there is a considerable gap between the characteristics of the majority within the state and the regional characteristics. A fundamental feature of the majority—ethno-culture, socioeconomic, or idea—can find itself to be of a regional minority. In the Baltic countries or in Ukraine, for example, the non-Russian majority lives in countries bordering the powerful Russian Federation. The idea that these countries should admit massive Russian immigration is perceived as dangerous by the majorities. While it is impossible to provide an Archimedean point from which one can exactly identity a regional-minority majority, some factors may be considered: the level of the cultural gap and its manifestation; the numerical ratio between the majority and the neighboring countries, as well as the size of the minorities joined by the immigrants; the strength of the majority culture; geographic proximity; the potential scale of immigration from neighboring countries; and the level and pace of integration of newcomers into the majority culture. The point is a sense of anxiety on the part of the majority group that is not purely subjective, but is supported by evidence.

The conception of a regional-minority majority is recognized in law and theory, yet thus far only within sovereign states. Referring to the issue of linguistic rights, the Council of Europe has clarified that minority rights should also be granted to "persons belonging to the majority population who reside in areas of the country where they constitute a minority." This means that when a majority becomes a regional minority within a state, it is entitled to linguistic minority rights: "The linguistic rights of these so-called 'majority in a minority' situations require . . . similar safeguards to those of persons belonging to national minorities."[64] Likewise, in Canada, the Supreme Court has provided minority protections to

[63] U.N., "The Right to Self-Determination," paras. 589–592 (n 8); Vrdoljak, p. 54 (n 10).

[64] Council of Europe, "Advisory Committee on the Framework Convention for the Protection of National Minorities: The Language Rights of Persons Belonging to National Minorities Under the

the English-speaking population in the province of Quebec, although it constitutes a majority in the Federation of Canada. In deciding who is a minority and who is a majority, the Canadian Supreme Court has zoomed in to the province of Quebec. The French-speaking population, which constitutes a minority in the Federation of Canada, has been labeled a "majority", while the English-speaking population, which is the federal majority, has been termed a "minority". The Court refers to the Francophone in Quebec as the "majority language community" and to the Anglophone as the "minority language."[65]

Existing concepts of "majorities" and "minorities" are state-based. This is less arbitrary than the loosely-defined notion of regional minorities, but it ignores the challenging reality posed by global migration. This should not lead to the conclusion that all national majorities are minorities now. It presents cases, however, where majorities feel like/are regional minorities.

The third case concerns *victimized majorities*; this relates to a situation in which the majority has a rich history of being persecuted. In the paradigmatic case, the history of victimization is comprehensively rooted in a preset group's identity and has become part of its collective memories, traumas, and ethos. Stories of victimization live "here and now": children learn about them in public schools; national holidays mark them; they appear in a society's constitutive documents; and they shape the group's foreign affairs policies. When the threats are persistent and empirically-grounded, more than just bad collective memories are at stake.

The notion that bad historical experiences shape legal rules and moral principles is not novel. History talks, in law and ethics. In comparative immigration law, a notable example is the preferential treatment granted by kin-states to ethnic Diaspora. Both the Finnish preferential immigration treatment toward Karelians and the Turkish policy toward Ahisha Turks from the Former Soviet Union have been justified on the basis of past sufferings under the communist regime.[66] Redress for past injustice

Framework Convention," Council Doc. ACFC/44DOC(2012)001 rev. 2012, para. 91. Compare to Parliamentary Assembly of the Council of Europe Recommendation 1201 of 1 February 1993 on an Additional Protocol on the Rights of National Minorities to the European Convention on Human Rights, Art. 13.

65 Supreme Court of Canada, *Gosselin (Tutor of)* v. *Quebec (Attorney General)*, 1 S.C.R. 238, para. 31, March 31, 2005.

66 Alexander Yakobson and Amnon Rubinstein, *Israel and the Family of Nations: The Jewish Nation-State and Human Rights* (New York: Routledge, 2008): pp. 126–133.

is one of the justifications of the Israeli Law of Return, granting automatic entry to Jews.[67] It is also one of the justifications given by European states for the preferential treatment to people from former colonies when issuing visas, residence permits, and citizenship status.[68] In the context of a victimized majority, the idea is a plea to consider its past or present exploitation when determining its proper immigration capacity.

The fourth case concerns *minoritized majorities*; this relates to a situation in which a national majority displays the state of mind of a national minority. Will Kymlicka, who has coined this term, defines minoritized majorities as "majorities that continue to think and act as if they are weak and victimized minorities and, therefore, continue to live in existential fear for their survival." These majorities were once national minorities, dominated by a foreign national majority, which is often the present national minority. Reality has changed, yet the majority retains the psychological state of mind of a minority. Kymlicka gives the example of the Slovak majority in Slovakia, which, although being a solid numerical majority of about 80 percent of the population, acts toward the Hungarian community, a small minority (about 10 percent of the population), with the state of mind of a minority. This is because, historically, Slovaks were a subordinate group within the Habsburg Empire, in which the Hungarians were part of the dominant majority. Hierarchy has been changed, but "memory remains." Kymlicka provides some other examples: the German minority in Poland, the Hungarian minority in Romania, the Russian minority in Ukraine and Moldova, the Serbian minority in Croatia and Bosnia, and the Turkish minority in Bulgaria. "In such cases," he observes, "minorities are seen (rightly or wrongly) as allies or collaborators with external powers that have historically oppressed the majority group, and the majority group, in turn, reacts as a 'minoritized' majority."[69] In these scenarios, further immigration of people sharing the minority background is perceived by the national majority as a threat to its territorial integrity and sovereignty.

[67] Asa Kasher, "Justice and Affirmative Action: Naturalization and the Law of Return," *Israel Yearbook on Human Rights* 15 (1985): pp. 101–112.

[68] Christian Joppke, *Selecting by Origin: Ethnic Migration in the Liberal State* (Cambridge: Harvard University Press, 2005): pp. 93–111, 144–156.

[69] Kymlicka, "The Internationalization of Minority Rights," pp. 26–27 (n 19); Kymlicka, *Multicultural Odysseys*, pp. 184–185, 255–257 (n 19).

These four cases are not a closed list. Other cases, such as when migrants join a potentially irredentist minority, are not discussed in this chapter. Various factors influence the question as to when a majority becomes "needy." Some factors relate to the characteristics of the majority group, while others concern the effects of migration and the characteristics of the existing minority joined by some of the migrants. In some cases the decline of the majority may bring about a fundamental *cultural* change, while in other cases it can endanger the *liberal*-democratic structure.

So far, this chapter has advanced the recognition of a new concept, "majority groups," and discussed three conceptions of majorities. It has identified four paradigmatic cases in which majorities may see themselves, or indeed are, more vulnerable than is commonly assumed. The remaining question is whether any of these cases justifies immigration restrictions in order to protect the majority's constitutive character.

Majority rights?

The majority's plea for cultural defense builds on an already-established literature on cultural minority rights. Some of the principles invoked to defend minority cultures may apply, with proper accommodation, to "needy" majority cultures. The argument is that majorities and minorities make a claim to "cultural defense" on the basis of a similar rationale and jargon, though in a different application (sub-state units vis-à-vis state-based frameworks). Thus far, the needy groups have been mostly minorities; yet, similar justifications can be applied to needy majorities.

Liberal theorists provide two primary justifications for cultural minority rights.[70] According to the first justification, culture is a prerequisite for the realization of personal autonomy. Culture provides a sufficient range of options from which individuals can choose to live and shape their lives. According to the second justification, culture is an essential component for the realization of personal identity. It provides attributes that are essential for people's identities to flourish, and thereby makes life meaningful.[71] In both cases, due to the erosive effect of a majority-controlled laissez-faire democracy, and the simple fact that

[70] See, generally, Chaim Gans, *The Limits of Nationalism* (Cambridge: Cambridge University Press, 2003): pp. 39–66; Chaim Gans, "Individuals' Interest in the Preservation of their Culture: Its Meaning, Justifications, and Implications," *Law & Ethics of Human Rights* 1, no. 1 (2007): pp. 6–16.

[71] Avishai Margalit and Moshe Halbertal, "Liberalism and the Right to Culture," *Social Research* 71, no. 3 (2004): pp. 529–548 at 539–540.

the public sphere reflects the majority culture, members of the minority groups "are unfairly disadvantaged in the cultural market-place."[72] This unequal situation creates an injustice that needs to be rectified by giving special protection to minority groups.

Cultural minority rights have paved the way for cultural majority rights. The moral interests of the majority in adhering to its culture and preserving fundamental elements of that culture are based on rationales which are similar to those that first justify the cultural rights of minority groups. Liberal theory and human rights law do not contain an explicit body of law on cultural majority rights, yet this is merely because, so far, the majority culture has been presumed able to take care of itself by virtue of being a majority; its culture is presumed to be secured. However, majorities, like minorities, have an interest in adhering to their culture and preserving at least some of it—maintaining a meaningful, yet distinctive, collective way of life. This interest is based on similar justifications of cultural minority rights—personal autonomy and identity. Subject to some conditions (see Chapter 6), a culturally needy majority may legitimately seek to restrict immigration for the purpose of "cultural defense" of some of its essentials. Will Kymlicka persuasively argues:[73]

> The fact is that national minorities are no different from the members of majority nations.... Anglophones in Ontario (or Illinois) are as deeply attached to their language and culture as Francophones in Quebec or the Flemish in Belgium. If the demographics were reversed, and Anglophones in the United States were outnumbered by Francophones or Hispanics, then they, too, would mobilize to gain official recognition and support for their language and culture.... were their identity to be threatened, national majorities would mobilize in just the same way as minorities.

In "The Case for Linguistic Self-Defense," George Fletcher argues that defending the national way of life is no less significant than defending state territory. A territory provides a physical platform on which people may express their identities, enjoy their culture, and live according to their desired form of government. According to Fletcher, "What makes territory worth fighting for, therefore, is the culture, the way of life, and the government that define the identity and the history of the inhabitants." Fletcher draws an analogy between the right to self-defense against a physical invasion and the right to linguistic self-defense. He presents a

[72] Kymlicka, *Multicultural Citizenship*, p. 109 (n 26).

[73] Kymlicka, "The Sources of Nationalism: A Commentary on Taylor," p. 62 (n 27).

hypothetical scenario in which, during World War II, the Nazis abandoned their plan to conquer England and instead concocted a way of substituting the use of the English language for the use of the German language so that to communicate with one another in print or through the media, "English-speaking people had to understand German." In this hypothetical scenario, Fletcher claims that:[74]

> If the English language is essential to the maintenance of English culture, the English legal system, and the specific traditions of the English constitution, then the imagined substitution of German for English would arguably be as serious a form of aggression as a physical invasion. The English would have as much a right to go to war for their language, I think, as they would have to fight for the flowered fields of Wiltshire or the white cliffs of Dover. They would, in brief, have a right of linguistic self-defense.

Fletcher's analogy is disputable and his provocative means of achieving linguistic defense—going to war—may seem radical, but his underlying principle is relevant to our discussion. In certain cases, some elements of the majority culture are worth protecting no less than physical territories.

What does majority "rights" mean? First and foremost, it entails that the cultural interests of the majority should be protected by law—that is, recognizing that some cultural interests of majorities, in some cases and subject to some limitations, are a sufficient reason for granting privileges to the majority and imposing duties on others in order to secure those interests.[75] Second, a distinction should be made between immigration context and non-immigration context. In the latter case, the majority does not usually need a "right" to protect its culture because it can utilize its numerical superiority to perpetuate its culture. Indeed, majorities employ ordinary means of cultural protectionism—public education, national ceremonies, limitations on cultural free trade, or criminal and civil sanctions, as in the case of abortion, animal slaughter, and circumcision. In the immigration context, however, majorities are less able of utilizing the forces of democratic decision-making, for the reasons that have already been discussed (see Chapter 1 and earlier in this chapter). Majority "rights," in this context, means a plea to consider the majority's cultural interests and special circumstances when determining the

[74] George Fletcher, "The Case for Linguistic Self-Defense," in *The Morality of Nationalism* (n 27), pp. 324–339 at 325–326.

[75] For the concept of "right," see generally Joseph Raz, "Legal Rights," *Oxford Journal of Legal Studies* 4, no. 1 (1984): pp. 1–21.

immigration capacity, either as a justification for a certain immigration policy or as an excuse for a deviation from a particular legal norm—a form of mitigating circumstances. And third, the legal formula can be varied according to the changing circumstances but, generally, it means that domestic law and international law should protect culturally "needy" (or vulnerable) groups, whether they are minorities or majorities.

What is the scope of the protection?[76] A distinction can be made between negative and positive defense. Negative defense focuses on cultural *preservation*. Positive defense focuses on cultural *development*. International law, under Article 1 of the ICCPR, speaks about the right of people to pursue their "cultural development." Development, by definition, involves change. This change, as Samuel Scheffler shows, is in the interest of the majority because "Cultures survive only by changing.... to prevent a culture from changing, if such a thing were possible, would not be to preserve the culture but rather to destroy it."[77] Cultural defense in the immigration context, thus, promotes neither a radical version of cultural nationalism in which immigrants must be harmonized with the majority culture nor a radical version of multiculturalism in which the entire culture of the immigrants is recognized. Instead, it allows cultural changes until a point at which further immigration may pose a threat to cultural essentials of the majority. Quite obviously, the scope of majority rights should be country-specific—depending on the overall circumstances of every state.

What factors should be considered when determining the scope of majority rights? One factor is the severity of the threat posed to the majority culture, the probability of it occurring, and its consequences. The threat must be real—a sense of threat is not sufficient—yet it relates not only to individual applications, but also to the volume and composition of migration given the regional, historical, and psychological circumstances, as well as geopolitical conditions, of the majority group—whether it constitutes a regional-minority majority, a victimized majority, or a minoritized majority. Other factors are the moral value of the culture of the majority (how much it is worth protecting?), its centrality in defining the majority's identity, and whether the majority culture encompasses only a single state, or different states in which it is realized. While the focus of these factors is the majority interest, other

[76] This issue is discussed in detail in Ch. 6.

[77] Samuel Scheffler, "Immigration and the Significance of Culture," *Philosophy & Public Affairs* 35, no. 2 (2007): pp. 93–125 at 104–107.

factors relate to justice: does the demographic change brought about by migration bring a more or less just society?[78] There are cases where the cultural effects of the demographic change brought about by migration are perceived to be for the worst; immigration restrictions are seen in these cases as "the lesser evil." In other cases, the cultural effects of the demographic change brought about by migration are perceived to create a more just society; in these cases, from a universal point of view, immigration restrictions are less justified. Yet the hard case, and the most prevalent, is when the cultural effects of the demographic change brought about by migration give rise to similar just institutions, but *different* ones; in this case, the majority seeks to restrict migration not in order to prevent harm to liberal-democratic principles and institutions, but in order to sustain its dominant status and privileged position in determining the particular outcome of those just institutions and their basic structure.

Why is a state-level, rather than a sub-state cultural defense, required? In a Utopian reality, where a majority culture can safely and independently flourish in sub-state political units, this may indeed be an option. However, there are cases in which there are grounds to believe that the majority, if it becomes a minority, may no longer be able to properly maintain its cultural essentials in sub-state arrangements. The fears of the Jewish majority in Israel are an apt example. A state-based cultural defense is viewed as essential for the physical security of Jews in Israel. The case of Member States in Europe is not identical to that of Israel, although in some states the claims and fears of right-wing parties resemble those of Jews in Israel.

Two final comments: first, majorities are not free of moral constraints and legal restrictions in the immigration context. Chapter 6 elaborates on these constraints in detail. Here, suffice it to say that a prerequisite for the majority's cultural defense is the assurance of cultural minority rights. And second, my focus is immigration law. I do not discuss other means by which the majority culture may lose its dominance or be marginalized, such as occupation or expulsion, nor do I address non-immigration related means by which the majority can strengthen its culture: for example, by public education, national ceremonies, or changes in the criteria determining who belongs to the majority group, such as who is "white" or who is "Jewish"?

[78] James L. Hudson, "The Ethics of Immigration Restriction," *Social Theory and Practice* 10, no. 2 (1984): pp. 201–239 at 212–236.

LIBERALISM AND MAJORITY RIGHTS

Liberal theorists are concerned with minority rights. This is justified given the infamous history of majority groups. If history teaches us anything, it is that the power of rulers must be restrained. Authority, as John Stuart Mill argues, should be restricted. In order to restrict the power of majorities, a democracy can apply different mechanisms: a bill of rights, checks and balances, judicial review, and federalism.[79] These mechanisms have not always been effective. Throughout the twentieth century, minorities have been discriminated against and deprived of their rights. The traditional liberal response to the "tyranny of the majority" has been tolerance—"letting minorities conduct themselves as they wish...so long as they do not interfere with the culture of the majority."[80] As a consequence of World War II, anti-discrimination laws on the grounds of race and religion have become part of human rights law and an additional limitation on the power of the majority; the majority can no longer exclude members of the minority from the public space (schools, jobs, residences, etc.). International law has sought to create a balance between the right of peoples to self-determination and the rights of persons belonging to minority groups to enjoy their own culture. International law has thereby enabled nation-states "to reproduce men and women of a certain sort: Norwegian, French, Dutch, or whatever," to quote Michael Walzer, on condition that they allow "minorities an equal freedom to organize their members, express their cultural values, and reproduce their way of life."[81]

During the 1980s and 1990s, a third liberal response to majority power became common: minority group rights and multiculturalism.[82] The rise of minority rights and multiculturalism, however, has produced a form of majority nationalism and brought about laws intended to protect the culture of the majority. Everyone who promotes minority rights must recognize that cultural minority rights, by definition, mean the existence of a distinctive cultural majority. When society is largely

[79] Michael A. Genovese, ed., "Federalist No. 51" (Madison), in *The Federalist Papers: Alexander Hamilton, James Madison, and John Jay* (n 2): pp. 119–122.

[80] Joseph Raz, "Multiculturalism: A Liberal Perspective," in *Ethics in the Public Domain: Essays in the Morality of Law and Politics* (Oxford: Clarendon Press, 1996): pp. 170–191 at 172.

[81] Michael Walzer, "Comment," in *Multiculturalism: Examining the Politics of Recognition* (n 24): pp. 99–103 at 101, 100, respectively.

[82] Natan Lerner, *Religion, Secular Beliefs and Human Rights*, 2nd ed. (Leiden: Martinus Nijhoff, 2012): pp. 99–116.

homogenous, the culture of the majority is taken for granted without according it too much attention. The majority hardly notices the pervasiveness of its own culture in the public sphere. It is the expansion of minority rights that gives rise to the revival of majority groups. As George Bernard Shaw once claimed, "A healthy nation is as unconscious of its nationality as a healthy man of his bones." But when its sense of nationality becomes insecure, "it will think of nothing else but getting it set again."[83]

Political theory and international law are ill-equipped to address the challenge of cultural defense policies. Law and theory focus on states, peoples, and nations, yet these concepts are not the appropriate ones by which to facilitate an understanding of the challenge to which cultural defense policies try to respond. The analysis of cultural defense policies reveals that their focus is the majority. They reflect its histories, stories, identities, values, interests, anxieties, and ways of life. The law uses terms such as "community," "society," and "the people," yet, in spite of this neutral jargon, it is quite obvious that it is concerned with the majority culture. Disregarding the interests of the majority is not just morally wrong but politically unwise, as it may enhance majority nationalism in the future.

Recognizing a principle—cultural majority rights in the immigration context—tells little about its application and manifestation. Every defense, if it wishes to be liberal, must be implemented within liberal-democratic theory. What is legitimate, and what is not? To this question I now turn.

[83] Bernard Shaw, *John Bull's Other Island and Major Barbara* (New York: Brentano's, 1916): p. xxxvi.

6

National Constitutionalism

> There is therefore a purely civil profession of faith... not exactly as religious dogmas, but as sentiments of sociability, without which it is impossible to be either a good citizen or a loyal subject.
>
> —Jean-Jacques Rousseau[1]

Constitutional theory has much in common with religious tradition. Western constitutional democracy and Western religious history not only share challenges and problems, but also language and concepts. "Many religions have faced the same problems of community and continuity and so have developed languages and concepts to deal with precisely these questions," Jack Balkin observes, and that is "why the language of religion is particularly useful in understanding" constitutional theory, "even if the constitutional project itself is secular."[2] In modern history, constitutional democracies have sought to formulate a "center" that holds people together in the community, and maintain it through generations. The center usually has collective narratives, alongside core beliefs, which must be affirmed by the public and function as the moral foundation for social unity. Rousseau eloquently dubbed it "civil religion."

Religious traditions have their parallels not only within constitutional theory, but also within Western citizenship theory. Religious conversion has been a central method of changing identity throughout history. In a sense, Western naturalization law can be seen as a form of "civic conversion" (see Chapter 4). Naturalization hinges on meeting substantive requirements and rituals as a prerequisite for membership. Applicants

[1] Jean-Jacques Rousseau, *On the Social Contract*, Christopher Betts, trans. (Oxford: OUP, 1994): p. 166 (Book IV, Ch. VIII).

[2] Jack M. Balkin, *Constitutional Redemption: Political Faith in an Unjust World* (Cambridge: Harvard University Press, 2011): p. 7; Sanford Levinson, *Constitutional Faith* (Princeton: Princeton University Press, 1988): p. 17.

are required to prove their worth and expected to conform to society's way of life. In so doing, liberal states are at constant risk of what Jack Balkin calls legal idolatry—"the idolatry of legal reason as a solution to all moral and social problems... and unreasoning forms of patriotism and nationalism"; the idols "insist that they are true, and that you should believe in them," in their laws, and institutions.[3] This tendency puts liberal democracies at continuous risk of becoming illiberal, even if their ultimate goal is to keep liberalism alive.

Liberal democracies have implemented a variety of cultural defense measures in order to protect the culture of the majority, as illustrated in Chapter 3. Some measures, as shown in Chapter 4, have become illiberal. This raises a fundamental question: is it morally defensible for a liberal state to protect the majority culture by imposing immigration restrictions? As explained in Chapter 5, such measures can be justified under certain conditions. But every restriction, if designed to be liberal, must be compatible with liberal-democratic theory. The devil is in the detail—in the application of cultural defense measures. From a liberal perspective, what information must be known as a prerequisite for joining a liberal state, and what essentials should one accept in the naturalization process?

In the following pages, I suggest a two-stage immigration process. In the first stage, immigrants would have to accept basic liberal-democratic principles as a prerequisite for admission; these principles are not culture-oriented but constitute a system of structural rules governing human behavior. In the second stage, as part of the naturalization process required to obtain citizenship of a specific state, immigrants would be asked to accept fundamental constitutional principles; these principles must be essential to citizenship and as just as one could reasonably expect, given the state's circumstances. I call this concept "national constitutionalism."

Admission criteria, anchored in political liberalism, and citizenship criteria, anchored in national constitutionalism, resemble each other. Yet their focus, aim, and justification differ. Admission criteria focus on political liberalism; national constitutionalism focuses on constitutional essentials. Admission criteria aim to defend liberal principles; naturalization criteria aim to protect constitutional identity. The justification for

[3] Jack M. Balkin, "Idolatry and Faith: The Jurisprudence of Sanford Levinson," *Tulsa Law Review* 38, no. 4 (2003): pp. 553–578 at 562–563.

accepting principles of political liberalism is grounded on the universal claim that "this is the way things ought to be done everywhere"; the justification for accepting constitutional essentials is grounded on the more particular claim that "this is the way we do things here."[4] Together, the above two-stage process seeks to provide a framework for immigration regulation that protects elements of the majority culture within the liberal discourse.

The two-stage immigration process provides a *narrow* defense for the majority culture. First, the focus is culture in the normative rather than anthropological sense (see introductory chapter). It centers on normative principles, values, and institutions, instead of actual practices, folkways, and cultural mores. Second, within the normative realm, the focal point is the national constitution, rather than sociological concepts of German living conditions, life in the United Kingdom, French *communauté*, or Dutch society. Moreover, the focus is only on core constitutional principles, the basic structure, and, exclusively, on those principles that are essential for citizenship in a given state. Third, there is no plea for moral identification, only for legal acceptance. The notion of acceptance is more demanding than cognitive knowledge—it requires some commitment—but less demanding than identification. Fourth, the majority culture must be just, in light of the state's circumstances; not every element of it is to be defended. And fifth, the majority is not a temporary political majority, represented by a political body, but a more permanent majority, reflected by the values of the constitution. It is a constitutional, rather than an electoral, majority.

SOCIAL BOND

Liberal thinkers agree that political communities must share *some* specific bond (tie, glue, attachment) that binds people together. For centuries, the bond was one which centered on religion. Today, the role that religion plays in binding people together in Western society is less central than in the past.[5] Churches are no longer the cornerstone of identity and politics. However, a bond of some kind is still perceived as

[4] Brian Barry, *Culture and Equality: An Egalitarian Critique of Multiculturalism* (Cambridge: Harvard University Press, 2001): pp. 284, 286.

[5] Peter Riesenberg, *Citizenship in the Western Tradition: Plato to Rousseau* (Chapel Hill: University of North Carolina Press, 1992): p. x.

essential. It is required for instrumental purposes—maintaining a liberal democracy.[6]

A mere social bond is insufficient; some level of commitment to it must exist. Fellow citizens should perceive the common project—at least in its essentials—as being worthy of respect, otherwise they may not be willing to obey the law and, eventually, the political regime may collapse. Put differently, some level of commitment to the social bond is an indispensable precondition for the realization of unity, required for the maintenance of a liberal state. Rousseau summarized this point by noting:[7]

> But when the social tie begins to loosen, and the state to weaken, when particular interests begin to make themselves felt, and smaller groupings influence the greater one, then the common interest no longer remains unaltered, but is met with opposition, the votes are no longer unanimous, and the general will no longer the will of all; contradiction and argument arise, and the best opinion is not accepted without dispute.... when in each man's heart the social bond is broken...then the general will falls silent.

The nature of the "center" required for achieving social unity or other goals—community cohesion, social stability, a sense of solidarity, etc.—is one of the greatest puzzles in political theory.[8] Every typology can be problematic—in the literature, there are often classifications such as civic nationalists, cultural nationalists, constitutional patriots, etc.—in view of the difficulty in capturing the nuances and variations of different societies and approaches. Still, liberal theorists have made great efforts in identifying a defensible bond that must be held for the sake of social unity. Some scholars have adopted different variations of political principles. For John Rawls, the source of social unity depends on the principle of justice and minimal liberal values: mainly, equality, freedom, and tolerance. Other scholars focus on a thicker bond, which includes different versions of culture—although scholars vary greatly as to the definition of culture and its manifestations. Some variants of this approach characterize Will Kymlicka's "societal culture," Michael Walzer's "communities of

[6] Anna Stilz, *Liberal Loyalty: Freedom, Obligation, and the State* (Princeton: Princeton University Press, 2009): pp. 27–84, 113–136.

[7] Rousseau, pp. 134–136 at 135 (n 1) (Book IV, Ch. I).

[8] See, e.g., the two opposite views of John Jay and James Madison: Michael A. Genovese, ed., "Federalist No. 2" (Jay) and "Federalist No. 10" (Madison), in *The Federalist Papers: Alexander Hamilton, James Madison, and John Jay* (New York: Palgrave Macmillan, 2009): pp. 37–40 and 49–54, respectively.

character," and David Miller's "public culture."[9] But whatever the bond may be, liberal theorists agree that there has to be a *minimum core* to which most citizens are attached. Citizens must share "something"—whether this is a concept of justice, language, cultural identity, or constitutional essentials.

Different social bonds require different demands of newcomers. Those who believe that the bond can be based on justice and liberal-democratic principles expect immigrants to uphold basic liberal values and comply with just institutions. They usually do not require immigrants to subscribe to common cultural traditions or demonstrate language proficiency unless these are an essential instrument for promoting just principles and institutions. In this view, language proficiency has an instrumental rather than intrinsic value. However, those who advocate a thicker bond typically demand that immigrants comply with a broader requirement—that they endorse some national cultural traditions and demonstrate language proficiency. In this view, the liberal state can legitimately promote some national cultures due to their intrinsic value. In between are those who do not necessarily celebrate the promotion of national cultural traditions, yet accept them as an unavoidable outcome of democracy. As the national culture is likely to be the dominant majority culture in a democracy, scholars suggest compensating members of minority groups for being disadvantaged in the marketplace by granting them special cultural rights. The first approach, often referred to as civic nationalism, seeks to uncouple the civic culture from the national culture of the majority; the second approach, often referred to as cultural nationalism, advocates the promotion of a national culture due to its intrinsic value; the third approach, often referred to as liberal nationalism, accepts the reality of a dominant majority culture, but seeks to rectify for its unequal outcome.

This chapter does not explore the puzzling issue of the social bond and its essentials—nation-states are currently struggling with this question in an attempt to define their Britishness or Frenchness (see Chapter 3)—or the means by which a social bond should be developed; instead, it explores the "core" that newcomers are expected to

[9] See, respectively, Will Kymlicka, *Multicultural Citizenship: A Liberal Theory of Minority Rights* (Oxford: Clarendon Press, 2000): pp. 77, 187–192; Will Kymlicka, "Multicultural Citizenship," in *The Citizenship Debates: A Reader*, Gershon Shafir, ed. (Minneapolis: University of Minnesota Press, 1998): pp. 167–188 at 168–169, 179–185; Michael Walzer, *Spheres of Justice: A Defense of Pluralism and Equality* (New York: Basic Books, 1983): p. 62; David Miller, *On Nationality* (Oxford: Clarendon Press, 1995): pp. 22–27, 41–45, 68–70.

accept before, and as a prerequisite for, joining a liberal state. In other words: what can a liberal state justifiably require newcomers to know and accept as a precondition for their admission and naturalization?

ADMISSION AND POLITICAL LIBERALISM

Political liberalism, at least in its Rawlsian version, requires the liberal state to be generally neutral on conceptions of the good; still, there should be an "overlapping consensus"—an area of agreement that essentially focuses on the principle of "justice as fairness."[10] This entails a platform that allows individuals to pursue their private way of life while respecting a society's basic structure in the political sphere. Political liberalism is not intrinsically "cultural"; it resembles a system of political principles governing human behavior. Although some of its versions are substantive, "justice as fairness," at its core, is procedural. It contains a procedural framework that governs human behavior and regulates political life. This includes a duty to obey laws passed by just institutions and equality before the law. It is considered "universal,"[11] though some local adaptations exist, arguably similar to traffic rules, which are "universal" yet local; in New York people drive on the right, while in London they drive on the left.

If living in a liberal democracy requires obedience to certain structural principles, the liberal state can require *knowledge* and *acceptance* of these principles as a prerequisite to admission. In addition, states can implement appropriate means to ascertain a person's knowledge and acceptance and, in their absence, deny admission. These principles should oblige every person who voluntarily moves to a new state, irrespective of the visa status.[12] Refusing to accept or failing to demonstrate knowledge of these principles, if required, may enable the state to legitimately prevent the issue of a residence visa. Moreover, if an applicant consistently violates liberal-democratic principles, the state can justifiably refuse to renew the permit to stay on a temporary basis and, if necessary, rescind the immigration status.

[10] John Rawls, *Political Liberalism: Expanded Edition* (New York: Columbia University Press, 2005): pp. 133–172; John Rawls, "Justice as Fairness in the Liberal Polity," in *The Citizenship Debates: A Reader* (n 9), pp. 53–72.

[11] The use of the term "universal" is not empirical—as a matter of fact, principles of political liberalism are mainly "Western" and do not apply in all countries—but rather normative, namely, that these principles ought to be universally accepted as a matter of law.

[12] The case of refugees, whose movement is not purely voluntary, requires a separate discussion.

Obeying the framework of principles is justified because the principles are considered just. In *A Theory of Justice*, John Rawls elaborates on the concept of "natural duties." Natural duties are *natural*; they apply to all moral persons as such simply by virtue of their status as human beings. In the "original position," people would opt for these natural duties in order to form a society.[13] It does not follow that people must adopt a particular way of life, only that they accept *some framework and procedures*, such as the duty to comply with just institutions. These duties are a precondition of freedom because freedom "depends on options which depend on [the] rules which constitute those options."[14] People should accept that under the rule of law, they must obey the law whether they like it or not,[15] comply with court decisions even if they disagree with them, and resolve conflicts by peaceful means. They are compelled to accept that certain laws may contradict their private beliefs, but that they are nevertheless obliged to obey them, and accept the right of other people to live accordingly. In this way, even when one disagrees with a certain outcome, one should at least recognize that the procedure leading to that outcome is equal and fair.

If acceptance of some "natural duties" can be a test for admission in the liberal state, exclusion may be justified when an immigrant does not accept those duties, or can reasonably be expected to reject them (under some probability test concerning the likelihood of the threat and its severity). The concept of natural duties creates a narrow area of agreement that must be tolerated by all people living in a liberal state. People who refuse to take on those duties should not be tolerated in the admission procedure. "Some cultures, or aspects of some cultures," Joseph Raz contends, "are unacceptable"; those cultures are communities that do not accept a legal system based on individual autonomy. The state should not tolerate them unless it is either "possible to neutralize their oppressive aspects," or they possess minimal standards, such as the existence of a right to opt out of the group and an ability to live in peace with other groups.[16]

The idea that the liberal state must not admit politically intolerant immigrants—intolerant not in their beliefs, but in their refusal to accept

[13] John Rawls, *A Theory of Justice* (Cambridge: Harvard University Press, 1971): pp. 114–117.

[14] Joseph Raz, "Multiculturalism: A Liberal Perspective," in *Ethics in the Public Domain: Essays in the Morality of Law and Politics* (Oxford: Clarendon Press, 1996): pp. 170–191 at 176.

[15] I do not discuss cases of civil disobedience on the basis of unjust or oppressive law.

[16] Raz, p. 184 (n 14).

the "natural duties"—has deep roots. "Unlimited tolerance must lead to the disappearance of tolerance," Karl Popper wrote years ago, and "if we are not prepared to defend a tolerant society against the onslaught of the intolerant, then the tolerant will be destroyed, and tolerance with them."[17] Similarly, Rousseau argued that each society has a "civil profession of faith ... sentiments of sociability, without which it is impossible to be either a good citizen or a loyal subject." While the sovereign cannot force citizens to believe in certain principles, "it can banish from the state anyone who does not believe them; he can be banished, not for impiety, but for being unsociable, and for being incapable of cherishing the laws and justice sincerely."[18] Nowadays, the idea of banishing from the state citizens whose dogmas contradict the duties of the citizen is considered outlandish, yet the principle that the state should not tolerate the intolerant remains relevant.

The question whether immigration poses a threat to basic liberal-democratic principles is empirical. To a large extent, the perceived threat to liberalism from immigration has been greatly exaggerated (see Chapter 2). However, in a few cases in Europe, immigrants and native Europeans hold significantly opposing views on basic principles of political liberalism, a gap that sometimes becomes even more acute in second and third-generation immigrants (see Chapter 1). The liberal proposition that there is an "overlapping consensus" on core issues does not always exist. This is a fundamental flaw in the theory of multiculturalism that tolerates and even encourages pluralistic societies on the assumption that there is an "overlapping consensus" on basic liberal principles. In practice, "the hegemony of [the] liberal discourse is often skin-deep."[19] The Hawaiian "aloha spirit," in which culturally and religiously diverse groups accept at least some framework and procedures and respect one another, is not always promoted merely by the invisible hand of the market—living in a liberal state.

Even those who disagree that, empirically, there are cases in Western societies in which immigration challenges principles of political liberalism may agree that, normatively, should such a case exist, a liberal state must not admit immigrants who are unwilling, at the bare minimum, to accept these principles. Thus, if there is tangible evidence that an immigrant is a fascist or a religious militant seeking to enter a country in order

[17] Karl R. Popper, *The Open Society and Its Enemies* (Princeton: Princeton University Press, 2013): p. 581.

[18] Rousseau, pp. 166–168 (n 1) (Book IV, Ch. VIII).

[19] John Gray, *Two Faces of Liberalism* (New York: The New Press, 2000): p. 13.

to destroy its liberal-democratic regime, it would be justifiable to deny his or her entry. This conclusion remains valid when the immigrant does not wish to accord rights to Blacks, Jews, or women; refuses to obey just institutions; a priori declares the supremacy of religious authority over state authority; or refuses to resolve conflicts by peaceful means. The state has the right not to admit people who do not accept, let alone reject, liberal principles on which the state is founded and which enable diverse cultural forms of life to live together and flourish—those principles that underpin its very existence.

If basic principles of political liberalism are so fundamental, why not require compliance with them from every native-born citizen? First, these duties are also expected of citizens, though liberal states do not generally banish citizens who fail to abide by such duties,[20] preferring instead to impose civil and criminal sanctions.[21] Second, empirically, there is a presumption that native-born citizens are not alien to basic principles of political liberalism by virtue of their birth and residence in a liberal state (a presumption that can obviously be challenged). Third, normatively, state obligations toward citizens and aliens are not identical. States may decide to take risks and admit intolerant immigrants, yet this is a political decision, neither a legal obligation of the state nor a legal right of the immigrant.

How can a state explore an applicant's intolerant attitudes and actions? As explained in Chapter 4, there are two options. One radical option is to ask applicants directly about their views, a policy that was implemented in its extreme form by the German *Land* of Baden-Württemberg in 2005. A second option is to refrain from intrusive questions, yet take into account an applicant's previous statements and actions when he or she voluntarily reveals them, or where they become known to the state authorities. In both options, there are two grounds for exclusion. Under one, politically intolerant *beliefs* are to be excluded on the assumption that people who hold such beliefs are not to be tolerated per se. Under the second, such beliefs are tolerated, yet the applicants who hold them are

[20] There are exceptions in cases of involvement in terrorism. See, e.g., Audrey Macklin and Rainer Bauböck, eds., "The Return of Banishment: Do the New Denationalisation Policies Weaken Citizenship?," EUI Working Paper RSCAS 2015/14, 2015.

[21] The question of how the liberal state should deal with illiberal groups deserves a separate discussion. See, e.g., Ayelet Shachar, "On Citizenship and Multicultural Vulnerability," *Political Theory* 28, no. 1 (2000): pp. 64–89; Menachem Mautner, "From 'Honor' to 'Dignity': How Should a Liberal State Treat Non-Liberal Cultural Groups?," *Theoretical Inquiries in Law* 9, no. 2 (2008): pp. 609–642; Bhikhu Parekh, "Minority Practices and Principles of Toleration," *International Migration Review* 30, no. 1 (1996): pp. 251–284.

excluded on the assumption that beliefs are likely to lead to intolerant *behavior*. In the latter case, exclusion is based upon a concern as to future behavior. These grounds are often interwoven. The dividing line is a difficult one as some actions (for example, the wearing of the *niqab*) may be a manifestation of beliefs up to the point that beliefs and behavior may become inseparable.

NATURALIZATION AND NATIONAL CONSTITUTIONALISM

Political liberalism says little about Britishness or Frenchness. It does not establish a special relationship between an immigrant and a specific country. This relationship may be required, for becoming a citizen means joining a concrete, well-defined political community—"here and now."

Under my approach, "national constitutionalism," immigrants would have to accept a state's essential constitutional principles before becoming citizens—as long as these principles are just, taking into account the state's circumstances. This formula has five elements: it refers to: (a) *constitutional* principles; (b) which are *fundamental*; (c) *essential* for obtaining citizenship; (d) *just, given the circumstances* of a particular state; and (e) need to be *legally accepted* by the immigrant. National constitutionalism may be viewed as a middle position between civic and cultural nationalism. On the one hand, it is more particular than civic nationalism and leaves room for constitutional exceptionalism—each state according to its own story and constitutional identity. On the other hand, it is more universal than cultural nationalism because it is divorced from romantic notions of national culture and focuses on just constitutional essentials. The controlling factor is the constitution, as long as it is just (a universal element), given a country's circumstances (a particular element).

National constitutionalism is justified for at least two reasons. First, it is based on consent. The decision to become a citizen of a particular country implies an explicit or tacit agreement with its constitutional essentialism.[22] Second, it is based on fairness. Persons who become citizens of a particular country enjoy its benefits, resources, and protection. It is only fair to ask them to accept its constitutional essentials in return.[23]

[22] David Martin, "Membership and Consent: Abstract or Organic," *Yale Journal of International Law* 11, no. 1 (1985): pp. 278–296.

[23] Jeremy Waldron, "Special Ties and Natural Duties," *Philosophy and Public Affairs* 22, no. 1 (1993): pp. 3–30 at 5–11.

Constitutional principles

National constitutionalism focuses on the constitution—not necessarily a formal legal document, but a constitution in the Aristotelian sense of the community's essential character and form of government. A constitution here means a set of fundamental principles and institutions according to which a state is organized and governed.[24] It means the de facto constitution, including judicial interpretations and unwritten conventions.[25]

Every state has a constitutional uniqueness reflecting its history, development, traditions, and contextual background. In order to understand a state's constitutional uniqueness, one should look at its formative documents, among them its constitution, preamble, and declaration of independence. These documents reflect the constitutional trademark, what George Fletcher calls "constitutional identity."[26] They tell a constitutional story, detail the constitutional understandings of the founding fathers, and specify the political aspirations of the community. In some cases, constitutional uniqueness is not necessarily found in a formal constitution. It is embodied in case-law, particularly in common law countries; civil codes, particularly in civil law countries; and fundamental statutes, such as the fundamental principles acknowledged in the laws of the Republic in France. In other cases, constitutional uniqueness is not expressed in juridical texts, but in uncodified constitutional conventions and unwritten constitutional understandings. Whatever the source is, every country has its own constitutional identity—"origins," "concepts," and "aspirations."[27]

There are three methods of viewing constitutional identity. One method focuses on unique *particular* identities; for example, there are many democratic countries, but only one is Jewish (Israel). A second method focuses on different interpretations and applications of *universal* principles.[28] Consider Germany: German constitutionalism is embodied in concepts of human dignity and Kantian morality. Other countries have a constitutional concept of human dignity, but it usually differs

[24] See, e.g., A.V. Dicey, *Introduction to the Study of the Law of the Constitution*, Roger E. Michener, ed., 8th ed. (Indianapolis: Liberty Fund Inc, 1982): pp. 22–23.

[25] Some countries, such as Israel or Britain, do not have a formal constitution, while other countries, such as the Netherlands, do not venerate their constitution as the focal point of identity. In both cases, the test of what counts as a constitution shall be substantive.

[26] George P. Fletcher, "Constitutional Identity," *Cardozo Law Review* 14, no. 3–4 (1993): pp. 737–746.

[27] Gary Jeffrey Jacobsohn, *Constitutional Identity* (Cambridge: Harvard University Press, 2010): p. 91.

[28] Jan-Werner Müller, *Constitutional Patriotism* (Princeton: Princeton University Press, 2007): pp. 65–66.

from the German *unantastbar* dignity. Similarly, the rule of law is a "universal" concept, but the German *Rechtsstaat* is quite different from the Anglo-American rule of law; it requires substantive and procedural fairness, an idea closer to American due process. The Social State, too, is a widely shared concept but, again, the German *Sozialstaat* has a local meaning—it requires affirmative acts to promote the public weal, similar to the American idea of the general welfare.[29] A third method centers on a different blend of *universal* principles. Each country offers a different mixture of universal values, and these mixtures yield different identities. In order to identify constitutional uniqueness, one must look at the system *as a whole.*[30] What makes the German Constitution uniquely *German* is not each discrete principle, but the entire Constitution, the whole package, and the unique mixture in which German constitutionalism is expressed.

National constitutionalism represents an abstract form of collective identity in the liberal state. Its object is the constitution, not the French *communauté* nor the German *Kulturnation*. It leaves room for constitutional particularity and is divorced from romantic conceptions of citizenship. It does not focus on single constitutional principles, but on the constitutional framework as a whole. It builds on Jürgen Habermas' Constitutional Patriotism, but in a slightly different direction. The motivation for national constitutionalism is not the creation of "a just constitutional regime" that "express[es] universal norms of justice and fairness in specific contexts";[31] rather, its *raison d'être* is to protect essential constitutional principles because they are *ours* and because *we*—the French, the German, the Dutch, etc.—have an interest in their preservation. Thus, national constitutionalism is less universal, among other things since it applies to naturalization, the second stage, whereas universal principles apply to the first stage—admission.

Habermas' Constitutional Patriotism is essentially universal; it is tied to universal moral principles. Its particularity is revealed when one looks at the concrete *interpretation* and *application* of universal principles in a particular state, and its particular constitutional *blend* (the second and third methods cited earlier). Constitutional Patriotism is nation-specific

[29] David P. Currie, *The Constitution of the Federal Republic of Germany* (Chicago: University of Chicago Press, 1994): pp. 1–32.

[30] Frank I. Michelman, "Morality, Identity and 'Constitutional Patriotism'," *Denver Law Review* 76, no. 4 (1999): pp. 1009–1028 at 1009, 1015.

[31] Müller, pp. 58–60 (n 28).

only in the sense of local implementation of universal values. In order to be a constitutional patriot, one should be dedicated to universal principles in a concrete national political culture and "interpret the universalistic content of the same constitutional principles in different ways, namely, against the background of the experiences that make up a national history and in light of historically prevailing tradition, culture, and form of life."[32] In this way, the particular identity is embodied in local political institutions, legal interpretations, and constitutional adjudication. Criminalizing Holocaust denial, for example, is a "concrete universal" of the principle of freedom of speech in Germany.[33] The "overlapping consensus," in Habermesian terms, centers on the *validity* of the principles themselves. Accordingly, citizens should accept the validity of universal principles, even though they may disagree over their interpretation and application.[34]

Compared with Constitutional Patriotism, the concept of national constitutionalism embraces a more direct inclusion of the particular by incorporating specific constitutional identities even if they are not merely universal (the first method cited earlier).[35] Most liberal states are *national* states; they hold principles and values that are not just different applications of the universal, but are rooted in an ethno-cultural history, religious heritage, and national traditions. Notable examples are states' official languages—the state language is usually a key feature of a society's constitutional identity,[36] whether it is explicitly anchored in the Constitution, as in France and Spain, or not, as in Germany; religious symbols and institutions, including the official or quasi-official status of the Church—as in England, Greece, Italy, Denmark, and Norway;[37]

[32] Jürgen Habermas, *The Inclusion of the Others: Studies in Political Theory*, Ciaran Cronin and Pablo De Greiff, eds. (Cambridge: The MIT Press, 1998): p. 144; Jürgen Habermas, *Habermas on Law and Democracy: Critical Exchanges*, Michel Rosenfeld and Andrew Arato, eds. (Berkeley: University of California Press, 1988): p. 400.

[33] Todd Hedrick, *Rawls and Habermas: Reason, Pluralism, and the Claims of Political Philosophy* (Stanford: Stanford University Press, 2010): p. 178.

[34] Michelman, "Morality, Identity and 'Constitutional Patriotism'," p. 1026 (n 30).

[35] Under Constitutional Patriotism, "the majority culture must give up its historical prerogative to define the official terms of the *generalized* political culture" and equally interact with other subcultures. See Jürgen Habermas, "The European Nation State. Its Achievements and Its Limitations. On the Past and Future of Sovereignty and Citizenship," *Ratio Juris* 9, no. 2 (1996): pp. 125–137 at 133.

[36] Azar Gat with Alexander Yakobson, *Nations: The Long History and Deep Roots of Political Ethnicity and Nationalism* (Cambridge: Cambridge University Press, 2013): pp. 328–379.

[37] Alexander Yakobson, "God and Religion in Modern Democratic Constitutions," in *Contemporary Challenges to the Nation State: Global and Israeli Perspectives*, vol. II, *The Nation State and Religion: The Resurgence of Faith*, Anita Shapira, Yedidia Z. Stern, and Alexander Yakobson, eds. (Eastbourne: Sussex Academic Press, 2013): pp. 1–13.

traditional national institutions, such as the institution of the monarchy in Britain and Scandinavia; cultural and religious identities in the public sphere—national holidays, symbols, and calendar; and particular national concepts, like the French *laïcité*. Some of these features are symbolic and have few normative or practical implications, as in the case of the official status of the Church in England; still, they reflect, to different degrees, normatively and practically, the majority's heritage, and sometimes its still-existing socio-cultural identity.

Thus far, the defense of majority-based constitutional identities has been performed indirectly (see introductory chapter). One common technique is "universalizing the particular." This technique justifies particular identities by attempting to "universalize" them. For example, the Italian government defends the display of the crucifix in public schools by claiming, among other things, that the crucifix is a "symbol of the principles and values which formed the basis of democracy and western civilisation." The crucifix is not just an Italian (or Catholic) symbol, but a universal moral principle; it is an expression of tolerance, equality, and liberty.[38] Similarly, in one of the numerous cases addressing the phrase "under God" in the Pledge of Allegiance in public schools, and its compatibility with the Establishment Clause of the U.S. Constitution, a U.S. Federal Court found that, although the phrase "under God" has a "religious connotation," it is primarily an expression of "the idea that our nation is founded upon the concept of a limited government.... In adding the words 'under God' to the Pledge, Congress reinforced the belief that our nation was one of individual liberties granted to the people directly by a higher power."[39] God, it seems, is an expression of the idea of inalienable rights. Alexander Yakobson rightly observes that a technique clothing "one's cultural particularity in universalist vestments" by making it as "universalist as possible" requires an unreasonable stretch of that concept. "Attempts to put the cross or the crucifix into the procrustean bed of state neutrality are misguided and offensive," Yakobson notes, because the message is that the minority's cultural particularity is "a deviation from universal moral standards and precepts—rather than just from the national mainstream," while the majority's cultural particularity is found to be an expression of universal morality: "Particularism clothed in universalist rhetoric, is apt, nowadays, to be more aggressive, and less accommodating to others, than particularism that frankly

[38] *Lautsi* v. *Italy* Application 30814/06 (E.Ct.H.R., March 18, 2011), para. 36.

[39] *Newdow* v. *Rio Linda Union School District* 597 F. 3d. 1007, p. 1032 (9th Cir. 2010).

acknowledges itself as such—provided, of course, that this particularism functions within a strong liberal framework."[40]

National constitutionalism, however, is more narrowly focused than national identity, societal culture, and similar concepts; its focal point is the constitution, substantively defined. It does not focus on cultural mores, lifestyles, folkways, ways of doing things, or popular culture. In Germany, for instance, national constitutionalism would not contain the symphonies of Beethoven, the writings of Nietzsche, or the paintings of Caspar David Friedrich, nor would it focus on "what do Germans traditionally do at Easter?" (see Chapter 3); these items might be considered part of the German *national* culture, rather than *constitutional* identity. In the United States, national constitutionalism would not include mountains, rivers, or popular culture, nor would it focus on questions such as "where is the Statue of Liberty?" The dividing line is not clear-cut; there are cases in which constitutional and national identities overlap, such as that of the United States.[41] In other cases, national constitutionalism may include some elements of national culture—values, principles, figures, and events—in so far as constitutional identity has become part of the national culture. Different states may reach different conclusions. Franklin may be of constitutional significance in the United States, the same as Kant in Germany, and Rousseau in France.

This is not to say that requiring immigrants to know certain national cultural traditions and social conventions, even if not legally formulated, is always unjustifiable. Immigrants can legitimately be expected to engage in some level of cultural adaptation. Brian Barry rightly points out that there are cases in which saying " 'This is the way we do things here' is a sufficient basis for the legitimacy of majoritarian collective decision-making with no provision for exceptions.... it was up to them [the immigrants] to check out well-established features of country life... before moving into the area."[42] When a person moves to a new country, he or she must realize that there are new expectations and commitments in the sense of local traditions and social conventions; the immigrant is "not in Kansas anymore." This is not unique to citizenship. Changing one's legal status, getting married for example, is usually

[40] Alexander Yakobson, "Muslims in Europe—Dilemmas of Secularism, Christian Heritage, 'Neutrality' and Religious Freedom," in *Muslim Minorities in Modern Times* (forthcoming, on file with the author). See also Christian Joppke, "A Christian Identity for the Liberal State," *British Journal of Sociology* 64, no. 4 (2013): pp. 597–616 at 606–607.

[41] Levinson, p. 95 (n 2).

[42] Barry, p. 287 (n 4).

followed by new obligations. However, while the defense of certain cultural traditions in the immigration context may be justified,[43] the focal point of national constitutionalism is the constitution as the *sine qua non* for becoming a citizen. Constitutional essentials usually reflect a consensus in a given society and lay down the basic structure of the polity; in addition, they provide more space for multiculturalism and a plural way of life in the liberal state compared to notions of national culture. To the extent that elements of the national culture become consensual, they may be seen as part of a community's essential character and, consequently, constitutional.

Constitutional essentialism

National constitutionalism focuses on fundamental constitutional principles essential for citizenship. The term fundamental constitutional principles, or "constitutional essentials" to use Frank Michelman's term, refers to the most basic values and principles of a given society, what constitutional law scholars call the "basic structure doctrine." It centers on the most fundamental pillars of the society, its constitutive character, "the general political philosophy of the Constitution," as labeled by U.S. courts.

How can fundamental constitutional principles be identified? While there is no foolproof method, a few options exist. First, some constitutions include "eternity clauses" that entrench values and principles which are considered perpetual and immutable. They cannot be altered, even by a constitutional amendment; such an attempt would be an "unconstitutional constitutional amendment." An example is article 79(3) of the German Constitution, which provides that certain principles and values can never be changed, among them the right to human dignity and the German form of government as a democracy, Federal Republic, and Social State. The German eternity clause was influenced by the traumatic events of the Weimar Republic and is aimed at preventing such a scenario from reoccurring. However, the idea of unamendable constitutional provisions exists in other states, directly—through a constitutional provision—and indirectly—through judicial interpretation.[44]

[43] See, e.g., David Miller, "Immigration: The Case for Limits," in *Contemporary Debates in Applied Ethics*, Andrew I. Cohen and Christopher Heath Wellman, eds. (Malden: Blackwell Publishing, 2005): pp. 193–206 at 199–201, 204; David Miller, "Immigrants, Nations, and Citizenship," *Journal of Political Philosophy* 16, no. 4 (2008): pp. 371–390; Yael Tamir, *Liberal Nationalism* (Princeton: Princeton University Press, 1995): pp. 57–94.

[44] Aharon Barak, "Unconstitutional Constitutional Amendments," *Israel Law Review* 44, no. 3 (2011): pp. 321–342.

Second, some constitutions allow the disqualification of political parties that undermine the basic structure of society, for instance, article 21(2) of the German Constitution and article 7a(a)(1) of the Israeli Basic Law: The Knesset. These provisions are seen as measures of "militant democracy," but their goal is often broader than protecting democratic principles; they aim to protect society from fundamental changes.[45] And third, constitutions often have a hierarchy of rights—in the constitution or through judicial interpretation. Such hierarchy signifies the importance of certain values and principles in a specific society.

The identification of constitutional essentials is country-specific and, in many cases, none of the above options exist. Take the United States: the core of American constitutionalism has been debated in American society since its foundation. For some, it centers on republican institutions, the American form of government, and the Bill of Rights. For others, it focuses on freedom of speech and the option of advocating even radical constitutional changes as long as they are promoted according to article V, the constitutional amendment procedure (see Chapter 4). For all, however, American constitutional essentials include the political beliefs drafted by Thomas Jefferson in the U.S. Declaration of Independence: "that all Men are created equal, that they are endowed by their Creator with certain unalienable Rights, that among these are Life, Liberty, and the Pursuit of Happiness." Abraham Lincoln regarded these words as scriptural:[46]

> The expression of that principle, in our Declaration of Independence.... was the word, *"fitly spoken"* which has proved an "apple of gold" to us. The *Union*, and the *Constitution*, are the *picture of silver*, subsequently framed around it. The picture was made, not to *conceal*, or *destroy* the apple; but to *adorn*, and *preserve* it. The *picture* was made *for* the apple—*not* the apple for the picture. So let us act, that neither *picture*, or *apple* shall ever be blurred, or bruised or broken.

Lincoln's metaphor expresses the idea that the U.S. Constitution is an instrument designed to achieve the superior vision of the U.S. Declaration of Independence, but his point is deeper—each society stands for something fundamental, whether we call it an "apple of gold," constitutional essentials, or basic structure. It can be a form of government (democracy, republic, monarchy), governmental structure (federalism, separation of

[45] Samuel Issacharoff, "Fragile Democracies," *Harvard Law Review* 120, no. 6 (2007): pp. 1405–1467.

[46] Roy P. Basler, ed., *The Collected Works of Abraham Lincoln*, vol. IV (New Brunswick: Rutgers University Press, 1953): pp. 168–169.

powers, the rule of law), character (religious identity, secularism, language), or rights and freedoms (equality, liberty, dignity). Some of these elements are universal; others are more particular. Sometimes the law helps in identifying the "apple of gold"; courts legally define it. In the United States, it may be a representative government, federalism, separation of powers, the rights to life, liberty, and private property, and due process of law; in Canada—it may be the principles of federalism, democracy, constitutionalism, the rule of law, and respect for minorities.[47]

There are two kinds of transformation in constitutional essentialism. The first kind is a constitutional amendment. A constitutional amendment affects the constitution as a normative set of rules; it can lead to significant reforms, but still retains the basic structure. Such changes in the constitution are a natural part of its evolution and development. The second kind is a constitutional metamorphosis; it means a repeal of the basic structure of the constitution—its core. "The word amend," Walter Murphy asserts, "means to correct or improve; amend does not mean 'to deconstitute and reconstitute,' to replace one system with another or abandon its primary principles." Therefore, he concludes, "changes that would make a polity into another kind of political system would not be amendments at all, but revisions or transformations.... amendments can operate only within the existing political system; they cannot deconstitute, reconstitute, or replace the polity."[48] The difference between an amendment and a metamorphosis is illustrated by Joseph Raz's analogy between a constitution and a house built centuries ago: "[the] house had been repaired, added to, and changed many times since. But it is still the same house and so is the constitution."[49] National constitutionalism seeks to protect constitutional essentials from a metamorphosis brought about by migration.

Essential for citizenship

National constitutionalism focuses on fundamental constitutional principles essential for obtaining citizenship in a given country. Not every

[47] See, respectively, *Re Saralieff* 59 F. 2d. 436, pp. 436–437 (E.D. Mo. 1932); Supreme Court of Canada, *Reference re Secession of Quebec*, 2 S.C.R. 217, August 20, 1998.

[48] Walter F. Murphy, "Merlin's Memory: The Past and Future Imperfect of the Once and Future Polity," in *Responding to Imperfection the Theory and Practice of Constitutional Amendment*, Sanford Levinson, ed. (Princeton: Princeton University Press, 1995): pp. 163–190 at 177.

[49] Joseph Raz, *Between Authority and Interpretation* (Oxford: OUP, 2009): p. 370.

element of a state's constitutional identity, even if fundamental, is essential to know or accept as a prerequisite for obtaining citizenship of that state.

Consider Britain: the United Kingdom's preparation book for the citizenship test includes questions on leisure culture, TV licenses, horse races, and dog owners. Other questions focus on peculiar issues. An example is the question "according to *Life in the UK*, where does Father Christmas come from?" Possible answers are Lapland, Iceland, and the North Pole. The answer to this question, which is more about mythology than history, is controversial. Some people might answer Lapland, while others might say the North Pole. Various societies tell different tales. Because the question explicitly refers to the handbook, the "correct" answer is the North Pole. The real question, however, is whether this information is essential for settling in the United Kingdom. The answer derives from the title of the test and its purpose—it is a test about *Life in the UK*. Thus, while common law tradition seems less essential for daily life in the United Kingdom, information about housing, childcare, and leisure is. This information is required if one believes, as Trevor Phillips asserts, that British identity is about "what people do.... 'British is as British does'" (see Chapter 3). But while this information may be socially important, citizenship tests are not a TV-game show "Who Wants to Be a Millionaire." Rather, they should set the threshold requirements for becoming a British citizen and not investigate whether immigrants can snap back random trivia about the Grand National or the Notting Hill Carnival. Thus, if a certain value, principle, figure, or event is of constitutional significance, and this knowledge is essential in order to become a citizen of a specific state, it would be legitimate to require this knowledge in the process of naturalization. So, the question is what does "essential" really mean? Under national constitutionalism, essential is not a catch-all category. Rather, it seeks to identify the *sine qua non* principles which are truly necessary for obtaining the citizenship of a particular state.

Under national constitutionalism, different states can ask different questions according to their essential contextual constitutionalism. Thus, state *Z* may demand a different answer than state *X*. Protecting the environment may be an essential constitutional principle in the Netherlands (article 21 of the Dutch Constitution), while it might not be so in other states. In addition, states may require immigrants to accept the same constitutional principles in diverse ways. Thus, immigrants in the Netherlands may be required to accept the lawfulness of abortion under Dutch constitutionalism, whereas they may be required to accept its unlawfulness under Irish constitutionalism. Hence, it would be appropriate to ask about history, so long as it is a constitutional history essential for obtaining citizenship. In the Netherlands, it would be legitimate to ask about constitutional monarchy and pillarization, but less so about Rembrandt and Huygens. In Germany, it would be legitimate to ask about Bismarck's 1871 Constitution, the Weimar Republic, and World War II, but less so about Beethoven, Karl Benz, and what Germans traditionally do at Easter. The challenge is to separate the items of national culture from the more specific items of constitutional identity.[50] In the European Union, because Member States' citizenship entails a European citizenship, it would be legitimate to expect would-be citizens to know and accept essential principles of European constitutionalism.

While testing immigrants about daily life (housing, employment, tax policies) or items of the national culture (Beethoven, Brigitte Bardot, cricket) is not unlawful per se, this information—which has some social value—can be supplied as orientation materials, rather than as mandatory knowledge that must to be tested. This is a matter of discretion and there are good reasons (see Chapter 4) to be more selective in the subject matter of the naturalization process by focusing on the topics that are truly essential for becoming a citizen. Immigrants can learn about Brigitte Bardot or the importance to the Dutch of bringing gifts for birthdays by living in the society. There were times when immigrants were taught by the U.S. Bureau of Naturalization how to decorate their homes, keep clothes clean and mended, and boil eggs (see Chapter 3). But those days have passed; the current U.S. naturalization process focuses on a few essentials: basic proficiency in the English language, an elementary knowledge of U.S. civics and history, and attachment to the principles of the U.S. Constitution. The American experience shows that not all knowledge ought to be mandatory.

A typology that may help is based on a distinction between questions that *must* be asked as a prerequisite to joining a liberal state, questions

[50] The American case is easier than the European because the history of the United States is the history of its Constitution. In Europe, it is much harder to separate the nation from the state (and its Constitution) since the history of European nation-states is deeply rooted in events, principles, and values that sometimes do not relate to the constitution.

that *may* be asked, and questions that *must not* be asked. In between questions that must or must not be asked there is an area of discretion. Examples include questions about rivers, Santa Claus, cricket, or the Statue of Liberty. This information may be important, but it can also be supplied as orientation material instead of as mandatory knowledge that must be tested.

Just, given a state's circumstances

Under national constitutionalism, universal principles, as expressed in a certain political community, must be just. However, the constitution as a whole must be just, not necessarily each separate principle. Legal rules are just when the entire legal system is just. As Frank Michelman notes in referring to Constitutional Patriotism, some principles may be "unjust and badly misguided, and nevertheless legitimate." However, when the system as a whole is morally "respect-worthy," the constitution is considered legitimate, "including even those [laws] that you or I...[judge] to be very bad and immoral ones."[51] There is no need to justify every single constitutional provision; rather, the basic structure, what Jan-Werner Müller calls "the deepest normative impulse," should be just.[52] Certain laws, or legal interpretations, may be seen as unjust, but the general framework of the political community must be perceived as legitimate.

The general constitutional framework should be just, "here and now," that is, at a particular time and place, and in a given circumstance. The question is whether the general constitutional framework as a whole is just, given the state's overall circumstances—its history, culture, demography, economy, tradition, and geopolitical situation (see Chapter 5). Thus, for instance, the question is not whether the French principle of *laïcité*, or the *burqa* ban, is just, but whether the French legal system as a whole is legitimate in the French circumstances, even if certain laws may be seen as unjust by other states. The same applies to the institution of the monarchy in Britain and Scandinavia, religious identities in Italy or Ireland, and a Jewish state in Israel. Justice, as other moral principles, differs from case to case, and legal rules of particular societies may apply it in different ways at different times.

[51] Frank I. Michelman, "Faith and Obligation, or What Makes Sandy Sweat?," *Tulsa Law Review* 83, no. 4 (2003): pp. 651–668 at 654.

[52] Müller, p. 53 (n 28). See also Balkin, p. 34 (n 2).

Legally accept

Suppose that there are some recognizable constitutional principles that are both fundamental and essential for obtaining citizenship in a certain society and that, on the whole, they are just, given the circumstances of the state; what does it mean to legally "accept" them? Acceptance is a type of commitment, but what sort of commitment, to what, and why? The notion of acceptance is tricky: one may accept things one does not like, yet one cannot be forced to like what one accepts. Does acceptance only mean compliance with the law, or does it also include a deeper obligation of faith in, or identification with, the law? Is it an obligation that is valid only at a certain moment, or does it also entail a promise of future behavior?

Under national constitutionalism, acceptance is a legal commitment, not a moral obligation. This issue touches upon the Kantian distinction between "recognition, respect" and "adherence, identification." The former are legal commitments; the latter are moral obligations. Under national constitutionalism, only the first can be involved in the processes of naturalization. Take the *Länder* tests: it is legitimate to inquire if would-be Germans accept Germany's constitutional principles, such as human dignity and the Social State, but the questions should be framed so as to ignore internal perceptions and instead focus on external respect for these principles. Thus, it is better to ask if one legally accepts gender equality than if one "considers gender equality to be a progressive concept." Similarly, a person's "opinion about homosexuals holding public office" in Germany is less essential in legal terms; what is essential is the applicant's acceptance of the legality of same-sex marriages in Germany. In the Netherlands, integration courses embarrass applicants by forcing them to see nude women and homosexuals. Yet the purpose of raising the issue should not be to explore a migrant's personal views of nudism and homosexuality, but whether he or she is willing to accept them as legal, if openly displayed, and respect other people's desire to adopt such lifestyles. There can be cases where a person may privately prefer (and identify with) one norm, yet honestly agree to accept and respect other norms in the public sphere. The focus, to use Ines Michalowski's distinction, should be on what is "right" (lawful/unlawful) rather than what is (morally) "good."[53]

[53] Ines Michalowski, "Citizenship Tests in Five Countries: An Expression of Political Liberalism?," Wissenschaftszentrum Berlin für Sozialforschung (WZB), 2009.

Should liberal democracies inquire into the reason for one's acceptance? The liberal response is, generally, "no." In *The Concept of Law*, H.L.A. Hart develops the idea of an "internal point of view."[54] Hart denies the notion that people who accept legal rules should accept their moral legitimacy; people comply because they accept the validity of a legal rule even if they do not accept its moral truth. Acceptance does not require a specific reason; people can accept a "thing" due to many considerations. One may accept a legal norm on moral grounds (one accepts its moral validity), epistemic grounds (one accepts the legitimacy of the framers), democratic grounds (one accepts that the norm reflects the will of the people), or self-interest (one accepts the norm due to a desire for citizenship). The reason for one's willingness to accept a norm or a principle ought not to be tested; it is analogous to the acceptance of a *fact*, an empirical thing, similar to accepting that there *are* sixteen *Länder* in Germany. One accepts the legal validity of a norm—the legitimacy of a legal rule—while its moral validity is discretionary. Acceptance means obedience, compliance, or conformity, not identification or belief. People may want to become citizens for various reasons—to save on inheritance taxes, travel on a certain passport, or enjoy welfare benefits—but these are personal choices that should not be the "business" of the government.

Under national constitutionalism, acceptance involves not only legal principles, but also their legal meaning in a certain society. The immigrant is required to accept abstract principles—equality, liberty, freedom of speech, etc.—*and* their particular legal meaning in a specific society, namely, what equality or liberty mean in legal terms in that society. This applies to universal principles, such as equality or liberty, and particular principles—such as *laïcité* or a constitutional monarchy. While the person may hold a different view on the meaning of these principles, he or she must accept their prevailing legal interpretation in a certain community. The immigrant is not required to morally agree with the interpretation, only to accept it as the law of the land. This does not solely mean accepting principles such as "all men are created equal," but also accepting the *particular* legal understanding of equality in a given society.

[54] H.L.A. Hart, *The Concept of Law*, Penelope A. Bulloch and Joseph Raz, eds., 2nd ed. (Oxford: Clarendon Press, 1994): pp. 88–91, 110–117, 198, 225–256. Hart focuses on officials, who work in the legal system, mainly judges, and says little about citizens. While officials must take an "internal point of view" of the law, citizens *may* take such a view. This is because officials work with the rules of recognition, and people in the citizen's role do not. For that latter role, in order to achieve stability, citizens must obey.

There can be different methods of demonstrating acceptance. One is a statement, oral or written, similar to naturalization oaths or integration contracts. For some, a mere statement is not sufficient due to the fear that people may lie. A second method can consist of demonstrating some pattern of behavior. In the United States, the requirement of attachment to the U.S. Constitution demands that the applicant demonstrates attachment through a certain "behavior for a period of five years" prior to the naturalization petition. In theory, this can be shown by demonstrating "positive" patterns of behavior or, alternatively, abstaining from "negative" patterns of behavior by avoiding one of the grounds of ineligibility, such as opposition to government or law, or membership in a totalitarian party. A third method can be a formal test. A legal system can require one or all of these methods, or indeed offer different alternatives for demonstrating actual acceptance.

THEORY AND PRACTICE

The two-stage immigration process attempts to provide a liberal framework that allows liberal democracies to protect their essential contextual constitutionalism by means of immigration law.[55] It departs from both communitarianism and cosmopolitanism theories of citizenship—the starting point is that a state is neither a club whose members enjoy the right of closure, nor a global village open "to all and sundry"—and seeks to offer a middle position that is both compatible with liberal principles and firmly grounded in the existing immigration trends in the liberal state.

On the practical level, the two-stage immigration process has certain implications. On admission, liberal states can legitimately require whoever wishes to enter the state on a non-visitor visa to know and accept the so-called "natural duties," which in essence are the most basic principles of political liberalism. These duties include obeying laws passed by just institutions—even if they contradict private beliefs or religious orders—and respecting the right of other people to live accordingly, resolving conflicts by peaceful means, and respecting the principle of equality before the law. For that purpose, the state can implement some measures to ascertain a person's knowledge and, at least declared,

[55] The two-stage regulation, distinguishing between admission and naturalization, can be further developed to include four stages: admission, temporary residency, permanent residency, and citizenship. See Seyla Benhabib, *The Claims of Culture: Equality and Diversity in the Global Era* (Princeton: Princeton University Press, 2002): p. 154.

acceptance. This implies that some pre-entry level of scrutiny may be necessary, whether by means of an interview, a course, an orientation day, a declaration, a contract, or even a cognitive, knowledge-based test. In principle, the idea of "integration from abroad" is not unjustified, though the process, under my approach, should be free of direct or indirect imposition of cultural adaptation. The objective of this stage is not to teach immigrants the host society's history, civics, culture, or constitutional essentials, but to verify that they know the "rules of the game" in a liberal society, accept them, and are ready to follow them.

On naturalization, liberal states can legitimately require immigrants who seek to become fellow citizens to know and accept fundamental and essential constitutional principles. This implies the following: first, the requirement of knowledge is cognitive, something that can be learnt, rather than "moral," a measure of one's inner belief (belief can be encouraged, but not imposed or mandated as a prerequisite for membership in a liberal society). Second, cognitive knowledge is not a blank check for the liberal state to implement policies without restraint. The focus should be on what is legally "right," rather than what is morally "good." Immigrants should not be expected to spell out how "great" nudity is, or how impolite it is to attend a birthday party without a present, even if these issues are cognitive and learnable. The idea that there is one "correct" way to behave in society runs against the liberal theory. It rules out many of the questions in the Dutch citizenship test, such as the following query: "Hanna runs into Sue. Sue asks: 'Do you want to stop by for a coffee some time?' What is the best thing Hanna can do? (a) schedule a proper time with Sue to come over for a coffee; (b) stop by whenever Hanna has time; or (c) wait until Sue again asks Hanna to come over."[56] It also rules out questions in the *Life in the UK Test* (a radical example is "Suppose you spill someone's pint in the pub. What, according to the book, usually happens next?") and in the federal test in Germany (one example is "What should parents of a 22-year-old girl do if they do not like her boyfriend?" (They must respect her decision)).[57] These questions are funny at best and absurd at worst. Third, even when the required knowledge is cognitive and focuses on what is legally "right," naturalization requirements should focus on what is essential for a newcomer to know in order to become a citizen. Is it really essential to know "How

[56] The "right" answer is (a); the question seeks to teach immigrants that people do not show up uninvited in the Netherlands.

[57] The parents' attempt to find another boyfriend for their daughter is "incorrect" according to the quiz.

might you stop young people playing tricks on you on Halloween?" or "Until what time do people play jokes on one another on April Fool's Day?" to give but two examples from the *Life in the UK Test*. Fourth, even if the knowledge is cognitive, legal, and essential, it should not necessarily be tested; there may be alternatives, such as distributing orientation materials on a mandatory orientation day. And fifth, even if a formal test is the most effective way to transmit this knowledge, it should be fair and equal. When a test is intentionally designed to exclude specific ethnic or religious groups, it may become discriminatory. Moreover, the procedure of the test must be fair. Among the pertinent issues are the test's level of difficulty, its cost, the existence of a preparation package (in the Netherlands, no study materials exist), as well as the number of times that the test can be retaken.[58]

Alongside knowledge, national constitutionalism requires "acceptance." The distinction between knowledge and acceptance is disputed in philosophical and psychological studies. Constitutional theory provides no useful definition of the notion of acceptance. One challenge is to determine whether acceptance is only an act of obedience, namely, that one accepts the law in the sense of not violating it, or does acceptance require some sort of commitment and, if so, which type? One view of acceptance is "procedural constitutionalism." Under this view, one should accept only the constitutional amendment procedure; he or she can act to repeal the constitution and its essentials as long as it is according to the method for amending the constitution. A second view of acceptance, which national constitutionalism embraces, requires, at the bare minimum, that an individual must not act against constitutional essentials, a society's basic structure, even by legal means. In this view, "acceptance" entails a promise of future behavior. True, citizens may have a legal right to repeal the constitution and establish an entirely different legal system through legal means—in some constitutions, this is legally impossible—but this does not imply that liberal constitutional democracies should give noncitizens a "license" (citizenship) to do it once they become citizens. Under national constitutionalism, thus, "acceptance" means the following: first, concerning admission, when a person is unwilling to (at least) declare acceptance of "natural duties" as the basis for life in a liberal democracy, entry may be denied. In addition, when a person acts against his or her statement once in the territory on an

[58] Christian Joppke, "Through the European Looking Glass: Citizenship Tests in the USA, Australia, and Canada," *Citizenship Studies* 17, no. 1 (2013): pp. 1–15 at 10–13.

immigration visa, the visa may not be renewed. Second, concerning naturalization, a person who is unwilling to (at least) declare acceptance of a society's basic structure in the sense of not fundamentally acting against it may be denied citizenship on the basis of lack of "attachment" to the constitution, to use the legal terminology of U.S. naturalization law. The level of scrutiny should be rigorous because, unlike employment decisions, in which a failure in *ex ante* rejection can be reversible by an *ex post* dismissal, naturalization decisions cannot be simply revoked. Generally, naturalized citizens cannot be denaturalized unless they acquired citizenship improperly; thus, for example, when citizenship was unlawfully procured or was procured by concealment, as in the case in which a candidate falsely declared acceptance, the person may be denaturalized due to fraud.

Every country has to decide immigration questions: whom to admit, how many, according to what criteria, and under which selection procedures? These are political questions reflecting political choices. In addressing them, a community must first explore the type of nation it wants to be. The prevailing view in liberal theory and human rights law has been that, subject to some conditions, a state has a "qualified right to limit immigration," to use the words of John Rawls.[59] The challenge has always been to grasp the nature of the legitimate qualifications to restrict immigration and access to citizenship. The two-stage immigration process suggested in this chapter seeks to achieve a meaningful, and yet liberal, immigration and naturalization process that goes beyond memorization of random trivia to require some commitment to a society's basic structure—its form of government and constitutional essentials. The exact way of doing it is the biggest challenge of the naturalization process.

[59] John Rawls, *The Law of Peoples, with "The Idea of Public Reason Revisited"* (Cambridge: Harvard University Press, 2001): p. 39 (note 48).

Conclusion:
Immigration Policy and Constitutional Identity

IMMIGRATION POLICY

Immigration has become the axis on which contemporary dilemmas in the liberal state meet. It is the topic of the day. Immigration affects concepts of sovereignty, self-determination, and the nation-state. The changes in the number, composition, and intensity of immigration, coupled with profound changes in Western society and in the world, yield one of the greatest challenges of the twenty-first century (see Chapter 1). Demographic changes have been so rapid and dynamic that there has been little opportunity to think about the impact of global immigration and the consequence of policies chosen to deal with it. Undoubtedly, the pros and cons of immigration will achieve better clarification in the next generation.

One visible effect of immigration occurs in majority-minority relations. The democratic theory assumes that the majority is able to "take care of itself"; it can perpetuate its culture by controlling entry into the community and by utilizing forces of democratic decision-making. Since democratic legislative institutions are dominated by the majority, they cannot be neutral toward the minority. In the real world, state neutrality is not a workable concept since liberal democracies inevitably promote the majority culture—vis-à-vis its language, holidays, symbols, political institutions, and perceptions of what is just or unjust. Therefore, a democracy must compensate for the unequal outcome of the routine democratic decision-making by granting special privileges to minorities. This is, in essence, the theory justifying cultural minority rights.

Minority rights have been an important development in liberal theory, yet in the intersection between cultural minority rights and the mass influx of immigrants, unexpected consequences have occurred—shifts in the power of majorities. The shift is not only demographic, but also normative—a gradual erosion of the majority culture as reflected in legal documents, judicial decisions, and common social conventions. In the age of immigration, the majority may become "needy." There is nothing unprecedented in the idea of a "needy" majority. This case is just not typically associated with immigration but, in a paradigmatic case, with occupation or a military defeat.[1] The connection between immigration and the majority culture is empirical. Thus far, the prevailing view has found that immigration does not pose a risk to the culture of the majority. However, as shown in Chapter 5, under certain circumstances, majorities, like minorities, have a strong interest in protecting their cultural rights, based upon rationales similar to those used to justify the cultural minority rights—personal autonomy and the right to identity. Will Kymlicka's idea alluding to minority cultures is well suited to the culture of the majority:[2]

> It should be up to each culture to decide when and how they adopt the achievements of the larger world. It is one thing to learn from the larger world; it is another to be swamped by it, and self-government rights may be needed for smaller nations to control the direction and rate of change.

The assumption that the majority can "take care of itself" is no longer self-evident. This is due to various reasons, among them the changes in the scale, composition, and pace of global immigration; the rise of cultural minority rights; the erosion of national identities and traditional ways of life as a result of globalization, transnationalism, and technological developments; and legal limitations that make it relatively more difficult for majorities to impose integration policies on newcomers and minorities. Majority groups in the West, particularly in Europe, have become smaller in size—numbers matter, especially in a democracy—and their culture has become more vulnerable and needy. This reality leads to a normative shift in majority-minority relations.

[1] Eric P. Kaufmann, "The Decline of the WASP in the United States and Canada," in *Rethinking Ethnicity: Majority Groups and Dominant Minorities*, Eric P. Kaufmann, ed. (New York: Routledge, 2004): pp. 54–73.

[2] Will Kymlicka, *Multicultural Citizenship: A Liberal Theory of Minority Rights* (Oxford: Clarendon Press, 2000): p. 104.

Existing legal concepts are simply unfit to address the challenge posed by global migration to the majority culture. The concept of the "majority" does not even exist in international law, which centers on "peoples" and apparently holds that the right of peoples to self-determination is sufficient to protect the culture of the majority. With no explicit concept, and a lack of direct legal protection, the majority finds indirect methods to defend its culture through a legal design of immigration criteria and by "legal white lies." One technique is protecting "state" interests (or using other terms: "common," "prevailing," "mainstream," "shared," etc.), as if this loaded language is not largely synonymous with the majority. Another technique is "universalizing the particular" in order to disguise the defense of particular cultural identities of the majority (see introductory chapter).

This book makes a case for defending cultural majority rights based on international law, moral philosophy, and constitutional theory. After distinguishing between "peoples," "nations," and "majorities," and presenting four cases of "needy" majorities (diminishing majorities, regional-minority majorities, victimized majorities, and minoritized majorities), it offers two justifications for cultural majority rights—personal autonomy and the right to identity. It then discusses the scope of these rights and provides factors to be considered in their implementation (see Chapter 5). The book then constructs a two-stage immigration process as a general framework for providing protection to the majority culture without slipping into illiberal immigration policies (see Chapter 6). Broadly speaking, the book seeks to protect a thin version of the majority culture, as reflected in a national constitution, substantively defined; this approach is labeled "national constitutionalism." In essence, it focuses on the basic structure of the constitution—fundamental values, conventions, and institutions. National constitutionalism, thus, is more narrowly focused than concepts of national identity and public culture. It is concerned with the fundamental constitutional identity of a given society and not with its ways of doing things, cultural mores, lifestyles, folkways, and popular culture.

CONSTITUTIONAL IDENTITY

The first rule to follow in drafting a constitution, Rousseau advised the people of Corsica, is that "each people has, or ought to have, a national character; if it did not, we should have to start by giving it one."[3] Yet, a national character (identity, culture, creed, etc.) is an elusive concept. Ask ten Britons what Britishness is—what are the most distinctive British features—or who is a "typical" Briton, and you may get ten different answers. Still, at a high level of abstraction, each people has a fundamental character. Britain, for example, is a constitutional monarchy, a parliamentary system, the birthplace of criminal justice, an English-speaking country, and a democracy that cherishes freedom, the rule of law, fairness, and tolerance—to name just a few identity elements included in a pie chart "What is Britishness?" published by the Commission for Racial Equality.[4]

Immigration policy is a mirror of constitutional identity. Naturalization requirements—the criteria that "they" must fulfill in order to join "us"—define "our" way of living, form of thinking, and mode of behavior. Much can be learned about collective identities by analyzing immigration and naturalization requirements. By investigating the legal ways to become a citizen, we can learn a great deal about who we are as a people (see Chapter 3).

What does immigration policy imply about constitutional identity? The obvious point is that nation-states are attempting to discover, or rediscover, their collective identity. They have established committees and asked the public to find a shared identity. The results are contradictory. On the one hand, nation-states have discovered that, imperceptibly, their collective identity has become less robust. National identity debates end up with trivial issues, items of popular culture like movies, carnivals, and lots of sports. This "Disneyfication of cultural difference," as termed by Will Kymlicka,[5] may be the clearest indicator of a national identity crisis. Political leaders in the West declare the death of multiculturalism and seek to focus on "our" culture, yet cannot pinpoint exactly what this culture is. In a sense, they find out that the shared culture is, at best, a particular version of political liberalism. Ironically, the cultural defense of the majority reveals how thin its culture has become; the majority culture is so diverse to a point at which it is hard to find a shared culture in the anthropological sense (see introductory chapter).[6] This identity crisis is reflected in Western immigration and

[3] Jean-Jacques Rousseau, *Constitutional Project for Corsica* (Whitefish: Kessinger Publishing, 2004): p. 12.

[4] Commission for Racial Equality, "Citizenship and Belonging: What is Britishness?," 2005: p. 34.

[5] Will Kymlicka, "The Rise and Fall of Multiculturalism? New Debates on Inclusion and Accommodation in Diverse Societies," in *The Multiculturalism Backlash: European Discourses, Policies and Practices*, Steven Vertovec and Susanne Wessendorf, eds. (New York: Routledge, 2010): pp. 32–49 at 34.

[6] The diversification of the majority culture is more visible on the municipal level, in big cities. See Christian Joppke, *Is Multiculturalism Dead? Crisis and Persistence in the Constitutional State* (forthcoming, on file with the author), Ch. 2.

naturalization policies, which, on the whole, have become more liberal than ever before.[7]

On the other hand, national identity debates sometimes end up with "high culture"—Rembrandt, Nietzsche, Molière, or Shakespeare. As a large percentage of the public is not well-versed in this information, this looks like a tendency to "romanticize" collective identity. It may be more what "we" think "we" are (ideal self), or want other people to think "we" are (ought-to-be self), than who we really are (actual self) (see Chapter 4). In addition, liberal democracies are thickening their liberal-democratic identity—as Sara Wallace Goodman observes, access to citizenship is more liberal, but thicker (or muscular) liberalism.[8] Liberal nationalism is becoming thicker by thickening the liberal-democratic integration requirements and providing them with cultural nuances rooted in a particular legal culture.

Talking about the protection of cultures in an age of globalization may seem a bit old fashioned. Trans-cultural diffusion is greater today than in any other period in human history. In the contemporary world, ideas come and go—through free markets, international media, and the Internet—and the notion of cultural exceptionalism faces multiple challenges. The "other" is present in national boundaries not just physically but spiritually. Cultures change, and they will continue to change more rapidly than ever. This reality is one of the triggers of cultural defense policies. Immigration law is still regarded as a "controllable" area and majorities try to design it in light of their cultural preferences. This reality is also one of the limitations of cultural defense. Even if a majority can control the flow of people, it can hardly control the flow of values and cultures. It is too early to predict whether we are witnessing the "swan song" of the old structure of national identity, or its transformation.

IMMIGRATION LAW AND CONSTITUTIONAL DESIGN

International law has traditionally provided states with a broad discretion in regulating immigration. In 2008, the British House of Lords reaffirmed this position by ruling that "It is one of the oldest powers of a sovereign state to decide whether any, and if so which, non-nationals shall be permitted to enter its territory, and to regulate and enforce the

[7] Christian Joppke, *Citizenship and Immigration* (Malden: Polity Press, 2010): pp. 34–67.

[8] Sara Wallace Goodman, "Integration Requirements for Integration's Sake? Identifying, Categorising and Comparing Civic Integration Policies," *Journal of Ethnic and Migration Studies* 36, no. 5 (2010): pp. 753–772 at 757, 762.

terms on which they may do so."[9] About a year later, the U.S. Court of Appeals for the D.C. Circuit held that "a nation-state has the inherent right to exclude or admit foreigners and to prescribe applicable terms and conditions for their exclusion or admission."[10] International courts have increasingly interfered in immigration issues, but admission and naturalization decisions, unless completely arbitrary or discriminating against a particular nationality, still enjoy a broad spectrum of judicial immunity. This is particularly the case where culture-based immigration selection is concerned.

Setting immigration criteria invites a discussion on constitutional identity—who "we" are, and what kind of nation "we" want to be. In particular, there should be a discussion on the function of immigration law in designing constitutional identity. There must be some clear goals for the immigration and naturalization law and a continuous exploration of whether immigration and naturalization means indeed advance the promotion of these goals. Quite often, however, immigration and naturalization requirements look like a "grab bag" with no underlying theory.

This book asks whether it is justified, from a liberal perspective, to defend the majority culture by means of immigration law and, if so, what can be the legitimate ways to achieve it. Descriptively, I point out an increasing appeal to immigration and naturalization policies in order to defend the majority culture. Analytically, I criticize some of these policies for approaching a point of being illiberal. Normatively, I argue that a narrow defense of the majority culture may often be justified.

The problems associated with immigration are as old as the Bible. The story of the Israelites in Egypt (see Chapter 2) reflects most of the ingredients of the modern crisis: economic immigration of persons ethnically and religiously different from the host society; a demographic change; suspicion and ensuing social tensions; excessive reaction; and the Exodus. In contemporary societies, the Exodus and the triumphant divine outcome are unlikely, yet the cultural challenges brought about by global immigration are here to stay for a long time.

[9] *R (BAPIO Action Ltd and anor)* v. *Secretary of State for the Home Department and anor* [2008] 1 A.C. 1003: p. 1007.

[10] *Kiyemba* v. *Obama* 555 F. 3d 1022, p. 1025 (D.C. Cir. 2009).

Bibliography

Introduction

Aristotle, *Politics*, Ernest Barker, trans. (Oxford: OUP, 1995).

Bader, V., "Associational Governance of Ethno-Religious Diversity in Europe: The Dutch Case," in *Citizenship, Borders, and Human Needs*, Rogers M. Smith, ed. (Philadelphia: University of Pennsylvania Press, 2011): pp. 273–300.

Barry, B., *Culture and Equality: An Egalitarian Critique of Multiculturalism* (Cambridge: Harvard University Press, 2001).

Brubaker, R., "Immigration, Citizenship, and the Nation-State in France and Germany," in *The Citizenship Debates: A Reader*, Gershon Shafir, ed. (Minneapolis: University of Minnesota Press, 1998): pp. 131–164.

Commission for Racial Equality, "Citizenship and Belonging: What is Britishness?," 2005.

Eisenstadt, S.N. and Giesen, B., "The Construction of Collective Identity," *European Journal of Sociology* 36, no. 1 (1995): pp. 72–102.

Gellner, E., *Nations and Nationalism* (Ithaca: Cornell University Press, 1983).

Glazer, N., *We Are All Multiculturalists Now* (Cambridge: Harvard University Press, 1997).

GOV.UK, "British Values: Article by David Cameron," June, 15, 2014 <http://www.gov.uk/government/news/british-values-article-by-david-cameron> [accessed 5 Sept,. 2015]

Hobsbawm, E.J., *Nations and Nationalism since 1780: Programme, Myth, Reality* (Cambridge: Cambridge University Press, 1990).

Home Office, "The New and the Old: The Report of the 'Life in the United Kingdom' Advisory Group," 2003.

Huntington, S.P., *Who Are We? The Challenges to America's National Identity* (New York: Simon & Schuster, 2004).

Kymlicka, W., *Multicultural Odysseys: Navigating the New International Politics of Diversity* (Oxford: OUP, 2007).

Miller, D., *On Nationality* (Oxford: Clarendon Press, 1995).

Orwell, G., *The Road to Wigan Pier* (New York: Harcourt, Brace and Company, 1958).

Rawls, J., *The Law of Peoples, with "The Idea of Public Reason Revisited"* (Cambridge: Harvard University Press, 2001).

Scruton, R., *Culture Counts: Faith and Feeling in a World Besieged* (New York: Encounter Books, 2007).

Smith, R.M., "Foreword," in *Immigration & Citizenship in the 21st Century*, Noah M.J. Pickus, ed. (Oxford: Rowman & Littlefield, 1998): pp. xi–xv.

Telegraph View, "The Core British Values that Define Our Nation," *Daily Telegraph*, June 11, 2014 <http://www.telegraph.co.uk/education/educationopinion/10889884/The-core-British-values-that-define-our-nation.html>

Chapter 1

Aristotle, *Politics*, Benjamin Jowett, trans. (New York: Dover Publications, 2000).

Aristotle, *The Athenian Constitution*, Peter J. Rhodes, trans. (New York: Penguin Books, 2004).

Barry, B., *Culture and Equality: An Egalitarian Critique of Multiculturalism* (Cambridge: Harvard University Press, 2001).

Bosniak, L., "Multiple Nationality and the Postnational Transformation of Citizenship," *Virginia Journal of International Law* 42, no. 4 (2002): pp. 979–1004.

Brettfeld, K. and Wetzels, P., "Muslime in Deutschland: Integration, Integrationsbarrieren, Religion und Einstellungen zu Demokratie, Rechtsstaat und Politisch-religiös Motivierter Gewalt," Bundesministerium des Inneren, 2007.

Buruma, I., *Murder in Amsterdam: Liberal Europe, Islam, and the Limits of Tolerance* (New York: Penguin Books, 2006).

Capacent, "Muslimer I Danmark: Resultater," DR, 2009 <http://www.dr.dk/NR/rdonlyres/2A053F15-C3EA-4A32-82DF-6EFB97F69314/1283022/Muslimunders%C3%B8gelse_endeligeresultaterformuslimeriD.pdf> [accessed 6 Sept. 2015]

Castles, S. and Miller, M.J., *The Age of Migration: International Population Movements in the Modern World*, 4th ed. (New York: Palgrave Macmillan, 2009).

Coleman, D., "Immigration and Ethnic Change in Low-Fertility Countries: A Third Demographic Transition," *Population and Development Review* 32, no. 3 (2006): pp. 401–446.

Coleman D. and Dubuc S., "The Fertility of Ethnic Minorities in the UK, 1960s—2006," *Population Studies: A Journal of Demography* 64, no. 1 (2010): pp. 19–41.

CSA Opinion Institutionnel, "Portrait des Musulmans: Rapport Final," 2006 <http://www.csa.eu/multimedia/data/sondages/data2006/opi20060823b.pdf> [accessed 6 Sept 2015]

CSA Opinion Institutionnel, "Islam et Citoyenneté," *Le Monde des Religions*, 2008 <http://www.csa.eu/multimedia/data/sondages/data2008/opi20080730-islam-et-citoyennete.pdf> [accessed 6 Sept. 2015]

Dalen, H.P.V. and Henkens, K., "Longing for the Good Life: Understanding Emigration from a High-Income Country," *Population and Development Review* 33, no. 1 (2007): pp. 37–66.

Dillingham, W.P., U.S. Immigration Commission, *Abstracts of Reports of the Immigration Commission, with Conclusions and Recommendations and Views of the Minority*, vol. I, *Reports of the Immigration Commission* (Washington: Government Printing Office, 1911).

Esposito, J.L. and Mogahed, D., *Who Speaks for Islam? What a Billion Muslims Really Think* (New York: Gallup Press, 2007).

European Commission, "Europe's Demographic Future: Facts and Figures on Challenges and Opportunities," 2007.

European Monitoring Centre on Racism and Xenophobia, "Racism and Xenophobia in the EU Member States: Trends, Developments, and Good Practice," 2005.

European Monitoring Centre on Racism and Xenophobia, "Muslims in the European Union: Discrimination and Islamophobia," 2006.

Fukuyama, F., "Identity, Immigration, and Liberal Democracy," *Journal of Democracy* 17, no. 2 (2006): pp. 5–20.

Gallup, "The Gallup Coexist Index 2009: A Global Study of Interfaith Relations: With an In-Depth Analysis of Muslim Integration in France, Germany, and the United Kingdom," 2009.

Gallup, "Islamophobia: Understanding Anti-Muslim Sentiment in the West," 2011.

Gallup, "The Abu Dhabi Gallup Forum: Research, Dialogue, and Solutions," 2011.

GfK NOP, "Attitudes to Living in Britain: Topline Findings," 2006 <http://www.stranieriinitalia.it/news/indaginegfk22nov2006.pdf> [accessed 6 Sept. 2015]

Goldin, I., Cameron, G., and Balarajan, M., *Exceptional People: How Migration Shaped Our World and Will Define Our Future* (Princeton: Princeton University Press, 2011).

Gorodzeisky, A. and Semyonov, M., "Terms of Exclusion: Public Views Towards Admission and Allocation of Right to Immigrants in European Countries," *Ethnic and Racial Studies* 32, no. 3 (2009): pp. 401–423.

Grant, J. et al., "Low Fertility and Population Ageing: Causes, Consequences, and Policy Options," RAND Corporation, 2004 <http://www.rand.org/content/dam/rand/pubs/monographs/2004/RAND_MG206.pdf> [accessed 6 Sept. 2015].

Gravelle, T.B. et al., "What Makes 700 Million Adults Want to Migrate," Gallup, February 18, 2010 <http://www.gallup.com/poll/126065/makes-700-million-adults-migrate.aspx> [accessed 6 Sept. 2015]

Gregoriou, P., Kontolemis, Z., and Matsi, M., "Immigration in Cyprus: An Analysis of the Determinants," *Cyprus Economic Policy Review* 4, no. 1 (2010): pp. 63–88.

Hamilton, B.E., Martin, J.A., and Ventura, S.J., "Births: Preliminary Data for 2010," *National Vital Statistics Report* 60, no. 2 (November 2011): pp. 1–26.

Haug, H.S., Müssig, S., and Stichs, A., "Muslim Life in Germany: A Study Conducted on Behalf of the German Conference on Islam," Federal Office for Migration and Refugees, 2009.

Hoorens, S. et al., "Low Fertility in Europe: Is There a Reason to Worry?," RAND Corporation, 2011.

Huntington, S.P., "The Hispanic Challenge," *Foreign Policy*, no. 141 (March/April 2004): pp. 30–45.

ICM Research, "Muslims Poll—February 2006," *Sunday Telegraph*, 2006 <http://www.icmresearch.com/pdfs/2006_february_sunday_telegraph_muslims_poll.pdf> [accessed 6 Sept. 2015]

INFO GmbH and Liljeberg Research International, "Erste Internationale Studie zur Wertewelt der Deutschen, Deutsch-Türken und Türken," 2009.

International Organization for Migration, *World Migration 2005: Costs and Benefits of International Migration* (Geneva: IOM, 2005).

International Organization for Migration, *World Migration 2008: Managing Labour Mobility in the Evolving Global Economy* (Geneva: IOM, 2008).

International Organization for Migration, *World Migration Report 2010: The Future of Migration: Building Capacities for Change* (Geneva: IOM, 2010).

Johansen, B. and Spielhaus, R., "Counting Deviance: Revisiting a Decade's Production of Surveys among Muslims in Western Europe," *Journal of Muslims in Europe* 1, no. 1 (2012): pp. 81–112.

Jones, R.P. et al., "What It Means to Be an American: Attitudes in Increasingly Diverse America 10 Years After 9/11," Brookings Institution & the Public Religion Research Institute, 2011.

Keeley, B., *International Migration: The Human Face of Globalisation* (Paris: OECD Publishing, 2009).

Kent, M.M., "Do Muslims have More Children Than Other Woman in Western Europe?," U.S. Population Reference Bureau, 2008.

Korteweg, A. and Yurdakul, G., "Islam, Gender, and Immigrant Integration: Boundary Drawing in Discourses on Honour Killing in the Netherlands and Germany," *Ethnic and Racial Studies* 32, no. 2 (2009): pp. 218–238.

Kymlicka, W., *Liberalism, Community and Culture* (Oxford: OUP, 1989).

Kymlicka, W., *Multicultural Citizenship: A Liberal Theory of Minority Rights* (Oxford: Clarendon Press, 2000).

Lanzieri, G., "Fewer, Older and Multicultural? Projections of the EU Populations by Foreign/National Background," Eurostat, 2011.

Legomsky, S.H., "Immigration, Equality and Diversity," *Columbia Journal of Transnational Law* 31, no. 2 (1993): pp. 319–336.

Levitt, P., *The Transnational Villagers* (Berkeley: University of California Press, 2001).

Lindsey, D., "Turkish Prime Minister Erdogan Wants to Be the Father," *Spiegel*, March 1, 2011 <http://www.spiegel.de/international/germany/the-world-from-berlin-turkish-prime-minister-erdogan-wants-to-be-the-father-a-748379.html> [accessed 6 Sept. 2015]

Lorant, K., "The Demographic Challenge in Europe," European Parliament, 2005.

Lüken-Klaßen D. and Heckmann F., "Intercultural Policies in European Cities," European Foundation for the Improvement of Living and Working Conditions, 2010.

Maliepaard, M., Lubbers, M., and Gijsberts, M., "Generational Differences in Ethnic and Religious Attachment and Their Interrelation. A Study among Muslim Minorities in the Netherlands," *Ethnic and Racial Studies* 33, no. 3 (2010): pp. 451–472.

Manchin, R., "Religion in Europe: Trust Not Filling the Pews," Gallup, September 21, 2004 <http://www.gallup.com/poll/13117/religion-europe-trust-filling-pews.aspx> [accessed 6 Sept. 2015]

Margalit, A. and Halbertal, M., "Liberalism and the Right to Culture," *Social Research* 71, no. 3 (2004): pp. 529–548.

Martin, P. and Midgley, E., "Immigration in America 2010," U.S. Population Reference Bureau, 2010.

Mirza, M., Senthilkumaran, A., and Ja'far, Z., "Living Apart Together: British Muslims and the Paradox of Multiculturalism," Policy Exchange, 2007.

Mogahed, D. and Nyiri, Z., "Reinventing Integration: Muslims in the West" *Harvard International Review* 29, no. 2 (2007): pp. 14–18.

Muenz, R., "Aging and Demographic Change in European Societies: Main Trends and Alternative Policy Options," SP Discussion Paper no. 0703, The World Bank, 2007.

Norris, P. and Inglehart, R., "Islam & the West: Testing the 'Clash of Civilization' Thesis," Harvard Kennedy School of Government, Faculty Research Working Paper Series RWP02-015, 2002.

Nyiri, Z., "Muslims in Berlin, London and Paris: Bridges and Gaps in Public Opinion," Gallup, 2007.

OECD, *Society at Glance 2009: OECD Social Indicators* (Paris: OECD Publishing, 2009).

OECD, *Pensions at a Glance 2011: Retirement-Income Systems in OECD and G20 Countries* (Paris: OECD Publishing, 2011).

Open Society Foundations, "Muslims in Amsterdam", 2010.

Open Society Foundations, "Muslims in Berlin," 2010.

Open Society Foundations, "Muslims in Europe: A Report on 11 EU Cities," 2010.

Open Society Foundations, "Muslims in Rotterdam," 2010.

Open Society Foundations, "Muslims in Copenhagen," 2011.

Open Society Foundations, "Muslims in London," 2012.

Ortman, J.M. and Guarneri, C.E., "United States Population Projections: 2000 to 2050," U.S. Census Bureau, 2009.

Pew Hispanic Center, "An Awakened Giant: The Hispanic Electorate is Likely to Double by 2030," 2012.

Pew Research Center, "Support for Terror Wanes Among Muslim Publics: Islamic Extremism: Common Concern for Muslim and Western Publics," 2005.

Pew Research Center, "Europe's Muslims More Moderate: The Great Divide: How Westerners and Muslims View Each Other," 2006.

Pew Research Center, "Muslim Americans: Middle Class and Mostly Mainstream," 2007.

Pew Research Center, "U.S. Religious Landscape Survey: Religious Affiliation: Diverse and Dynamic," 2008.

Pew Research Center, "Global Christianity: A Report on the Size and Distribution of the World's Christian Population," 2011.

Pew Research Center, "Muslim Americans: No Sign of Growth in Alienation or Support for Extremism," 2011.

Pew Research Center, "Muslims—Western Tensions Persist," 2011.

Pew Research Center, "The Future of the Global Muslim Population: Projections for 2010–2030," 2011.

Pew Research Center, "Faith on the Move: The Religious Affiliation of International Migrants," 2012.

Pew Research Center, "The Global Religious Landscape: A Report on the Size and Distribution of the World's Major Religious Groups as of 2010," 2012.

Pew Research Center, "The World's Muslims: Religion, Politics and Society," 2013.

Phillips, M., *Londonistan* (New York: Encounter Books, 2006).

Ray, J. and Esipova, N., "More Adults Would Move for Temporary Work Than Permanently," Gallup, March 9, 2012 <http://www.gallup.com/poll/153182/adults-move-temporary-work-permanently.aspx> [accessed 6 Sept. 2015]

Rheault, M. and Mogahed, D., "Cartoons and Controversy: Free Expression or Muslim Exceptionalism in Europe?," *Harvard International Review* 30, no. 2 (2008): pp. 68–71.

Rhodes, P.J., *A Commentary on the Aristotelian Athenaion Politeia* (Oxford: Clarendon Press, 1981).

Roy, O., *Globalized Islam: The Search for a New Ummah* (New York: Columbia University Press, 2004).

Savage, T.M., "Europe and Islam: Crescent Waxing, Cultures Clashing," *The Washington Quarterly* 27, no. 3 (2004): pp. 25–50.

Schirrmacher, C., "Muslims in Germany," Federal Ministry of the Interior, 2008.

Scruton, R., *The West and the Rest: Globalization and the Terrorist Threat* (Wilmington: ISI Books, 2002).

Shakespeare, W., *The Oxford Shakespeare: Coriolanus*, R.B. Parker, ed. (Oxford: OUP, 2008).

Stalker P., "Migration Trends and Migration Policy in Europe," *International Migration* 40, no. 5 (2002): pp. 151–179.

Thorne, J. and Stuart, H., "Islam on Campus: A Survey of UK Student Opinions," Centre for Social Cohesion, 2008.

TNS Gallup, "Holdninger til Integrasjon og Internasjonale Konflikter Blant Muslimer I Norge og den Norske Befolkning Generelt," TV 2, 2006 <http://pub.tv2.no/multimedia/TV2/archive/00248/TNS_Gallup_-_muslim_248757a.pdf> [accessed 6 Sept. 2015]

Ulram, P.A., "Integration in Österreich: Einstellungen, Orientierungen, und Erfah- Rungen von MigrantInnen und Angehörigen der Mehrheitsbevölkerung," GfK-Austria GmbH, 2009.

U.N., Department of Economic and Social Affairs, Population Division, "World Marriage Patterns 2000," 2000.

U.N., Department of Economic and Social Affairs, Population Division, "Replacement Migration: Is It a Solution to Declining and Ageing Populations?," U.N. Doc. ST/ESA/SER.A/206, 2001.

U.N., Department of Economic and Social Affairs, Population Division, "World Population Ageing 1950–2050," U.N. Doc. ST/ESA/SER.A/207, 2002.

U.N., Department of Economic and Social Affairs, Population Division, "World Economic and Social Survey 2004: International Migration," U.N. Doc. E/2004/75/Rev.1/Add.1, 2004.

U.N., Department of Economic and Social Affairs, Population Division, "World Population to 2300," U.N. Doc. ST/ESA/SER.A/236, 2004.

U.N., Department of Economic and Social Affairs, Population Division, "The Diversity of Changing Population Age Structure in the World," U.N. Doc. POP/PD/2005/1, 2005.

U.N., Department of Economic and Social Affairs, Population Division, "World Population Prospects: The 2006 Revision, Highlights," U.N. Doc. ESA/P/WP.202, 2007.

U.N., Department of Economic and Social Affairs, Population Division, "World Fertility Data 2008," U.N. Doc. POP/DB/Fert/Rev2008, 2008.

U.N., Department of Economic and Social Affairs, Population Division, "Trends in International Migrant Stock: The 2008 Revision," U.N. Doc. POP/DB/MIG/Stock/Rev.2008, 2009.

U.N., Department of Economic and Social Affairs, Population Division, "World Marriage Data 2008: Annual Number of Divorces and Crude Divorce Rate," U.N. Doc. POP/DB/Marr/Rev2008, 2009.

U.N., Department of Economic and Social Affairs, Population Division, "International Migration Report 2009: A Global Assessment," U.N. Doc. ST/ESA/SER.A/316, 2011.

U.N., Department of Economic and Social Affairs, Population Division, "World Fertility Report 2009," U.N. Doc. ST/ESA/SER.A/304, 2011.

U.N., Department of Economic and Social Affairs, Population Division, "World Mortality 2011," U.N. Doc. ST/ESA/SER.A/308, 2011.

U.N., Department of Economic and Social Affairs, Population Division, "World Population Prospects: The 2010 Revision," U.N. Docs. POP/DB/WPP/Rev.2010/01/F01 and POP/DB/WPP/Rev.2010/01/F05-1, 2011.

U.N., Department of Economic and Social Affairs, Population Division, "Population Ageing and Development 2012," U.N. Doc. ST/ESA/SER.A/323, 2012.

U.N., Department of Economic and Social Affairs, Population Division, "Trends in International Migrant Stock: Migrants by Destination and Origin," U.N. Doc. POP/DB/MIG/Stock/Rev.2012, 2012 <http://esa.un.org/MigOrigin/UN_MigStock_Origin.xls> [accessed 6 Sept. 2015]

U.N., Department of Economic and Social Affairs, Population Division, "World Mortality Report 2011," U.N. Doc. ST/ESA/SER.A/324, 2012.

U.S. Census Bureau, "2008 National Population Projections," 2008 <http://www.census.gov/population/projections/data/national/2008.html> [accessed 6 Sept. 2015]

U.S. Census Bureau, "Table 1. Projections of the Population and Components of Change for the United States: 2010 to 2050," 2008 <http://www.census.gov/population/projections/data/national/2008/summarytables.html> [accessed 6 Sept. 2015]

U.S. Census Bureau, "Methodology and Assumptions for the 2012 National Projections," 2012.

U.S. Census Bureau, "Most Children Younger than Age 1 are Minorities, Census Bureau Reports," May 17, 2012 <http://www.census.gov/newsroom/releases/archives/population/cb12-90.html> [accessed 6 Sept. 2015]

U.S. Population Reference Bureau, "Transitions in World Population," *Population Bulletin* 59, no. 1 (March 2004): pp. 1–41.

Westoff, C.F. and Frejka, T., "Religiousness and Fertility among European Muslims," *Population and Development Review* 33, no. 4 (2007): pp. 785–809.

White, R.C. Jr., *A. Lincoln: A Biography* (New York: Random House, 2009).

World Values Survey Association, "World Values Survey 2005–2008: Official Data File," 2009, results of question V186 of the WVS questionnaire on religious service attendance <http://www.wvsevsdb.com/wvs/WVSAnalizeSample.jsp> [accessed 6 Sept. 2015]

Chapter 2

Comprehensive Immigration Reform: Becoming Americans—U.S. Immigrant Integration: Hearing Before the Subcommittee on Immigration, Citizenship, Refugees, Border Security, and International Law of the Committee on the Judiciary, House of Representatives, 110th Congress, 1st Session (Washington: Government Printing Office, 2007): pp. 57–65 (prepared statement of John Fonte).

"French Minister Slammed for 'Unequal Civilisations' Comment," France 24, February 5, 2012 <http://www.france24.com/en/20120205-france-minister-slammed-unequal-civilisations-politics-gueant> [accessed 6 Sept. 2015]

"Immigration: Hearings Before the Subcommittee on Immigration and Naturalization of the Committee on the Judiciary United State Senate, on S. 500. 89th Congress, 1st Session" (February 10, 1965), in *Immigration and Nationality Acts: Legislative Histories and Related Documents*, vol. 11, Oscar M. Trelles and James F. Bailey, eds. (Buffalo: Hein, 1979): pp. 1–41.

"Nicolas Sarkozy Joins David Cameron and Angela Merkel View that Multiculturalism Has Failed," *Daily Mail*, February 11, 2011 <http://www.dailymail.co.uk/news/article-1355961/Nicolas-Sarkozy-joins-David-Cameron-Angela-Merkel-view-multiculturalism-failed.html> [accessed 6 Sept. 2015]

Baer, S., "A Closer Look at Law: Human Rights as Multi-Level Sites of Struggles Over Multi-Dimensional Equality," *Utrecht Law Review* 6, no. 2 (2010): pp. 56–76.

Bawer, B., *While Europe Slept: How Radical Islam is Destroying the West from Within* (New York: Doubleday, 2006).

Bernstein, E., "Netanyahu: To Exclude the Infiltrators, They Threaten National Identity," *Maariv*, May 20, 2012 <http://www.nrg.co.il/online/1/ART2/369/825.html> [accessed 6 Sept. 2015]

Blankley, T., *The West's Last Chance: Will We Win the Clash of Civilizations?* (Washington: Regnery Publishing, 2005).

Borjas, G.J., *Friends or Strangers: The Impact of Immigrants on the U.S. Economy* (New York: Basic Books, 1990).

Bowen, J.R., *Can Islam Be French? Pluralism and Pragmatism in a Secularist State* (Princeton: Princeton University Press, 2010).

Brimelow, P., *Alien Nation: Common Sense About America's Immigration Disaster* (New York: Harper Perennial, 1996).

Buchanan, P.J., *State of Emergency: The Third World Invasion and Conquest of America* (New York: Thomas Dunne Books, 2006).

Buruma, I., *Murder in Amsterdam: Liberal Europe, Islam, and the Limits of Tolerance* (New York: Penguin Books, 2006).

Caldwell, C., *Reflections on the Revolution in Europe: Immigration, Islam, and the West* (New York: Doubleday, 2009).

Carroll, R. and Prickett, S., eds., *The Bible: Authorized King James Version with Apocrypha* (Oxford: OUP, 2008).

Charles, R.H., ed., *Pseudepigrapha*, vol. II, *The Apocrypha and Pseudepigrapha of the Old Testament* (Oxford: Clarendon Press, 1913).

Chavez, L.R., *The Latino Threat: Constructing Immigrants, Citizens, and the Nation* (Stanford: Stanford University Press, 2008).

Chin, G.J., "The Civil Rights Revolution Comes to Immigration Law: A New Look at the Immigration and Nationality Act of 1965," *North Carolina Law Review* 75, no. 1 (1996): pp. 273–346.

Daniels, R., *Coming to America: A History of Immigration and Ethnicity in American Life*, 2nd ed. (Princeton: Perennial, 2002).

Erlanger, S., "French Mosque's Symbolism Varies With Beholder," *New York Times*, December 27, 2009 <http://www.nytimes.com/2009/12/28/world/europe/28marseille.html?pagewanted=all> [accessed 6 Sept. 2015]

European Monitoring Centre on Racism and Xenophobia, "Muslims in the European Union: Discrimination and Islamophobia," 2006.

Ferguson, N., "Eurabia?," *New York Times*, April 4, 2004 <http://www.nytimes.com/2004/04/04/magazine/04WWLN.html> [accessed 6 Sept. 2015]

Ferguson, N., "The Widening Atlantic," *Atlantic Monthly* 295, no. 1 (January–February 2005): pp. 40–44.

Franklin, B., "Observations Concerning the Increase of Mankind, Peopling of Countries, etc," in *The writings of Benjamin Franklin*, vol. III, Albert Henry Smyth, ed. (New York: The Macmillan Company, 1905): pp. 63–73.

Furlong, R., "Germans Argue over Integration," BBC News, November 30, 2004 <http://news.bbc.co.uk/2/hi/4056109.stm> [accessed 6 Sept. 2015]

Gibson, C. and Jung, K., "Historical Census Statistics on Population Totals By Race, 1790 to 1990, and By Hispanic Origin, 1970 to 1990, For The United States, Regions, Divisions, and States," U.S. Census Bureau, 2002.

Glazer, N., "The Closing Door," *The New Republic* 209, no. 26 (December 1993): pp. 15–20.

GOV.UK, "PM's Speech at Munich Security Conference," February 5, 2011 <http://www.gov.uk/government/speeches/pms-speech-at-munich-security-conference> [accessed 6 Sept. 2015]

Grieco, E.M. and others, "The Size, Place of Birth, and Geographic Distribution of the Foreign-Born Population in the United States: 1960 to 2010," U.S. Census Bureau, 2012.

Higham, J., *Strangers in the Land: Patterns of American Nativism, 1860–1925* (New Brunswick: Rutgers University Press, 2002).

Huntington, S.P., *American Politics: The Promise of Disharmony* (Cambridge: Harvard University Press, 1982).

Huntington, S.P., "Reconsidering Immigration: Is Mexico a Special Case?," Center for Immigration Studies, 2000 <http://www.cis.org/articles/2000/back1100.html> [accessed 6 Sept. 2015]

Huntington, S.P., "One Nation, Out of Many: Why 'Americanization' of Newcomers is Still Important," *The American Enterprise* 15, no. 6 (September 2004): pp. 20–25.

Huntington, S.P., "The Hispanic Challenge," *Foreign Policy*, no. 141 (March/April 2004): pp. 30–45.

Huntington, S.P., *Who Are We? The Challenges to America's National Identity* (New York: Simon & Schuster, 2004).

Israel Central Bureau of Statistics, "Back to School: Selected Data from 'Society in Israel—Report No. 5' and CBS Data," 2012 <http://www.cbs.gov.il/reader/newhodaot/hodaa_template.html?hodaa=20120622> [accessed 6 Sept. 2015]

Israel Population and Immigration Authority, "Data About Aliens in Israel," 2013 <http://www.piba.gov.il/PublicationAndTender/ForeignWorkersStat/Documents/%D7%90%D7%A4%D7%A8%D7%99%D7%9C%202013.pdf> [accessed 6 Sept. 2015]

Jefferson, T., *Notes on the State of Virginia* (London: John Stockdale, 1787).

Kaufmann, E.P., *The Rise and Fall of Anglo-America* (Cambridge: Harvard University Press, 2004).

Kennedy, D., "Can We Still Afford to Be a Nation of Immigrants?," *Atlantic Monthly* 278, no. 5 (November 1996): pp. 52–68.

Kern, S., "France's Tottery Effort to Reverse Creeping Islamization," Gatestone Institute, January 2, 2012 <http://www.gatestoneinstitute.org/2719/france-creeping-islamization> [accessed 7 Sept. 2015]

Kettner, J.H., *The Development of American Citizenship, 1608–1870* (Chapel Hill: University of North Carolina Press, 1978).

Klausen, J., *The Islamic Challenge: Politics and Religion in Western Europe* (Oxford: OUP, 2005).

Krikorian, M., *The New Case Against Immigration: Both Legal and Illegal* (New York: Sentinel, 2008).

Laqueur, W., *The Last Days of Europe: Epitaph for an Old Continent* (New York: Thomas Dunne Books/St. Martin's Press, 2007).

Leiken, R.S., *Europe's Angry Muslims: The Revolt of the Second Generation* (Oxford: OUP, 2011).

Lowell, J.R., *Literary and Political Addresses*, vol. VI, *The Writings of James Russell Lowell* (Boston: Houghton, Mifflin and Company, 1890).

Marquand, D., *The End of the West: The Once and Future Europe* (Princeton: Princeton University Press, 2011).

Massey, D.S., "The New Immigration and Ethnicity in the United States," *Population and Development Review* 21, no. 3 (1995): pp. 631–652.

Mayer, J.F., "In the Shadow of the Minaret: Origins and Implications of a Citizens' Initiative," in *The Swiss Minaret Ban: Islam in Question*, Patrick Haenni and Stéphane Lathion, eds., Tom Genrich, trans. (Fribourg: Religioscope Institute, 2011): pp. 10–16.

Miller, J.J., *The Unmaking of Americans: How Multiculturalism Has Undermined America's Assimilation Ethic* (New York: Free Press, 1998).

Ministry of the Interior, "Advisory Committee for the Review of Israel's Immigration Policy 2006," 2006.

Motomura, H., *Americans in Waiting: The Lost Story of Immigration and Citizenship in the United States* (Oxford: OUP, 2006).

Neuman, G.L., *Strangers to the Constitution: Immigrants, Borders, and Fundamental Law* (Princeton: Princeton University Press, 1996).

Norton, A., *On the Muslim Question* (Princeton: Princeton University Press, 2013).

Open Society Foundations, "Muslims in Europe: A Report on 11 EU Cities," 2010.

Paltiel A. et al., "Long-Range Population Projections for Israel: 2009–2059," Israel Central Bureau of Statistics, 2012.

Perea, J.F., "'Am I an American or Not?' Reflections on Citizenship, Americanization, and Race," in *Immigration & Citizenship in the 21st Century*, Noah M.J. Pickus, ed. (Oxford: Rowman & Littlefield, 1998).

Perea, J.F., "A Brief History of Race and the U.S.-Mexican Border: Tracing the Trajectories of Conquest," *UCLA Law Review* 51, no. 1 (2003): pp. 283–312.

Pew Hispanic Center, "A Demographic Portrait of Mexican-Origin Hispanics in the United States," 2013.

Portes, A. and Rumbaut, R.G., *Legacies: The Story of the Immigrant Second Generation* (Berkeley: University of California Press, 2001).

Roy, O., *Globalized Islam: The Search for a New Ummah* (New York: Columbia University Press, 2004).

Roy, O., "Islam in Europe: An Ordinary Religion Like Any Other," in *The Swiss Minaret Ban: Islam in Question*, Patrick Haenni and Stéphane Lathion, eds., Tom Genrich, trans. (Fribourg: Religioscope Institute, 2011): pp. 90–95.

Schuck, P.H., "The Emerging Political Consensus on Immigration Law," *Georgetown Immigration Law Journal* 5, no. 1 (1991): pp. 1–34.

Schuck, P.H., *Diversity in America: Keeping Government at a Safe Distance* (Cambridge: Harvard University Press, 2003).

Sharvit, N., Libeskind, K., and Segal, H., "Loyal to His Approach: The Minister of Justice Talks," *Maariv*, February 17, 2012 <http://www.nrg.co.il/online/1/ART2/337/305.html> [accessed 7 Sept. 2015]

Skerry, P., *Mexican Americans: The Ambivalent Minority* (New York: The Free Press, 1993).

Smee, J., "The World from Berlin: Merkel's Rhetoric in Integration Debate is 'Inexcusable,'" *Spiegel*, October 18, 2010 <http://www.spiegel.de/international/germany/the-world-from-berlin-merkel-s-rhetoric-in-integration-debate-is-inexcusable-a-723702.html> [accessed 7 Sept. 2015]

Smith, R.M., *Civic Ideals: Conflicting Visions of Citizenship in U.S. History* (New Haven: Yale University Press, 1999).

Steyn, M., *America Alone: The End of the World as We Know It* (Washington: Regnery Publishing, 2006).

Swain, C.M., *The New White Nationalism in America: Its Challenge to Integration* (Cambridge: Cambridge University Press, 2004).

Syrett, H.C., ed., *July 1800–April 1802*, vol. XXV, *The Papers of Alexander Hamilton* (New York: Columbia University Press, 1977).

Weil, P., "Races at the Gate: A Century of Racial Distinctions in American Immigration Policy (1865–1965)," *Georgetown Immigration Law Journal* 15, no. 4 (2001): pp. 625–648.

Weiler, J.H.H., "State and Nation; Church, Mosque and Synagogue—the Trailer," *International Journal of Constitutional Law* 8, no. 2 (2010): pp. 157–166.

Yakobson, A., "Joining the Jewish People: Non-Jewish Immigrants from the Former USSR, Israeli Identity and Jewish Peoplehood," *Israel Law Review* 43, no. 1 (2010): pp. 218–239.

Yakobson, A., "God and Religion in Modern Democratic Constitutions," in *Contemporary Challenges to the Nation State: Global and Israeli Perspectives*, vol. II,

The Nation State and Religion: The Resurgence of Faith, Anita Shapira, Yedidia Z. Stern, and Alexander Yakobson, eds. (Eastbourne: Sussex Academic Press, 2013): pp. 1–13.

Yakobson, A. and Rubinstein, A., *Israel and the Family of Nations: The Jewish Nation-State and Human Rights* (New York: Routledge, 2008).

Ye'or, B., *Eurabia: The Euro-Arab Axis* (Cranbury: Fairleigh Dickinson University Press, 2005).

Yerushalmi, S., "Eli Yishai in a Special Interview: It's We or They," *Maariv*, June 1, 2012 <http://www.nrg.co.il/online/1/ART2/373/346.html> [accessed 7 Sept. 2015]

Zolberg, A.R., *A Nation by Design: Immigration Policy in the Fashioning of America* (Cambridge: Harvard University Press, 2008).

Chapter 3

"France to Ban Full Face Veil, Says Ruling Party Chief," RFI, December 16, 2009 <http://www.rfi.fr/actuen/articles/120/article_6211.asp> [accessed 7 Sept. 2015]

"Germany's Immigration Debate: Politician Demands IQ Tests for Would-Be Immigrants," *Spiegel*, June 28, 2010 <http://www.spiegel.de/international/germany/germany-s-immigration-debate-politician-demands-iq-tests-for-would-be-immigrants-a-703328.html> [accessed 7 Sept. 2015]

Adam, C. and Devillard, A., *Comparative Study of the Laws in the 27 EU Member States for Legal Immigration* (IOM: Geneva, 2008).

Adamo, S., "Northern Exposure: The New Danish Model of Citizenship Test," *International Journal on Multicultural Societies* 10, no. 1 (2008): pp. 10–28.

Adamo, S., "What is the Point? Policies on Immigration and the Language Issue in Denmark," RECODE Working Paper Series no. 04, 2012.

Adams, E.W., *A Community Civics: A Text-book in Loyal Citizenship* (New York: Charles Scribner's Sons, 1920).

Aristotle, *Politics*, Benjamin Jowett, trans. (New York: Dover Publications, 2000).

Assemblée Nationale, "Rapport d'Information: Au Nom de la Mission d'Information sur la Pratique du Port du Voile Intégral sur le Territoire National," 2010.

Banting, K. and Kymlicka, W., "Is There Really a Retreat from Multiculturalism Policies? New Evidence from the Multiculturalism Policy Index," *Comparative European Politics* 11, no. 5 (2013): pp. 577–598.

Bennhold, K., "A Veil Closes France's Door to Citizenship," *New York Times*, July 19, 2008 <http://www.nytimes.com/2008/07/19/world/europe/19france.html?pagewanted=all&_r=0> [accessed 7 Sept. 2015]

Besselink, L.F.M., "Integration and Immigration: The Vicissitudes of Dutch *'Inburgering,'*" in *Illiberal Liberal States: Immigration, Citizenship and Integration in the EU*, Elspeth Guild, Kees Groenendijk, and Sergio Carrera, eds. (Burlington: Ashgate, 2009): pp. 241–257.

Brooks, T., "The 'Life of the United Kingdom' Citizenship Test: Is It Unfit for Purpose?," Durham University, 2013.

Buruma, I., *Murder in Amsterdam: Liberal Europe, Islam, and the Limits of Tolerance* (New York: Penguin Books, 2006).

BVA, "La Démission de Jérôme Cahuzac—La laïcité," i>TELE, 2013 <http://www.bva.fr/data/sondage/sondage_fiche/1258/fichier_bva_actu_-_cahuzac_-_laicite34131.pdf> [accessed 7 Sept. 2015]

Caron, J.F., "Understanding and Interpreting France's National Identity: The Meanings of Being French," *National Identities* 15, no. 3 (2013): pp. 223–237.

CDU, "Arbeitsgrundlage für die Zuwanderungs-Kommission der CDU Deutschlands," 2000.

CDU and CSU, "Umfassendes Gesetz zur Steuerung und Begrenzung der Zuwanderung sowie zur Förderung der Integration jetzt vorlegen," 2001.

Committee for the Development of the Dutch Canon, *A Key to Dutch History: Report by the Committee for the Development of the Dutch Canon* (Amsterdam: Amsterdam University Press, 2007).

Consumerfieldwork GmbH, "Meinungsumfrage zur Buchveröffentlichung von Thilo Sarrazin: Hat Sarrazin Recht, oder Hat Sarrazin nicht Recht?," 2010 <http://www.consumerfieldwork.de/pdf/chartbericht_pressemitteilung_umfrage_sarrazin_buch.pdf> [accessed 7 Sept. 2015]

Crist, R.F., U.S. Department of Labor, Bureau of Naturalization, *Student's Textbook: A Standard Course of Instruction for Use in Public Schools of the United States for the Preparation of the Candidate for the Responsibilities of Citizenship* (Washington: Government Printing Office, 1918).

Dillon, H., *How British Are You? Questions from the British Citizenship Test* (London: Red Squirrel Publishing, 2008).

Ersbøll, E., "Country Report: Denmark," European University Institute, 2013.

Etzioni, A., "Citizenship Tests: A Comparative, Communitarian Perspective," *The Political Quarterly* 78, no. 3 (2007): pp. 353–363.

Extramiana, C. and Avermaet, P.V., "Language Requirements for Adult Migrants in Council of Europe Member States: Report on a Survey," Council of Europe, 2011.

Fisher, D., "Split Between Britain, U.S. Seen as 'Inevitable': Foreign Policy: The Conservative Party Chairman Fears that a 'Less European' America Will Provide the Wedge," *Los Angeles Times*, April 19, 1990 <http://articles.latimes.com/1990-04-19/news/mn-2009_1_conservative-party> [accessed 7 Sept. 2015]

Fletcher, A., *How to Be German in 50 Easy Steps: A Guide from Apfelsaftschorle to Tschüss*, Ingo Herzke, trans. (Munich: C.H. Beck, 2013).

Franklin, F.G., *The Legislative History of Naturalization in the United States from the Revolutionary War to 1861* (Chicago: University of Chicago Press, 1906).

Giesen, P., "Nederlander heeft Weinig Kaas Gegeten van Historie," *de Volkskrant*, March 26, 2008 <http://www.volkskrant.nl/binnenland/nederlander-heeft-weinig-kaas-gegeten-van-historie~a885241/>

Glendinning, L., "Citizenship Guide Fails Its History Exam," *The Guardian*, April 29, 2006 <http://www.theguardian.com/uk/2006/apr/29/immigration.immigrationpolicy> [accessed 7 Sept. 2015]

Goldman, S., ed., *Brandeis on Zionism: A Collection of Addresses and Statements by Louis D. Brandeis* (Washington: Zionist Organization of America, 1942).

Goldsmith, Q.C., "Citizenship: Our Common Bond," Ministry of Justice, 2008.

Goodhart, D., "Too Diverse?," *Prospect Magazine* 95 (February 2004): pp. 30–37.

Goodman, S.W., "Integration Requirements for Integration's Sake? Identifying, Categorising and Comparing Civic Integration Policies," *Journal of Ethnic and Migration Studies* 36, no. 5 (2010): pp. 753–772.

Goodman, S.W., "Naturalisation Policies in Europe: Exploring Patterns of Inclusion and Exclusion," European University Institute, 2010.

Goodman, S.W., "Controlling Immigration through Language and Country Knowledge Requirements," *West European Politics* 34, no. 2 (2011): pp. 235–255.

Goodman, S.W., "Fortifying Citizenship: Policy Strategies for Civic Integration in Western Europe," *World Politics* 64, no. 4 (2012): pp. 659–698.

Gordon, S.M., "Integrating Immigrants: Morality and Loyalty in US Naturalization Practice," *Citizenship Studies* 11, no. 4 (2007): pp. 367–382.

GOV.UK, "New Life in the UK Test Goes Live," March 25, 2013 <https://www.gov.uk/government/news/new-life-in-the-uk-test-goes-live--2>

Halbertal, M., *People of the Book: Canon, Meaning, and Authority* (Cambridge: Harvard University Press, 1997).

Hasan, M., "Testing Makes a Mockery of Britishness," *New Statesman*, July 4, 2012 <http://www.newstatesman.com/blogs/politics/2012/07/testing-makes-mockery-britishness> [accessed 7 Sept. 2015]

Hawley, C., "Muslim Profiling: A German State Quizes Muslim Immigrants on Jews, Gays and Swim Lessons," *Spiegel*, January 31, 2006 <http://www.spiegel.de/international/muslim-profiling-a-german-state-quizes-muslim-immigrants-on-jews-gays-and-swim-lessons-a-397482.html> [accessed 7 Sept. 2015]

Higham, J., *Strangers in the Land: Patterns of American Nativism, 1860–1925* (New Brunswick: Rutgers University Press, 2002).

Home Office, "Building Cohesive Communities: A Report of the Ministerial Group on Public Order and Community Cohesion," 2001.

Home Office, "Community Cohesion: A Report of the Independent Review Team Chaired by Ted Cantle," 2001.

Home Office, "The New and the Old: The Report of the 'Life in the United Kingdom' Advisory Group," 2003.

Home Office, *Life in the United Kingdom: A Journey to Citizenship*, 1st ed. (London: TSO, 2005).

Home Office, "Knowledge of Life in the UK Settlement Q&A," 2007.

Home Office, *Life in the United Kingdom: A Journey to Citizenship*, 2nd ed. (London: TSO, 2007).

Home Office, "The Path to Citizenship: Next Steps in Reforming the Immigration System," 2008.

Hurst G., "Maverick Streak Makes Mockery of Hunt for a British Motto," *The Times*, 22 November 2007 <http://www.thetimes.co.uk/tto/news/politics/article2024244.ece>

InfraForces and Obea, "Français et l'Identité Nationale," *20 Minutes*, 2010 (on file with the author).

Institut für Demoskopie Allensbach, "Meinung zu Sarrazins Thesen," 2010 (on file with the author).

Islamic Human Rights Commission, "The Über-Citizen and German Kulturkampf—s.10 German Naturalisation Law: A Front?," 2007.

Jacobs, D. and Rea, A., "The End of National Models? Integration Courses and Citizenship Trajectories in Europe," *International Journal on Multicultural Societies* 9, no. 2 (2007): pp. 264–283.

James, K., "French Commission Recommends Banning the Burqa," *Deutsche Welle*, January 26, 2010 <http://www.dw.de/french-commission-recommends-banning-the-burqa/a-5169860> [accessed 7 Sept. 2015]

Johnson, N., ed., "Britishness: Towards a Progressive Citizenship," Smith Institute, 2007.

Joppke, C., "Exclusion in the Liberal State: The Case of Immigration and Citizenship Policy," *European Journal of Social Theory* 8, no. 1 (2005): pp. 43–61.

Joppke, C., "Comparative Citizenship: A Restrictive Turn in Europe?," *Law & Ethics of Human Rights* 2, no. 1 (2008): pp. 1–41.

Joppke, C., "The Role of the State in Cultural Integration: Trends, Challenges, and Ways Ahead," Migration Policy Institute, 2012.

Joppke, C. and Torpey J., *Legal Integration of Islam: A Transatlantic Comparison* (Cambridge: Harvard University Press, 2013).

Kite, M., "Immigrants to Be Taught How to Queue," *Daily Telegraph*, February 13, 2010 <http://www.telegraph.co.uk/news/uknews/immigration/7230274/Immigrants-to-be-taught-how-to-queue.html> [accessed 7 Sept. 2015]

Kostakopoulou, D., "The Anatomy of Civic Integration," *Modern Law Review* 73, no. 6 (2010): pp. 933–958.

Kymlicka, W., "Multiculturalism: Success, Failure, and the Future," Migration Policy Institute, 2012.

Lancaster, P. and Coull, M.A., *Life in the United Kingdom Test: Citizenship Study Guide* (Horton: Lancaster and Coull, 2007).

Laurence, J. and Goodliffe, G., "The French Debate on National Identity and the Sarkozy Presidency: A Retrospective," *The International Spectator: Italian Journal of International Affairs* 48, no. 1 (2013): pp. 34–47.

Le Bars, S., "Une Marocaine en Burqa se Voit Refuser la Nationalité Française," *Le Monde*, July 11, 2008 <http://www.lemonde.fr/societe/article/2008/07/11/une-marocaine-en-burqa-se-voit-refuser-la-nationalite-francaise_1072401_3224.html> [accessed 7 Sept. 2015]

Le Bars, S., "Vivre sans Voile Intégral, le Nouveau Départ de Faiza," *Le Monde*, December 22, 2010 <http://www.lemonde.fr/societe/article/2010/12/22/vivre-sans-voile-integral-le-nouveau-depart-de-faiza_1456635_3224.html> [accessed 7 Sept. 2015]

Legomsky, S.H., "Immigration, Equality and Diversity," *Columbia Journal of Transnational Law* 31, no. 2 (1993): pp. 319–336.

LH2, "L'Observatoire de l'Opinion," *Le Nouvel Observateur*, 2010 <http://www.ladocumentationfrancaise.fr/var/storage/rapports-publics/134000405/0000.pdf> [accessed 7 Sept. 2015]

Marchand, P. and Ratinaud, P., *Etre Français Aujourd'hui: Les Mots du "Grand Débat" sur l'Identité Nationale* (Paris: Les Liens qui Libèrent, 2012).

Mason, A., "Citizenship Tests: Can They Be a Just Compromise?," *Journal of Social Philosophy* 45, no. 2 (2014): pp. 137–161.

Mautner, M., *Law and the Culture of Israel* (Oxford: OUP, 2011).

Meyer, K.E., "Who Gets to Be French?," *New York Times*, April 11, 2012 <http://www.nytimes.com/2012/04/12/opinion/who-gets-to-be-french.html> [accessed 7 Sept. 2015]

Michalowski, I., "Required to Assimilate? The Content of Citizenship Tests in Five Countries," *Citizenship Studies* 15, no. 6–7 (2011): pp. 749–768.

Miller-Idriss, C., *Blood and Culture: Youth, Right-Wing Extremism, and National Belonging in Contemporary Germany* (Durham: Duke University Press, 2009).

Ministère de l'Intérieur, "Intervention de M. Eric Besson Lors de la Conclusion de la 1ère Étape du Grand Débat sur l'Identité Nationale, le Vendredi 5 Février 2010," February 5, 2010 <http://www.immigration.interieur.gouv.fr/Archives/Les-archives-du-Cabinet-de-M.-Eric-Besson-2009-2010/Les-discours-du-Cabinet-de-M.-Eric-Besson-2009-2010/Fevrier-2010/Intervention-de-M.-Eric-Besson-lors-de-la-conclusion-de-la-1ere-etape-du-grand-debat-sur-l-identite-nationale-le-vendredi-5-fevrier-2010>

Ministère de l'Intérieur, "Accueil des Nouveaux Citoyens Français," October 19, 2012 <http://www.interieur.gouv.fr/Archives/Archives-Manuel-Valls-mai-2012-avril-2014/Interventions-du-Ministre/Accueil-des-nouveaux-citoyens-Francais>

Mitchell, M., *Life in the United Kingdom: Official Practice Questions and Answers* (London: TSO, 2013).

Neuman, G.L., "The Lost Century of American Immigration Law (1776–1875)," *Columbia Law Review* 93, no. 8 (1993): pp. 1833–1901.

O'Hagan, A., "Short Cuts," *London Review of Books* 28, no. 22 (November 2006): p. 22.

Orgad, L., "Liberalism, Allegiance, and Obedience: The Inappropriateness of Loyalty Oaths in a Liberal Democracy," *Canadian Journal of Law & Jurisprudence* 27, no. 1 (2014): pp. 99–122.

Peucker, M., "Similar Procedures, Divergent Function: Citizenship Tests in the United States, Canada, Netherlands and United Kingdom," *International Journal on Multicultural Societies* 10, no. 2 (2008): pp. 240–261.

Pew Research Center, "Most Americans Disapprove: Widespread Support for Banning Full Islamic Veil in Western Europe," 2010.

Phillips, M., *Londonistan* (New York: Encounter Books, 2006).

Phillips, T., "Britishness and Integration," in *Britishness: Towards a Progressive Citizenship*, Nick Johnson, ed., Smith Institute, 2007: pp. 37–46.

Pickus, N., *True Faith and Allegiance: Immigration and American Civic Nationalism* (Princeton: Princeton University Press, 2007).

Pickus, N., "Laissez-Faire and Its Discontents: US Naturalization and Integration Policy in Comparative Perspective," *Citizenship Studies* 18, no. 2 (2014): pp. 160–174.

Regev, M., "To Have a Culture of Our Own: On Israeliness and Its Variants," *Ethnic and Racial Studies* 23, no. 2 (2000): pp. 223–247.

Rogers, B. and Muir, R., "The Power of Belonging: Identity, Citizenship and Community Cohesion," Institute for Public Policy Research, 2007.

Roosevelt, T., "True Americanism," in *True Americanism: Four Essays* (New York: Kessinger, 2006): pp. 27–57.

Rousseau, J.J., *On the Social Contract*, G.D.H. Cole, trans. (Mineola: Dover Publications, 2003).

Roy, O., *Secularism Confronts Islam*, George Holoch, trans. (New York: Columbia University Press, 2007).

Sandison, G. and Dillon, H., eds., *Life in the UK Test: Study Guide: The Essential Study Guide for the British Citizenship Test*, 7th ed. (London: Red Squirrel Publishing, 2013).

Sarrazin, T., *Deutschland Schafft sich ab: Wie wir unser Land aufs Spiel setzen* (Munich: Deutsche Verlags-Anstalt, 2010).

Scheffer, P., "Het Multiculturele Drama," *NRC Handelsblad*, January 29, 2000 <http://retro.nrc.nl/W2/Lab/Multicultureel/scheffer.html> [accessed 7 Sept. 2015]

Schuck, P.H., "The Reevaluation of American Citizenship," in *Citizens, Strangers, and In-Betweens: Essays on Immigration and Citizenship* (Boulder: Westview Press, 1998): pp. 176–206.

Schuck, P.H., *Diversity in America: Keeping Government at a Safe Distance* (Cambridge: Harvard University Press, 2003).

Scott, J.W., *The Politics of the Veil* (Princeton: Princeton University Press, 2007).

Sela-Sheffy, R., "'What Makes One an Israeli?' Negotiating Identities in Everyday Representations of 'Israeliness,'" *Nations and Nationalism* 10, no. 4 (2004): pp. 479–497.

Sen, A., *Identity and Violence: the Illusion of Destiny* (London: Penguin Books, 2006).

Simon, P., "French National Identity and Integration: Who Belongs to the National Community?," Migration Policy Institute, 2012.

Spiro, P.J., *Beyond Citizenship: American Identity After Globalization* (Oxford: OUP, 2008).

Spotti, M., Avermaet, P.V., and Extra, G., eds., *Language Testing, Migration and Citizenship: Cross-National Perspectives on Integration Regimes* (London: Continuum, 2009).

Statistisches Bundesamt, "Statistisches Jahrbuch 2010: Für die Bundesrepublik Deutschland mit Internationalen Übersichten," 2010.

Statistisches Bundesamt, "Bevölkerung und Erwerbstätigkeit Bevölkerung mit Migrationshintergrund—Ergebnisse des Mikrozensus 2011," 2012.

TNS Sofres, "Les Français et l'identité Nationale," *La Croix*, 2009 <http://www.tns-sofres.com/etudes-et-points-de-vue/les-francais-et-lidentite-nationale> [accessed 7 Sept. 2015]

U.S. Citizenship and Immigration Services, "USCIS Introduces New Naturalization Test," *USCIS Monthly* (October 2007): pp. 1–8.

U.S. Citizenship and Immigration Services, "Civics (History and Government) Questions for the Redesigned (New) Naturalization Test," 2008.

U.S. Citizenship and Immigration Services, "Learn About the United States: Quick Civics Lessons for the New Naturalization Test," 2013.

U.S. Commission on Immigration Reform, *Becoming an American: Immigration and Immigrant Policy* (Washington: Government Printing Office, 1997).

U.S. Department of Homeland Security, Task Force on New Americans, *Building an Americanization Movement for the Twenty-first Century: A Report to the President of the United States from the Task Force on New Americans* (Washington: Government Printing Office, 2008).

U.S. Immigration and Naturalization Service, *Federal Textbook on Citizenship: The Gardners Become Citizens: A Supplementary Literacy Reader* (Washington: Government Printing Office, 1943).

U.S. Immigration and Naturalization Service, *Federal Textbook on Citizenship: The Business of Our Government* (Washington: Government Printing Office, 1944).

U.S. Immigration and Naturalization Service, *Federal Textbook on Citizenship: Our Constitution and Government*, Catheryn Seckler-Hudson, ed. (Washington: Government Printing Office, 1969).

Van Oers, R., De Hart, B., and Groenendijk, K., "The Netherlands," in *Country Analyses*, vol. 2, *Acquisition and Loss of Nationality: Policies and Trends in 15 European Countries*, Rainer Bauböck et al., eds. (Amsterdam: Amsterdam University Press, 2006): pp. 391–434.

Van Oers, R., Ersbøll, E., and Kostakopoulou, D., eds., *A Re-definition of Belonging? Language and Integration Tests in Europe* (Leiden: Martinus Nijhoff, 2010).

Vasileva, K., "6.5% of the EU Population are Foreigners and 9.4% are Born Abroad," *Eurostat Statistics in Focus* 34 (2011): pp. 1–7.

Vinocur, J., "From the Left, a Call to End the Current Dutch Notion of Tolerance," *New York Times*, November 29, 2008 <http://www.nytimes.com/2008/12/29/world/europe/29iht-politicus.3.18978881.html> [accessed 7 Sept. 2015]

Wales, J., *Life in the United Kingdom: Official Study Guide* (London: TSO, 2013).

Walzer, M., "What Does it Mean to Be an 'American'?," *Social Research* 57, no. 3 (1990): pp. 591–614.

Weil, P., *How to Be French: Nationality in the Making since 1789*, Catherine Porter, trans. (Durham: Duke University Press, 2008).

Weinmann, M., Becher, I., and Gostomski, C.B.V., "Einbürgerungsverhalten von Ausländerinnen und Ausländern in Deutschland sowie Erkenntnisse zu Optionspflichtigen: Ergebnisse der BAMF-Einbürgerungsstudie 2011," Federal Office for Migration and Refugees, 2012.

Wetenschappelijke Raad voor het Regeringsbeleid, *Identificatie Met Nederland* (Amsterdam: Amsterdam University Press, 2007).

Wolfrum, R. and Röben, V., "Gutachten zur Vereinbarkeit des Gesprächsleitfaden für die Einbürgerungsbehörden des Landes Baden-Württemberg mit Völkerrecht," 2006 <http://www.igmg.org/fileadmin/pdf/integration_dialog/mpi_gutachten_einburgerungsleitfaden_bw_marz_2006.pdf> [accessed 7 Sept. 2015].

Zick, A., Küpper, B., and Hövermann, A., "Intolerance, Prejudice and Discrimination: A European Report," Meredith Dale, ed. and trans., Friedrich-Ebert-Stiftung, 2011.

Chapter 4

Bader, V., *Secularism or Democracy? Associational Governance of Religious Diversity* (Amsterdam: Amsterdam University Press, 2007).

Balkin, J.M., *Constitutional Redemption: Political Faith in an Unjust World* (Cambridge: Harvard University Press, 2011).

Barry, B., *Culture and Equality: An Egalitarian Critique of Multiculturalism* (Cambridge: Harvard University Press, 2001).

Bauböck, R., "Sharing History and Future? Time Horizons of Democratic Membership in an Age of Migration," *Constellations* 4, no. 3 (1998): pp. 320–345.

Bauböck, R., "Civic Citizenship: A New Concept for the New Europe," in *Managing Integration: The European Union's Responsibilities Towards Immigrants*, Rita Süssmuth and Werner Weidenfeld, eds. (Washington: Migration Policy Institute and Bertelsmann Stiftung, 2005): pp. 122–138.

Bianco, J.L., "Point D'étape sur les Travaux de l'Observatoire de la Laïcité," Premier Ministre, 2013.

Broder, D.S., "One Nation No More?," *Washington Post*, July 3, 2008 <http://www.washingtonpost.com/wp-dyn/content/article/2008/07/02/AR2008070202352.html> [accessed 7 Sept. 2015]

Danish Immigration Service and Danish Agency for Labour Market and Recruitment, "Ombedømmelse af Indfødsretsprøven Spørgsmål 10," Nyidanmark.dk, February 24, 2009 <http://www.nyidanmark.dk/da-dk/nyheder/nyheder/integrationsministeriet/2009/februar/ombedoemmelse_af_indfoedsretsproeven_spoergsmaal_10.htm> [accessed 7 Sept. 2015]

Ellison, N., Heino, R., and Gibbs, J., "Managing Impressions Online: Self-Presentation Processes in the Online Dating Environment," *Journal of Computer-Mediated Communication* 11, no. 2 (2006): pp. 415–441.

Ersbøll, E., "On Trial in Denmark," in *A Re-definition of Belonging? Language and Integration Tests in Europe*, Ricky Van Oers, Eva Ersbøll, and Dora Kostakopoulou, eds. (Leiden: Martinus Nijhoff, 2010): pp. 107–152.

Goodman, S.W. and Wright, M., "Does Mandatory Integration Matter? Effects of Civic Requirements on Immigrant Socio-economic and Political Outcomes," *Journal of Ethnic and Migration Studies* 41 no. 12 (2015): pp. 1885–1908.

Gray, J., *Two Faces of Liberalism* (New York: The New Press, 2000).

Hailbronner, K., "Nationality in Public International Law and European Law," in *Comparative Analyses*, vol. 1, *Acquisition and Loss of Nationality: Policies and Trends in 15 European Countries*, Rainer Bauböck et al., eds. (Amsterdam: Amsterdam University Press, 2006): pp. 35–104.

Hamburger, P., "Illiberal Liberalism: Liberal Theology, Anti Catholicism, & Church Property," *Journal of Contemporary Legal Issues* 12, no. 2 (2002): pp. 693–726.

Intercollegiate Studies Institute, "Our Fading Heritage: Americans Fail A Basic Test on Their History and Institutions," 2008.

Islamic Human Rights Commission, "The Über-Citizen and German Kulturkampf—s.10 German Naturalisation Law: A Front?," 2007.

Joppke, C., "How Liberal are Citizenship Tests?" and "How Liberal are Citizenship Tests? A Rejoinder," in *How Liberal are Citizenship Tests?*, Rainer Bauböck and Christian Joppke, eds., EUI Working Paper RSCAS 2010/41, 2010: pp. 1–4 and pp. 39–41.

Joppke, C., "The Retreat is Real—But What is the Alternative? Multiculturalism, Muscular Liberalism, and Islam," *Constellations* 21, no. 2 (2014): pp. 286–295.

Joppke, C. and Torpey J., *Legal Integration of Islam: A Transatlantic Comparison* (Cambridge: Harvard University Press, 2013).

Kymlicka, W., "Multicultural Citizenship," in *The Citizenship Debates: A Reader*, Gershon Shafir, ed. (Minneapolis: University of Minnesota Press, 1998): pp. 167–188.

Law, D.S. and Versteeg, M., "The Declining Influence of the United States Constitution," *New York University Law Review* 87, no. 3 (2012): pp. 762–858.

Legomsky, S.H., "Rationing Family Values in Europe and America: An Immigration Tug of War Between States and their Supra-National Associations," *Georgetown Immigration Law Journal* 25, no. 4 (2011): pp. 807–858.

Leibowitz, Y., *On Just About Everything: Talks with Michael Shashar* (Jerusalem: Keter Publishing House, 1987).

Leibowitz, Y., *Judaism, Human Values, and the Jewish State*, Eliezer Goldman, ed. and Eliezer Goldman et al., trans. (Cambridge: Harvard University Press, 1992).

Levinson, S., *Constitutional Faith* (Princeton: Princeton University Press, 1988).

Macedo, S., *Diversity and Distrust: Civic Education in a Multicultural Democracy* (Cambridge: Harvard University Press, 2003).

Margalit, A., "Revisiting God's Authority," *Social Research* 80, no. 1 (2013): pp. 77–100.

Neuman, G.L., "Justifying U.S. Naturalization Policies," *Virginia Journal of International Law* 35, no. 1 (1994): pp. 237–278.

Neuman, G.L., *Strangers to the Constitution: Immigrants, Borders, and Fundamental Law* (Princeton: Princeton University Press, 1996).

Orgad, L., "Creating New Americans: The Essence of Americanism Under the Citizenship Test," *Houston Law Review* 47, no. 5 (2011): pp. 1227–1298.

Rawls, J., "Justice as Fairness in the Liberal Polity," in *The Citizenship Debates: A Reader*, Gershon Shafir, ed. (Minneapolis: University of Minnesota Press, 1998): pp. 53–72.

Raz, J., "Multiculturalism: A Liberal Perspective," in *Ethics in the Public Domain: Essays in the Morality of Law and Politics* (Oxford: Clarendon Press, 1996): pp. 170–191.

Roy, O., *Globalized Islam: The Search for a New Ummah* (New York: Columbia University Press, 2004).

Scheffler, S., "Immigration and the Significance of Culture," *Philosophy and Public Affairs* 35, no. 2 (2007): pp. 93–125.

Schuck, P.H., "The Disconnect Between Public Attitudes and Policy Outcomes in Immigration," in *Debating Immigration*, Carol M. Swain, ed. (Cambridge: Cambridge University Press, 2007): pp. 17–31.

Smith, R.M., *Stories of Peoplehood: The Politics and Morals of Political Memberships* (Cambridge: Cambridge University Press, 2003).

Spiro, P.J., "A New International Law of Citizenship," *American Journal of International Law* 105, no. 4 (2011): pp. 694–746.

Taylor, C., *Sources of the Self: The Making of the Modern Identity* (Cambridge: Harvard University Press, 1989).

U.S. Citizenship and Immigration Services, "USCIS Announces New Naturalization Test," September 27, 2007 <http://www.uscis.gov/sites/default/files/files/pressrelease/NatzTest_27sep07.pdf> [accessed 7 Sept. 2015]

U.S. Citizenship and Immigration Services, USCIS Policy Manual, vol. 12: Citizenship & Naturalization, Part D: General Naturalization Requirements, 2014.

Weil, P., *The Sovereign Citizen: Denaturalization and the Origins of the American Republic* (Philadelphia: University of Pennsylvania Press, 2013).

Weiler, J.H.H., "In Defence of the Status Quo: Europe's Constitutional *Sonderweg*," in *European Constitutionalism Beyond the State*, J.H.H. Weiler and Marlene Wind, eds. (Cambridge: Cambridge University Press, 2003): pp. 7–23.

Wolfrum, R. and Röben, V., "Gutachten zur Vereinbarkeit des Gesprächsleitfaden für die Einbürgerungsbehörden des Landes Baden-Württemberg mit Völkerrecht," 2006 <http://www.igmg.org/fileadmin/pdf/integration_dialog/mpi_gutachten_einburgerungsleitfaden_bw_marz_2006.pdf> [accessed 7 Sept. 2015].

Chapter 5

Ackerman, B.A., *Social Justice in the Liberal State* (New Haven: Yale University Press, 1981).

Adams, J., *A Defence of the Constitutions of Government of the United States of America*, vol. III (London: John Stockdale, 1794).

Anderson, B., *Imagined Communities: Reflections on the Origin and Spread of Nationalism* (London: Verso, 2006).

Appiah, K.A., *The Ethics of Identity* (Princeton: Princeton University Press, 2005).

Barnard, F.M., "National Culture and Political Legitimacy: Herder and Rousseau," *Journal of the History of Ideas* 44, no. 2 (1983): pp. 231–253.

Bossuyt, M.J., *Guide to the "Travaux Préparatoires" of the International Covenant on Civil and Political Rights* (Leiden: Martinus Nijhoff, 1987).

Carens, J.H., "Aliens and Citizens: The Case for Open Borders," *Review of Politics* 49, no. 2 (1987): pp. 251–273.

Carmi, N., "Immigration Policy: Between Demographic Considerations and Preservation of Culture," *Law & Ethics of Human Rights* 2, no. 1 (2008): pp. 1–29.

Cassese, A., *Self-Determination of Peoples: A Legal Reappraisal* (Cambridge: Cambridge University Press, 1995).

Cohen, A., *Non-Jewish Jews in Israel* (Jerusalem: Shalom Hartman Institute and Keter Publishing House, 2006).

De Tocqueville, A., "Tyranny of the Majority," in *Democracy in America*, Henry Reeve, trans. 3rd ed. (New York: George Adlard, 1839): pp. 255–268.

Fletcher, G., "The Case for Linguistic Self-Defense," in *The Morality of Nationalism*, Robert McKim and Jeff McMahan, eds. (Oxford: OUP, 1997): pp. 324–339.

Gagnon, A.G., Lecours, A., and Nootens, G., eds., *Contemporary Majority Nationalism* (Montreal: McGill-Queen's University Press, 2011).

Gans, C., *The Limits of Nationalism* (Cambridge: Cambridge University Press, 2003).

Gans, C., "Individuals' Interest in the Preservation of their Culture: Its Meaning, Justifications, and Implications," *Law & Ethics of Human Rights* 1, no. 1 (2007): pp. 6–16.

Gat, A. with Yakobson, A., *Nations: The Long History and Deep Roots of Political Ethnicity and Nationalism* (Cambridge: Cambridge University Press, 2013).

Genovese, M.A., ed., "Federalist No. 10" (Madison), in *The Federalist Papers: Alexander Hamilton, James Madison, and John Jay* (New York: Palgrave Macmillan, 2009): pp. 49–54.

Genovese, M.A., ed., "Federalist No. 51" (Madison), in *The Federalist Papers: Alexander Hamilton, James Madison, and John Jay* (New York: Palgrave Macmillan, 2009): pp. 119–122.

Gladney, D.C., "Introduction: Making and Marking Majorities," in *Making Majorities: Constituting the Nation in Japan, Korea, China, Malaysia, Fiji, Turkey, and the United States*, Dru C. Gladney, ed. (Stanford: Stanford University Press, 1998): pp. 1–9.

Glazer, N., *We Are All Multiculturalists Now* (Cambridge: Harvard University Press, 1997).

Hudson, J.L., "The Ethics of Immigration Restriction," *Social Theory and Practice* 10, no. 2 (1984): pp. 201–239.

Joppke, C., *Selecting by Origin: Ethnic Migration in the Liberal State* (Cambridge: Harvard University Press, 2005).

Joseph, S. and Castan M., *The International Covenant on Civil and Political Rights: Cases, Materials, and Commentary*, 3rd ed. (Oxford: OUP, 2013).

Kasher, A., "Justice and Affirmative Action: Naturalization and the Law of Return," *Israel Yearbook on Human Rights* 15 (1985): pp. 101–112.

Kaufmann, E. and Haklai, O., "Dominant Ethnicity: From Minority to Majority," *Nations and Nationalism* 14, no. 4 (2008): pp. 743–767.

Kelsen, H., "The Preamble of the Charter—A Critical Analysis," *The Journal of Politics* 8, no. 2 (1946): pp. 134–159.

Kymlicka, W., "The Sources of Nationalism: Commentary on Taylor," in *The Morality of Nationalism*, Robert McKim and Jeff McMahan, eds. (Oxford: OUP, 1997): pp. 56–65.

Kymlicka, W., *Multicultural Citizenship: A Liberal Theory of Minority Rights* (Oxford: Clarendon Press, 2000).

Kymlicka W., *Multicultural Odysseys: Navigating the New International Politics of Diversity* (Oxford: OUP, 2007).

Kymlicka, W., "The Internationalization of Minority Rights," *International Journal of Constitutional Law* 6, no. 1 (2008): pp. 1–32.

Lerner, N., *Group Rights and Discrimination in International Law*, 2nd ed. (The Hague: Martinus Nijhoff, 2003).

Lerner, N., *Religion, Secular Beliefs and Human Rights*, 2nd ed. (Leiden: Martinus Nijhoff, 2012).

Margalit, A. and Halbertal M., "Liberalism and the Right to Culture," *Social Research* 71, no. 3 (2004): pp. 529–548.

Mill, J.S., *On Liberty* (New York: Dover Publications, 2002).

Parekh, B., *Rethinking Multiculturalism: Cultural Diversity and Political Theory*, 2nd ed. (New York: Palgrave Macmillan, 2006).

President's Committee on Civil Rights, *To Secure These Rights: The Report of the President's Committee on Civil Rights* (Washington: Government Printing Office, 1947).

Raz, J., "Legal Rights," *Oxford Journal of Legal Studies* 4, no. 1 (1984): pp. 1–21.

Raz, J., "Multiculturalism: A Liberal Perspective," in *Ethics in the Public Domain: Essays in the Morality of Law and Politics* (Oxford: Clarendon Press, 1996): pp. 170–191.

Scheffler, S., "Immigration and the Significance of Culture," *Philosophy & Public Affairs* 35, no. 2 (2007): pp. 93–125.

Schnapper, D., "The Concept of 'Dominant Ethnicity' in the Case of France," in *Rethinking Ethnicity: Majority Groups and Dominant Minorities*, Eric P. Kaufmann, ed. (New York: Routledge, 2004): pp. 90–102.

Shachar, A., *The Birthright Lottery: Citizenship and Global Inequality Birthright Citizenship* (Cambridge: Harvard University Press, 2009).

Shaw, B., *John Bull's Other Island and Major Barbara* (New York: Brentano's, 1916).

Skrentny, J.D., *The Minority Rights Revolution* (Cambridge: Harvard University Press, 2002).

Smith, A.D., *The Ethnic Origins of Nations* (Malden: Blackwell, 1988).

Smith, A.D., *National Identity* (Reno: University of Nevada Press, 1991).

Smith, A.D., *Nations and Nationalism in a Global Era* (Cambridge: Polity Press, 1995).

Smith, A.D., "Ethnic Cores and Dominant Ethnies," in *Rethinking Ethnicity: Majority Groups and Dominant Minorities*, Eric P. Kaufmann, ed (New York: Routledge, 2004): pp. 15–26.

Smith, A.D., *Nationalism: Theory, Ideology, History* (Malden: Polity Press, 2010).

Tajfel, H., *Human Groups and Social Categories: Studies in Social Psychology* (Cambridge: Cambridge University Press, 1981)

Taylor, C., "The Politics of Recognition," in *Multiculturalism: Examining the Politics of Recognition*, Amy Gutmann, ed. (Princeton: Princeton University Press, 1994): pp. 25–73.

U.N., *Documents of the United Nations Conference on International Organization San Francisco, 1945*, vol. VI (New York: United Nations Information Organizations, 1945).

U.N., "Annotations on the Text of the Draft International Covenants on Human Rights," U.N. Doc. A/29291, 1955.

U.N., "Study on the Rights of Persons Belonging to Ethnic, Religious and Linguistic Minorities," U.N. Doc. E/CN.4/Sub.2/384/Rev.I, 1977 (study prepared by Francesco Capotorti).

U.N., "The Right to Self-Determination: Historical and Current Development on the Basis of United Nations Instruments," U.N. Doc. E/CN.4/Sub.2/404/Rev.1, 1981 (study prepared by Aureliu Cristescu).

U.N. Commission on Human Rights, "Report to the Economic and Social Council on the Work of the Sixth Session of the Commission, Held at Lake Success, New York, 27 March–19 May 1950 (E/1681)," 1950.

U.N. Commission on Human Rights, "Commentary of the Working Group on Minorities to the United Nations Declaration on the Rights of Persons

Belonging to National or Ethnic, Religious and Linguistic Minorities," U.N. Doc. E/CN.4/Sub.2/AC.5/2005/2, 2005.

U.N. Permanent Forum on Indigenous Issues, "Frequently Asked Questions: Declaration on the Rights of Indigenous Peoples," 2006.

UNESCO, "International Meeting of Experts on Further Study of the Concept of the Rights of Peoples," UNESCO Doc. SHS-89/CONF.602/7, 1990.

Vrdoljak, A.F., "Self-Determination and Cultural Rights," in *Cultural Human Rights*, Francesco Francioni and Martin Scheinin, eds. (Leiden: Martinus Nijhoff, 2008): pp. 41–78.

Waldron, J., "Minority Cultures and the Cosmopolitan Alternative," *University of Michigan Journal of Law Reform* 25, no. 3–4 (1992): pp. 751–794.

Walzer, M., *Spheres of Justice: A Defense of Pluralism and Equality* (New York: Basic Books, 1983).

Walzer, M., "Comment," in *Multiculturalism: Examining the Politics of Recognition*, Amy Gutmann, ed. (Princeton: Princeton University Press, 1994): pp. 99–103.

Yakobson, A. and Rubinstein, A., *Israel and the Family of Nations: The Jewish Nation-State and Human Rights* (New York: Routledge, 2008).

Yakobson, A. and Rubinstein, A., "Joining the Jewish People: Non-Jewish Immigrants from the Former USSR, Israeli Identity and Jewish Peoplehood," *Israel Law Review* 43, no. 1 (2010): pp. 218–239.

Chapter 6

Balkin, J.M., "Idolatry and Faith: The Jurisprudence of Sanford Levinson," *Tulsa Law Review* 38, no. 4 (2003): pp. 553–578.

Balkin, J.M., *Constitutional Redemption: Political Faith in an Unjust World* (Cambridge: Harvard University Press, 2011).

Barak, A., "Unconstitutional Constitutional Amendments," *Israel Law Review* 44, no. 3 (2011): pp. 321–342.

Barry, B., *Culture and Equality: An Egalitarian Critique of Multiculturalism* (Cambridge: Harvard University Press, 2001).

Basler, R.P., ed., *The Collected Works of Abraham Lincoln*, vol. IV (New Brunswick: Rutgers University Press, 1953).

Benhabib, S., *The Claims of Culture: Equality and Diversity in the Global Era* (Princeton: Princeton University Press, 2002).

Currie, D.P., *The Constitution of the Federal Republic of Germany* (Chicago: University of Chicago Press, 1994).

Dicey, A.V., *Introduction to the Study of the Law of the Constitution*, Roger E. Michener, ed., 8th ed. (Indianapolis: Liberty Fund Inc, 1982).

Elliot, J., ed., *The Debates in the Several State Conventions on the Adoption of the Federal Constitution*, vol. IV (Philadelphia: J.B. Lippincott Company, 1941).

Fletcher, G.P., "Constitutional Identity," *Cardozo Law Review* 14, no. 3–4 (1993): pp. 737–746.

Gat, A. with Yakobson, A., *Nations: The Long History and Deep Roots of Political Ethnicity and Nationalism* (Cambridge: Cambridge University Press, 2013).

Genovese, M.A., ed., "Federalist No. 2" (Jay) and "Federalist No. 10" (Madison), in *The Federalist Papers: Alexander Hamilton, James Madison, and John Jay* (New York: Palgrave Macmillan, 2009): pp. 37–40 and 49–54.

Gray, J., *Two Faces of Liberalism* (New York: The New Press, 2000).

Habermas, J., *Habermas on Law and Democracy: Critical Exchanges*, Michel Rosenfeld and Andrew Arato, eds. (Berkeley: University of California Press, 1988).

Habermas, J., "The European Nation State. Its Achievements and Its Limitations. On the Past and Future of Sovereignty and Citizenship," *Ratio Juris* 9, no. 2 (1996): pp. 125–137.

Habermas, J., *The Inclusion of the Others: Studies in Political Theory*, Ciaran Cronin and Pablo De Greiff, eds. (Cambridge: The MIT Press, 1998).

Hart, H.L.A., *The Concept of Law*, Penelope A. Bulloch and Joseph Raz, eds., 2nd ed. (Oxford: Clarendon Press, 1994).

Hedrick, T., *Rawls and Habermas: Reason, Pluralism, and the Claims of Political Philosophy* (Stanford: Stanford University Press, 2010).

Issacharoff, S., "Fragile Democracies," *Harvard Law Review* 120, no. 6 (2007): pp. 1405–1467.

Jacobsohn, G.J., *Constitutional Identity* (Cambridge: Harvard University Press, 2010).

Joppke, C., "A Christian Identity for the Liberal State," *British Journal of Sociology* 64, no. 4 (2013): pp. 597–616.

Joppke, C., "Through the European Looking Glass: Citizenship Tests in the USA, Australia, and Canada," *Citizenship Studies* 17, no. 1 (2013): pp. 1–15.

Kymlicka, W., "Multicultural Citizenship," in *The Citizenship Debates: A Reader*, Gershon Shafir, ed. (Minneapolis: University of Minnesota Press, 1998): pp. 167–188.

Kymlicka, W., *Multicultural Citizenship: A Liberal Theory of Minority Rights* (Oxford: Clarendon Press, 2000).

Levinson, S., *Constitutional Faith* (Princeton: Princeton University Press, 1988).

Macklin, A. and Bauböck, R., eds., "The Return of Banishment: Do the New Denationalisation Policies Weaken Citizenship?," EUI Working Paper RSCAS 2015/14, 2015.

Martin, D., "Membership and Consent: Abstract or Organic," *Yale Journal of International Law* 11, no. 1 (1985): pp. 278–296.

Mautner, M., "From 'Honor' to 'Dignity': How Should a Liberal State Treat Non-Liberal Cultural Groups?," *Theoretical Inquiries in Law* 9, no. 2 (2008): pp. 609–642.

Michalowski, I., "Citizenship Tests in Five Countries: An Expression of Political Liberalism?," Wissenschaftszentrum Berlin für Sozialforschung (WZB), 2009.

Michelman, F.I., "Morality, Identity and 'Constitutional Patriotism,'" *Denver Law Review* 76, no. 4 (1999): pp. 1009–1028.

Michelman, F.I., "Faith and Obligation, or What Makes Sandy Sweat?," *Tulsa Law Review* 83, no. 4 (2003): pp. 651–668.

Miller, D., *On Nationality* (Oxford: Clarendon Press, 1995).

Miller, D., "Immigration: The Case for Limits," in *Contemporary Debates in Applied Ethics*, Andrew I. Cohen and Christopher Heath Wellman, eds. (Malden: Blackwell, 2005): pp. 193–206.

Miller, D., "Immigrants, Nations, and Citizenship," *Journal of Political Philosophy* 16, no. 4 (2008): pp. 371–390.

Müller, J.W., *Constitutional Patriotism* (Princeton: Princeton University Press, 2007).

Murphy, W.F., "Merlin's Memory: The Past and Future Imperfect of the Once and Future Polity," in *Responding to Imperfection the Theory and Practice of Constitutional Amendment*, Sanford Levinson, ed. (Princeton: Princeton University Press, 1995): pp. 163–190.

Parekh, B., "Minority Practices and Principles of Toleration," *International Migration Review* 30, no. 1 (1996): pp. 251–284.

Popper, K.R., *The Open Society and Its Enemies* (Princeton: Princeton University Press, 2013).

Rawls, J., *A Theory of Justice* (Cambridge: Harvard University Press, 1971).

Rawls, J., "Justice as Fairness in the Liberal Polity," in *The Citizenship Debates: A Reader*, Gershon Shafir, ed. (Minneapolis: University of Minnesota Press, 1998): pp. 53–72.

Rawls, J., *The Law of Peoples, with "The Idea of Public Reason Revisited"* (Cambridge: Harvard University Press, 2001).

Rawls, J., *Political Liberalism: Expanded Edition* (New York: Columbia University Press, 2005).

Raz, J., "Multiculturalism: A Liberal Perspective," in *Ethics in the Public Domain: Essays in the Morality of Law and Politics* (Oxford: Clarendon Press, 1996).

Raz, J., *Between Authority and Interpretation* (Oxford: OUP, 2009).

Riesenberg, P., *Citizenship in the Western Tradition: Plato to Rousseau* (Chapel Hill: University of North Carolina Press, 1992).

Rousseau, J.J., *On the Social Contract*, Christopher Betts, trans. (Oxford: OUP, 1994).

Shachar, A., "On Citizenship and Multicultural Vulnerability," *Political Theory* 28, no. 1 (2000): pp. 64–89.

Stilz, A., *Liberal Loyalty: Freedom, Obligation, and the State* (Princeton: Princeton University Press, 2009).

Tamir, Y., *Liberal Nationalism* (Princeton: Princeton University Press, 1995).

Waldron, J., "Special Ties and Natural Duties," *Philosophy and Public Affairs* 22, no. 1 (1993): pp. 3–30.

Walzer, M., *Spheres of Justice: A Defense of Pluralism and Equality* (New York: Basic Books, 1983).

Yakobson, A., "God and Religion in Modern Democratic Constitutions," in *Contemporary Challenges to the Nation State: Global and Israeli Perspectives*, vol. II, *The Nation State and Religion: The Resurgence of Faith*, Anita Shapira, Yedidia Z. Stern, and Alexander Yakobson, eds. (Eastbourne: Sussex Academic Press, 2013): pp. 1–13.

Yakobson, A., "Muslims in Europe—Dilemmas of Secularism, Christian Heritage, 'Neutrality' and Religious Freedom," in *Muslim Minorities in Modern Times* (forthcoming, on file with the author).

Conclusion

Carens, J.H., "Aliens and Citizens: The Case for Open Borders," *Review of Politics* 49, no. 2 (1987): pp. 251–273.

Commission for Racial Equality, "Citizenship and Belonging: What is Britishness?," 2005.

Goodman, S.W., "Integration Requirements for Integration's Sake? Identifying, Categorising and Comparing Civic Integration Policies," *Journal of Ethnic and Migration Studies* 36, no. 5 (2010): pp. 753–772.

Joppke, C., *Citizenship and Immigration* (Malden: Polity Press, 2010).

Joppke, C., *Is Multiculturalism Dead? Crisis and Persistence in the Constitutional State* (forthcoming, on file with the author).

Kaufmann, E.P., "The Decline of the WASP in the United States and Canada," in *Rethinking Ethnicity: Majority Groups and Dominant Minorities*, Eric P. Kaufmann, ed. (New York: Routledge, 2004).

Kymlicka, W., *Multicultural Citizenship: A Liberal Theory of Minority Rights* (Oxford: Clarendon Press, 2000).

Kymlicka, W., "The Rise and Fall of Multiculturalism? New Debates on Inclusion and Accommodation in Diverse Societies," in *The Multiculturalism Backlash: European Discourses, Policies and Practices*, Steven Vertovec and Susanne Wessendorf, eds. (New York: Routledge, 2010): pp. 32–49.

Laurence, J., *The Emancipation of Europe's Muslims: The State's Role in Minority Integration* (Princeton: Princeton University Press, 2012).

Rousseau, J.J., *Constitutional Project for Corsica* (Whitefish: Kessinger Publishing, 2004).

Schuck, P.H., *Diversity in America: Keeping Government at a Safe Distance* (Cambridge: Harvard University Press, 2003).

Name Index

Subject Index

Tables are indicated by an italic *t* following the page number.

Printed and bound by CPI Group (UK) Ltd, Croydon, CR0 4YY